Contents

Feminist Readings/ Feminists Reading

2nd edition

Sara Mills and Lynne Pearce

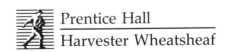

Prentice Hall
Harvester Wheatsheaf

London New York Toronto Sydney Tokyo Singapore
Madrid Mexico City Munich

First published 1996 by
Prentice Hall Europe
Campus 400, Maylands Avenue
Hemel Hempstead
Hertfordshire, HP2 7EZ
A division of
Simon & Schuster International Group

Typeset in 9½/11½ pt Palatino
by Photoprint, Torquay, Devon

Printed and bound in Great Britain by T.J. Press (Padstow) Ltd

Library of Congress Cataloging-in-Publication Data

Mills, Sara, 1954–
    Feminist readings/feminists reading / Sara Mills and Lynne Pearce.—2nd ed.
    p. cm.
    Rev. ed. of: Feminist readings/feminists reading / Sara Mills . . . [et al.], 1989
    Includes bibliographical references and index.
    ISBN 0–13–375395–6
    1. English fiction—Women authors—History and criticism—Theory, etc.
2. American fiction—Women authors—History and criticism—Theory, etc.
3. Hardy, Thomas, 1840–1928. Tess of the d'Urbervilles. 4. Feminism and
literature. 5. Women and literature. I. Pearce, Lynne. II. Feminist readings/
feminists reading. III. Title.
PR830.W6M55   1996
813.009′352042—dc20
                                                                            96–6899
                                                                            CIP

British Library Cataloguing in Publication Data

A catalogue record for this book is available from the British Library
ISBN 0–13–375395–6

1 2 3 4 5   00 99 98 97 96

Acknowledgements

We would like to thank all those people who have given this book their support in both the first and the second editions: our students, for whom it was written; Jackie Jones at Harvester Wheatsheaf for her enthusiasm and consideration through all stages of its first production, and Christina Wipf for seeing it through the second.

Thanks, too, to our families and friends for providing us with the time and space necessary in which to meet and work; and especially the following individuals for their unfailing understanding, inspiration, care, patience . . . and most of all for their sense of fun: Tony Brown, Gabriel Mills-Brown, Rowena Murray, Gordon Fairbairn and Les Millard.

We would also like to acknowledge the very material input of friends, colleagues and students at the various institutions to which we have been affiliated. At Loughborough University: thanks to the Feminist Research Group, especially Elaine Hobby, Christine (Drama) White, Christine (English) White, Chris Christie, Gillian Spraggs, Marion Shaw and also to Mick Mangan and Mick Wallis. At Sheffield Hallam University: thanks especially to Jill LeBihan, Judy Simons, Robert Miles and Keith Green. At Lancaster: thanks to members of the MA module in 'Feminist Theory and Textual Practice' (1995) who participated in the making of the second edition; to all members of the 'Prayer Group', near and far; and to Jackie Stacey and Hilary Hinds (the latter not at Lancaster, but very respected nevertheless) for their comments on early drafts of Chapter 7.

The authors and publishers wish to thank the following, who have kindly given permission for the use of copyright material:

David Higham Associates Ltd for extracts from *The Color Purple* by Alice Walker, published by The Women's Press, 1983.
Andre Deutsch Ltd for extracts from *Surfacing* by Margaret Atwood, 1984.
Penguin Books for extracts from *Wide Sargasso Sea* by Jean Rhys, 1968.
For extracts from *The Magic Toyshop*, by Angela Carter, copyright © Angela Carter 1967. Reproduced by permission of The Estate of Angela Carter, c/o Rogers, Coleridge and White Ltd. 20 Powis Mews, London W11 1JN.

Introduction

Sara Mills and Lynne Pearce

Feminist literary theory: history and development

In the ten years since we originally began work on the first edition of *Feminist Readings* there have been many interesting, and heartening, developments in the dissemination of feminist theory within literary criticism. Since the late 1980s, for example, 'theory' – including feminist theory – has become part of the core curriculum in the majority of institutions of Higher Education and it is expected that most students' work will be informed by a knowledge of contemporary theoretical debates concerning language, authorship, subjectivity, gender and so on.

Whilst teachers of literary studies still observe the difficulty of getting students to put this theoretical knowledge into practice (in their readings of literary and other texts), perhaps the biggest challenge those of us committed to feminist criticism and pedagogy now face is maintaining its radical, and subversive, profile. For students on the more general 'introduction to theory' courses, feminism can sometimes seem no more than another (optional) way of reading a text, and the passion and excitement experienced by those of us who were introduced to the transgressive possibilities of 'feminist reading' ten or fifteen years ago is no longer present. This slide towards familiarity and 'assimilation' is, of course, part of the challenge that faces '90s feminism generally, and it is consequently our hope that this revised edition of *Feminist Readings* will alert a new generation to the risks and rewards of 'reading as a feminist'.

By understanding a little about the history of academic feminism over the past thirty years and, in particular, its impact on literary studies, new readers will hopefully perceive their place in a strong, yet dynamic tradition of radical textual practice. Despite the fact (discussed below and in a number of the chapters) that the issue of what constitutes a female/feminist identity has become increasingly complex in recent years, to effect a feminist reading of a text of any kind is still necessarily to express a political commitment to the fight against women's oppression in patriarchal culture(s). How literature and/or literary criticism engages with such oppression in the 'material world' remains, of course, a complicated issue, but most of us who identify as feminist theorists and critics believe there *is* a connection, thus ensuring that there is also an abiding *purpose* to our scholarship. It is fair to say, however, that some of the developments within feminist theory over the past ten years have obscured the political cutting edge of our practices even as others have sharpened it, and in the next few pages we offer a brief overview of some of the major changes that have occurred. Before that, however, we reproduce our account of Julia Kristeva's framework of the development of feminist criticism from 1960 to 1980 since this somewhat idealistic projection of how things have progressed (or *ought* to have progressed) will be useful for readers coming to the field of feminist theory for the first time.

Kristeva's framework, elaborated in her article 'Women's time', traces three stages in the development of feminist literary theory: first, a critique of male canonical writings; secondly, a concentration on the establishment and tracing of a female literary tradition, re-valuing those texts that had been written by women; and thirdly, a calling into question of gender difference in the work of both male and female authors.[1]

Phase 1: Feminist critique of male-authored texts

According to Kristeva, the concern of the earliest feminist critics was to scrutinize a shared canon of literary 'greats' in order to try to account for the absence of a significant body of women's writing. Tillie Olsen's *Silences* catalogues the limitations placed on the creativity of both men and women, using testimonies from their letters and diaries.[2] She focuses particularly on the difficulty women have had in finding space and time for their work, including her own struggle to be a woman writer. The struggle for space has been a consistent theme in accounts of writing women.[3]

Feminist literary criticism became a theoretical issue with the publication of Kate Millett's *Sexual Politics* in 1969.[4] This book concentrates on 'discovering' sexist assumptions in male-authored texts: identifying patriarchy as the source of women's textual as well as material oppression. As is recorded in Chapter 1, it was the polemical nature of this text which distinguished it from the equally provocative though more cautious studies that had gone before, such as Mary Ellmann's *Thinking About Women* (1968), and situated it in the foreground of a new public debate that linked women's fight for equality in the material world with the sexism inherent in both literature and literary criticism.[5] This book sparked off a good deal of controversy and interest in feminist literary criticism, and together with other texts such as Arlyn Diamond and Lee Edward's edited collection *The Authority of Experience* (1977) aimed to criticize the images of women characters which were presented in male-authored texts.[6]

Shortly after this, critics began to make generalizations about feminist literary theory as a whole: for example, Josephine Donovan's collection entitled *Feminist Literary Criticism* (1975).[7] In this collection, Cheri Register wrote an article entitled 'American feminist literary criticism' which also marked another turning point in its suggestion that feminist criticism should be *prescriptive*: that critics should suggest ways in which writers could produce 'literature which is good from a feminist viewpoint'.[8] A culmination of this trend of examining primarily male-authored texts can be seen in Judith Fetterley's *The Resisting Reader* (1978) which suggests that much of American literature has been addressed to an exclusively male audience.[9] Inevitably, therefore, female readers when reading these texts have either had to position themselves as males, or have 'resisted' the reading position that they have been allocated.

However, although the analytical work which was done on male-authored texts became increasingly sophisticated, many feminists felt that rather than challenging the status of these texts, they were perhaps perpetuating some of the problems. Thus feminists began to move away from the analysis of male writing, and embraced a new commitment to the reading and analysis of texts by women.

Phase 2: Establishing a female literary tradition

Elaine Showalter, in her book *A Literature of Their Own* (1977), and Ellen Moers, in *Literary Women* (1976), started a new phase in feminist literary scholarship by turning their attention away from a critique of male writing and towards the establishment of a female tradition.[10] These authors concentrated their energies both on a re-reading of 'classic' women writers such as Jane Austen, the Brontës, and Emily Dickinson, and on extending 'the canon' (see Glossary) to include previously little-known women writers such as Maria Edgeworth and

Aphra Behn. In these books the aim was to show how much of a tradition of women's writing there had been in the past which had nevertheless been ignored in general histories of British and American literature. They argued that rather than literary women being isolated exceptions they formed significant communities: corresponding, exchanging manuscripts, reacting against and consciously referring to each other's work. As late as 1986, critics like Dale Spender were still working in this mode (see *Mothers of the Novel*), and, as will be discussed in Chapter 7, such reclamation projects continue to be important to Black and lesbian readers and critics.[11]

In an article entitled 'Feminist criticism in the wilderness' (1981), Elaine Showalter then went on to detail some of the work that was then being done in feminist criticism, arguing that the 'feminist critique' (described here as a feature of 'Phase 1') was being supplanted by a new 'Gynocriticism' which not only sought to make visible the women writers 'hidden from history' in the way just described, but also worked to define the specificity of women's writing: i.e. to ask the question 'Do women write differently from men, and if so, why?' (see Chapter 3).[12]

As will be seen in Chapter 4, Sandra Gilbert and Susan Gubar were also interested in examining the ways in which women's writing differed from men's . Their readings of nineteenth-century women's writing in *The Madwoman in the Attic* (1979) suggest that common themes found in those women's writing stem from their ambivalent relationship to their male predecessors and the fact that women writers in the nineteenth century had no *female* literary tradition to subscribe to; hence, they had to reuse male writing strategies to their own distinctly female ends.[13]

Phase 3: New interrogations of gender

In France, during the 1960s and 1970s, French feminists like Hélène Cixous, Luce Irigaray and Julia Kristeva developed a system of analysis which was radically different to that which had been practised in the United Kingdom and the United States.[14] In these French works, theories of writing take precedence over the selection and rereading of specific literary texts. The writers construct a critique, not of the representation of women's experience in literature, but (as will be explained in Chapter 5) the nature of female subjectivity (see Glossary) and the language through which it is constructed and symbolized. Through the related academic disciplines of linguistics, psychoanalysis and philosophy, each of these theorists moves away from an analysis of writing based on the sex of the author, to a naming of 'masculine' and 'feminine' elements in the writings of both men and women. Central to all the French feminisms is a knowledge of Saussurian linguistics and Lacanian theories of 'the subject' as constituted in language. Language, they argue, in privileging the phallus, suppresses what is 'feminine', subjecting it to the symbolization of a patriarchal system of naming and categorization.[15] For Kristeva, the suppressed feminine emerges in both men's and women's writing of the modernist *avant-garde* which, with its self-conscious focus on language, displays subjectivity in the process of construction. For Irigaray and Cixous, meanwhile, writing 'woman' is a more utopian quest to bring into being that which has not yet been written. As part of this project, they employ the phrase 'to write the body', which caused major suspicion amongst many Anglo-American feminists because of its connotations of the kind of biological essentialism ('anatomy is destiny') that such feminism has seen as its major target.[16] In practice, however, much of their writing is distinctly anti-essentialist, working to unpick existing binary oppositions of male/female, rational/irrational, heard/silenced and so on, and using the symbolism of fluidity and female sexuality to confront the phallogocentricism (see Glossary) of Western philosophical writings. Their writing practices, moreover, though not in themselves readings of literary texts, have provided literary theorists with a model for reading texts as discursive constructs (see 'discourse' in Glossary) rather than reflections of an individual author's experience. These feminist theorists have used the sophisticated verbal and philosophical strategies of Lacan and Derrida in order to establish the notion of gender positions within texts, and their methods have been further developed by more recent Anglo-American feminist critics such as Peggy Kamuf, Alice Jardine, Gayatri Spivak and Shoshana Felman.[17]

As we noted in the first edition, throughout these three phases of development in feminist criticism there have been other voices continually struggling to make themselves heard, and whilst the complex calling into question of gender difference envisaged by Kristeva as the 'third phase' is recognizable as part of the general 'post-structuralist' revolution (see Glossary), the 1980s and 1990s have witnessed a continued commitment to the work of phases 1 and 2 from feminists who believe it is too soon to abandon the earlier practices of consciousness-raising, sexual political criticism (see Chapter 1), and the reclamation of women writers 'hidden from history' (see Chapter 3). Indeed, in this last respect, other developments in literary theory and criticism in the 1980s – like 'New Historicism' and 'Cultural Materialism' – have provided new legitimation for archival research and a resituating of authors and their works in the context of production.[18] What many of us now feel is that this important work of making female-authored texts visible (campaigning for equal representation of male and female authors on university syllabuses, for example) needs to be sustained alongside the more sophisticated interrogations of gender in *all* texts. In this context, it is fair to say that for lesbian and Black critics especially, a premature abandonment of the gynocritical project (see Chapters 3 and 7) would be disastrous: visibility is still an issue for these groups, and Black and lesbian readers require access to a pool of texts addressed explicitly to them before (or as well as) the interrogation of 'heterosexuality' and/or 'whiteness' now being practised by poststructuralist theorists.[19]

The latter developments, meanwhile, centre primarily on a newly self-conscious concern with *difference*: a concern predicated both on the poststructuralist models of language and subjectivity that inform Kristeva's vision of the third phase, and a more material sense of the differences (cultural, historical, 'racial', etc.) that distinguish women from one another and productively frustrate our ability to talk about ourselves as a homogeneous group. White/heterosexual/middle-class feminists have had to become more critically aware of the privileges which accrue to them simply because of their status; they have had to reconsider the narrowness of much early feminist theory and many have enthusiastically embraced the new possibilities in current theory developed by lesbian, Black and post-colonial feminist theorists. White/heterosexual/middle-class feminists have also begun to theorize their own position more fully, so that the work of lesbian, Black and post-colonial theorists is not simply added on to a base which consists of the concerns of the 'dominant' group, but rather forces a crisis which leads to greater theoretical sophistication at all levels of debate.[20]

Together with this concern with difference has come an increased questioning of the category 'woman' – so fundamental to a movement such as feminism. This has been a vital issue since *what constitutes a woman* was given little consideration in early theoretical work and the dominant group has tended to characterize 'woman' in their own guise. The move to question this narrowness has led to an instability *vis-à-vis* the term 'woman' which theorists like Judith Butler and Diana Fuss have explored in some detail.[21] Rather than simply railing against 'essentialist' models of womanhood, they have forced feminists seriously to engage with the definition of 'woman' from a number of different perspectives, with the result that many now doubt that the category 'woman' should be used at all. This said, feminists like Tania Modleski in *Feminism without Women* have anticipated a number of problems that will occur if feminism dispenses with the term 'women' too easily.[22] Without this 'given', feminism – which arose as a movement to improve conditions for women as a whole – no longer has anything to organize itself around. On the ground, this must lead (and, indeed, has led) to the factionalization of the movement into special interest groups which must be divisive unless a politics of coalition is actively invoked.[23] For feminist criticism, too, as we indicated above, a premature de-centring of 'women's writing' could mean that important texts disappear from the shelves of our bookshops and libraries (the Virago Classics, for example) only a few years after their arrival.[24]

The spread of poststructuralist and postmodernist thought through-out the academic world has also eradicated the gulf that formerly existed between Anglo-American and French theory, although the division still remains a useful heuristic device when establishing the history and development of contemporary feminist criticism. What has happened is that few Anglo-American theorists are now opposed to 'theory' (as characterized/caricatured by an obsessive focus on 'textuality'), although there are still many who oppose theory which wilfully excludes others through its obfuscatory language and unglossed technical terms. However, the value of theorizing one's own critical position seems to be one that is now acknowledged by *most* academic feminists. Few Anglo-American critics, indeed, now engage in unproblematized autobiographical/'authentic realist' accounts of literature. Instead, there has been a recent move to theorize autobiography and textuality more fully: in particular, the value of autobiography as an enunciative strategy and 'method'.[25] Elspeth Probyn, in her book *Sexing the Self* (1994), has also examined the notion of 'experience' and the 'sexed subject' in ways which have enabled many feminists to reconsider and recuperate the use of autobiography in theoretical and critical writing. Thus, Anglo-American criticism is no longer the poor country cousin to the more sophisticated French feminist theory.

The theorization of Anglo-American criticism has also involved a more positive approach to the feminist appropriation of 'male-theory'. One of the most repeated criticisms of French theory by Anglo-American critics in the early days, for example, was its overdepend-ence on the founding 'fathers' of contemporary thought (in particular, Sigmund Freud, Jacques Lacan, Jacques Derrida and Michel Foucault), and 1970s 'gynocriticism' originally presented itself as an alternative to this.[26] Since the mid-1980s, however, such suspicions of the 'male-stream' have been gradually eroded (if not totally erased), as feminists have felt increasingly confident about appropriating such theory for their own purposes – often significantly rewriting it in the process.[27] The feminist rescripting of Lacan and Foucault, in particular, has become big business in recent years and it could be argued that these reconstructed theorists are now often the most visible mark of one's 'identity' as a (feminist) scholar. 'Is she a Foucauldian or a Lacanian?' could possibly be a quicker way of establishing someone's theoretical 'roots' than asking them directly about their feminist identity. This annexing of male-authored 'high' theory has had both positive and negative effects. On the positive side, it has made these 'master-discourses' the legitimate object of feminist enquiry and given visibility to feminist issues in so-called mainstream debates, especially since there are now very few male theorists who have not been subjected to this feminist critique (see note 27). More negatively, it has had the effect of making some feminists consider that they need a male 'mentor' in order to be taken seriously either in feminist circles or in the mainstream. For the present, however (as evidenced by any survey of publishers' catalogues) the feminist dialogue with these 'master-discourses' shows little sign of abating.

One erstwhile metanarrative which has, however, been put under severe pressure since the first publication of this book is Marxism. Indeed, the recent assault on Marxist politics (in literary theory as in the world) must be considered *the* intellectual (counter) revolution of our time, and those of us formerly (or still) identified as 'Marxist-feminists' have been left reeling. The reason for this challenge to what has long been one of the best supported, best documented, social and intellectual movements of the twentieth century lies with the collapse of the Soviet Union, marked, symbolically, by the removal of the Berlin Wall in 1990. Despite the fact that most Marxist intellectuals had long disassociated themselves from Soviet politics *per se* (or, indeed, from Communist governments elsewhere in the world), events in Eastern Europe seemed fundamentally to undermine the designation 'Marxist'. Thus, at a public lecture in 1990, Catherine Belsey became (to our knowledge) one of the first British feminists to disclaim a Marxist identity, stating plainly that the changes taking place in Eastern Europe made it impossible to continue using the term.[28] To the concern of many (then) still Marxist-identified participants in the audience, she announced that she would now describe herself as a 'materialist': a term that has since become a euphemism for the erstwhile Marxist academic, as well as for Foucauldian and 'New Historicist' critics who pledge some concern with the historical specificity of literary/textual production and connections (however complexly conceived) between the text and the lives of men and the women in the 'material world'.

To be a 'materialist', however, is *not* the same as being a Marxist – even in the post-Althusserian, poststructuralist sense that we our-selves adopt in Chapter 6. Whereas Marxist criticism was, however tangentially, tied to a programme of revolutionary social change based on a 'belief' in the primacy of the economic base in the oppression of all 'minority' groups (including women), materialist criticism (especially that influenced by Foucault) refuses to privilege the economic in this way and also lacks any concrete model for the analysis of oppression. Although, as Jeremy Hawthorn observes in his book *Cunning Passages* (1996), Foucauldians, like Marxists, agree that texts need to be understood in relation to the 'institutions, economic and social processes, behavioural patterns, systems of norms, techniques, types of classification, modes of characterization' by which they are inscribed, they refuse (unlike Marxists) to organize these discourses/ideologies according to a hierarchy.[29] Whilst this decentring of the economic base has undoubtedly been useful to feminists wishing to push questions of gender to the fore, some might argue that it has also been at the expense of disassociating gender from the class and economic factors which continue to be instrumental in the oppression of women throughout the world. What this shift has translated into in terms of textual practice, meanwhile, is a certain lack of interest in the representation of women as members of (economically disadvantaged) social groups or communities and an emphasis, instead, on the discourses that produce *individual* female subjectivities (notably psychoanalysis).[30]

Needless to say, as authors of the original Marxist-feminist chapter of this book, we share some concern with this too-easy sublimation of the Marxist into the materialist and would argue that feminists still need to hold on to all that was valuable in the Marxist critique of history and culture (and its representation in literature). It could also be argued that this dismissal of Marxism by a relatively small group of Western intellectuals pays no attention to how the changes have been experienced by Marxist and feminist academics still living in Eastern Europe and elsewhere. In addition, as will become clear in Chapter 6, Marxist literary criticism has provided feminists with many useful tools/strategies for textual analysis as well as with a political framework for that analysis, and much of our criticism is still indebted to the 'method' of 'symptomatic reading' instigated by the French Marxist, Pierre Macherey, and made popular by the writings of critics like Terry Eagleton.[31] We feel, too, that the complaints of some feminists that Marxism *had* to be discredited because of its failure to recognize the competing claims of race and sexuality in women's oppression have been somewhat overstated. British Marxism, post-Raymond Williams, has been fully cognisant of the claims of competing ideologies in the construction of both individuals and societies, and the late 1980s saw some excellent feminist work which brought issues of race, sexuality and colonialism within Marxist frameworks of analysis.[32]

Since the first publication of *Feminist Readings/Feminists Reading*, then, some major changes have occurred in the world of academic feminism: both with respect to the intellectual frameworks and discourses to which that feminism is affiliated, and with respect to the institutional superstructures which now recognize feminist and Women's Studies courses as part of their curriculum. The speed with which Women's Studies, as a legitimate and respected academic discipline, has spread in both Britain and the United States during this period is, indeed, a cause for major celebration. During the past five years the number of universities and colleges in the United Kingdom offering Women's Studies courses (including single-honours degree schemes) at both undergraduate and postgraduate level has mushroomed dramatically, and we are now entering a phase in which many Women's Studies Centres are becoming independent budget-centres or departments and employing their own Women's Studies staff. Such an institutionalization of the feminist project has been inevitably double-edged, however; not least because of the dangers of assimilation and ghettoization. This is linked to the problem that feminism in general, and academic feminism in particular, is threatened by a counter-movement in which individuals (male and female) and institutions are arguing that since 'equality' has now been achieved it is unhelpful for women to continue to represent themselves as the 'victims' of patriarchy. The relationship between this so-called 'post-feminism' and a more straightforward reactionary backlash (a return to 'femininity', 'family values', etc.) is, indeed, a complex and dangerous one, and it is significant that figures like the American writer Camille Paglia are perceived to be feminist, postfeminist and anti-feminist by different interest groups.[33] No matter how complex these contemporary politics become, however, it is clear that, for better or worse, feminism and, by extension feminist literary criticism, is even more diverse than it was in the late 1980s when the book was first published. Whilst we welcome the new attention to 'difference' that has been partly responsible for bringing this about (see above), we also believe in the need for feminism to retain a sense (however imaginary) of itself as a movement with its own history and identity. It is in this spirit that we have produced this new edition of *Feminist Readings/Feminists Reading*, and hope that its chapters – by introducing readers new to the field to some of the key landmarks in the history and development in feminist literary criticism – will constitute a base for today's textual practice.

Guide to the Chapters

As the reader will now have gathered, the format of each chapter is tripartite: the actual reading of the literary text is sandwiched between an introductory section (Part I) which offers a summary and positive evaluation of the critical approach concerned, and a retrospective critique (Part III) which attends to the problems that have arisen as a part of the reading. This final section also offers suggestions as to how the individual theories may be revised/appropriated for use by present-day readers.

Our choice of both literary and theoretical texts has been necessarily selective. While acknowledging the problem of dealing with only token aspects of a theorist's/group of theorists' work, the parameters of the project made it inevitable that we concentrate on just one or two key theoretical texts per chapter, although the introductory sections make reference to the general theoretical context within which the reading is made. Our choice of literary texts has been similarly restricted to a total of seven. These are as follows: Emily Brontë's *Wuthering Heights* (1847); Thomas Hardy's *Tess of the d'Urbervilles* (1891); Jean Rhys's *Wide Sargasso Sea* (1966); Charlotte Perkins Gilman's 'The Yellow Wallpaper' (1899); Angela Carter's *The Magic Toyshop* (1967); Alice Walker's *The Color Purple* (1983); and Margaret Atwood's *Surfacing* (1972). In this selection we have tried to achieve a balance between established 'classics' (such as Hardy and Brontë), recently reclaimed feminist 'classics' (Rhys and Gilman), and popular contemporary writing (Walker, Carter, Atwood). Each chapter will focus on two of these texts; thus each one will be read or referred to by at least two different theoretical positions. In this way it is hoped that readers will begin to differentiate between theories, and also to establish a sense of critical dialogue between them. It will be noted that all the literary texts are by women, with the exception of Hardy's *Tess*, which is included in the chapter on 'Sexual Politics', since Millett was herself primarily concerned with the critique of male texts. When this structure was originally decided upon, we were also well aware of the problems entailed in choosing 'literary texts' to analyze – given women's relative exclusion from 'literary status' – and we remain committed to challenging the canonical mechanism whereby certain texts are privileged over others and are considered to be of more value. In the first edition, we also expressed a hope that, in the not too distant future, it would be possible to discuss women's science fiction, romance, travel writing and political writing *alongside* that which has been regarded as 'high literature'; and , indeed, this incursion into multiple genres has been one of the most notable changes to university syllabuses in the last ten years. For the purposes of this volume, however, our primary concern was accessibility, and we therefore selected texts – from the nineteenth-century to the present-day – which have established themselves as important within a tradition of women's writing. It is interesting to reflect, however, that some of the literary texts we chose to work with – in particular, Alice Walker's *The Color Purple* – are significantly *less* popular now than they were in the mid-1980s, perhaps indicating that the feminist canon is less rigid and fixed than its mainstream counterpart.

In terms of style, our main aim was, and remains, one of clarity and accessibility. Some of the approaches we describe/engage with are notoriously difficult for new readers, and we have avoided using any academic vocabulary which is not fully explained. At the same time, we have endeavoured not to oversimplify the complexity of these arguments and, to assist the new reader, we have supplied a Glossary at the end of the book (which has, of course, been supplemented for the new edition). In this regard, we believe, like Deborah Cameron that, where possible, feminist theoretical discussion should aim to avoid 'mystification' and should appeal to as broad a readership as possible.[34]

The second edition

Behind the reissue of this volume is the recognition that there is still a dearth of books that are (a) truly accessible to readers new to the field of feminist theory and (b) that *demonstrate* the 'engagement' of that theory in the analysis of literary texts.

Feminist Readings/Feminists Reading was first conceived partly in response to the Nottingham University Critical Theory Group's collection of essays, *Literary Theory at Work* (1986).[35] This was one of the first volumes seriously to tackle the question of how theories of language, subjectivity, gender and so on, translate into textual practice, and its focus on the analysis of just three literary texts was a novel way of exploring how very different readings could be made of the same material. While we do, of course, register our acknowledgement of this enterprise, the critical hindsight provided by that book's reception was equally valuable in defining our own project and in helping us to negotiate certain problems. First, we are aware of the problems attending any simplistic notion of 'application' in our analysis of the relationship between theoretical model and literary text. We consequently preferred to think of our own book as supplying the reader with working examples of how particular theoretical positions look in actual readings; and here the word 'example' is used advisedly, since neither 'theoretical position' nor 'reading' could claim to be prescriptive in any way. The function of our chapters is thus primarily to acquaint the reader with *some aspect* of a particular theoretical approach, and then to offer a reading based upon it. However, rather than being content with a reading of a literary text by a theoretical text, we also determined to read the theoretical text *with/through/against* the literary text in a concluding section in each chapter. In this way we hoped to ensure that the theoretical text was not privileged over the literary text in any absolutist or reductive way. This sense of text and theory being *in dialogue* with one another has since become a popular way of conceiving textual practice as is evidenced by a number of books and series which begin from this premise (see, for example, the Edward Arnold 'Interrogating Texts' series and the Open University's 'Theory in Practice' series), but the notion of theory that can be mechanically 'applied' to texts is still dangerously inscribed on the syllabuses of many university 'Introduction to theory' courses.[36]

Response to the Tallack collection of essays, *Literary Theory at Work*, also alerted us to the charges of political ineffectiveness that could be levelled at a textbook which appears to offer the reader a seemingly arbitrary choice of reading positions. As a collective, we all felt strongly that a theoretical position which does not inform a reading strategy in a manifestly feminist way, or change the way the reader approaches that text (or, indeed, the way she thinks about herself and her life) has ultimately little to offer. As Chris Weedon has observed: 'These political questions should be the motivating force behind feminist theory which must always be answerable to the needs of women in our struggle to transform patriarchy'.[37] In other words, our textual practices must, *in the last analysis*, be informed and supported by our feminist belief in a programme for change in the material world. In the Introduction to the first edition, we were consequently concerned to point out that each of the theoretical positions explored in the book could not be mechanically adopted and/or discarded by readers like a change of clothes: part of one's responsibility as a feminist reader/critic is to make informed *choices* between such positions, and for this reason we have worked hard to make visible the political assumptions behind each of the theories with which we engage.

At the same time, a volume such as this one will hopefully prove helpful in demonstrating *how* the same text can solicit a range of different interpretations: how, in particular, literary meaning is determined through the complex interaction of *author*, *text* and *reader*. All the theories considered here, for example, place a slightly different emphasis on each of these terms in the production of meaning (i.e. where the text's meaning is located). Whilst 'Authentic realism', Millett's 'Sexual Politics', and Gilbert and Gubar's criticism thus depend upon a close association between *reader* and *author* in the production of meaning, most of the other theories display a struggle between *reader* and *text* in which sometimes one, and sometimes the other, has the upper hand. It is the variable authority granted these three terms, and the relationship between them, which allows for the wide variations in interpretation that are now associated with literary criticism.[38]

Another problem with the *Literary Theory at Work* essays which we risked replicating with our own volume was the impression that contemporary literary criticism could be neatly carved up into the 'approaches' somewhat artifically manufactured by our own, discrete chapters. As has become increasingly evident in the ten years since the first edition of *Feminist Readings/Feminists Reading*, much feminist textual practice is broadly eclectic in the theories, theorists, and approaches it draws upon, and individual readings are rarely as easily classifiable as we suggest here. This, again, is why the *contextualizing* introductions and conclusions to our own readings are so important, and why – as we move into a new era of theory and criticism – we would prefer to think of these chapters as an *archaeology* of contemporary feminist theory: an exploration of the recent history of criticism that will help new readers identify the 'roots' of our current complex textual practices in order to be more aware of the theoretical assumptions which underlie our current work.

A final potential criticism of volumes like this and *Literary Theory at Work* is that they 'reduce' literary and cultural theory to a concern with interpretation and reading, when the wider remit of such theory is to engage with debates on the status of knowledge, rhetoric, textual structure, canonicity and so on. In other words, theories should, to some extent, be allowed to be theories, and *not* be bound to a narrow explicatory function. Once again, we have responded to this charge – and with renewed attention in this second edition – in the introductory and concluding sections of the chapters in which we attempt to set the theory in its broader epistemological context. We would also reiterate, too, our belief that engaging theories with texts is as useful in reviewing the status of the theory as it is in explicating the texts: often making visible the blind spots of more abstract debate.

Apart from attempting to address, even more directly, many of the problems present in the first edition, however, there were other pressing reasons why this volume needed to be revised. First, there was the need to keep abreast with the changes that have taken place in feminist theory and criticism in the past ten years and to integrate these into the new and revised chapters. The theoretical approaches featured in the first edition of *Feminist Readings/Feminists Reading* were, for the most part, 'historical' by the time the volume was published in 1989; that is to say, they represented critical practices from the 1970s and early 1980s which were already in the process of being challenged, revised and supplemented through poststructuralist developments within feminism. That we, as authors, were ourselves presenting the theories through this revisionary (poststructuralist) lens is something we attempted to spell out in the Introduction to the first edition, but the hindsight of another decade has inevitably enabled us to problematize the approaches even more precisely. What we understand by a 'poststructuralist' framework has also undergone transformation during this period, but the main tenets which we ascribed to are in essence unchanged: namely, a post-Saussurean view of language; a post-Lacanian and post-Althusserian view of subjectivity; a belief in a non-essentialist, and predominantly 'social' construction of gender; a basic rejection of author-intentionality in the production of meaning (see discussion above); and a questioning of certain liberal-humanist views (see Glossary) on the value of (English) literature. Since 1989, these fundamental poststructuralist principles have been augmented by an ever-deepening respect for 'difference' in feminist politics (see discussion in Chapters 7 and 8), and a further destabilizing of 'the (female) subject' as theorists like Judith Butler have challenged the status of all 'identity'.[39]

We maintain, however, that the historical survey of feminist criticism represented by the six original chapters is extremely useful to students coming new to the subject-area. These earlier theories (which, to an extent, have been held artificially separate from one another in our 'applications') have formed the basic building-blocks on which many, more recent, feminist critics have constructed new theoretical positions and textual practices. At the same time, we acknowledge that other aspects of feminist theory have developed in direct *conflict* with the earlier models (the post-colonial feminist critic's problematization of a homogenizing gynocriticism, for example: see Chapter 8), and in these cases a familiarity with the political blind spots of the former generation will help new readers understand the logic (and passion!) of the contemporary debates.

Whilst it is extremely difficult, meanwhile, to prevent a survey-guide such as this one from becoming dated (by the time of going to press, even the most recent theories we discuss here will already be history), our new chapters on lesbian and post-colonial theory will hopefully offer some indication of how the earlier theories have been taken up, revised and/or rejected under these two, demonstrably hybrid theoretical configurations. For as Chapters 7 and 8 make abundantly clear, radically opposing theoretical models of text and subject have been engaged in the service of both of these interest groups, and despite the unresolved tensions between, in particular, materialist and psychoanalytic discourses, some very exciting, very challenging, new criticism has emerged.

Needless to say, we are also aware that that there have been many other developments in feminist theory – and many more inspiring illustrations of theoretically hybrid textual practice – that are *not* featured in this new edition. Apart from the type of feminist criticism associated with New Historicism and Cultural Materialism, mentioned above (see note 18 below) which has produced excellent new feminist readings of Shakespeare and Foucauldian-based engagements with literature from a whole range of other historical periods, we should also acknowledge the feminist revisions of contemporary literature and culture provided by postmodernist feminist critics such as Linda Hutcheon and Patricia Waugh, together with the American 'deconstructionist' reworking of French feminist and post-Lacanian theory by critics such as Elizabeth Meese and Shari Benstock, and the engagement of object-relations theory by many psychoanalytic writers looking for an alternative to the Freudian/Lacanian tradition.[40] In addition, there have been rapid and radically destabilizing developments in Black feminist theory and criticism quite apart from those discussed here under the heading of post-colonial theory, not least through a new focus on the politics of 'whiteness'.[41] As this cursory list itself indicates, however, it is becoming increasingly difficult for the feminist scholar to define any of these more recent projects as a discrete theoretical approach, and we have probably arrived at the stage of literary theoretical history where no number of volumes of this kind would adequately cover the range, and mix, of critical practices now available. In this respect, the new Chapters 7 and 8 are perhaps best regarded as indices of the complexity and hybridity of most contemporary feminist theory and textual practice, and the difficulty we would now have in grouping theorists – even those united by a common political interest, such as race or sexuality – under one heading. As far as *future* feminist theory goes, therefore, it seems unlikely that we would be able to produce an introductory guide of this kind that is any way useful. The 'standpoints' of contemporary feminist theory are simply too diverse.

The first edition of *Feminist Readings* was written over a two-year period when the four original authors (Sara Mills, Lynne Pearce, Sue Spaull and Elaine Millard) were all postgraduate students based in Glasgow, Birmingham, London and Nottingham. We had met because of our connections with Birmingham and Nottingham Universities, and had all been involved in, and were active in, feminist discussion groups and mainstream theory groups (for example, the long-established David Lodge seminar at Birmingham University; feminist theory groups at Birmingham and Nottingham Universities; and the Nottingham University Critical Theory group). The idea for the book developed out of discussions we had with each other about the lack of an introductory textbook on feminist theory which we could use, either with students, or with other people outside the academic world who were new to the field. Once we had the contract for the book, and started writing our draft chapters, we began to work as a collective: meeting at each other's houses and at conferences, and sending material to each other on disc. We also talked to each other over the phone and extensively rewrote (and/or commented on) each other's material. Although this process of collective writing was stressful at times, it was also immensely productive in teaching us about collaborative work and ways of writing which did not privilege one author at the expense of another. Although now, in 1996, we are based in different parts of the country (Sheffield, Lancaster, London and Nottingham) and our professional and personal lives have changed greatly, we still regularly keep in touch. From being postgraduate students, two of us (Sara and Lynne) are based in English and Cultural Studies Departments, Elaine works in an Education Department, and Sue works as a housing adviser in London. Despite the divisive individualism of Thatcherite politics, both within academia and in British society generally, we have all maintained our commitment to feminism, and our lives continue to be informed and enriched by feminist thought. Two of us (Lynne and Sara) have taken responsibility for this new edition of *Feminist Readings/Feminists Reading*, largely because of the logistic difficulty of co-ordinating a 'rewrite' when we are no longer able to meet up as easily as we did previously. Elaine and Sue have, however, played a significant role in the revision process and have been consulted throughout in terms of the revision of material which started life as theirs. We have made the decision to attribute the chapters to whoever was most fundamentally instructive in writing them (whilst also noting which of us was primarily responsible for the revisions). The extent to which we have amended or rewritten the text varies considerably from chapter to chapter, but it will be seen that our most substantive revisions have, in every case, been to the introductory and concluding sections where we were committed to recontextualizing the theory and (as far as possible) bringing it up-to-date. Aside from this, we have drawn upon our experience of using the text in the seminar room to clarify points which have proved difficult or confusing to student readers. We appreciate now, even more than we did with the first publication of the volume, how bewildering a theoretical vocabulary can be to readers coming new to this type of writing, and have therefore worked to eradicate any assumptions of prior knowledge. Because a good deal of basic theoretical terminology occurs in every chapter, however, we have cross-referenced definitions, or directed readers to the Glossary, rather than repeating material in every instance.

In terms of its production, we realize that such a hybrid text as this has now become rare in scholarly writing, but rather than apologizing, we hope that this alternative, collaborative mode of textual production will encourage our readers to participate more fully in the dialogues and debates that are represented in the text. And because there can be no final word on how feminists read, we are happy to entrust the future of these debates to each new generation of feminist readers.

Lynne Pearce and Sara Mills
1996

Notes

1. Julia Kristeva, 'Women's time', in Toril Moi (ed.), *The Kristeva Reader* (Blackwell, Oxford, 1986); see also Toril Moi's *Sexual/Textual Politics* for a discussion of these stages (pp. 12–13).
2. Tillie Olsen, *Silences* (Virago, London, 1980).
3. See, for example, Virginia Woolf, *A Room of One's Own* (Granada, London, 1977).
4. Kate Millett, *Sexual Politics* (Virago, London, 1977).
5. Mary Ellmann, *Thinking About Women* (Harcourt, New York, 1968).
6. Arlyn Diamond and Lee R. Edwards (eds), *The Authority of Experience: Essays in Feminist Criticism* (University of Massachusetts Press, Amherst, 1977).
7. Josephine Donovan (ed.), *Feminist Literary Criticism: Explorations in Theory* (University of Kentucky Press, Lexington, 1975).
8. Cheri Register, 'American feminist literary criticism: a bibliographical introduction' in Donovan (see note 7), p. 10.
9. Judith Fetterley, *The Resisting Reader: A Feminist Approach to American Fiction* (Indiana University Press, Bloomington, 1978).
10. Elaine Showalter, *A Literature of their Own: British Women Novelists from Brontë to Lessing* (Princeton University Press, Princeton, 1977); Ellen Moers, *Literary Women: The Great Writers* (Women's Press, London, 1976).
11. Dale Spender, *Mothers of the Novel* (Pandora, London, 1986). See also Jane Spencer, *The Rise of the Woman Novelist* (Blackwell, Oxford, 1986).
12. Elaine Showalter, 'Feminist criticism in the wilderness' in Elaine Showalter (ed.), *The New Feminist Criticism: Essays on Women, Literature and Theory* (Virago, London, f. publ. 1981).
13. Sandra Gilbert and Susan Gubar, *The Madwoman in the Attic: The Woman Writer and the Nineteenth-Century Literary Imagination* (Yale University Press, New Haven, 1979).
14. See Elaine Marks and Isabelle de Courtivron, *New French Feminisms* (Harvester Wheatsheaf, Hemel Hempstead, 1980) and Toril Moi, *French Feminist Thought* (Blackwell, Oxford, 1987).
15. An explanation of these concepts and terms is provided in Chapter 5; readers should also refer to the Glossary for brief summaries. See also

Elizabeth Wright (ed.), *Feminism and Psychoanalysis: A Critical Dictionary* (Blackwell, Oxford, 1992).

16. Freudian theory in particular seemed to propose that women's anatomy predisposed them to certain types of psychic structures, most notably hysteria. Early Anglo-American feminists (e.g. Kate Millett: see Chapter 1) were highly critical of such assumptions, stressing instead the socially constructed nature of both bodily experience and psychic structures. For a critical review of this anti-essentialist tendency see Diana Fuss's *Essentially Speaking* (Routledge, London, 1989).

17. See Shoshana Felman, 'Women and madness: the critical phallacy', *Diacritics*, vol. 5, no. 4, 1975; Alice Jardine, *Gynesis: Configurations of Women and Modernity* (Cornell University Press, Ithaca, 1985). Although we have characterized this division as primarily French, Toril Moi has shown that there is a substantial amount of work being done in the United Kingdom and the United States by what she terms 'French Americans'. See Moi, 'Feminism, postmodernism, and style: recent feminist criticism in the US' (paper given at Strathclyde University, 1989).

18. New Historicism is probably best thought of as an umbrella term which refers to the renewed interest in, and legitimation of, reading texts in their historical context which began in Europe and America in the early 1980s. New Historicism differs from the earlier engagements of literature and history through its broadly poststructuralist view of the text, and by regarding history itself as a configuration of discourses rather than a quasi-objective database of facts and figures. Cultural Materialism has developed as the largely British wing of New Historicism, and unlike the American-based Cultural Poetics, puts a particular emphasis on making connections between the historical context in which a text was produced and present-day discourses in its interrogation of various types of power-relation. Cultural poetics focuses more specifically on relating texts to the discursive fields in which they were originally produced and consumed. See Jeremy Hawthorn, *Cunning Passages: New Historicism, Cultural Materialism and Marxism* (Edward Arnold, London, 1996).

19. With respect to the interrogating of heterosexuality see Judith Butler, *Gender Trouble* (Routledge, London and New York, 1990) and *Bodies that Matter* (Routledge, London and New York, 1993) and Eve Kosofsky Sedgwick, *Epistemology of the Closet* (Harvester Wheatsheaf, Hemel Hempstead, 1991) and *Tendencies* (Routledge, London and New York, 1994) (both these theorists are discussed in Chapter 7). With respect to 'whiteness' see Ruth Frankenberg, *White Women, Race Matters: The Social Construction of Whiteness* (Routledge, London, 1993) and helen (charles), 'Whiteness – the relevance of politically colouring the "non" ', in *Working Out: New Directions for Women's Studies*, ed. Hilary Hinds *et al.* (Falmer, London and Washington DC, 1991), pp. 29–35).

20. See, for example, Sara Mills, *Discourses of Difference: An Analysis of Women's Travel Writing and Colonialism* (Routledge, London and New

York, 1991); Laura Donaldson, *Decolonizing Feminisms: Race, Gender and Empire Building* (Routledge, London and New York, 1993); and Chela Sandoval, 'Third World feminism', in *Genders*, no. 10, Spring 1991, pp. 1–24.

21. See Judith Butler's two books cited in note 19 above and Diana Fuss, *Essentially Speaking* (Routledge, London and New York, 1989).

22. Tania Modleski, *Feminism without Women: Culture and Criticism in a 'Postfeminist' Age* (Routledge, London and New York, 1991).

23. In the United States, especially, some feminists see 'coalition politics', both within feminism, and between feminism and other interest groups, as the only effective means of bringing about change. See, for example, Kathy E. Ferguson, *The Man Question: Visions of Subjectivity in Feminist Theory* (University of California Press, Berkeley, 1993).

24. At the time of writing, the leading feminist publishers Virago are themselves the subject of a takeover bid by Random House, and many smaller presses have recently been bought out or are struggling for survival.

25. See Elspeth Probyn, *Sexing the Self* (Routledge, London and New York, 1993) and also the essays in *Feminist Subjects, Multi-Media: Cultural Methodologies*, ed. Penny Florence and Dee Reynolds (Manchester University Press, Manchester, 1994). An excellent example of the 'new autobiography' in action is Annette Kuhn's *Family Secrets* (Routledge, London and New York, 1995).

26. See especially Elaine Showalter's essay 'Towards a feminist poetics', in *The New Feminist Criticism* (see note 12 above).

27. See, for example: Jana Sawicki, *Disciplining Foucault: Feminism, Power and the Body* (Routledge, London and New York, 1991); Caroline Ramazanoglu, *Up Against Foucault* (Routledge, London and New York, 1993); Elizabeth Grosz, *Jacques Lacan: A Feminist Introduction* (Routledge, London and New York, 1990); Kelly Oliver, *Womanizing Nietzsche* (Routledge, London and New York, 1994); Johanna Meehan, *Habermas and Feminism* (Routledge, London and New York, 1995); Alison Assister, *Althusser and Feminism* (Pluto, London, 1990).

28. Catherine Belsey made this pronouncement at the Gillian Skirrow Memorial Lecture, Strathclyde University, 1990. Belsey stated that it was visits to the United States that first drove her to avoid using the term 'Marxist' where it was repeatedly confused with communism. Other Marxist-feminists have, however, chosen to retain the term, and some useful reflective work has been done by critics around the relative merits of the terms 'Marxist' and 'Materialist'. See, for example, Donna Landry and Gerald MacLean, *Materialist Feminisms* (Blackwell, Oxford, 1993) and Rosemary Hennessy, *Materialist Feminism and the Politics of Discourse* (Routledge, London, 1993).

29. Hawthorn, *Cunning Passages* (see note 18 above).

30. See Sandoval, note 20 above.

31. See Pierre Macherey, *A Theory of Literary Production* (Routledge and Kegan Paul, London, 1978) and Terry Eagleton, *Against the Grain: Essays 1975–1985* (Verso, London, 1986). These reading practices are discussed in detail in Chapter 6.

32. See Raymond Williams, *Marxism and Literature* (Oxford University Press, Oxford, 1977), p. 125. Texts following the Williams model include Lynne Pearce's *Woman/Image/Text* (Harvester Wheatsheaf, Hemel Hempstead, 1991) and much of the feminist theory discussed in Terry Lovell's edited Reader, *British Feminist Thought* (Blackwell, Oxford, 1990). As Lovell states in the Introduction to the latter: 'While it was American feminism which, historically, provided the major point of reference for radical feminist thought, therefore acting as a powerful detonator of the British movement, socialist feminism conversely owes its greatest debt to British feminism' (p. 4).

33. Camille Paglia became a celebrity figure with the publication of her books *Sexual Personae* (Yale University Press, New Haven, 1990) and *Sex, Art and American Culture* (Penguin, Harmondsworth, 1994).

34. Deborah Cameron, *Feminism and Linguistic Theory* (Macmillan, Basingstoke, 1985).

35. Douglas Tallack (ed.), *Literary Theory at Work: Three Texts* (Batsford, London, 1986). This book is a collection of readings of three literary texts using a range of literary theoretical positions; for example, structuralist, Marxist, feminist. Elaine Millard was one of the contributors to the volume ('Feminism II: reading as a woman', pp. 135–57) and Sara Mills sat in on several of the discussion sessions for the book. We feel this book has served an extremely important function, since many students who feel intimidated by literary theory have felt enabled by an approach which gives concrete examples of reading practices: what literary theory can enable you to *say* about a literary text. Further examples of this kind of book include Alan Durant and Nigel Fabb's *Literary Theory in Action* (Routledge, London, 1990) and Dave Murray's *Literary Theory and Poetry* (Batsford, London, 1989).

36. Books already published in the Edward Arnold 'Interrogating Texts' series include: Patricia Waugh's *Practising Postmodernism, Reading Modernism* (Edward Arnold, London, 1992); Lynne Pearce's *Reading Dialogics* (Edward Arnold, London, 1994); Linda Williams's *Critical Desire: Psychoanalysis and the Literary Subject* (Edward Arnold, London, 1995); and Jeremy Hawthorn's *Cunning Passages* (see note 18 above). The Open University 'Theory in Practice' series, edited by Tony Davies, Barbara Rasmussen and Nigel Wood aims to read one canonical text through/against a range of different theoretical perspectives; each volume is thus focused on one literary text. Titles currently available include *Don Juan, Mansfield Park, A Passage to India, The Prelude* and *The Waste Land*.

37. See Chris Weedon, *Feminist Practice and Post-structuralist Theory* (Blackwell, Oxford, 1987), pp. 1–2.

38. For further discussion of the roles of author, text and reader in the production of meaning see Lynne Pearce's ' "I" the reader: text, context and the balance of power' in *Feminist Subjects, Multi-Media: Cultural Methodologies*, ed. Penny Florence and Dee Reynolds (Manchester University Press, Manchester and New York, 1995, pp. 160–170 and also *Feminism and the Politics of Reading* (Edward Arnold, London, 1997). Another volume devoted to this subject is *Gendering*

the Reader, ed. Sara Mills (Harvester Wheatsheaf, Hemel Hempstead, 1994).

39.   See Judith Butler, note 19 above. Butler's assault on 'identity politics' is discussed in Chapter 7.

40.   See Linda Hutcheon, *A Poetics of Postmodernism: History, Theory, Fiction* (Routledge, London and New York, 1990); Patricia Waugh, *Practising Postmodernism/Reading Modernism* (Edward Arnold, London, 1992); Shari Benstock, *Textualizing the Feminine* (University of Oklahoma Press, Norman, 1991) and Elizabeth Meese, 'Theorizing lesbian: writing – a love letter' in *Lesbian Texts and Contexts*, ed. Karla Jay and Joanne Glasgow (New York University Press, New York, 1990), pp. 70–87.

41.   See note 19 above.

1
Sexual politics

Lynne Pearce

Kate Millett: *Sexual Politics*
Thomas Hardy: *Tess of the d'Urbervilles*
Emily Brontë: *Wuthering Heights*

I

The 1977 Virago edition of Kate Millett's *Sexual Politics* has emblazoned across its cover the words, 'World Bestseller'.[1] This, indeed, it was, and today, almost three decades after its original publication in 1969, it is sometimes easy for feminists to forget its initial impact: what Toril Moi has described as a 'powerful fist in the solar plexus of patriarchy'.[2] Reviews in the popular press conspired with the sensationalism of its marketing, proclaiming it 'breathtaking in its command of history and literature' (*New York Times*) and 'One of those rare books that can change your outlook and force you to re-examine the way you live . . .' *New Statesman* (quoted on the cover of the 1977 Virago edition). With Germaine Greer's *The Female Eunuch* (1971), *Sexual Politics* was the text that relaunched the modern Women's Movement in both its popular and academic manifestations. It was a manifesto for revolution whose challenge to patriarchy is implicit in all subsequent feminist writing.

The reason why *Sexual Politics* was instantly received as a revolutionary text is no mystery: it simply proclaimed itself as such. As recent critics like Toril Moi have observed, it was the polemical nature of Millett's text that distinguished it from other contemporary, more circumspect studies (such as Mary Ellmann's *Thinking About Women*, 1968: see Bibliography) and ensured its popular attention. *Sexual Politics* came waving its own red flag.

Any assessment of *Sexual Politics* consequently needs to account for not only its analysis of patriarchy, which has been severely challenged in recent years, but also the legitimacy of polemic as a critical genre.

23

Most criticism of Millett's work by other feminists, in literary criticism in particular, has been essentially a quarrel with this one problem. Thus, while Moi begins by applauding Millett for the revolutionary impact of polemic on reading practice:

> The most striking aspect of Millett's critical studies . . . though, is the boldness with which she 'reads against the grain' of the literary text . . . Millett's importance as a literary critic lies in her relentless defence of the reader's right to posit her own viewpoint, rejecting the received hierarchy of text and reader,

she subsequently condemns her for bias, inaccuracy and 'rhetorical reductionism' (pp. 24–5). Cora Kaplan, who concentrates in particular on Millett's selective misreadings of Freud, concludes: 'She looks for, and in most cases finds, a concrete reading, ties it to the text and heaves it over the side'.[3] The practical problems which can, indeed, be shown to result from a polemical approach will become manifest in the course of this reading. Here, however, I feel it necessary to defend the role of polemic both in Millett's text and in future feminist criticism. Polemic is by definition biased and controversial, and as Ann Jones has observed, Millett's text never claims to be anything else:

> Millett's application of sexual political theory to texts was not designed to produce subtler or more complete readings of, for example, D. H. Lawrence. Instead it sought to highlight certain tendencies and assumptions within his work in the first wave of feminist consciousness raising.[4]

Before proceeding with a summary of *Sexual Politics* itself, I will therefore attempt to resituate this type of writing in the context of 1990s feminism.

The role of polemical writing within the feminist movement has become an issue, once again, in the mid-1990s. American writers like Naomi Wolf (*The Beauty Myth*, 1991, and *Fighting Fire with Fire*, 1993) have defended their own, unashamedly polemical commentaries on the role of women in 'postmodernist'/'postfeminist' society by arguing that each *new* generation of women requires its own 'consciousness raising'.[5] Although we might hope that the feminist movement, as a movement, has achieved *some* improvements in women's lives in the past thirty years, there are many injustices of patriarchy that each new generation needs to discover for itself; or this, at least, is how Wolf has met the criticism that the 'scandals' dealt with in *The Beauty Myth* are 'old-hat'. Whilst I would certainly not wish to give my wholehearted support to the work of the so-called 'American new-wave feminists' (and writers like Naomi Wolf, Susan Faludi, Katie Roiphe and Camille Paglia are often unproblematically and unfairly yoked together under this heading), I do accept the reasoning that feminism (including academic feminism) needs a popular and, on occasion, evangelical voice.[6] The problem of finding a space for such voices within academia is, however, frustrated by the movement towards an ever-increasing anxiety and defensiveness within theoretical writing: an anxiety prompted, partly, by new standards of 'political correctness' (especially over issues such as 'essentialism', but also by the solipsistic mode that characterizes many recent (post-1990) texts). Instead of a writer presenting an argument which invites/provokes a 'dialogic' response, most of us feel that our academic credibility will be jeopardized if we 'lay ourselves open' in such a way.[7] As a consequence, our theses, as I have discussed elsewhere, have become almost agonizingly cautious and self-reflexive: 'one step forwards followed by two steps back'.[8] Within academic feminism, alas, polemic is no longer an accepted, rhetorical mode and this is why it is the journalists, marketed as feminists, that are stealing the show. Of all these 'new wave' texts, meanwhile, the one that bears the closest resemblance to *Sexual Politics* is Susan Faludi's *Backlash* (see note 6), to which it was directly compared in the 'hype' that surrounded its publication.

In the remainder of this introductory section, I offer a summary and assessment of *Sexual Politics*. I shall describe the organization of the book, its central theoretical premises and the main features of Millett's literary analyses. With respect to the latter, I shall pay special attention to her readings of Thomas Hardy's *Jude the Obscure* from what she has designated the period of the 'Sexual Revolution', and to her reading of D. H. Lawrence from the 'Counter-Revolution'. At all times, my reading will be directed towards revealing hypotheses and techniques that have a practical application in feminist criticism and which will hopefully be demonstrated in my own readings of Thomas Hardy's *Tess of the d'Urbervilles* and Emily Brontë's *Wuthering Heights*.

Millett's text is divided into three main sections: 'Sexual politics', 'Historical background' and 'The literary reflection'. The first of these opens with a sub-section entitled 'Instances of sexual politics', where quotation of some of the most pornographic scenes from the work of Henry Miller and Norman Mailer could also have had something to do with the book's instant popular recognition. By selecting such overtly 'crude' and covertly misogynistic examples, Millett was able to demonstrate the fascist potential of heterosexual relations with little critical elucidation. Framed by a few ironic asides, Millett allows the texts to speak for themselves. This technique has been widely imitated by feminist critics since, especially in the realm of media studies. Numerous books and articles have exposed the sexism and porno-graphy of images simply by reproducing them in a critical context.[9] While such an approach has not been without its problems, its central role in feminist consciousness-raising cannot be denied. Sexual political criticism is based on the principle of *exposing* patriarchal authority, and Millett's window on these bedroom scenes anticipates many famous 'naked apes'. Successful sexual political criticism begins with the art of incriminating quotation.

It is in the second section of the first part of the book that Millett outlines her 'theory of sexual politics'. This has already been summarized by other feminist readers who concentrate, rightly, on two key aspects of her argument: her definition of politics and her conception of patriarchy. The first of these is accounted for by the following oft-quoted sentence: 'The term "politics" shall refer to power-structured relationships, arrangements whereby one group of persons is controlled by another.'[10] Consequently, 'sexual politics' is to do with the potential oppression of one sex by another in the same way that racial politics is to do with the assumed authority of one racial group, or class politics with the ascendency of a particular class. Particularly important is the fact that politics in all these instances is an exercise of power which is not officially inscribed in state legislature. Those who govern have not been elected, and their 'subjects' are entirely without representation: 'For it is precisely because certain groups have no representation in a number of recognized political structures that their position tends to be so stable, their oppression so continuous' (Millett, p. 24). They are political institutions, in other words, which do not officially exist.

Yet although Millett aligns sexual oppression with racial and class oppression, her whole argument depends on the assumption that patriarchy comes first; that it subsumes all other categories of oppression: 'While the same might be said of class, patriarchy has a still more tenacious and powerful hold through its successful habit of passing itself off as nature' (p. 58). It is this view of patriarchy as a transcendent and monolithic force, the *origin* of all capitalist and class oppression, that has proved a central target for Millett's critics. While the exact relationship between patriarchy and the other forms of oppression is still far from being resolved (see Chapter 6 for further discussion of this), feminist critics like Kaplan and Moi have attacked Millett's thesis for being too simplistic. Millett does not, in Moi's words, allow that capitalism is itself 'a contradictory construct, marked by gaps, slides and inconsistencies' (p. 26), but conceives of it rather as a 'conscious, well-organised male conspiracy' (p. 28). Patriarchy, as the political institution by which one sex is oppressed by another, is the template for all forms of oppression. In a later section on the polemical manifestation of the sexual revolution, Millett underlines this point by invoking the similar conclusions of Marx and Engels, which she summarizes thus:

Under patriarchy, the concept of property advanced from its simple origins in chattel womanhood, to private ownership of goods, land and capital. In the subjection of female to male, Engels (and Marx as well) saw the historical and conceptual prototype of all subsequent power systems, all invidious economic relations, and the effect of oppression itself. (p. 121)

Yet if Millett's conception of patriarchy can be seen as monolithic (and her simplification of the Marxist analysis is undeniable), her enumeration of the *means* by which that patriarchy is manifested in modern society is not. In the chapter on the theory of sexual politics, she proceeds to examine eight ways in which patriarchy is both realized and sustained, namely: 'ideology', 'biology', 'sociology', 'anthropology', 'psychology', 'economics and education', 'force' and 'class'. These 'notes towards a theory of patriarchy', which draw upon a number of sociological and other texts, provide the reader with useful categories with which to produce a sexual political reading of a text, some of which will be employed in the following reading of *Tess* and *Wuthering Heights*. Most original is Millett's specification of the 'psychological', the omission of which she feels was crucial in earlier theories of patriarchy. To correct this deficiency, she draws parallels with the work done on 'racial' minorities to argue that the ideology of patriarchy 'goes deeper' than economic oppression.[11] Supported by a biological determinism which regards the social dependency of the female as 'natural', patriarchy effects 'ego damage' on the female through subtle psychological pressure:

When in any group of persons the ego is subjected to such invidious versions of itself through social beliefs, ideology and tradition, the effect is bound to be pernicious. This coupled with the persistent though subtle denigration women encounter daily through personal contacts, the impressions gathered from the images and the media about them, and the discrimination in matters of behaviour, employment, and education which they endure, should make it no special cause for surprise that women develop group characteristics common to those who suffer minority status and a marginal existence. (p. 55)

This notion of female inferiority is held by both sexes in a set of shared, but mostly unspoken, 'beliefs' that women (like Black people) are intellectually inferior, emotional rather than rational, primitive and childlike, more sensually and sexually oriented. They are also assumed to have a 'contentment with their own lot', 'a wily habit of deceit, and concealment of feeling' (p. 57). These assumptions in turn force the victims into a number of 'accommodational tactics', because they are thought to be weak, they can win attention only through 'ingratiating or supplicatory behaviour', because they are thought to be ignorant, they have to appear it. We will see examples of such behaviour in the female characters in *Tess of the d'Urbervilles* and *Wuthering Heights*.

The second section of Millett's book records political, polemical and literary participation in the two historical periods Millett has designated 'The sexual revolution' (1830–1930) and 'The counter-revolution' (1930–60). For the feminist literary critic, the most interesting aspect of this analysis is its reading of selected literary texts from the period of the Sexual Revolution. In contrast with polemical texts like John Stuart Mill's *On the Subjection of Women* or John Ruskin's 'Of Queen's Gardens' which 'had a definite stand to take for or against the sexual revolution', the literature of the period was 'confused in its response' (p. 29). Millett interprets this ambivalence as being due to the fact that writers were 'afraid, delighted and guilty' of the sexual revolution their works 'reflected', and, because their response was not properly formulated theoretically, they were able to 'explore sexual politics at an inchoate primary level' (p. 129). This recognition of indeterminacy on the part of the authors concerned prepares the way for her readings of Thomas Hardy, George Meredith and Charlotte Brontë, whom she presents as enlightened, if confused and inconsistent, in their portrayal of relationships between the sexes. Consequently, Hardy's 'nervousness' in his treatment of Sue Brideshead in *Jude the Obscure* is put down to the fact that while he perceived, he did not fully understand, the combination of social and psychological forces at work in the New Woman:

> At the other pole [from Arabella] stands Sue – pure spirit. They [she and Arabella] are the familiar Lily and Rose, but Sue is a lily with a difference – she has a brain. Yet she is repelled by sense, for Sue is not only the New Woman, but a complex set of frequently unsympathetic defences, at times convincing, and at times only a rather labored ambivalence of Hardy's own – she is the Frigid Woman as well. Hardy is disgusted by Arabella, appalled, if intrigued, by her crude and terrible vitality. He champions Sue through a series of uningratiating manoeuvers, but he is always slightly nervous of her. (p. 130)

It must be said that the confusion Millett accredits to Hardy here can as easily be seen as the result of her own reading method which, starting from the premise that literature is a 'reflection' of the real world, is unable to decide how much or how little responsibility to give the author. Hardy may well have been ambivalent about his own response to the sexual revolution, but this does not disguise the fact that Millett's own reading position is equally confused. On the one hand, she is eager to praise Hardy for his 'insight' into Sue's character (as though she were an objectified 'real' person); on the other, she criticizes some incredible or inconsistent twist in the plot ('This is not to say that the portrait is without flaws. Sue is broken by the arbitrary death of her children; Hardy's murder – their own suicide' (p. 131)). In other words, she is unclear about Hardy's authorial relation to 'his' characters and to what extent she should make his 'intentions' the basis for her own evaluation of the text. I will return to these problems in my critique of Millett's theory in Part III. Here, however, I wish to offset these difficulties with a summary of the ways in which Millett's reading does constitute a significant feminist perspective on Hardy's novel. First, and perhaps most importantly, she reveals the way in which the mystery surrounding Sue's sexuality is *related* to her feminist opposition to 'a number of patriarchal institutions, principally marriage and the church' (p. 131). Her tragedy is the direct result of her inability to have the courage of her own convictions: she deplores the institutions oppressing her, but is unable to fulfil her sexual life outside them because she still fears them. She desires sexual revolution, but she cannot quite believe in it. As Millett writes:

> The moment her children are dead Sue breaks like a straw . . . All her shaky but hard-earned faith in her own intelligence and the critical analysis it had accomplished on the society she had inhabited was assailed by collapses before what she confesses is her 'awe and terror of conventions I don't believe in. It comes over me at times like a creeping paralysis'. (p. 132)

Millett also uses her analysis of the psychological effects of patriarchy to note that both Sue and Isabella exhibit the 'self-hatred and contempt' common to all oppressed groups. This self-hatred is personal, but is also collective; like the majority of women in patriarchal society, they 'despise womanhood'. Indeed, it could be argued that one of the reasons Sue's rebellion failed was that, although it attacked patriarchy, it was not supported by any compensatory love or respect for women. Along with this general lack of self-respect, Millett also shows that Sue suffers from a specific sexual guilt. Her 'terror of conventions' (mentioned above) is essentially the belief (product of the biological, anthropological and psychological tenets of patriarchy) that 'sex is female and evil' (p. 131). Her resulting masochism is, as we shall see, of a similar order to Tess's. Millett quotes the line, 'I cannot humiliate myself too much. I should like to prick myself all over with pins and bleed out the badness that's in me' (pp. 132–3).

Millett considers George Meredith's writings in a similar vein to her analysis of Hardy. *The Egoist* (1879), like *Jude the Obscure*, is a shrewd analysis of sexual political relations, but is similarly confused in its conclusion, in this case, marriage: 'This hardly seems satisfactory. It would be a splendid thing if the bitter generality of sexual politics were all to be solved in marrying the right person, and the sexual revolution confined and completed by a honeymoon in Switzerland' (p. 139). And it is for this very reason – that is, the resistance to a happy ending in marriage – that Millett singles out Charlotte Brontë's *Villette* (1853) as a true 'expression of revolutionary sensibility' (p. 147). This particular reading is one that has been repeatedly attacked by Millett's critics for its 'creative misreading'. Even what Millett reads as its resistance to conventional closure (i.e. marriage) is, according to Moi, totally unfounded, since: 'Brontë leaves the question of Paul's death unsettlingly open' (p. 30). Whether or not we accept Millett's reading, we are thus returned to the question of polemical discourse, and what limitations, if any, we seek to impose upon it. As long as we understand that Millett is not claiming her reading to be the only one, it may be considered liberating. By suggesting that Lucy Snowe actively resists the authority of M. Paul in this final manoeuvre, Millett posits an alternative to popular sentimental readings of the text. I shall engage a similar position in my own reading of *Wuthering Heights*, where the hero status of male characters does not absolve them of patriarchal tyranny.

In the following section of *Sexual Politics*, Millett describes how the incipient challenge of these nineteenth-century texts was silenced by the reactionary forces of the Counter-Revolution (1930–60). Apart from surveying the political events in Europe which supported this change (the aftermath of the revolution in the USSR and ascendency of the Third Reich in Nazi Germany), Millett mounts what Moi describes as a 'savage demolition' (p. 27) of Freud and psychoanalytic theory. This is the section of *Sexual Politics* that was probably of most lasting influence on the development of feminism in the 1970s and 1980s. As Moi acknowledged (in 1985): 'Millett's denunciation of psychoanalysis is still widely accepted by feminists both inside and outside of the women's movement' (p. 29). It is also the part of the study that has been most vigorously attacked by feminist psychoanalytic critics in recent years.[12]

It should be remembered that at the time Millett was writing, Freudian theory had effected a major social revolution in the Western world. Acknowledging that Freud's influence in the United States was 'almost incalculable', Millett was intent on exposing what she believed to be the pernicious sexual politics behind his theory: 'The effect of Freud's work, that of his followers, and still more, that of his popularizers, was to rationalize the invidious relationship between the sexes; to ratify traditional roles, and to validate temperamental differences' (p. 178). Although criticized by feminists like Juliet Mitchell (see note 12) for misreading Freud's work, Millett does (albeit in passing) pay tribute to his 'major contribution' to the understanding of the unconscious and infant sexuality, and she also acknowledges that 'vulgar Freudianism . . . exceeded the man's original intentions' (p. 178). Indeed, what her analysis does is attack this 'vulgar Freudianism', which by 1969 had become the popular understanding of penis-envy, in particular. In a series of subtle (her critics would say 'deceitful') manoeuvres, Millett represents Freudian theory as both descriptive and prescriptive. Freud's most serious impact, she argues, was the implication that women were not only sexually disadvantaged, but that the only way for them to meet that disadvantage was to accept it, and to sublimate their desires in the alternative desire for children. Millett concludes that Freud had totally failed to recognize the *social* causes for the female's envy of the male:

> Confronted with so much evidence for the male's superior status, sensing on all sides the depreciation in which they are held, girls envy not the penis, but what the penis gives one social pretensions to. Freud appears to have made a major and rather foolish confusion between biology and culture, anatomy and status. (p. 187)

Ultimately, too, Freudian theory had the effect of supporting the easy association of 'masculinity and femininity with the genetic reality of the male and the female' (p. 203), which was particularly important in Millett's own readings of Lawrence, which we will now briefly consider.

In departments of English literature, *Sexual Politics* is known primarily for its readings of Lawrence. This, indeed, is how I first came across it, directed by a tutor who tactfully suggested I balance my own post-'A'-Level 'mystical' readings of the texts with something more materialist or political. Being placed in this context (i.e. as a 'reference' for students of Lawrence), has caused *Sexual Politics* to be identified primarily with twentieth-century counter-revolutionary texts; the inference being that a sexual political reading is a strategy to be applied to male writers like Lawrence who were *consciously* promoting patriarchal oppression. Such a narrow interpretation of Millett's project in *Sexual Politics* is, as I hope I have shown, unwarranted. Many of the accusations of negativity levelled against the book would be mitigated if more attention had been paid to her readings of texts from the Revolutionary period cited above. The sensational exposés of modernist sexism, for which *Sexual Politics* is famous, take place *alongside* enthusiastic, if confused, readings of Hardy, Meredith and Brontë.

Millett's reading of Lawrence, as already noted, is part of the third section of the book which also considers Henry Miller, Norman Mailer and Jean Genet as part of what Millett terms 'The literary reflection'. Millett describes Lawrence himself as 'the most talented and fervid of sexual politicians' (p. 239). As she ranges through his oeuvre, Millett argues that Lawrence's patriarchal tendencies pass through five

distinct phases: devotional, Oedipal, transitional, fraternal and ritual-
istic. This forms itself into a profile of increasing misogyny and homoeroticism; a gradual exorcizing of women to the point when they are
no longer needed. Millett uses this thesis to link together her analysis
of a number of key extracts. These episodes are carefully chosen and
(to return to the importance of quotation discussed at the beginning of
the chapter) expertly framed. Her readings of the sexual power-
politics involved in, for example, the episode in *Sons and Lovers* (1913)
when Paul Morel throws his 'pencil' at Miriam must now be ranked
amongst the 'classics' of literary criticism. This particular analysis, like
many of the others, is explicitly Freudian in its symbolic interpretation
and, indeed, Millett's whole vilification of Lawrence depends, to a
large extent, on *her* reading of Lawrence's reading of Freud. Millett is
also particularly concerned with the way in which the misogyny of
Lawrence's texts is expressed through force (one of her aspects of
patriarchy listed earlier). Many of the power confrontations she cites
are openly sadistic and brutal, a theme I will return to in my own
subsequent reading of *Wuthering Heights*. According to Millett's thesis,
this violence towards women moves inexorably through the patriarchal phases listed above until, in the late novels like *The Plumed
Serpent* (1926), it culminates in a sexual fascism that converts the earlier
'sacrificial' humiliation of women into their murder. In line with a
great deal of contemporary pornography, Millett shows how Lawrence uses the erotic desire of women (for example, Kate, in *The
Plumed Serpent* (1928)) as an invitation to abuse and, ultimately,
murder. I quote here the conclusion to Millett's reading of *The Woman
Who Rode Away*:

> All sadistic pornography tends to find its perfection in murder.
> Lawrence's movie priests themselves seem to understand the
> purpose of the rites and are 'naked and in a state of barbaric ecstasy',
> as they await the moment when the sun, phallic itself, strikes like a
> phallic icicle, and signals the phallic priest to plunge the phallic knife
> penetrating the female victim and cutting out her heart – the death
> fuck. (p. 292)

This passage illustrates not only the way in which Millett's polemical
hypotheses are brought to dramatic conclusions, but also many other
features of her style. Typical is the unequivocal, provocative opening
sentence: a statement which challenges, questions, but at the same
time defies questioning. Typical, too, is the recourse to irony and
ridicule; Millett undermines the sinister power of the Lawrentian male
by describing him as a 'movie priest'. In a similar vein, she acidly
parodies Lawrence's own style: his long cumulative sentences; his
mystical repetition of the sanctified 'phallic'. Finally, she at once
parodies and defies her subject with her own crudity. Millett, as her

novels like *Flying* (1974) and *Sita* (1980) also show, is not afraid to meet male machismo on its own terms. Her text proclaims her 'knowledge' of the sexual practices she writes about and her vocabulary is similarly aggressive, 'street-wise'.

In conclusion, I would like to remind the reader of some of the features of Millett's text outlined here that would be of particular consequence in any sexual-political reading. First, there is her analysis of patriarchy itself, which, in the categories she invents for its articulation ('ideology', 'class', 'force', etc.), provides the reader with a framework with which to approach any text, whether or not overtly patriarchal. Secondly, there are her own distinctive techniques for revealing these features in texts, including a decisive use of incriminating quotation, 'creative misreading' and the unproblematic identification of fictional characters with their authors. Finally, and incorporating all these other features, is her use of polemical rhetoric, which, as in the reading of Lawrence just quoted, produces a style of writing that dazzles and damns without compunction. The limitations of such an approach as an effective feminist reading method I will return to in the final section. I offer next my own sexual political account of *Tess of the d'Urbervilles* and *Wuthering Heights*.

II

Both of the texts chosen for this reading, Thomas Hardy's *Tess of the d'Urbervilles* (1891) and Emily Brontë's *Wuthering Heights* (1847), belong historically to the period of Millett's Sexual Revolution. This in itself registers something of an aberration in the expected target-area of Millett's theory since, as was suggested at the end of the previous section, the popular notion of sexual political readings is as a critique of twentieth-century male authors. By focusing on these earlier texts (one by a woman), I therefore hope to redress the balance in the common perception of what Millett's critical work is about and thus emphasize its potential as a positive reading strategy. To this end, I will assess the contribution of both books to a critical undermining of patriarchy at the same time as elucidating the aspects of male authority and sexism they nevertheless 'reflect'. One of the problems with Millett's theory, to be discussed in Part III, is, of course, the fact that these two positions are not always easily separated. Whether a text is reflecting, condoning or criticizing a particular social relation depends, in Millett's terms, on what one considers to be the 'intentions' of the author. The reason she approves of Hardy, Meredith and Brontë is that she identifies in these texts an authorial voice critical of the institutions being described. The reason she disapproves of Lawrence,

Miller and Mailer is because she believes their author-narrators to be condoning the sexual politics they participate in. In my own readings, I have therefore combined explication of aspects of the texts which would seem simply to reflect patriarchy, with others (through the working of plot, character, sexual relationships) which challenge it. The problems and difficulties of such major shifts in perception, supported only by an assumption of authorial intent, I will discuss at the end of the chapter.

I have organized my reading relatively simply by considering both texts simultaneously under four headings based on Millet's own analysis of patriarchy described in the previous section. These are images of women, force, class and socio-economic oppression, and the psychological effects of patriarchy.

Images of women

Sexual political criticism can be thought of most simply as an analysis of the images of women perpetrated by patriarchal culture. In this form, it has been the motivation behind all the readings of sexist representations of women: in the visual arts, in film and advertising, as well as in 'high culture'.[13] While 'images of women' is therefore a concept that could be used to describe the whole of Millett's enterprise, in this section I limit it to an analysis of specifically 'physical' representations of the women concerned.

A great deal has already been written on the physical characterization of Tess, both by feminist and non-feminist critics (see notes 14 and 16 below). Indeed, in so far as Tess's tragedy is popularly read as the direct result of her appearance, a consideration of her physical attractions is central to any reading. From the start, readers realized only too clearly the connection between her sexual appeal and her fate, and Hardy had not even finished his first version of the text before he was attacked for the potential amorality of these implications. Mary Jacobus in her essay, 'Tess: the making of a pure woman', quotes the following indictment from Mowbray Morris, the editor of *Macmillan's Magazine*:

> Even Angel Clare . . . has not yet got beyond a purely sensuous admiration for her person. Tess herself does not appear to have any feelings of this sort about her; but her capacity for stirring up and by implication for gratifying these feelings in others is pressed rather more frequently and elaborately than strikes me as altogether convenient . . . You use the word *succulent* more than once to describe the general appearance of the Frome Valley. Might I say that the general impression left on me by reading your story . . . is one of rather too much succulence.[14]

What is of most interest in this particular assessment is Morris's perception that Tess's sexuality is defined exclusively by the men who look at and desire her. He notes that she herself 'does not appear to have any feelings of this sort about her'. Often, it is true, Tess is seen specifically through the eyes of one of the male characters. In the scene where Tess is working on the rick at Flintcombe-Ash, for example, we are shown her body – its objectified appeal and its objectified vulnerability – through d'Urberville's appraising eyes:

> Of course you have done nothing but retain your pretty face and shapely figure. I saw it on the rick before you saw me – that tight pinafore-thing sets it off, and that wing-bonnet – you field-girls should never wear those bonnets if you wish to keep out of danger.[15]

What is particularly disturbing about d'Urberville's voyeurism is not only its objectification of Tess's body (note that he refers to her face and figure as 'it'), but the sexual threat it immediately arouses ('you field-girls should never wear those bonnets if you wish to keep out of danger'). Tess's body has been seen and approved from a distance with the eyes of a dealer. She is seen to comply with a certain critical standard, to have 'passed the test', and d'Urberville is prepared to 'put in a bid' (though, as his last sentence warns, such purchases can be made simply by force if necessary). Indeed, the class politics in d'Urberville's statement is (as elsewhere in the text) virtually synonymous with the sexual politics. His reference to 'field-girls' (socially as well as sexually 'inferior') establishes a distance between them which is the distance of power. It is d'Urberville's sex and class, although the first alone would be sufficient, that allows him to make this judgement of Tess. And it is patriarchy's psychological transference of sexual guilt to the woman that enables him to abdicate the responsibility for his sexism by blaming it on her: 'What a grand revenge you have taken! I saw you innocent, and I deceived you. Four years after, you find me a Christian enthusiast; you then work upon me, perhaps to my complete perdition!' (p. 377). In the previous chapter, d'Urberville transfers this blame even more unashamedly by referring to Tess as his 'dear damned witch of Babylon' (p. 370).

Elsewhere in the text, Tess is seen *indirectly* through the eyes of the male characters. In the erotic dawn meeting in the dairy, for example, Tess is described as Angel was seeing her as he held her in his arms:

> Tess's excitable heart beat against his by way of reply; and there they stood upon the red-brick floor of the entry, the sun slanting in by the window upon his back, as he held her tightly to his breast; upon her inclining face, upon the blue veins of her temple, upon her naked arm, and her neck, and into the depths of her hair. Having been lying down in her clothes she was as warmed as a sunned cat. (p. 210)

Once again, however, this intimate appraisal is preceded by a voyeuristic impression. Angel Clare is given his opportunity to enjoy the unsuspecting Tess, just as d'Urberville is:

> She had not heard him enter, and hardly realised his presence there. She was yawning, and he saw the red interior of her mouth as if it had been a snake's. She had stretched one arm so high above her coiled-up cable of hair that he could see its satiny delicacy above the sunburn; her face was flushed with sleep, and her eyelids hung heavy over their pupils. (p. 210)

Common to both these descriptions is the erotic concentration on specific *parts* of Tess's body: the reader is variously directed to her mouth, her arm, her neck, her hair. This is, of course, an aspect of the sexual representation of women that has received a good deal of attention in recent years, particularly in film and media studies where the fetishization of the particular parts of the female body is obvious.[16] As other commentators have observed, Tess consists of a whole series of memorable anatomical details, some of which appear to have specific sexual-symbolic overtones. The most commonly quoted of these is the description of Tess's mouth (interestingly cross-referenced with the description just quoted) when she accepts the fateful strawberry from d'Urberville ('and in slight distress she parted her lips and took it in', p. 70).

Yet apart from being represented directly or indirectly through the gaze of the male characters, Tess is also 'reflected' in mirrors, through the women characters (in particular her mother), and by the narrator himself. The role of the narrator in this respect (who Millett would assume to be Hardy himself) poses something of a problem, since it will inevitably affect our final verdict as to whether *Tess of the d'Urbervilles* is a truly 'revolutionary' text in sexual-political terms. Unfortunately, as Penny Boumelha has shown, the narrator of Tess would seem to share in the erotic voyeurism of the male characters. Her explanation for this is complex and stands outside a sexual-political reading, but her summary of narratorial involvement would seem persuasive:

> The phallic imagery of pricking, piercing and penetration which has repeatedly been noted, serves not only to create an image-chain linking Tess's experiences from the death of Prince to her final penetrative act of retaliation, but also to satisfy the narrator's fascination with the interiority of her sexuality, and his desire to take possession of her.[17]

The extent of narratorial collusion with the lust of the male characters does indeed make the theory that Hardy was merely 'reflecting' the patriarchal sexism of the age problematic. It is a question to which we will return in our final assessment of the sexual-political perspective of the novel, but it will already be realized that to claim for the text a more critical perspective would require a more sophisticated understanding of the relation between narrator and authorial intention than Millett's reading position allows.

Wuthering Heights, meanwhile, with its complex interchange of narrators, allows for a similar multi-perspective on the visual appearance of the female characters. Here the only overtly sexist (and sexual) descriptions come via the urbane gaze of Lockwood, the new tenant at the Grange. His description of the second Catherine at the beginning of the novel is stereotyped and sentimental, and instantly rendered ridiculous by its subject, whose hostile rejection of compliments completely undermines his fanciful image of her:

> Her position before was sheltered from the light: now I had a distinct view of her whole figure and countenance. She was slender, and apparently scarcely past girlhood; an admirable form, and the most exquisite little face that I ever had the pleasure of beholding; small features, very fair; flaxen ringlets, or rather golden, hanging loose on her delicate neck; and eyes – had they been agreeable in expression, they would have been irresistible.[18]

Later in the same scene, Lockwood refers to Catherine even more ridiculously as the 'benificent fairy' (p. 55). Such a compliment is ridiculous, not only because Catherine is herself indifferent to it, but because life at the Heights, entirely cut off from polite society, is oblivious to such gendered civilities. Indeed, when assessing the claims of *Wuthering Heights* to be a revolutionary text, this foil to the chivalry of ordinary middle-class expectation could be accounted one of its major successes. Certainly, the permanent male residents at the Heights – Hindley, Heathcliff and Hareton – are more reticent in their compliments to the females. The only occasion on which Heathcliff considers Cathy's appearance with anything like objectivity is in his childhood description of her, when she is seen through the window of the Grange:

> Afterwards, they dried and combed her beautiful hair, and gave her a pair of enormous slippers, and wheeled her to the fire, and I left her, as merry as she could be, dividing her food between the old dog and Skulker, whose nose she pinched as she ate; and kindling a spark of spirit in the vacant blue eyes of the Lintons – a dim reflection from her own enchanting face – I saw they were full of stupid admiration; she is so immeasurably superior to them – to everybody on earth; is she not, Nelly? (p. 92)

There are two occasional references here to conventional standards of beauty – her 'beautiful hair' and 'enchanting face' – but the description is in no way sexually voyeuristic. What stimulates Heathcliff's admiration is not sensuous passivity as we see in the descriptions of Tess, but Cathy's 'kindling spark of spirit'.[19] While a shift from sexual to moral appraisal does not automatically absolve the speaker from sexism, Heathcliff's perception of Cathy would seem to be motivated by an esteem that is essentially asexual.

The same, however, cannot be said of Heathcliff's attitude towards Isabella, whose sexual attractions he both acknowledges and repels with a misogynistic distaste as violent as anything Millett cites in Lawrence, Miller or Mailer:

> 'And I like her too ill to attempt it' [that is, take possession of Isabella], said he, except in a very ghoulish fashion. You'd hear of odd things, if I lived alone with that mawkish, waxen face, the most ordinary would be painting on its white the colours of the rainbow and turning the blue eyes black, every day or two; they detestably resemble Linton's. (p. 145)

Heathcliff's sadistic hatred of all women apart from Cathy is inevitably one of the major problems facing anyone wishing to make a positive feminist reading of *Wuthering Heights*. This is, after all, violence against women carried to considerable extremes. As we will argue presently, *Wuthering Heights* exists on one level as a novel about wife-battering. In this description, however, we find a possibility for, if not excusing his behaviour, then at least aligning it to the radical position on gender adopted by the book as a whole. I propose that Heathcliff's hatred is not of the female, but of *femininity*. Throughout the text we find references to his distaste for the Linton characteristic of blue eyes and blonde hair. These genetic traits irritate him not only in the first generation (Edgar and Isabella), but also in his son and the second Catherine. They are represented as being conterminous, indeed, with weakness and effeminacy; and this, we know, incites the hero to violence:

> It's odd what a savage feeling I have to anything that seems afraid of me. Had I been born where laws are less strict, I should treat myself to a slow vivisection of those two [Catherine and Linton] as an evening's amusement. (pp. 301–2)

In terms of a critique of femininity, this may be regarded as either revolutionary or reactionary. On the one hand, it could be read as a simple repetition of the homosexual misogyny Millett found in Lawrence's writing; on the other (suspending the rather questionable degree of violence involved), it could be seen to advance the cause of the sexual revolution by championing the removal of the oppressive 'feminine', and proposing instead ungendered, equal relationships based on the true sharing of power.

Heathcliff's distaste for gender difference is further evinced in the scene in which Cathy returns from the Grange, newly feminized. As other commentators have noticed, it is this rite of passage – social and sexual – that establishes the first (and fatal) difference between the two. Before this time, their relationship with one another was undefined in these terms, and possibly one way of understanding their subsequent relationship (which is puzzlingly ambiguous in sexual terms) is an attempt to recover the asexual, ungendered equality of childhood. Cathy's famous pronouncements such as 'I *am* Heathcliff' (p. 122) and 'That is not *my* Heathcliff. l shall love mine yet; and take him with me – he's in my soul' (p. 196) could be read effectively in this light: love not as the union of male and female, but as a transcendence of sexual difference altogether.

The images contained in *Wuthering Heights* may thus be seen to be more interrogating of patriarchal sexual politics than those found in *Tess of the d'Urbervilles*. The fact that neither text offers a consistent, ideological critique of these practices, however, makes their relative 'revolutionary' worth difficult to assess. This was, of course, the problem Millett herself encountered in her readings of Hardy and Brontë, and we will return to them at the end of the chapter.

Force

Several feminist critics have observed that, in *Tess of the d'Urbervilles*, there is very little essential difference between Clare and d'Urberville in their attitude towards Tess, despite their superficial characterization as 'angel' and 'devil'. As we saw in the previous section, the apprehension of both men is primarily sensual: Clare's desire cannot be described as spiritual, it is simply a little more socially refined. There is no essential difference, either, in the power politics of each relationship. Tess is always dependent: always subordinate. This power is exercised through all the various agencies of patriarchy that Millett outlines in her theoretical chapter, but the one I wish to focus on first is force.

Tess is full of episodes in which the heroine is seen to be physically controlled by her male suitors. Probably the most famous of these are the occasions on which she is forced to ride with d'Urberville; either on his horse or in his gig. The downhill gallop in which he first delivers Tess to Trantridge is a particularly vivid instance of male power politics (p. 84). It is interesting to reflect with Penny Boumelha, however, that Clare, like d'Urberville, also drives Tess in traps and seduces her with berries:

> It is not only Alec who is associated with the gigs and traps that, on occasion, literally run away with Tess; it is during a journey in a wagon driven by Angel that he finally secures Tess's acceptance of his proposal . . . It is noticeable, too, that during their wagon ride,

Angel feeds Tess with berries that he has pulled from the trees with a whip, recalling the scene at The Slopes when Alec feeds her with strawberries. (p. 132)

On two other memorable occasions, Clare claims physical possession of Tess by carrying her in his arms. The first is on the walk to church when he carries her across the flooded road (p. 185); the second, on their wedding night, when, sleep-walking, Clare carries her to the ruined abbey and places her in an empty stone coffin.

Unlike *Wuthering Heights*, *Tess* contains few examples of this exercise of force degenerating into physical violence (leaving aside the rape itself, which is not described). It is continually *threatened*, however, either by d'Urberville, or through the casual sexual harassment Tess suffers on her movement around the country. D'Urberville's second seduction, moreover, includes a scene in which this violence/violation is seen to be barely contained. Mocking her position as a deserted wife, he feels once again in a position to take advantage of her, and demonstrates this by roughly seizing her hand:

> In an impulse he turned suddenly to take her hand; the buff glove was on it and he seized only the rough leather fingers which did not express the life or shape of those within.
> 'You must not – you must not!' she exclaimed fearfully, slipping her hand from the glove as from a pocket, and leaving it in his grasp. 'O will you go away – for the sake of me and my husband – go, in the name of your own Christianity!'
> 'Yes, yes; I will,' he said abruptly, and thrusting the glove back to her turned to leave. Facing round, however, he said, 'Tess, as God is my judge, I meant no humbug in taking your hand'. (p. 365)

Despite d'Urberville's parting reassurances, Tess's evident terror betrays the fact that she knew exactly what the gesture had meant; indeed, what it had been symbolic of.

Such threat of assault is mild, however, compared with what is actually performed in *Wuthering Heights*. Isabella and the second Catherine are ruled by Heathcliff through the perpetual threat of physical violence, and even Nelly suffers her fair share of assault in the course of duty. The instances of battering are too plentiful to enumerate, so I will consider one particularly graphic example.

The marriage between Linton and Catherine is achieved through an act of wilful imprisonment. Physically assisting Nelly through the door, Heathcliff locks his guests inside, and there ensues a bitter and violent fight between himself and the second Catherine. This struggle is significant, not only as an example of the blatant violence against women that Heathcliff perpetrates, but also for the way in which Catherine fights back. Although Heathcliff must inevitably win in physical terms, Catherine is prepared to fight equally physically, and, when that fails, to employ the arts of the oppressed (see discussion of Millett above) to win a reprieve:

> Regardless of this warning, she captured his closed hand and its contents again.
> 'We will go!' she repeated, exerting her utmost efforts to cause the iron muscles to relax; and finding that her nails made no impression, she applied her teeth pretty sharply. (p. 302)

> Heathcliff glanced at me a glance that kept me from interfering a moment. Catherine was too intent on his fingers to notice his face. He opened them, suddenly, and resigned the object of dispute; but, ere she had secured it, he seized her with his liberated hand, and, pulling her on his knee, administered with the other, a shower of terrific slaps on both sides of the head, each sufficient to have fulfilled his threat, had she been able to fall. (p. 302)

> 'I've given over crying; but I'm going to kneel here, at your knee; and I'll not get up, and I'll not take my eyes from your face, till you look back at me! No, don't turn away! *do* look! You'll see nothing to provoke you. I don't hate you. I'm not angry that you struck me. Have you never loved *anybody*, in all your life, uncle? *never*? Ah! you must look once – I'm so wretched – you can't help being sorry and pitying me.' (p. 307)

Although he reacts violently to this feminine appeal ('I'd rather be hugged by a snake. How the devil came you to dream of fawning on me?' – p. 307), Heathcliff is clearly knocked off guard by this intelligent appeal to his emotions. It is significant, moreover, that in their future relationship, while Heathcliff regains ultimate control over Catherine through the threat of physical violence, she continues to challenge and oppose his authority, both in words, and in her insolent reluctance to do what he tells her to do. We will return to this question of women's power in the novel later. Heathcliff's use of force is most extreme, however, in his treatment of Isabella. I have already quoted his premarital determination to paint her face 'the colours of the rainbow', and this he clearly proceeds to do. When Isabella eventually flees the Heights, it is, indeed, as a battered wife.

What, then, is the feminist reader to make of all this undisguised violence against women in the novel? Surely there is no way to claim that this is anything other than a manifestation of patriarchy by force at its most extreme? Indeed there is not; but the problems of authorial intention then reassert themselves. By aligning Emily Brontë with the 'sane' disapproval of Nelly, we could perhaps make a case for the novel being a critique of such violence. We could also suggest, in line with the example quoted above, that the female characters also oppose this tyranny and exercise their own violence. Ultimately, however, it must be conceded that a sexual political reading, while exposing the utilization of patriarchal force and violence as one of the key features of both novels, can come to no clear moral judgement about their meaning, since the 'authorial intention' is nowhere as clear as Millett thinks it is.

Class and economic oppression

Virtually all existing feminist readings of *Tess* acknowledge the very obvious connection that exists between sexual and economic exploitation. In a reference to the gig episode already discussed in the previous section, Mary Jacobus observes the way in which Tess's lack of physical control over her body is merely a factor of her total socio-economic oppression:

> Alec's gig . . . is not simply the equivalent of a sports-car, his badge of machismo, wealth and social status. It is also a symbolic expression of the way in which Tess is to be deprived of control over her own body, whether by Alec himself or by the alien rhythms of the threshing machine at Flintcombe-Ash, in a scene where sexual and economic oppression are as closely identified as they had been in her seduction. (pp. 82–3)

At all points in the narrative we are reminded that Tess's treatment by both Clare and d'Urberville depends not only on the fact that she is a female, but also a socially inferior female. I have already quoted d'Urberville's denomination of her as a field girl, and his inference there echoes many earlier reproofs, such as the occasion on which he first attempts to kiss her: 'You are mighty sensitive for a cottage girl' (p. 85). Similar assumptions undoubtedly influence Clare's treatment of her. Although he exercises what he considers to be respectful restraint in his behaviour, there is no doubt that their romance is more demonstrably physical than it would have been were Tess his social equal. All the passes he makes are made under the assumption that, as a milkmaid, Tess has literally 'no rights' to be offended. It is unthinkable, for example, that he would have presumed to carry Mercy Chant across a flooded road.

In terms of the plot, too, it is important to remember that the reasons for Tess going to Trantridge were economic. The family desperately needed money and her responsibility for the death of Prince – 'the bread-winner' – forced her to comply with her mother's plan against her own better judgement (see pp. 64–5). From this position of dependency, d'Urberville was able to blackmail Tess with his charity time and time again, and the various symbolic replacements for Prince haunt her throughout the narrative.

A further interesting mixture of sexual and economic exploitation appears in the person of Farmer Groby, Tess's master at Flintcombe-Ash. Groby knows about her history at Trantridge and recognizes her on two subsequent occasions: once with Clare at an inn, and again, after her abandonment, on the road from Emminster. On this second occasion, his familiarity, which begins as mild sexual harassment, quickly develops into something more malicious when he recognizes her:

> She had reached the top of a hill . . . when she heard footsteps behind her back, and in a few moments she was overtaken by a man. He stepped alongside Tess and said 'Good-night, my pretty maid', to which she civilly replied. The light still remaining lit up her face, though the landscape was nearly dark. The man turned and stared hard at her. 'Why, surely it is the young wench who was at Trantridge awhile – young squire d'Urberville's friend? . . . Be honest enough to own it, and that what I said in the town was true, though your fancy-man was so up about it – hey, my sly one? You ought to ask my pardon for that blow of his, considering.' (p. 322)

On this occasion Tess escapes what is clearly another sexual assault by taking to her heels. She meets an alternative revenge, however, when she has the misfortune to end up in the employment of the same man. The blackmail he was unable to effect sexually, he now exacts through economic tyranny. Having bullied her for her slow work-rate he declares triumphantly: 'But now I think I've got the better of you' (p. 337). This invidious chain of events illustrates well Millett's formulation of the relationship between patriarchy and class. The two forms of oppression not only mirror, but collude with one another to render Tess, a working-class woman, liable to all manner of oppression, exploitation, abuse and blackmail.

According to Millett's thesis, the economic oppression of women is inscribed in marriage: the institution that ante-dated all other capitalism by reducing women to chattel status. In support of this analysis, there are several instances in Hardy's novel where Tess is referred to as a chattel quite blatantly. It is, moreover, a representation of herself in which Tess colludes. For while she actively resists becoming d'Urberville's 'creature' (p. 112), she submissively desires to be Clare's: 'I am so glad to think – of being yours, and making you happy!' (p. 231). Clare, himself, meanwhile, believes such a state of affairs to be equally natural and proper: 'It is in every way desirable and convenient that I should carry you off as my property' (p. 244). The degree of subjection Tess then seems willing to suffer within marriage, we will return to in the section on the psychological effect of patriarchy. It is worth noting in conclusion, however, that true to Millett's analysis, Tess's economic dependence is never free from her patriarchal oppression. Unmarried, her sexuality is a condition of service; married, she would merely have been expected to add housekeeeping to her prostitution.

Traditionally read as a love story, *Wuthering Heights*'s virtually feudal formulation of the institution of marriage has been generally overlooked. While we reflect upon the psycho-sexual power struggles taking place between the protagonists, it is easy to forget the economic reality of that power. The two households of the Heights and the Grange are best understood as mini-kingdoms, similar to those of the Gondal and Angrian sagas, and all sexual alliances – either marital or adulterous – exist to support, modify or undermine the existing order.[20] Both kingdoms are, moreover, unreservedly patriarchal. The only woman who stands to inherit any property in her own right is the second Catherine, and this Heathcliff quickly robs her of through marriage to his son who, at this time, is still a minor. (During this period, women surrendered all claim to money and property to their husbands upon marriage) (see p. 325). The first Cathy never had, or stood to have, any property of her own, since the Earnshaw inheritance passed automatically to Hindley. Consequently, like all women living under nineteenth-century patriarchal law, her only exercise of economic judgement was through her marriage. This is another factor that has been seriously underrated in her reasons for marrying Edgar. In the conversation with Nelly in which she first reveals her decision to marry, she is quite unashamedly Machiavellian in her motives. She sees the move as expedient, not only for herself, but also for Heathcliff: 'Nelly, I see now, you think me a selfish wretch, but did it never strike you that, if Heathcliff and I married, we should be beggars? whereas, if I marry Linton, I can aid Heathcliff to rise, and place him out of my brother's power?' (p. 122). From the point of view of the plot, it is also worth noting that this explanation takes place *after* Heathcliff has already left the room. Therefore, despite Cathy's confidence that Heathcliff 'comprehends in his person my feeling for Edgar and myself' (p. 122), much of his later jealousy and torment ('*Why* did you despise me? *Why* did you betray your own heart . . . ? – p. 197), could be traced to his belief that Cathy chose Edgar not for reasons of economics, but for reasons of *class*. As Nelly notes in her significant aside, Heathcliff left the room when 'he heard Catherine say it would *degrade* her to marry him' [my italics] (p. 121).

The relationship of class politics to gender indeed forms one of the novel's most complex responses to the patriarchal institution. Unlike *Tess*, which simply reflects the traditional prescription that class oppression colludes with patriarchy in the particular exploitation of working-class women, *Wuthering Heights* demonstrates that patriarchy does indeed *exceed* class in the exercise of power. For although the mystery of Heathcliff's birth exiles him to the kitchen during Hindley's tyranny, the fact that he is a man allows him to go out into the world, make his fortune and ultimately establish his own hegemony. Needless to say, a woman would never have been able to *earn* power in this way. Against his patriarchal authority, moreover, the class superiority of first, Isabella, and then the second Catherine is no defence. Both, in turn, suffer ridicule and humiliation when they attempt to use their status as 'ladies' to win respectful treatment. Just as Heathcliff was previously, so too are they banished to the servants' quarters. The supreme machismo of life at the Heights is well illustrated by Isabella's description of her first night there, during which she 'listened (in vain) to detect a woman's voice in the house' (p. 176). Both she and Catherine after her enter a kingdom in which the male reigns supreme, subsuming all other forms of authority.

In the second generation, the relationship between sex and class becomes more complex. Catherine, raised at the Grange, and with the advantage of education, appears to be of a higher social class than Hareton, who speaks and behaves like a servant. However, as Nelly keeps reminding her, they are, in fact, cousins, and their relationship can be seen as a coming to terms with that equality. Catherine has to learn to surrender her sense of class superiority; Hareton, the patriarchal 'birth-right' he uses to counter it: 'I'll see thee damned, before I be *thy* servant!' (p. 320). Thus, in the second generation, the sex and class differences which separated Heathcliff and Cathy are renegotiated and ultimately transcended. One of the last impressions we have of Catherine and Hareton (witnessed by Lockwood), as the former teaches the latter to read, is as the two children Cathy and Heathcliff once were; blissfully forgetful of both class and gender difference. Thus a sexual-political reading, while acknowledging *Wuthering Heights* as a ruthless exposition of patriarchal inheritance, may nevertheless find, in the second generation, a possible critique of the institution that had (in Heatheliff's words), forced Cathy to 'betray (her) own heart'.

The psychological effects of patriarchy

I turn now to a consideration of the psychological internalization of the effects of patriarchy on the female characters of both texts, contrasting the total self-abnegation of power in *Tess* with the resistance of the two Catherines in *Wuthering Heights*.

For the feminist reader, clearly one of the most distressing features of *Tess* is the heroine's unrelieved humility. Apart from a brief period towards the end of the novel in which she expresses slight bitterness at the injustice of her lot (pp. 404–5), Tess is never anything but a victim. She appears to be motivated only by guilt (activated, in the narrative, by the death of Prince), and all her actions are performed in the spirit of sacrifice, culminating in her last, symbolic 'offering' on the 'altar' at Stonehenge. This extreme passivity can, as Mary Jacobus (see note 14) has shown, be partly explained by Hardy's anxiety about her purity. To absolve her from any responsibility for her downfall, he was forced to render her naive and helpless, sometimes to the point of stupidity. She is denied, as Jacobus observes, 'the right of participation in her own life' (p. 78).

Tess accepts her role as victim from the very beginning of the novel. Indeed, her fatalistic view of life ('We live on a blighted star'), is philosophized even before the death of Prince. Her later outburst, 'Once victim, always victim – that's the law!' (p. 379) is therefore not something she has learnt through experience so much as a confirmation of what she already knew. There is no evidence, moreover, that Tess ever understood her oppression to be sexual and economic. Her unease at going to Trantridge is apparently based on pride (not wishing to beg), rather than any suspicion of the dangers of her own sexuality. Indeed, if we follow Jacobus's argument, it is expressly important that she is ignorant in these matters. Her conversation with her mother on her return to Marlott reassures us that she truly knew nothing of the 'danger in men-folk' (p. 117).

Tess's lack of education undoubtedly contributed to her own low opinion of herself and made her collude with the patriarchal assumption that women are of innately lower intelligence. Her relationship with Clare confirms all the popular Ruskinian beliefs that the female mind is intuitive and emotional rather than rational: a thesis brought to a truly sensational conclusion in her subsequent murder of d'Urberville.[21] When Clare offers to teach her history, for example, her reply indicates that she knew intuitively all there was to be known; that the lives of women like herself were always tragic 'Because what is the use of learning that I am one of a long row only – finding out in some old book somebody just like me and to know that I shall only act her part making me sad, that's all' (p. 165). At the same time, she regards Clare's intellectual knowledge as altogether 'natural' and admirable: 'When I see what you know, what you have read, and seen, and thought, I feel what a nothing I am!' (p. 164).

Because of this almost pathological sense of her own insignificance, Tess's desire (were she not too guilty to admit it) is simply to abandon all her consciousness of herself in becoming Angel's wife. Unfortunately, the debasement she feels as the result of being a 'fallen woman' combines with this 'instinctive' feminine humility, making even the dream of being a servant to Clare seem beyond what she can honestly expect. The psychological consequences of this mixture of moral guilt and natural humility are given their most nauseating expression in Tess's supplication to Clare after their marriage. She immediately accepts her rejection as just punishment, and only wishes to do what will be most convenient for him:

> I shan't ask you to let me live with you, Angel, because I have no right to! . . . I shan't do anything, unless you order me to; and if you go away from me I shall not follow 'ee; and if you never speak to me any more I shall not ask why, unless you tell me I may . . . I will obey you like your wretched slave, even if it is to lie down and die. (p. 272)

In the days that follow the marriage, Tess makes a laudable attempt to honour these vows. Quite beside herself as to how she should best discharge her wifely duty, she alternatively vacillates between the idea of killing herself, running away, or getting Clare's dinner. The only thing that prevents her from taking her own life is the fear of the scandal it might cause to *his* name.

Tess's psychological assumption of patriarchal values is nicely corroborated by her male suitors. Various comments reveal that both d'Urberville and Clare considered her to be rather stupid. Reacting to her various suggestions for releasing him from the marriage, Clare exclaims: 'O Tess – you are too, too – childish – unformed – crude, I suppose! I don't know what you are. You don't understand the law – you don't understand' (p. 281). This charge of incomprehension would also appear to be corroborated by the narrator, who groups Tess with the lower animals when he remarks: 'To fling elaborate sarcasms at Tess, however, was much like flinging them at a dog or cat. The charms of their subtlety passed by her unappreciated, and she only received them as inimical sounds which meant that anger ruled' (p. 273). Later in the narrative, Tess receives similar contempt from d'Urberville. Aware of the irony of the situation, he mocks her for her parrot-like repetition of Clare's religious views, which put an end to his own 'conversion'. He remarks, scathingly: 'The fact is . . . whatever your dear husband believed you accept, and whatever he rejected you reject, without the least reasoning or inquiry on your part. That's just like you women. Your mind is enslaved to his' (p. 368). And though he appears to accept the 'naturalness' of Tess's inferior intelligence on other occasions (for example, the references to cats and dogs quoted above), the narrator here chooses to share in d'Urberville's contempt by ridiculing her 'simplicity of faith in Angel Clare that the most perfect man would hardly have observed, much less her husband' (p. 368).

This apparent ambiguity in the narrational stance causes serious problems when we come to consider, once again, whether the novel is truly revolutionary in its prognosis, or merely a reflection of incontrovertible 'fact'. Could it be that the author-narrator is really as irritated by Tess's victimization as we are? Is that why she is allowed the final existential action of murdering d'Urberville? Possibly; but then we are returned to the problem that her acts of retaliation are without consequence or, worse, give rise to even greater punishment. On the only other occasion on which she fights back by hitting d'Urberville with her glove, she awaits instant retribution as her just desserts: 'Now, punish me! . . . Whip me, crush me . . . I shall not cry out!' (p. 370). As I will argue in my concluding remarks, Tess's attempts at retaliation merely compound her impotence. Her own diagnosis, 'Once victim, always victim' is never really challenged.

In *Wuthering Heights*, by contrast, a text which demonstrates a patriarchal ideology every bit as strict as that 'reflected' in *Tess*, the female characters do resist their psychological oppression. The fact that, like Tess, they cannot win, would seem to matter less than the fact that they try. The similarity in spirit between the two Catherines in the text is notable. One only has to examine the relationship Nelly has with each of her protegées to understand this: mother and daughter are equally wilful, each determined to get what they want.[22] Both women, too, make the most of their limited education. Cathy's education gives her a temporary advantage over Heathcliff as does Catherine's over Hareton. Both, moreover, are keenly articulate, and it is worth observing that the illusion of Cathy's power in her relationships with Linton and Heathcliff owes largely to her ability to match them verbally. Although without economic independence or physical strength, Cathy shares none of Tess's doubt in her own intellectual ability. Unsupported in other ways, words are her principal weapon. The rhetoric which she summons up on her death-bed reduces even the mighty Heathcliff to tears. Her wishes convert to threats and her threats to curses. Heathcliff, certainly, is aware that her words will live to haunt him: 'Are you possessed with a devil to talk in that manner to me, when you are dying? Do you reflect that all those words will be branded in my memory, and eating deeper eternally, after you have left me?' (p. 196). To condemn her husband and her lover to earthly damnation, therefore, is the realization of Cathy's power. It will be seen as a pyrrhic victory, nonetheless, since her blackmail can only be properly effected through her death. Other feminist writers such as Sandra Gilbert and Susan Gubar have also commented on Cathy's recourse to illness and suicide as her only means of protest and revolt.[23] In sexual-political terms, it is simply an inevitable factor in a power struggle between the master and the dispossessed. Having realized that she will never be allowed to have her own way and keep Heathcliff as a 'friend', she is quite prepared to give her own life in the cause of revenge: 'If I were only sure it would kill him . . . I'd kill myself directly' (p. 159). Suicide, after all, is the only exercise of power left to those who have nothing, and Cathy, like

Tess, has power over nothing but her own body. But whereas Tess's suicide is entertained as an acknowledgement of her own worthlessness, Cathy's is undertaken to re-establish superiority. Her decision is as calculated and as expedient as her reason for marrying Edgar. To Nelly she remarks coolly: 'Well, if I cannot keep Heathcliff for my friend – if Edgar will be mean and jealous, I'll try to break their hearts by breaking my own. That will be a prompt way of finishing all, when I am pushed to extremity!' (p. 155). This fundamental difference in the regard of self between Cathy and Tess is one of the main reasons why it would be easier for the feminist to proclaim *Wuthering Heights* a revolutionary text than *Tess*, and in the following section I will attempt some conclusions *vis-à-vis* this point.

Revolution or reaction?

At the end of each of the preceding sections, 1 have tried to assess whether the texts' approach to the various agents of patriarchy would classify them as 'revolutionary' in Millett's terms. Usually, as we have seen, this will depend on our interpretation of the author's intention: is the writer condoning or critical of the practices he or she describes? Is it implied that an alternative relationship between the sexes would be preferable?

The difficulty for the feminist reader looking for a revolutionary critique of patriarchy in *Tess* rests, as we have seen, with her victimization. While it is easy to infer criticism of d'Urberville's exploitation or Clare's hypocrisy, we are still left with the sense that Tess's passivity, like her sexuality, is involuntary and 'natural'.

The censure of the book would seem to be aimed not at the patriarchal institution that constituted Tess and her unfortunate sexual appeal as a liability, but simply at the men who would take advantage of it. It is also implied, however, that such restraint is too much to expect. The responsibility is returned to Tess and her overabundant charms. As Penny Boumelha has observed, Tess's sexuality is simply too provocative, and the implications are that her fate, if tragic, is inescapable:

> Tess . . . is trapped by a sexuality that seems at times almost irrelevant to her own experience and her sense of her own identity. She is doomed by her 'exceptional physical nature' (p. 269) and the inevitability of an erotic response from men . . . Her sexuality, provocative without intent, seems inherently guilty by virtue of the reactions it arouses in others. (p. 125)

By substituting the sensuous Tess with the more ethereal Liza-Lu at the end of the novel, Hardy seems to have been admitting not only that Tess's own fate was unavoidable, but that the only way to avoid similar tragedies was somehow to rid the world of such unfortunate sexual provocation. The adolescent, asexual Liza-Lu stands as an example of a new kind of woman who will engage men's devotion without arousing their lust. Read in this way, *Tess of the d'Urbervilles* would seem to come closer to the reaction of Ruskin than the revolution of John Stuart Mill (see note 21).

Written by one of the family of 'half-mad sisters' that, according to Millett, had sole claim to a 'revolutionary sensibility' amongst the women writers of the nineteenth century, *Wuthering Heights* has fair claim to be considered a book of the Sexual Revolution. My own reading here would seem to confirm this, though there is equal scope, as we have seen, to condemn it as one of the most violent and fascist representations of male tyranny ever written. Where the individual reader will finally decide to stand will depend, once again, on what she feels the author's position to be. While this is difficult in a book with so many different narrators (none of whom would appear to represent an objectified authorial viewpoint), there is the opportunity, as we have seen, for reading both character and plot as a powerful critique of patriarchal oppression. While it is true that Heathcliff establishes a patriarchal hegemony, the feminist reader can read his abuse of power as his revenge on the class difference that separated him from Cathy in the first instance. She can equally see his sadistic hatred of 'the feminine' as a desire to subvert traditional gender definition and return to his old, asexual relationship with Cathy. Both these hypotheses, moreover, would seem to have their justification in a second generation where, as we have seen, Hareton and the second Catherine learn to overcome their 'inherited' class and gender prejudice, and to form a new, equalized 'brother and sister' relationship of the kind Cathy and Heathcliff enjoyed as children.

Such a positive reading of a text is not what sexual-political criticism is famous for, and part of my purpose here has been to show how it might be engaged in that way. That quite opposite sexual political readings are possible for both these texts is one of the problems I now turn to in a closing critique on Millett's methodology.

III

Millett's understanding of literary texts starts, as we saw in Part I, from the assumption that they 'reflect' the real world (hence her section title: 'The literary reflection'). 'To reflect' can, of course, mean 'to consider' as well as 'to mirror', but even on this basic point it is unclear what Millett's exact perception of the relationship between X and Y is. Her confusion is most noticeable in her approach to the texts of the

Sexual Revolution since, as we observed, she saw them as being only *partly* conscious of their mission. While she was able to present the texts of the Counter-Revolution as unproblematic 'reflections' (literally, 'mirrors') of male chauvinism, Hardy, Meredith *et al.* uncomfortably exposed the weakness of her hypothesis. The confusion she consequently accredits to Hardy as author (did Sue's behaviour really challenge patriarchy, or did her nervous recapitulation merely condone it?) is clearly her own. She is torn between implying that these novels *unconsciously* reflect patriarchal society and showing that they are *consciously* critical of it. She is unable to decide, in other words, the exact role of the author in relation to the text, and the exact role of the text to the patriarchy it is engaged with.

This, likewise, is the problem that my own readings of *Tess* and *Wuthering Heights* encountered. While it was relatively easy to describe the various workings of patriarchy in the texts, it was difficult to decide how to interpret them. Like Millett, I found myself faced with the choice of presenting the texts as proto-revolutionary (as conscious critiques of patriarchal oppression) or regarding their 'reflection' of that patriarchy as essentially conservative. And while for each text either position is equally tenable, l was also aware that I was more disposed towards a positive reading of the female-authored text. Although one of the most significant aspects of Millett's theory is that it is not biologically determined in terms of author, I believe that she is likewise disposed in her own comparison of Hardy and Charlotte Brontë. In Millett's readings, the problem of authorial intention is made even more prominent by her systematic conflation of author and narrator. Although I manage to avoid such a reduction in my own readings (which would, in the case of *Wuthering Heights*, be extremely difficult), my final evaluations (as outlined in the final section of Part II) depend on the construction of a particular *author position* that is always only one step away from Hardy and Brontë. While I therefore sidestep the worst excesses of the biographical fallacy by avoiding reference to the authors' own lives, I nevertheless conceive for them a particular position *vis-à-vis* the Sexual Revolution. My information may have come from the texts themselves rather than from anything I have read about Hardy's own erotic susceptibilities or Brontë's 'incestuous' relationship with her brother and sisters, but my interpretations depend on the construction of an 'originating source' nevertheless.

Before passing on to some concluding comments on how Millett's reading practice may be seen to persist, stripped of all these problems of author-intentionality, in the work of subsequent materialist-feminists, it is perhaps necessary to consider why – even when literary theory has taught us we ought to know better – we still, on occasion, feel a desire to nail authors to their texts in the way Millett did thirty years ago.

Recognizing the force of this Luddite attitude in my own 'unofficial' (i.e. non-academic) reading practice, I am in the habit of asking the students who discuss this chapter as part of their MA module in Feminist Literary Theory which contemporary text/author they would like to 'deal with' (!) in the manner Millett deals with Lawrence? The recommendations have been as wide-ranging as they have been impassioned, but over the years I have observed that women experience a particular problem with offensive *visual* texts (most often ones depicting violence against women) and especially with those which are part of popular culture (e.g. films). Where women are most offended and threatened, it seems, they feel a strong need to make *someone* – whether author, producer, or distributor – responsible. My students have also expressed a strong reaction against the male authors such as Martin Amis and Brad Easton Ellis who, like Henry Miller before them, insist that their texts are 'critiques' of misogyny rather than its perpetrators.[24] For many women, however (and I would suggest that this means *most of us*, at least *some* of the time) such apparent abnegations of author-responsibility (sanctioned, of course, by poststructuralist theory) are not adequate, and we respond, however naively, by conflating text and author in precisely the same way as Millett did all those years ago. Thus, despite the fact that such a reaction is frequently difficult to defend in terms of the poststructuralist and postmodernist theoretical world we now inhabit, we should perhaps acknowledge that anger often *is* unsophisticated, but that occasionally we will need to make authors and producers, rather than ideologies or discourses, accountable for the 'crimes' of patriarchy that continue to be perpetrated against us.

In terms of *academic discourse*, however, the developments in Marxist-feminism in the late 1970s and early 1980s meant that it became possible for readers and critics to explicate and analyze the representation of 'patriarchy' in texts from all historical periods, and texts authored by women as well as men, *without* floundering in the muddy waters of author-intentionality. This was because post-Althusserian theories of ideology (see Chapter 6), promoted a model of the text as a site of conflicting and competing ideologies that not only 'reflected', but were also 'productive' of, the cultural struggles of the society with which the text engaged. 'Patriarchy', rather than the fixed monolith conceived of by Millett, thus came to be seen as the congruence of multiple *contradictory* ideologies, which the authors of texts could not expect to be fully aware of themselves. Explication of these contradictions thus became the business of the critic (see Chapter 6), whose consequent dismantling of texts was seen as important political work. Not only did such criticism provide new insight into the workings of the texts in question, but also into the workings of 'power' itself.

In the hands of its more sophisticated exponents – literary critics like Cora Kaplan, Catherine Belsey, or the art-historian Griselda Pollack – this new brand of Marxist or materialist textual practice might, at first, seem a million miles away from Millett's feisty, but crude, assault on selected texts and authors.[25] Millett's critiques can, however, be seen as the prototype for a good deal of the ideological/discourse-based analysis which has followed, demonstrating, as it did, the complex way in which texts reflect/reproduce the oppressions of the dominant culture.[26] The passion and anger with which she dealt with such misogyny, moreover, was itself a timely 'call to arms' for the burgeoning feminist movement of the late 1960s, and whilst today's critics may feel the targets of her assault misplaced (she blames authors rather than institutions), such political *purpose* within literary criticism is something no generation should lose sight of.

Notes

1. Kate Millett, *Sexual Politics*, 1969 (Virago, London, 1977). The label 'World Bestseller' appears on the cover of the 1977 Virago edition.
2. Toril Moi, *Sexual/Textual Politics: Feminist Literary Theory* (Methuen, London, 1985), p. 26. All further page references are given after quotations in the text.
3. Cora Kaplan, 'Radical feminism and literature: re-thinking Millett's *Sexual Politics*', *Red Letters*, vol. 9, 1979, pp. 4–16.
4. Ann Jones, 'Feminism 1: Sexual politics – Henry James, "In the cage"', in Douglas Tallack (ed.), *Literary Theory at Work* (Batsford, London, 1986), p. 85. All further references are given after quotations in the text.
5. Naomi Wolf, *The Beauty Myth: How Images of Beauty are Used Against Women* (Vintage, London, 1991) and *Fighting Fire with Fire: The New Female Power and How It Will Change the 21st Century* (Chatto and Windus, London, 1993).
6. Susan Faludi, *Backlash: The Undeclared War against Women* (Chatto and Windus, London, 1992); Katie Roiphe, *The Morning After: Sex, Fear and Feminism* (Penguin, Harmondsworth, 1994); Camille Paglia, *Sexual Personae: Art and Decadence from Nefertiti to Emily Dickinson* (Yale University Press, New Haven, 1990); and *Sex, Art and American Culture* (Penguin, Harmondsworth, 1994).
7. For an interesting discussion of the factors inhibiting the writing on academic feminists see the round-table discussion between Jane Gallop, Marianne Hirsch and Nancy K. Miller in *Conflicts in Feminism*, ed. Marianne Hirsch and Evelyn Fox Keller (Routledge, London and New York, 1990).
8. See Lynne Pearce, ' "I" the reader: text, context and the balance of

power' in *Feminist Subjects, Multi-media: Cultural Methodologies*, ed. Penny Florence and Dee Reynolds (Manchester University Press, Manchester, 1995), p. 164.

9.   See Rosemary Betterton (ed.), *Looking On: Images of Femininity in the Arts and Media* (Pandora, London, 1987). This is a collection of essays on images of women in the media and in the visual arts.

10. Kate Millett, *Sexual Politics* (Virago, London, 1977), p. 23. All further page references are given after quotations in the text.

11. Millett later indicates that it was failure to recognize this fact that caused the sexual revolution to fail in the Soviet Union. Although the revolution sought to remove patriarchy by redressing the economic dependence of women, it failed to set up a new psychic structure in its members to replace that of patriarchy (p. 173).
        Earlier sociological texts that Millett draws upon which exclude the 'psychological' factor include: William J. Goode, *The Family* (Prentice Hall, New Jersey, 1964) and Bronislaw Malinowski, *Sex. Culture and Myth* (Harcourt, New York, 1962).

12. See Juliet Mitchell, *Psychoanalysis and Feminism* (Penguin, Harmondsworth, 1975).

13. See *Looking On* (note 9 above).

14. Mary Jacobus, 'Tess: the making of a pure woman', in Susan Lipshitz (ed.), *Tearing the Veil: Essays on Femininity* (Routledge and Kegan Paul, London, 1978), p. 80. All further page references are given after quotations in the text.

15. Thomas Hardy, *Tess of the d'Urbervilles* (New Wessex edition, Macmillan, London, 1974), p. 377. All further page references are given after quotations in the text.

16. See *Looking On* (note 9 above).

17. Penny Boumelha, *Thomas Hardy and Women: Sexual Ideology and Narrative Form* (Harvester Wheatsheaf, Hemel Hempstead, 1982). All further page references are given after quotations in the text.

18. Emily Brontë, *Wuthering Heights* (Penguin Classics, London, 1965), p. 53. All further page references are given after quotations in the text.

19. In contrast, Penny Boumhela draws attention to the fact that Tess's sexuality is most exposed and vulnerable when she loses consciousness of herself, through sleep, or otherwise (see p. 121).

20. In 1826 Branwell Brontë was given a box of toy soldiers as a present from his father, and he allowed each of his sisters to choose a soldier for her own. The soldiers were named after popular heroes of the day such as the Duke of Wellington, and the explorer, William Edward Parry, and the children soon involved them in an elaborate saga of group games known collectively as 'The young men's play'. For these characters, the children invented imaginary kingdoms fraught with constant war and romance. The adventures were recorded in the form of poems, letters, magazines and newspapers, all produced on a miniature scale to correspond to the size of the soldiers themselves. The individual kingdoms the characters carved out for themselves were at first united in a confederation known as 'Glasstown', but after Charlotte's removal to school, the games fragmented and a schism occurred when Emily and Ann developed their own

independent saga based on the kingdom of 'Gondal', and Branwell and Charlotte created the new kingdom of 'Angria'. All these kingdoms were run as feudal monarchies and were essentially patriarchal, although Gondal was ruled for a while by a queen.

21. See John Ruskin's 'Of Queen's Gardens' (1865) in *Sesame and Lilies* (Homewood, Chicago, 1902).

22. Compare Cathy's means of getting hold of Nelly when she wishes to entertain Edgar alone (pp. 110–11), and Catherine's wile in getting to see Linton at the Heights.

23. See Sandra Gilbert and Susan Gubar's *Madwoman in the Attic: The Woman Writer and the Nineteeth-Century Literary Imagination* (Yale University Press, New Haven, 1979).

24. All Amis's novels have solicited concern from certain feminists, whilst the publication of Brad Easton Ellis's *American Psycho* (Picador, London, 1991) reopened the censorship debate (i.e. should texts depicting this degree of violence against women be banned?). Those who supported the text's right to publication (feminists included) argued strongly against any association between the author and the serial killer depicted in the text and suggested that the story was essentially a *critique* of the alienating effects of contemporary society. See Sara Mills, 'Working with sexism: what can feminist text analysis do?', 1995, for an analysis of Martin Amis's *London Fields*.

25. See, for example, Cora Kaplan's *Sea Changes: Culture and Feminism* (Verso, London, 1986); Catherine Belsey's *John Milton: Language, Gender, Power* (Blackwell, Oxford, 1988); Griselda Pollock, *Vision and Difference: Femininity, Feminism and the History of Art* (Routledge, London, 1988).

26. See, for example, Catherine Belsey, *John Milton: Language, Gender, Power* (Blackwell, Oxford, 1988); Linda Nead, *Myths of Sexuality* (Blackwell, Oxford, 1988); Lynne Pearce, *Woman/Image/Text* (Harvester Wheatsheaf, Hemel Hempstead, 1991).

2

Authentic realism

Sara Mills

Arlyn Diamond and Lee Edwards (eds):
The Authority of Experience
Alice Walker: *The Color Purple*
Emily Brontë: *Wuthering Heights*

I

For many feminists, authentic realism is distinguished as a critical approach that, through an exchange of experience between author, text and reader, can promise to 'change your life'. As such, it is not so much a fully articulated theoretical position, but rather a reading strategy, or a model of the relation between text and world. Its proponents believe that women's writing can be usefully discussed in terms of how texts relate to women's experience. Within this perspective, literature is seen as a potential vehicle for change in women's lives, since it can serve as a catalyst for consciousness-raising, and a basis for constructing models for other ways of living. This model of reading became particularly popular during the 1970s but it is still drawn upon now by many women for strategic political purposes. It is often used by those readers who experience a sudden shock of 'recognition' in relation to a character in a text; thus, those readers, for example disabled women, Black women, lesbians, working-class women, straight women, who have become used to texts presenting a stereotypical view of what is seen as their identity, may draw on this strategy to describe the feeling that is evoked by a literary text which counters such stereotypes, presenting images which seem closer to their sense of who they are. Whilst many feminist theorists reject this type of reading position, I hope to show that its strategic use may be productive.[1]

There are several collections of essays which have been written within this theoretical position: for example, Josephine Donovan's

Feminist Literary Criticism (1975), and the text which will be discussed here in detail, *The Authority of Experience* (1977) edited by Arlyn Diamond and Lee Edwards.[2] This collection can be broadly defined as 'liberal feminist', since it attempts to demand equality of treatment for women: for example, Maurianne Adams says in an essay in this collection 'women feel just as men feel; they need exercise for their faculties and a field for their efforts as much as their brothers do' (p. 145). The essays, although diverse in terms of subject matter – ranging from the depiction of women in Chaucer and Shakespeare to female characters in women's literature – share certain presuppositions which we can term authentic realism. In the following section, I will describe the development of this critical position and then attempt to detail its central tenets.

This critical approach developed at the time of, and in response to, the consciousness raising movement of the 1970s, where the state-ment 'the personal is political' originated.[3] Women began meeting in groups to discuss their experiences, in order to demonstrate that these experiences were not peculiar to them as individuals, but were rather a part of larger scale patriarchal oppression. Listening sympathetically to each other's troubles led to a changing of consciousness, so that other women were seen as potential allies, as sisters, rather than as potential competitors for the attention of men. Women's literature played an important role in awakening them to an awareness of their oppression as women, since while dealing with the individual experiences of characters, literature could also be seen as having a wider reference. Many of the texts which were written at this time and which were read by women were used as part of a consciousness-raising process, and even now they are used for such purposes.[4] This process helped women to use literature as a means of gaining some political insight into their own lives, and into the ways in which patriarchy limits women's possibilities. The texts were dis-cussed in terms of how they related to individual women's lives, and how far women identified with the female characters. In the United Kingdom now, there are still many such reading groups, often consisting of women who have left education to have children, but who want to discuss and meet with other women within a feminist context.

Authentic realism also developed as a response to a growth in fictional writing by women which was positioned as highly autobio-graphical.[5] These texts may or may not be autobiographical: indeed the question of the constructed, fictional nature of autobiography has become a focus of feminist theoretical work in recent years.[6] However, the fact remains that they appear to have been written according to the conventions of such texts, in that, first, they are generally written in the first person as if confessing to the events in the character's life, and secondly, they often include events and information which bear striking resemblance to the author's life.[7] Given this type of text which positions itself as autobiographical, a critical position which draws on this link is, in many ways, invited. It is more difficult to discuss the text in the way one would a text which was positioned as a straightforward third-person narrated novel, simply because the voice of the narrator/author seems so much at the forefront of the text. These texts address women readers in a different way to the way texts conventionally address the reader, and they may affect our view of the world – they are not simply pleasurable, they have a material effect on the way that readers think about themselves and may lead to concrete changes in readers' lives.[8]

Authentic realism developed at a moment when feminist criticism was attempting to carve out a space for itself within both academic circles and outside, and it is significant that one of the strategies which was developed stressed the importance of *being* a woman in order to read appropriately. This had the effect of excluding male critics who seemed to be intent on muscling in on these new reading groups, which women had difficulty in maintaining as women-only spaces. The stressing of the importance of experience staked out this form of criticism as one which only women could do.[9] Thus, for all of these reasons, women critics felt a different critical strategy was called for in the analysis of texts which seemed to be addressing them in particular, personal ways. In the following section, I shall describe the following aspects of an authentic realist reading: first, its anti-theoretical nature; secondly, its treatment of the relation between female characters and women's experience; thirdly, its concern with the author; and finally, its emphasis on the pleasure of reading.

Authentic realism is used by many women when discussing literary texts, employed as if it were mere common sense and self-evidently the proper method for analyzing women's texts; however, it is important to see it as a position which is historically situated and which is a theoretical position like any other.[10] Since many women, if not the majority of women, have at some time considered this a useful way to discuss texts, it must be treated seriously, and not simply discounted as unacademic and theoretically naive.

To a greater or lesser degree many of the critics adopting this position have stated that they are purposefully anti-theoretical, since they feel that theory is elitist and specifically prevents women from participating in debate. Because many women have been prevented, through marriage, child-rearing, or through being actively discouraged, from continuing their education, theoretical issues around women's writing often do not address the very audience they are aimed at. Some groups, such as the Dalston study group, suggest that any feminist work should be written in such a way that all women will be able to understand it and put it into practice. Complex theoretical terms should not be used, since this type of language and approach to knowledge is typically patriarchal; in the way in which it excludes women, it has historically been one of the elements in their oppression. They say, 'The language used . . . [has] the effect of making large numbers of women feel inadequate, stupid or angry . . . the process we identify in education as a process of socialization which often makes women, blacks, working-class people, etc., unconfident and suspicious of intellectual work, and makes them doubt the strength and potential of their own language. It also perpetuates the split between the undervalued day-to-day language of such groups . . . and the impoverished depersonalized analytical language of intellectuals.'[11]

This anti-theoretical position can best be understood as arising for several reasons.[12] At the time when this position developed, New Criticism and structuralism were becoming popular in university departments in Great Britain and the United States, and mainstream critics seemed intent on making literary criticism appear as 'scientific' and rigorous as possible; this often led to an analysis of text which refused to refer to the author or 'real life' in any form. Many women saw this professionalization of English studies as yet another attempt to exclude women from jobs and discussion, and also an attempt to undermine the importance of so many texts by women which seemed to refer to the author's life and women's experience in general. To counteract this type of development, many of the feminist essays written at this time therefore attempt to write in a way which is easily accessible to other women who may not have had a university education, without patronizing them. Indeed, it was a central tenet of much feminist theory at this time that it is possible to express and understand very complex issues using relatively simple language.

Many women draw on elements of authentic realism when they are reading texts for pleasure, and thus it cannot and should not be dismissed lightly. If women find it useful to discuss texts in this way and they can gain solidarity and insight into their position through using it, then although an anti-theoretical stance needs to be problematized, it should be given credit for being a position which many women are able to put into practice. However, it should be remembered that one of the difficulties with this position is that it is sometimes difficult to encourage women to read in any other way. It is one theoretical position amongst many, and is politically useful in certain contexts, but should not necessarily be seen as a 'universal' reading strategy.[13]

The critics in *The Authority of Experience* collection attempt to write in a non-academic way: they write in the main with little reference to other critics, except to attack the misguidedness or prejudice of male critics when discussing female-authored texts. They use little jargon or technical terms, and write in a very personal, conversational manner. Lee Edwards, for example, instead of writing in a calm, academic way about the text she is discussing, describes the emotions she felt: 'Having reached these conclusions I can, even now, feel an inward churning of those emotions which the novel raised in me when I first read it, and flung the book away with expressions of dismay' (p. 175). In many ways, this is a challenging shift towards a new intimacy between critic and reader, moving away from conventional critical writing, with its careful academic footnoting practices and distinct 'objective', distanced position of the critic. Maurianne Adams states that when she read *Jane Eyre* she was surprised to come to the following conclusion:

> Now that the burden of trying to pretend to a totally objective and value-free perspective has finally been lifted from our shoulders, we can all admit, in the simplest possible terms, that our literary insights and perceptions come in part at least, from our sensitivity to the nuances of our own lives and our observations of other people's lives. Every time we rethink and reassimilate *Jane Eyre* we bring to it a new orientation. For women critics, this orientation is likely not to focus particular attention upon the dilemmas of the male, to whom male critics have already shown themselves understandably sensitive, but rather to Jane herself and her particular circumstances. (pp. 140–1)

Adams feels that other critics have written from the perspective of being male and simply not admitted that fact; she feels that it is now time for critics to admit how much their position is determined by their personal prejudices, their backgrounds and presumably, their gender. This self-revelation on the part of the critic also serves the purpose of stressing the solidarity which these feminists have with their women readers, and serves to break down the conventional distance and hierarchical relation between critic and reader.

A second element in an authentic realist reading is that it is necessarily concerned with the text's reference to experience. Many of the women who use this type of approach suggest that there *is* such a thing as women's experience which we can refer to: in that all women are oppressed by patriarchy, there are common experiences which women can draw on. There are certain biological functions such as menstruation, the menopause, potential child-bearing and child-rearing, which all women experience. All women suffer, to a greater or lesser extent, discrimination because of patriarchy, and experience oppression at the hands of men: for example, on the simplest level, women fear violence, rape, or sexual harassment by men. This results in women's freedom being curtailed, since we feel unable to walk or travel when we want to. These are problems which many women can recognize as widespread amongst women.[14] Women's literary texts of the 1960s and 1970s often refer to these common experiences, and give as much seriousness to depictions of women's lives as to men's, as much importance to the onset of menstruation, for example, as to the rite of passage of male puberty, often depicted in male-authored texts as the first sexual experience. It is this which can be discussed to give all women within a group an experience of sisterhood and a sense of belonging. It is this common denominator of events that is termed 'experience' which makes women's consciousness radically different to men's, and which makes certain women's texts demand a different treatment by the critic.

Some of the critics in this collection of essays examine the representation of female characters within male texts, since, as Arlyn Diamond says, 'The parts we play in literature are not unconnected with the parts we are permitted to play in life' (p. 2). They look at these women characters and attempt to redress the balance of negative male criticism of them. For example, Marcia Lerenbaum tries to recuperate Moll Flanders and show that she is a truly 'feminine' character, in that she can be seen to undergo many female biological changes, such as child-birth, the menopause and so on. Other critics in this collection of essays consider female characters and ask whether they are feminist or not, as Fries does in her essay on Chaucer's Criseyde. This character is described as a 'would-be feminist, and as victim of her . . . society' (p. 45). In this way, characters are discussed as if they were real people existing in the time in which the text was produced. As Lerenbaum says, characters are 'created out of everyday fact and human psychology' (p. 102).[15]

There is a sense in which characters are judged according to an ideal of female representation: for example, Katherine Rogers compares Samuel Richardson's representation of women characters to that of Henry Fielding, and she finds that Richardson is more sympathetic to women, 'Genuinely convinced that women's minds were as worthy of development as men's, Richardson praised qualities that most of his contemporaries either could not see or did not value in women' (p. 118). She shows that Richardson is in fact remarkable for his 'conclusion that women are better off unmarried' (p. 128), which she considers a pro-feminist position. In his texts he presents female characters who are 'equal or superior to their male counterparts' (p. 130). In this account Richardson is seen to 'identify with women, to see things from their point of view' (p. 134). Thus, male writers are judged as to whether they are sympathetic to women or not, on the basis of the way they portray female characters in their text. A more subtle approach is that of Judith Fetterley who, in considering Ernest Hemingway's *A Farewell to Arms*, shows how much of a male point of view is presented, and she suggests that this leads to the implied reader of the text being constructed as male. She says, 'All our tears are ultimately for men because in the world of *A Farewell to Arms* male life is what counts' (p. 262); the female characters do not elicit our sympathy as readers because of the way the text is written.

Female characters are considered important in authentic realist criticism, because they are thought to affect the female reader's self-image.[16] Since women read and identify with characters, however problematic the notion of identification is, these characters should, according to authentic realist critics, be strong and resourceful to serve as role-models. Marcia Landy says, 'the image of herself in literature she has been asked to appreciate, is that of silence, receptivity, and responsiveness to the needs of the man' (p. 20). Landy draws attention to the image of women as silent and passive which men have constructed, because she feels it needs to be challenged and replaced by another which is closer to her view of the reality of women's lives. Indeed, she says, 'we expect affirmation . . . in a work of art' (p. 17). By affirmation she means that our feelings about ourselves and others are ratified by representations. This position can be reduced to absurdity, where, as Toril Moi says, 'Instead of strong happy tractor drivers and factory workers [which is the supposed requirement of socialist realism], we are now presumably, to demand strong happy *women* tractor drivers', simply because women readers would like strong representations.[17]

However, there is some truth in the assertion that there was a need at this time for strong representations of females, to counteract the effect of the weak, emotional representations that were common in both male and female writing. Not only are textual images important for what is classified as women's experience in general but for the reader as an individual woman; many of the critics discuss themselves as individuals and, more particularly, the lack of 'fit' between the images they are offered in male texts and the image they have of themselves. Arlyn Diamond, when discussing criticism of Chaucer's *Wife of Bath*, disagrees with many critics who feel that the wife of Bath offers insight into the female character in general. She says, 'My disbelief is based on my inability to recognise myself, or the women I know, or have known in history, in this figure compounded of masculine insecurities and female vices as seen by misogynists' (p. 68). Having encountered such stereotypical images of women in literature, it is therefore important to be able to describe the 'shock of recognition'

that results from reading a narrative which challenges these stereotypes and which presents characters in strikingly new roles.

This is the central tenet of authentic realist criticism. The most
extreme version of this type of character criticism is perhaps Cheri
Register's article, in which she states that feminist criticism should be
prescriptive; that is, it should tell women writers what type of
characters women readers would like to have.[18] The reason for this is
so that texts are produced which contain depictions of women which
are positive, and which have inspiring role models to follow.

Thus, authentic realist critics share a notion of what women are
really like, and representations are measured against this, and judged
deficient or accurate accordingly. If the representation seems to accord
with our notions of what women are like, then the characters and the
writing are deemed authentic or true to life. Male writers have
portrayed women as stereotypes or as mythical figures in the past, and
authentic realist critics demand a change to figures which are closer to
the way women are in real life. This position has led to demands for a
reform in the way women are portrayed in children's books and in
advertisements, so that women, instead of being represented simply
as housewives or sex objects, are seen as individuals who can have a
range of occupations and modes of being. For some, the notion of
authenticity is problematic, as I will discuss later in this chapter, but
this group of critics has highlighted the way women have been
portrayed by men in the past, and the changes which women writers
have often brought when portraying women characters themselves.
Thus, if we were to approach Thomas Hardy's *Tess of the d'Urbervilles*
from this perspective, we would discuss the degree to which we
thought that the central character Tess and other female characters
approximated to our notion of an authentic female experience and to
our own experience.[19]

Some authentic realist critics in this collection of essays turn from an
analysis of male texts to the work of male critics on women's writing,
and they attempt to defend such writing from male neglect or attack.
Lynn Sukenick makes this point clearly when she says, 'Elements of
women's writing which have been unappreciated or denigrated by
male critics may appear in a different light once the prejudices of these
critics have been named as such' (p. 44). Reaction to such treatment by
male critics can result in statements like that of Dale Spender, who
believes that women should not respond to each other's work in a
negative way, since at this particular historical moment, women
should only be positive about other women's work.[20] The fact that
women's writing has been described in negative terms is seen as a
result of the negative views of critics about women in general. Thus,
the feminist critic's role here is to point out the partiality of the view of

male critics. For example, Priscilla Allen devotes her article to a discussion of the negative male criticism of Kate Chopin's *The Awakening*. For her, it is a case of showing how the critics have 'misread' the text because of their gender-bias (p. 225); they have tended to sympathize with the male characters and have therefore been unsympathetic towards the central character Edna. Allen shows that women reading this text read it in quite a different way. She asks: 'Is the novel about *men* coping with Edna, one might ask, or are Edna's problems with them central?' (p. 228). An authentic realist reading would stress that with such a woman-centred text, it is a misreading to concentrate on anything other than the problems of the central character, Edna.

Although some of the critics analyze the work of male writers and criticize the work of male theorists, there is a sense in which the central aim of this approach is a turning away from 'images of women' criticism, since merely attacking literary representations seems to them to be 'barren' and not 'fruitful'.[21] In turning from men's texts, many found that they could not apply the usual critical terminology to women's writing. It was no longer interesting to talk simply about the structure of the text, the narrative technique and so on. Many women felt and still feel split when talking about women's texts: they use a theoretical position for men's texts, and yet they feel uncomfortable using such a model for women's texts, and some of them turn to a more untheorized model.[22] Taking a gendered position foregrounds some of the problems of male texts, and shows the elements which have been ignored throughout literary criticism. Attention is moved to considering the representation of women characters in women's writing and how authentic the content of such texts appears to readers. Having seen that men writing about women are often unsuccessful in portraying women characters, often reproducing stereotypical images, there is a move to consider the women characters in women's texts. As Mary Cohen says, 'It is vitally important that the protagonists in Lessing's longest and most significant works . . . are women, women whose personal lives have been painful and at times even debilitating' (p. 179). The reason it is so vitally important is that, for Cohen, this depiction reflects women's experience in the real world and is thus authentic. Very frequently these characters are discussed as if they were people, and when they are convincing as people, they are seen as authentic.

The reason why these critics discuss the relation between female characters and women's experience is that they believe that literature has a very close relationship to life in a broad political sense. Literary representations have some effect on what people do in the real world; as Arlyn Diamond says, literature embodies 'a society's most deeply held convictions, sometimes questioning these values, sometimes disguising an artist's ambivalence with regard to these matters, but never disengaged from the claims of time or social order' (p. 1). She goes on to say that a simple shift of attention from male characters to female characters is not enough: 'The critics represented here do not rest with the description of an author's techniques or the stance of a particular work, but instead point constantly to the need to measure literary reality on the one side against historical and personally felt reality on the other' (p. 2). Reality is seen as something which is 'reflected' in literature, and since reality is different for women and for men, the 'reflection' of this in literature must be equally different.

Many of these critics weigh literature against their own experience; for example, Lee Edwards says, when discussing Virginia Woolf's *Mrs Dalloway*: 'Let me note that Virginia Woolf, Clarissa Dalloway, and I share two common characteristics: our sex and, in the broadest sense, our class' (p. 196). She then goes on to discuss what these characteristics have meant for all three – character, author and critic – in terms of the limitations on what they have been able to do. She refers to the three as 'we' throughout this discussion, again breaking down the distinction between text and reality, and problematizing conventional critical distance. All three have felt the limitations of their class and gender and all have tried to break free from these restrictions. In another essay in the collection, Dawn Landy also refers to her personal history and her reasons for writing the article:

> I suppose I began to compose this essay on women in the wilderness long ago, when I was a girl living in the desert and dust of Southern Arizona and later in the irrigated central valley at Phoenix, and I suppose that now I am not in the beginning of consciousness, but somewhere in the middle, and am only elaborating upon an earlier response to the flat landscape and coarse uninhabited mountains. (p. 94)

She goes on to describe her life in this area, and her experience at university, where she studied literature which dealt with the wilderness:

> Repeatedly, however, I could find no place for myself and for my pleasure in the wilderness in the traditionally recorded images of women on the frontier . . . I did not see myself in this image and could not believe that it fully communicated the character of the frontier woman (pp. 195–6).

This involvement of the critic and self-revelation is important for criticism, since, in conventional criticism, the critic as a person is notably absent. These interventions by the critic change the nature of criticism from what had seemed to many to be dry scientific reports to something which affects women as individuals.[23]

A third element in an authentic realist reading is a concern with the author and her relation to the text. For many of the critics in this collection, it is important to discuss the author's life, especially when the text is written by a woman. The author is seen to have a close relationship with her characters, and with the content of the text. Often author and character are conflated. Adams relates the content of Charlotte Brontë's texts to the author's life, and shows how the limitations which the characters suffer in Brontë's texts are ones which Brontë herself suffered in real life. She says: 'Some women's lives have always pursued this course [education], likely enough with similar sacrifice, in Brontë's time and earlier; Charlotte Brontë is herself an instance, in her life, if not in her fiction' (p. 157). The distinction between author and character becomes, in many of the essays, almost insignificant.

A final element in authentic realist criticism is that these women critics discuss their pleasure in the texts, something which was notably lacking from male theorizing of the time. All of the theorists state what they found most enjoyable or most traumatic in the text, sometimes recounting a particularly exciting episode in the plot. And whilst pleasure is discussed in an untheoretical way, it is important that the pleasure in reading is not pushed into the background when analyzing texts, since many of the texts considered in this collection have been read compulsively and repeatedly by many women. This approach takes reading and the effects of reading seriously in terms of female identification. Some of these texts offer potential models of fantasy for women readers, offering alternative ways of living, and ways of experiencing. Very little work had been undertaken at this time on the notion of pleasure and the reasons why certain texts move their readers so forcefully.[24]

To sum up, the central features of an authentic realist reading of a literary text consist of relating elements of the text to women's experience in order to make women more aware of their oppression as a group; literature is seen as a powerful vehicle for changing women's self-image. In this type of analysis, female characters are described as successful if they are seen to depict women's lives in an authentic way, and if they seem to reflect the experience of the author. Literature and life are thus seen to be connected in the most intimate of ways.

II

The books which will be used for this analysis are *The Color Purple* by Alice Walker and Emily Brontë's *Wuthering Heights*.[25] Both of these books have been read and reread by many women. They are obviously important books in the formative years of many women's lives and later. They are books which women have used in discussion groups and which have been of fundamental importance to women individually and also to women as a group, in terms of constructing a tradition of women's writing. In the course of this analysis, I sent a questionnaire to a range of women, from academic and non-academic backgrounds, to ask them what it was they liked about these books and why they felt the books were important to them. I will draw on their responses in this section.[26]

Both of these texts seem to have been written for a female audience and women have claimed them as part of a female tradition. *Wuthering Heights* has also been claimed as part of the mainstream canon, and *The Color Purple* has been awarded the Pulitzer Prize and been made into a feature film by Spielberg. Thus, they have both a male and female audience; however, they are primarily women's texts, i.e. it is women who read and reread them. Many women in my survey remarked on the importance of *Wuthering Heights* to them in adolescence, and *The Color Purple* seemed important for its overtly feminist content. Many of the women readers remarked on the fact that they felt deeply involved by these texts to the extent that they cried when they read them, even when they had reread them several times. Some also felt that these were texts which 'changed your life'. Even Anne, who did not like *Wuthering Heights*, 'because I couldn't identify with any of the characters', said that she had still read it several times.

I shall therefore offer some suggestions for the popularity of these texts among women readers and relate the experience of my interviewees to the recurrent features of authentic realist criticism, which many of them seem to be using. There are several elements in *The Color Purple* to which an authentic realist reader would respond. The most important of these are the depiction of sexuality, strong female characters, the form and language of the novel, and the relation of the text to the author and to experience, and I will deal with these in turn.

The Color Purple attempts to look at women's sexuality in a different way to that in which it is conventionally seen, since it gives very negative portrayals of heterosexual love, and very positive portrayals of lesbian love, both sexual and non-sexual. In contrast to lesbian sexuality, the depictions of heterosexual love-making are often presented as disgusting. The first event which confronts the reader in the text is the fact that Celie has been sexually abused by her stepfather; his sexuality is seen as indiscriminate and violent, and the reader is shocked that a 14-year-old girl is subjected to incest. However, this is not portrayed as an isolated instance of aberrant sexuality, since Sophia also admits that she had to become physically strong as a girl in order to ward off such attacks from male members of her family. Because of her experiences, Celie consequently becomes revolted by male sexuality and admits finally that men's genitals remind her of frogs (p. 215). She likens sex to going to the toilet and refers to her husband 'doing his business' (p. 68). Again, this is not an isolated response to male sexuality, since Sophia becomes bored by Harpo's mechanical love-making, and he does not notice her lack of response; she says: 'He git up there and enjoy himself just the same. No matter what I'm thinking. No matter what I feel. It just him. Heartfeeling don't even seem to enter into it' (p. 59). Shug attempts to convince Celie that sex with men does not have to be unfeeling and unpleasurable; however, Celie remains unconvinced, and it is her point of view which dominates the text – it is Celie that the reader is encouraged to identify with. It is interesting therefore that the relationship which Celie has finally with Mr — is more like the relationship of brother and sister; we assume that it is not a sexual one.

In stark contrast to this negative portrayal of heterosexual love, relationships between women are portrayed in a very positive way. Lillian Faderman shows how lesbianism has been portrayed in men's literature through the ages, and discusses the misconceptions there have been about what women actually *do* together.[27] Even in lesbian novels like *The Well of Loneliness*, by Radclyffe Hall, the actions of lesbians are confined to vague embraces and yearnings, and lesbianism is described as 'inversion' – a medical term for a genetic predisposition which is viewed as an illness.[28] In the past, there have been frequent depictions of lesbianism as a problem, and this is one of the few occasions in a mainstream text where lesbianism was celebrated.[29] Here it is seen as a liberating experience which does not entail guilt; instead, Celie's love-making with Shug is described as:

> Little like sleeping with mama, only I can't hardly remember ever sleeping with her. Little like sleeping with Nettie, only sleeping with Nettie never felt this good. It warm and cushiony, and I feel Shug's big tits sorta flop over my arms like suds. It feels like heaven is what it feels like, not like sleeping with Mr — at all. (p. 98)

It is interesting that lesbianism is described not in terms of how it is similar to heterosexuality; there is little mention of penetration, but instead, Shug tells Celie that, 'Lot of sucking go on, here and there she say. Lot of finger and tongue work' (p. 69). Lesbianism is also described in terms of the way it is similar to other forms of female love: Celie's love for her mother and her sister, as in the above quotation, or as similar to her love for her children: 'Then I feels something real soft and wet on my breasts, feel like one of my little lost babies mouth. Way after while, I act like I a little lost baby too' (p. 97).

It is also one of the few texts where lesbianism is portrayed not as something which is necessarily biologically determined, but as a choice women can make as an alternative to oppressive sexual relations with men. Lesbianism here is not described in a voyeuristic way as in men's literature. Faderman notes that much of the portrayal of lesbians in literature has been for a male audience and for male sexual stimulation. This depiction at least shows lesbianism as an alternative to the unfeeling and aggressive sexuality of the males in the text. Shug and Celie make love in a very caring way, and Shug initially makes love to Celie to show her about clitoral stimulation, which Celie had not discovered. The love between these women is not seen as primarily sexual, although that plays an important part in their relationship, but they are seen to love one another and care for one another in the manner of 'romantic friendship' as described by Faderman. The strength of their emotional involvement is of greater importance than their sexual relationship. Shug dedicates a song to Celie and helps her when she needs to set up her own business; she is also aware enough of the problems in male–female relationships not to allow Celie to become her maid. At certain points the sexual side of their relationship becomes less important: 'Us sleep like sisters, me and Shug' (p. 124) and they find enjoyment in hugging and cuddling. The fact that Shug sleeps with Celie's husband is almost irrelevant; Celie does not feel jealousy about this because it does not seem very important. I found this emphasis on female friendship in the face of oppressive male relations very heartening, and among the interviewees, Sandra said: 'Despite being heterosexual I felt I could really relate to it – and felt very moved by it'; Kay also described the love scenes as 'very moving'. It is the emotional side of the relationship between Shug and Celie which is of importance, and their love-making is seen as an expression of this love; their relationship is seen to be of the same order as the relationship Celie has with her sister Nettie. The important permanent sexual and non-sexual relations are those between women; all the other male–female relationships are seen as temporary. In this respect, I feel *The Color Purple* is a significant realignment of many heterosexual women's worlds, which are often centred around relations with men, and it points to ways in which women could reconsider these relations and these priorities.

However, some of the women readers found the depiction of sexuality between women to be slightly problematic. I, like some of the interviewees, felt it was good to have a representation of female sexuality in terms of other women, rather than in terms of penetration by men, and it was also important that the representation is of clitoral rather than vaginal stimulation. Linda said: 'I can't honestly say I liked the bits where Celie "discovers" her sexuality. I found the emphasis on experimentation – all the references to "magic buttons" etc. rather whimsical and irritating.' The depiction of sexuality in the text is weighed against readers' notions of what they feel female sexuality is like, and found either to be accurate or deficient.[30]

A second element in an authentic realist reading of this book is the fact that this is a woman-centred or 'womanist' text: the focus of interest is not only on one Black woman character but it is on the relations between women characters.[31] The women are not defined in terms of their relationships with men, i.e. as sister, mother, wife of a man. Relationships with men are seen as temporary and almost as incidental. You may have had children by a man, but in this text the important relationship is with the children and not with their father. The central relationships for Celie are those she has with her sister and with Shug; her marriage and her traumatic childhood relationship with her father are not the focus of attention. Further, when Celie learns that her 'father' is in fact her stepfather, she is not particularly moved by the news. She is far more concerned, as are the other women in the text, with her relationship with her children and women friends. She loves Nettie so much that she is prepared to offer herself to the man she thinks is her father, rather than have him abuse Nettie. Despite the fact that she does not see or hear from her sister for twenty years, they send letters to each other regardless; and even though Shug leaves her to have an affair with a man, Celie still continues to love her. It is this intensity of relationship with other women and the solidarity between women which many women readers find affirming.

Men are mentioned as oppressors, lovers, deceivers and, like Grady, disappear once the relationship is finished; but the real focus of interest is on the women. Few of the women characters are shown in a negative light. The women support each other through trouble and help each other to cope. For example, Mr —'s sister, Kate, gets him to buy Celie clothes and forces Harpo to do more work around the house. Celie makes Harpo call his new girlfriend by her real name Mary Agnes, rather than by a nickname which belittles her. Shug will not consider leaving Celie 'until I know Albert won't even think of beating you' (p. 67). Mary Agnes sleeps with the prison warder so that Sophia is let out of prison. When one of the women needs to leave home or is forced to leave, the other women look after her children.

There is even a shift in the text so that Celie's letters, which were at first written to God, are, in the later section of the book, addressed to Nettie, when Celie realizes that God is a part of white patriarchy: a change in the text from living within and being oppressed by a male-dominated society, to a position where women make their own choices and discover sisterhood. When the solidarity of women is betrayed, it is presented in a negative light; for example, Celie tells

Harpo to hit Sophia to make her obey him, and she becomes ill as a consequence. It is only when she admits this to Sophia and begs her forgiveness that Celie recovers (p. 37).

There are depictions of strong women throughout the text: the women are seen to do all the work – Sophia mends the roof of their house, and Celie chops cotton single-handedly on the farm when her husband is too obsessed with Shug to work. Sophia is described as very physically strong: 'Arms got muscle. Legs too. She swing that baby about like it nothing' (p. 32). Sophia and her sisters are described as Amazons, and they carry her mother's coffin to her funeral. Sophia has to be so aggressive because she was brought up amongst aggressive males, and this was the only way she could survive. Irene commented that: 'Sophia's statement about women in her family needing weight to ward off male members of the family is . . . close to many women's experience.' However, Sophia's physical strength and aggression is seen to be, at least in part, the cause of her own downfall: strength has to be tempered. Kay said: 'I will *never* forget the woman who is imprisoned for striking out. She stands up to her husband and patriarchal white society and is dealt with accordingly. I could weep everytime I think about that big, strong independent woman being crushed'. Several of the readers mentioned how important Shug was for them; she is portrayed as so powerful as to be almost frightening. Naima said how much she enjoyed seeing: 'a woman full of life who lives her passions as *she* likes and not as the conventions suggest she should [these are of course to men's benefit]. She is a woman, free, strong, generous *and* full of talent.'

Celie shows another type of strength – not the physical strength which is associated with men, but a strength of will. She is not a strong character at the beginning of the novel, and generally does as she is told by the male characters. Shug scolds her for being so subservient to her husband and finally Celie gains enough self-confidence and power to stand up to Mr —; she faces him with the fact that he has treated her badly, by withholding the letters from her sister. Naima says about Celie: 'She seems to have achieved a certain awareness, a certain consciousness through her own experience, nothing drawn from a theory or indoctrinating of some kind. It made me feel respect for this woman who becomes aware of her identity as a woman through a hard life.' When Celie leaves her husband, she manages to achieve financial independence from men by setting up her own small-scale clothing firm. Irene commented on this: 'Mainly it is the women's capacity to *survive* the subjugation by men that makes the novel enjoyable.'

The reader sees another element of Celie's power in the scene where she confronts her husband with having withheld letters from her sister, since she curses him: 'Until you do right by me, everything you touch will crumble' (p. 176). Her strength is supernatural, since a miraculous dust devil springs up at her words, and the reader is led to believe, because of Shug's rather frightened intervention, that Celie's curse would really have had an effect on Mr —, if it had not been stopped.

In contrast to the strength of the female characters, the men are described in terms which are essentially negative. When they are not straightforwardly evil, they are shown to be weak. Celie's step-father and Mr — are portrayed as cruel, selfish and unfeeling in their treatment of Celie and other women. Shug calls Mr — 'a weak little boy' (p. 43), since he did not have the strength to disobey his father and marry her. Instead he marries Celie as his father wishes, whilst continuing to see Shug. Harpo is described as equally weak: when he wants to make his wife Sophia obey him, he decides to hit her; Celie notes: 'Next time us see Harpo his face is a mess of bruises' (p. 35). On another occasion, Celie sees Harpo and Sophia 'fighting like two mens' (p. 36). Harpo cannot conceive of any relationship with a woman which does not involve the woman obeying her husband completely. Finally, he eats massive amounts of food so that he will be as big as Sophia, and he is surprised to find that this has no effect either. He cries to Celie like a baby. This bears comparison with Shug, since all the men she has affairs with are weak: Grady does not work and she has to keep him, and she pays for Germaine, her young lover, to go to college.

None of the men stand up for the women when they are in trouble; for example, in church, Mr — does not defend Shug when the preacher calls her a slut. Celie says: 'Somebody got to stand up for Shug, I think. But he don't say nothing' (p. 40). Men treat women as property, as, for example, in the scene where Mr — is given Celie as a wife instead of Nettie; he refers to her as 'that one' and she is made to turn around for him, as if she were livestock. Her father even throws a cow into the bargain to induce him to take Celie, and this seems to be one of the major elements which makes Mr — decide to marry her.

Although these male characters are weak as individuals, the power of patriarchy makes them strong and enables them to behave in a way which disadvantages others. We are presented with a depiction of the power of men to prevent women from fulfilling themselves: Celie is the victim of incest and her children are taken from her by her stepfather; her sister leaves her because of her husband's sexual harassment; even Nettie's letters are kept from Celie by her husband.[32]

It is only towards the end of the book that Celie's husband comes to some realization of how badly he has behaved, and he is then presented as a reasonable character with whom we can imagine Celie continuing to live. For Irene, this reconciliation is important, as she says: 'It presented us with women who suffer because of their relationship with men and yet ends with a friendship being formed between a man and a woman.' Thus, although the text is largely very critical of heterosexuality, it seems to shy away from rejecting it altogether.

A third element which an authentic realist reader would draw attention to is the form and language which are used, since they lead the reader to feel close to the characters and the events in the text. Linda drew attention to the special intimacy created by the novel's epistolary form. The second person singular (you) is by definition the most intimate form of address, opening itself to the reader as well as to the addressee. Linda observed that letterwriting, along with diaries and other 'confessional' forms, represent the crucial 'sub-genres' of the female literary tradition, and had been central to her own life-experience: 'Letters have played a major – the major? – role in my relationships, and this seems to have been generally true for women throughout history.' Letters *between* women, in particular, have often (as in *The Color Purple*) assumed the nature of, as Linda puts it: 'a secret conspiracy against men', and become a 'symbol of faith and promise between women'. This is why Albert's act of concealing Nettie's letters is perceived by women readers as such a despicable betrayal. Linda remarked: 'I shared in the murderous instinct – absolutely! I suppose it's because the episode is symbolic of the absolute power of the male in keeping women apart.'

The letters do not have the structure of a conventional letter or of conventional chapters – they are based around anecdotal events in the life of Celie, and in this way one can imagine the character of Celie writing these letters late at night before going to sleep. The events are not narrated in the conventional way of situating the narrator at a particular point in time describing the events in chronological order: here the narrator is situated at the same point in time as the events – they are described as they happened with the lack of hindsight and foreshadowing which letters or a diary would have. For example, when Celie's baby goes missing, she at first thinks that 'God took it', and it is only in the next chapter that she finds that it is her father who has abducted the baby. Celie has the same knowledge as the reader, and this makes us empathize more with her as a character.

The language in the text is also very important in this type of reading. The fact that Walker has decided to use Black American vernacular as the language of Celie's letters also makes the novel seem more authentic. The text is full of conversations rather than the narration of events; for example, in the early parts of the book, in one of her letters to God, she writes: 'Dear God, Harpo want to know what to do to make Sophia mind. He sit out on the porch with Mr —. He say, I tell her one thing, she do another. Never do what I say. Always backtalk' (p. 34). In this way, conversations are reported through the medium of Celie's writing, and even the narrative voice is based on the model of spoken language: the sentences are short, and reflect the way sentences are constructed in conversations, rather than being filtered through a standard narrative voice. Thus, the novel is less like a series of letters, but rather like a series of conversations. The reader is aware of the voices of the characters throughout the text; there seems to be a reflection of the speech patterns of certain people in reporting conversations with the repeated 'I say', and 'he say'. For example: 'I tell her she can't be all the time going to visit her sister. Us married now, I tell her. Your place is here with the children. She say, I'll take the children with me. I say, Your place is with me. She say, You want to come?' (p. 34).

This conversational tone is added to by the fact that Celie writes words as they would be pronounced, for example 'kine' for kind (p. 3), 'git' for get, 'ast' for ask, etc. The fact that she uses certain words such as 'titties', 'thing', 'pussy', which would normally only be used in intimate settings or in jokes, also draws the reader to the figure of Celie; she uses the words of intimacy, because this writing is constantly addressed to an interlocutor – she does not have to use the impersonal terms of written forms.

On the first page there is an added element which makes us feel that this is an authentic depiction of a diary written by an adolescent, since it begins: 'Dear God, I am fourteen years old. I ~~am~~ have always been a good girl' (p. 3). The fact that the 'I am' is crossed out in the text means that we read this to be a depiction of the type of error a young girl would make in writing a diary. The events are described with the limitations that a 14-year-old's consciousness would have; for example, she is unable to articulate her father's assaults on her, and when she is pregnant, she is surprised when the baby appears: 'When I start to hurt and then my stomach start moving and then that little baby come out of my pussy chewing on it fist you could have knock me over with a feather' (p. 4).

A fourth element which authentic realist readers remarked upon is that they felt that the book related to women's experience. Kay said that she wept openly as she read this book: 'I did feel it reflected women's experience, *all* women's experience because it was about suffering, humiliation, degradation *and* joy, love, strength and celebration.' The fact that the novel related to experience also made a strong impression on her: 'For me, Celie's emergence from her terrible life as a strong and intelligent woman inspired me and saddened me at the same time.' For some of the women, the question of race was important, although as Lizzie said: 'Sometimes I was aware that Celie was a black woman, sometimes just that she was a woman.' And Irene said that she felt it 'reflected the experience of lots of women – white as well as black'. Thus, these readers, the majority of whom are white, feel that they can read the text as reflecting the experience of all women oppressed under patriarchy.

An authentic realist reading is also concerned with the author and her life and the relation to the text; in this case, it is important that *The Color Purple* was written by a woman of colour.[33] On the last page of the book is written: 'I thank everybody in this book for coming, A. W. author and medium' (p. 245), which leads the reader to assume that Alice Walker feels that she has composed the book in a less structured way than most novelists; she has almost written by allowing voices to be heard. This supposed lack of conscious control makes the text less of an artefact, more of a 'confessional'. The fact that she has included this comment also leads one to assume that the author feels she has a close relation to her text. She describes, in an article entitled 'Writing *The Color Purple*', the way in which the characters in the story invaded her life: the characters of Shug and Celie would tell her what to do in her life, and would refuse to appear when she wanted to start writing.[34] For example, she writes:

> Just as summer was ending, one or more of my characters – Celie, Shug, Albert, Sofia or Harpo – would come for a visit. We would sit wherever I was sitting, and talk. They were very obliging, engaging, and jolly. They were, of course, at the end of their story but were telling it to me from the beginning. Things that made me sad often made them laugh. Oh, we got through that; don't pull such a long face, they'd say. (p. 45)

Because Alice Walker is herself Black, the depiction of Black American characters has a more authentic feel for white readers than if they had been depicted by white writers, male or female. The white authentic realist reader assumes that Walker must know more about Black people and therefore she must be qualified to discuss them and portray them. The fact that this text was written by a woman is important, that it was written by a woman of colour is even more so. Much structuralist and poststructuralist work, in particular the work of Roland Barthes and Michel Foucault, has attempted to show that the author is of no importance in the discussion of texts; the author is effectively 'dead'.[35]. However, many feminists would disagree with this type of theoretical position, since the gender of the author is of vital importance, both in terms of the way the text is received by male critics and the way it is read by female readers. For critics such as Patricia Waugh it is rather striking that the concept of the self is questioned so radically just as feminists are claiming a particularly feminine self.[36] And Black theorists like Barbara Christian have criticized the so-called 'death' of the author because, as she states,

> Now I am told that philosophers are the ones who write literature; that authors are dead, irrelevant, mere vessels through which their narratives ooze; that they do not work nor have they the faintest idea what they are doing – rather they produce texts as disembodied as angels.[37]

This erasing of the author is particularly important for all those women writers who have struggled to gain acceptance by the mainstream. *The Color Purple*, in particular, is read in a different way because it was written by a woman of colour than if it had been written by, for example, a white male. Written by a female, it can be read as an attempt at a redefinition of women's experience, and a celebration of that experience. But written by a man it would be yet another attempt to take over radical positions and neutralize them. There would also be the charge of potential racism and voyeurism if the book had been written by a white male. Many proponents of authentic realism would also say that only women can write effectively about women's experience, because only they have undergone such experience.[38] Thus, within this type of reading, because Walker is Black, white readers assume that she can write about Black characters in a way which convinces them of their authenticity.

To sum up, this novel has served as a vehicle of consciousness-raising for many women, white and black; many ordinary women, when reading this book, find that they can relate the experiences of the female characters to their own lives, and enjoy the depiction of strong female characters. In reading such texts in this way, they become aware that the problems they face are not simply individual problems, but are ones faced by other women.

Wuthering Heights is a novel which has also been extremely important for women readers. Most women have read it at some time in their lives, and many have reread the novel several times. In this authentic realist reading of the text, the following elements will be concentrated on: strong female characters, identification with the characters, the depiction of love, and language and form. Beginning with strong female characters, we find, just as in *The Color Purple*, that they are limited by their male oppressors: Cathy is as wild and adventurous as Heathcliff as a child, and Kay remarks that 'Cathy's wildness was exciting'. Cathy runs across the moor with Heathcliff and stays out with him; as Nelly Dean says in the novel: 'from the hour she came downstairs, till the hour she went to bed, we had not a minute's security that she wouldn't be in mischief. Her spirits were always at high-water mark, her tongue always going – singing, laughing and plaguing everybody who would not do the same' (p. 83). She is an extremely wilful child, and after her father's death, she spends her time on the moors with Heathcliff despite the punishment which ensues. However, her freedom is gradually curtailed, especially after an incident where she goes to Thrushcross Grange with Heathcliff to torment the Linton children. On running away, she falls and is bitten by the Lintons' dog. The Lintons look after her, and when she returns from Thrushcross Grange, she has changed:

> instead of a wild, hatless little savage jumping into the house, and rushing to squeeze us all breathless, there lighted from a handsome black pony a very dignified person, with brown ringlets falling from the cover of a feathered beaver, and a long cloth habit which she was obliged to hold up with both hands that she might sail in. (p. 93)

This move by Cathy into the world of adult femininity was seen by many of the women surveyed as a limit on her as a person, because: 'while her eyes sparkled joyfully when the dogs came bounding up to welcome her, she dare hardly touch them lest they should fawn upon her splendid garments' (p. 93). It is in this way that Cathy's wildness is tamed, and she is also weaned away from the person she loves most, because Heathcliff is not of the same social class. When Heathcliff reluctantly comes to shake her hand: 'She gazed concernedly at the dusky fingers she held in her own, and also at her dress; which she feared had gained no embellishment from its contact with his' (p. 95). From this moment onwards in the text, the relationship with Heathcliff is discouraged, and Cathy's wildness is subdued, in an attempt to make her a perfect wife for Edgar Linton.

Her daughter Catherine is also strong and wilful; she forces Nelly to let her go out on the moor alone. However, she is tricked by Heathcliff, and lured into his house. Once there, she is forced to marry Linton against her will. Catherine's first reaction to Heathcliff's threat is to consider burning the door down, for she knows that her dying father will be worried by her absence. Gradually, she realizes that she must comply with his wishes, and marries Linton, who says to Nelly:

> Papa . . . says I'm not to be soft with Catherine; she's my wife, and it's shameful that she should wish to leave me. He says, she hates me and wants me to die, that she may have my money; but she shan't have it; and she shan't go home! She never shall! – she may cry and be sick as much as she pleases' (p. 311)

In this way, by being forced into a feminine role and by being forced to marry, the strong women characters in the text are tamed by male characters, and this taming is sanctioned by society.

Many of the readers said that they identified with characters within the text; surprisingly some of them identified with Heathcliff – which may be because he feels so strongly. Linda said: 'My identification with the thwarted tormented relationships which comprise the book is simply as thwarted tormented relationships!' She also remarked that she felt a 'perverse attraction to Heathcliff's jealousy and Catherine's selfishness' and explained this by saying that it was the result of 'being brought up in a society where absolute love is regarded as single exclusive, obsessive, etc.'. Linda also mentioned that she had read the book as analogous to her own relationship with a woman and saw the obstacles thrown in the path of Cathy and Heathcliff as similar to the obstacles imposed on lesbian relationships; she remarks: 'I wonder if other lesbians have responded to the text in this way, or whether they are unable to transcend the fact that Cathy and Heathcliff are male and female'. She stated that for her the book's enduring fascination lay in its transcendence of sexuality: 'the ancient Romantic idea that there is a "higher spiritual soul-communion" [I suspect lots of women are attracted to this book for this reason]'. She also acknowledged, however, that the appeal of such transcendence was clearly a form of wish-fulfilment ('romance' in the popular sense of the word), coterminous with the limitations placed upon relationships in real life. She admitted to seeing the predestined yet socially impossible relationship between Cathy and Heathcliff as an analogy to her own repressed friendship with another woman, and observed that, for this reason, *Wuthering Heights* probably had a special meaning for lesbians and other groups (mistresses, partners-in-incest, etc.) whose love would never be sanctioned by the society in which they lived. For Sandra, the gender implications were also problematic: 'I experienced conflicting emotions. I was both attracted to and repelled by Catherine and Heathcliff; they are so impressively yet terrifyingly powerful. Perhaps what I felt most was sympathy for Catherine; her rejection of Edgar's conformity and her attraction to freedom and equality with Heathcliff.'

The third issue which many of the interviewees drew attention to in their appraisal of this book was the fact that love is of such intensity that it survives even death. As in much romance, love is seen to be of central importance both to the female and male characters.[39] Here, it is Heathcliff who suffers from love, arguably far more than Cathy. He is driven to deceitful and violent acts by his love for her, to the point where he is likened to a 'devil'. The love between Cathy and Heathcliff is not like other earthly loves; Heathcliff describes his love for Cathy and compares it to Edgar's love for her:

> every thought she spends on Linton, she spends a thousand on me
> . . . I was a fool to fancy for a moment that she valued Edgar
> Linton's attachment more than mine – If he loved with all the
> powers of his puny being, he couldn't love as much in eighty years,

as I could in a day. And Catherine has a heart as deep as I have; the sea could be as readily contained in that horse-trough, as her whole affection be monopolised by him. (p 186)

Such is his love for Cathy that on her death he prays that she will haunt him:

> I pray one prayer – I repeat it till my tongue stiffens – Catherine Earnshaw, may you not rest as long as I am living! You said I killed you – haunt me, then! The murdered do haunt their murderers, I believe – I know that ghosts have wandered on earth. Be with me always – take any form – drive me mad! only do not leave me in this abyss, where I cannot find you! Oh God! it is unutterable! I cannot live without my life! I cannot live without my soul!' He dashed his head against the knotted trunk; and lifting up his eyes, howled, not like a man, but like a savage beast getting goaded to death with knives and spears. (p. 204)

Many of the women interviewed remarked on how attractive they found the prospect of a man loving them with such intensity. They remarked on how this often contrasted starkly with their own lives. As Mandy described the book: 'All pash and nothing about the rent.' And Sandra described the feeling of 'the fantastically intense and passionate atmosphere of the whole book'. Other readers also mentioned the appeal of the emotional depth portrayed in the novel; for example, Lizzie said: 'I loved this book both times I read it, first as a schoolgirl and then more recently. Both times what impressed me was the whole range of emotions expressed and the vividness of the turmoil the characters were plunged into. This book still haunts me.' Linda suggested a reason for this: 'Probably what appeals to me (and other women) in a love that defies present circumstance, survives the grave, etc., etc., is that it gives this transcendent reality to what is impossible on earth.'

The language and form of the text are also important for the feeling of authenticity that some readers are aware of. The text is written as if told by a variety of characters: Mr Lockwood is related the tale by Nelly Dean, who on occasion hears gossip from other characters such as Zillah. In this way the text is, like *The Color Purple*, a form of reported conversation rather than straightforward narrative prose. The reader receives information that is reported through conversations, rather than being presented with 'facts' and the information is given only in a piecemeal fashion. The reader is also engaged in the text, since she soon realizes that the main source of information, Nelly Dean, is not reliable; the reader is involved and has to be astute and to weigh up Nelly's judgements on events. The sources of information are all women, who have to attempt to find out what has happened without the men discovering. Nelly passes notes to Cathy from

Heathcliff, and is given information by Zillah; all this has to be kept secret from the male figures.

To sum up, an authentic realist reading of this text finds the depiction of love of great importance to women readers; this is the element which gives readers pleasure and makes them reread the text, and which involves them most in the events of the novel.

III

The central problems of authentic realism have been described in detail by Toril Moi in her discussion of this position.[40] First, there is a problem with any position which supposes that it is untheoretical, since this is in fact a theoretical position, whether one is aware of it or not. Many of the critics writing within an authentic realist framework claim not to be holding a theoretical position at all, but this is obviously an illusion; theory cannot be escaped in this way, and the theoretical origins of authentic realism have been traced convincingly by Toril Moi. However, it must be said that an avoidance of jargon and addressing one's writing to a non-academic female audience has great advantages for feminist discussions, though that in no way rules out explicit theoretical positions.

A further serious shortcoming of this approach is one which I drew attention to in the first section: the notion of women's experience. Experience is clearly not the same for all women: even our biological similarities are not constructed in the same way by society. Menstruation might be roughly the same physical process for all women, but the way it is constructed and treated within each society and social group differs radically. In a similar way, our expectations and the limitations on our behaviour differ according to social class, 'race', and ethnic origin: no one can fail to be aware that upper-class women are less restricted than working-class women.[41] What seems to be counted as experience within authentic realism is what counts as middle-class white heterosexual experience; the best examples of theoretical work on authentic realism's universalizing tendencies can be found in Diana Fuss and Judith Butler's work.[42] Discussion of experience by many of these critics veers dangerously close to prescriptivism: that is, because a novel does not seem to deal with *my* experience, it is not authentic. Authenticity itself is a problematic term, since it is unclear by whom the experience is being validated. With many of the assumptions underlying this position, common sense is being drawn on, and for feminists who know well the perils of common sense views about women this must surely be avoided.

Furthermore, the notion of identification with characters must be further scrutinized. Identifying seems such a common sense activity when reading; yet critical analysis highlights the way in which we as readers are often manipulated into positions by textual means. If we take the example of identifying with characters who are representing romantic love as in *Wuthering Heights*, although it may seem pleasurable to 'identify' with Cathy and/or Heathcliff, this may not in fact be in our interests as individuals. Romance scenarios such as these render us passive victims of circumstances, out of control, unable to act, prey to our emotions and to others.[43] Whilst this may be pleasurable (we take our pleasure where we find it), as Frigga Haug has shown, masochism is often presented to women as a 'natural' choice, but that is not to say that it is in our interests to take that choice.[44]

There is a related problem that the demand for realism, truth to life, clashes with the demand for role models, since the reader cannot ask for a reflection of reality, if at the same time she is asking for something idealized. In terms of 'race', it is certainly not the case that the way experience is constructed by different 'racial' groups is the same; many women of colour resent the way in which white middle-class feminists assume that they share sisterhood simply because they are women. Cora Kaplan in her article on *The Color Purple* has stressed that it is a mistake to read it as a text which refers to women's experience in general; instead it must be read with reference to its historical background and specificity, as a Marxist-feminist reading would.[45] In this case it is the history of Black people and their literature in the United States which must be addressed, and it would be a mistake to read it as referring to women's experience as a whole, or women's sexuality as a whole. In order to discuss *The Color Purple* as relating to women's 'experience', for white women, it is necessary to leave out the whole section on Nettie's travelling to Africa, which is central for its depiction of the roots of Black Americans, and the continued exploitation of Africa by whites.[46] Similarly, if we read *Wuthering Heights* uncritically as solely about romantic love, we have to erase the economic forces which largely determine the course of the emotional relationships and marriages within the novel.

A further related problem which Cora Kaplan points to, is that if we refer texts to our experience, we have to ignore the whole question of textuality, of novels as textual entities which refer to other writing and are constructed within the conventions of other books.[47] She shows that *The Color Purple* was written in reaction to novels by Black male writers, such as Eldridge Cleaver and James Baldwin, who portrayed the life of Black American men without reference to Black women. Leaving out the textual history of a novel involves us in omitting a major textual determinant. Thus the text is seen as a simple reflection, and language is seen as a simple transparent medium through which meanings pass. More recent poststructuralist criticism questions this 'transparency' of language, and suggests that the textual determinants, like genre, are more important in the production of the text.[48]

Although authentic realism can be readily used in the discussion of books which are written within the realist tradition, it is rather more difficult to apply it to texts like those of Christine Brooke Rose, Monique Wittig or Gertrude Stein (although that does not stop critics from trying). Modernist and postmodernist texts cannot be referred to an 'experience' which we all share, since it is textuality rather than 'reality' which is the focus of attention. Even when discussing novels written within the realist tradition, the textual nature of literature is not addressed.

A related problem is the fact that although literature is important for determining how people conceive of themselves as individuals, it is not the only element, and perhaps not even the most important. Books like *Wuthering Heights* and *The Color Purple* are obviously central for many women but they are only elements in a larger social enterprise which is much more powerful; for example, education, parenting and the media define women's roles much more pervasively than literature. Perhaps the problem here is giving literature a centrality which in real life it does not necessarily have. Women critics who work in literature departments often find it difficult to see literature in perspective, as one element which provides role models for women. Linda also remarked upon the dangers of this type of criticism if it is taken too seriously, since women readers can begin to identify and perhaps emulate disenabling characters; she noted the 'perils of giving adolescent girls D. H. Lawrence to read' for this reason.[49]

The importance of authentic realism for 1990s feminists is that it can be a useful political stage in the changing of women's consciousness and hence women's position in society. Gayatri Spivak has suggested that perhaps this type of reading strategy is a temporary position that might be taken up in certain circumstances.[50] She also notes that in certain circumstances it is necessary to 'take the risk of essence'; that is, to occupy the position of 'experience' strategically.[51] This may seem a paradoxical position, since in most definitions, 'essence' is something at the core of one's being, which cannot be adopted strategically. However, Spivak argues that with multiple positionings of the self, this sense of strategy is important. At times it is important and necessary to stake out a claim for yourself as a particular type of subject.

The problem with this strategic adoption of a subject position is that it is a *risk*; Black writing, both male and female, is very frequently read as autobiographical, as is women's writing in general, and reappropriating positions which have been assigned to you by society runs the risk of reaffirming you in your subjected position.[52] And as Peggy Kamuf has noted

> How is one supposed to understand essence as a risk to be run when it is by definition the non-accidental and therefore hardly the apt term to represent danger or risk? Only over against and in impatient reaction to the deconstruction of the subject can 'essence' be made to sound excitingly dangerous and the phrase 'the risk of essence' can seem to offer such an appealing invitation . . . 'Go for it' the phrase incites. If you fall into [essence] you can always say it was an accident.[53]

A more useful way of utilizing authentic realism might involve an exploration of the textual nature both of characters *and* identities, so that in the process of reading characters as people, one's identity is transformed into a character, which is subject to change and revision/ rewriting.[54] As Jonathan Culler states:

> For a woman to read as a woman is not to repeat an identity or an experience that is given but to play a role she constructs with reference to her identity as a woman, which is also a construct, so that the series can continue: a woman reading as a woman reading as a woman.[55]

Whilst I do not see Culler's reductiveness as particularly useful, there is a sense in which the critical distance which his statement demarcates between the self/identity and the representation of the self can be used by feminists to distance themselves from even those representations and selves which seem closest to who we think we are. Some of the interesting theoretical work currently being undertaken by feminists is precisely focused on critically analyzing who white heterosexual women think they are and the benefits which they accrue from holding these subject positions. As Mary Crawford shows, in discussing experience, white heterosexual women often assume that their identity is the norm and erase the privileges that they have:

> No one hassles me at my child's school, at the doctor's office or at work. No one tells me I'm an unfit mother. Because I'm legally married, my job provides health care for my partner and family . . . Wills and mortgages, taxes and auto insurance, retirement pensions and school enrollment for the children – all the ways that individuals ordinarily interface with social structures – are designed to fit people like me and my partner.[56]

Much feminist work now aims to make experience 'strange', to analyze even those elements of our personalities which seem most clearly 'us', in order to develop ways of being and thinking which are not exclusionary.[57]

We need to question the reasons for identification and for holding onto singular selves which have homogeneous experience; as June Jordan so tellingly asks 'What is your identity *for?*'[58] Perhaps, when reflecting on the exclusionary practices involved in constructing the notion of an authentic women's experience, readers will be led to consider the uses to which identities, however provisional, may be put, and they may be able to construct more productive narratives for themselves and others than are represented within literary texts. Whilst dispensing with the notion of the homogeneous self or using it only provisionally may seem a loss to many feminist readers, its destabilizing may lead to more productive dialogues across our differences as women.

Notes

1. It is certainly a method of reading which we as teachers have tried to discourage our students on Women's Studies courses from using. Its often unreflective nature can pose problems on courses where the importance of critical awareness is stressed. In certain circumstances it may lead readers to assume that they know what their identity is, where perhaps that stability of identity might be more usefully explored. Particularly for white middle-class women, the givenness of identity is built on the exclusion of other categories of identity, and it is this process which needs often to be focused on. See for example Ruth Frankenberg, *White Women, Race Matters: The Social Constructedness of Whiteness* (Routledge, London, 1993); Vron Ware, *Beyond the Pale: White Women, Racism and History* (Verso, London, 1992), and Laura Donaldson, *Decolonizing Feminisms: Race, Gender and Empire-Building* (Routledge, London, 1992). These theorists are critical of the universalizing tendencies of white middle-class women and have documented the ways in which white women's concerns with experience and identity have not been simply positive and anti-patriarchal. However, whilst being very aware of the limitations which this type of reading strategy may involve, we have come to recognize its importance for many women as a catalyst in the development of a political consciousness.

2. Arlyn Diamond and Lee R. Edwards (eds) *The Authority of Experience: Essays in Feminist Criticism* (University of Massachusetts Press, Amherst, 1977). Since it is a tendency rather than a position, there are many feminist positions which draw on the assumptions of authentic realism.

3. 'The personal is political' is a slogan used to describe that change in consciousness which many feminists underwent in the 1960s and 1970s whereby the very nature of the political changed. Instead of politics being located in the public sphere, concerned with party

politics, it was a revelation to many that the very nature of women's daily lives was political: who did the washing up or who looked after children was no longer a seemingly trivial personal issue, which had to be negotiated between individuals, but was a serious political matter which concerned women as a group, class or caste (see Anne Phillips, *Hidden Hands: Women and Economic Policies* (Pluto, London, 1983) and Michèle Barrett and Mary McIntosh, *The Anti-social Family* (Verso, London, 1982).

4. Some of the texts which were read in the 1970s were novels such as Marilyn French, *The Women's Room* (Sphere, London, 1977); Erica Jong, *Fear of Flying* (Granada, Frogmore, 1974); Kate Millett, *Sita* (Virago, London, 1977); Doris Lessing, *The Golden Notebook* (Granada, Frogmore, 1962). More recently, novels by Alice Walker, Jeannette Winterson, Toni Morrison, Margaret Atwood, Angela Carter have been read and discussed by groups of women.

5. For example, Doris Lessing, *The Golden Notebook* (Granada, Frogmore, 1962); Dorothy Richardson, *Pilgrimage* (Virago, London, 1915–35); Sylvia Plath, *The Bell Jar* (Faber, London, 1963); Agnes Smedley, *Daughter of Earth* (Virago, London, 1977)

6. See, for example, work by Nancy K. Miller, 'Changing the subject: authorship, writing and the reader', *Feminist Studies/Critical Studies*, ed. Teresa de Lauretis (Indiana University Press, Indiana, 1986), pp. 102–20; and *Getting Personal: Feminist Occasions and Other Autobiographical Acts* (Routledge, London, 1991); Liz Stanley's edited collection, *Feminist Praxis: Research, Theory and Epistemology in Feminist Sociology* (Routledge, London, 1990) contains a section on autobiography; her later work *The Auto/Biographical I* (Routledge, London, 1994) provides an overview of current textual theorizing of autobiography.

7. A good example of this is Agnes Smedley's *Daughter of Earth* (Virago, London, 1977), which bears striking resemblances to her autobiography, *Battle Hymn of China* (Pandora, London, 1974). This should not necessarily lead us to assume that the novel is therefore a simple transcription of Smedley's life, since, as I have noted, that autobiography is itself textual.

8. As Judith Fetterley has shown in *The Resisting Reader: A Feminist Approach to American Fiction* (Indiana University Press, Bloomington, 1978), many texts address us as males. See also Sara Mills ed., *Gendering the Reader* (Harvester Wheatsheaf, Hemel Hempstead, 1994), for a further analysis of the ways in which texts gender us in the reading process. For a discussion of the way texts may bring about material changes, see Rosalind Coward, 'This novel changes lives', in Mary Eagleton (ed.), *Feminist Literary Theory: A Reader* (Blackwell, Oxford, 1986), pp. 155–60. By realizing, through literature, that an event in their lives, such as violence, incest, or rape was not unique, many women changed their view of their lives and radically restructured their relationships and their sense of their personal histories.

9. As the essays in such collections as Alice Jardine and Paul Smith's *Men in Feminism* (Methuen, London, 1987) show, the relation

between men attempting to do feminist criticism and women has often been an extremely fraught one.

10. By seeing it as a theoretical practice, and tracing the history of its development, we at least partly eliminate the troubling 'naturalness' or 'common sense' which this approach assumes for itself. See Catherine Belsey's *Critical Practice* (Methuen, London, 1980) for an analysis of the problems entailed in the use of common-sense assumptions.

11. Dalston study group, 'Was the patriarchy conference "patriarchal"?', in Papers on Patriarchy, cited by Deborah Cameron, *Feminism and Linguistic Theory* (Macmillan, Basingstoke, 1985), p. 135.

12. By the term anti-theoretical I mean not that the approach is necessarily untheoretical but rather that it is working against the idea of theoretical knowledge (see Glossary).

13. It is often taught or encouraged in schools, and for those who have no further literary training, it may present itself as a common-sense way to read, simply because it is the only one available.

14. However, as I shall discuss later in this chapter, even those elements which seem to be universal to all women, in the final analysis, seem to be very much more the concerns of white Western middle-class women than any other group. For example, fear of sexual attack when in the public sphere is much more a problem for Western women in urban contexts, than it is for, say, Asian rural women. See, for further analysis of this, some of the essays in *Gender, Place and Culture*, vol 1/1 and 1/2, 1993.

15. But this notion of characters being created from the same material as real people is highly problematic and as we shall see later in this chapter, it is important to in fact turn this statement on its head and recognize the way in which people's sense of their identity is textually constructed.

16. In this, it is very similar to the work of John Berger, *Ways of Seeing* (Penguin, Harmondsworth, 1972); and Judith Williamson in her work on reader-positioning, *Decoding Advertisements: Ideology and Meaning in Advertising* (Boyars, London, 1978). See also, for a fuller discussion of the relation between representations and self-image, Rosemary Betterton (ed.) *Looking On: Images of Femininity in the Arts and Media* (Pandora, London, 1987) and Deirdre Pribram (ed.) *Female Spectators: Looking at Film and Television* (Verso, London, 1988).

17. Toril Moi, *Sexual/Textual Politics* (Methuen, London, 1985).

18. See Cheri Register, 'American literary criticism: a bibliographical introduction', in Josephine Donovan (ed.), *Feminist Literary Criticism, Explorations in Theory* (University of Kentucky Press, Lexington, 1975), pp. 1–28.

19. In all of these examples, we have in our teaching, in various educational contexts, found that this type of reading strategy evokes very strong reactions from students. In reading *Tess of the d'Urbervilles*, female students refer to similar emotional crises they have undergone or to the emotions they experience when 'identifying' with Tess.

20. Dale Spender, *Women of Ideas and What Men Have Done to Them* (Ark,

London, 1982). Toril Moi in *Sexual/Textual Politics*, has shown how this is a very dangerous stance, since it can lead to women producing second-rate work and being praised for it in a patronizing way by other women. However, during the 1970s and 1980s it was an important statement of solidarity with other women, and it was also a realization that it was not necessary to produce similar criticism to that of male academics, i.e. with combative and merciless comments on other critics. Discussions with Elaine Hobby have made me recognize how important it is to build critically on other feminist critics' work and to acknowledge earlier, sometimes relatively untheorized work, rather than assuming that our own work necessarily supersedes theirs.

21. 'Images of women' criticism analyzes the negative portrayals of female characters in male texts, and demands changes (see Chapter 1).

22. This may be because 'theoretical' implies 'critical', but it may also be that women readers feel that these texts address them in a different way to male-authored texts. It is difficult to analyze them using theoretical models which pay no attention to gender difference, or the way the reader is positioned as male or female. This may point up a more general difficulty with mainstream theory which does not consider gender in analysis.

23. This inclusion of personal information has been used by other feminist critics such as Toril Moi and Deborah Cameron who in their academic work have provided elements of their personal histories so that the reader is aware of the political position within which their writing is produced. Vron Ware, in *Beyond the Pale* (Verso, London, 1992) has also explored this method of integrating theoretical and personal information, without resorting to the banality of the anecdotal, in her investigation of white women and racism.

24. See, for example, Roland Barthes, 'The pleasure of the text', in Susan Sontag (ed.), *Barthes: Selected Writings* (Fontana, London, 1982) pp. 404–14. Pleasure has since been considered central by many feminist theorists, particularly by film theorists such as Annette Kuhn, *Women's Pictures* (Routledge and Kegan Paul, London, 1982) and Laura Mulvey, 'Visual pleasure and narrative cinema', *Screen*, vol. 16, no. 3, 1975, pp. 6–18.

25. Alice Walker, *The Color Purple* (The Women's Press, London, 1983); Emily Brontë, *Wuthering Heights* (Penguin, Harmondsworth, 1982 f. pub. 1847). All further references are given after quotations in the text.

26. I would like to thank all of the women who replied to the questionnaire, especially the following whose comments I have used in this chapter: Anne, Mandy, Linda, Naima, Kay, Irene, Lizzi, Sandra. The interviewees were chosen to represent a range of variables such as race, class, age and sexual preference.

27. Lillian Faderman, *Surpassing the Love of Men: Romantic Friendship and Love Between Women from the Renaissance to the Present* (Morrow, New York, 1981). Authentic realism is drawn upon by many lesbian critics. See Lynne Pearce's discussion of this in Chapter 7; Bonnie Zimmerman, 'What has never been: an overview of lesbian feminist

criticism', in Gayle Greene and Coppelia Kahn (eds), *Making a Difference* (Methuen, London, 1986); and Elaine Hobby and Chris White (eds), *What Lesbians Do in Books* (The Women's Press, London, 1991).

28. Radclyffe Hall, *The Well of Loneliness* (Virago, London, 1982 f. pub. 1928).

29. Even in contemporary texts, there are still examples of lesbianism being depicted as a painful and unhappy experience. Notable exceptions, however, are Ellen Galford's *Moll Cutpurse* (Stramullion, Edinburgh, 1985) and *The Fires of Bride* (The Women's Press, London,1986); Barbara Burford's *The Threshing Floor* (Sheba, London, 1985); Jeanette Winterson's *Oranges are not the only Fruit* (Pandora, London, 1985); and *Serious Pleasure: Lesbian Erotic Stories* (Sheba, London, 1989) and *More Serious Pleasure* (Sheba, London, 1990) both edited by the Sheba Collective.

30. It is interesting that lesbian sexuality was one of the elements which was significantly played down in the Steven Spielberg film of *The Color Purple* and reduced to coy embraces. See Darryl Pinkney, 'Black victims: Black villains', *New York Review*, 29 January 1987, pp. 17–20, for a discussion of the relation between the film and the book.

31. Alice Walker developed the term 'womanist' to refer to a Black feminist writing practice and criticism which worked against the racism implicit in the term feminist (see Glossary).

32. This 'man-hating' nature of the book is often remarked upon by critics; see Pinkney, note 30.

33. I use both the term 'woman of colour' and 'Black'. Some women prefer to use the former since it refers to women from a wide range of ethnic origins; however, since Alice Walker identifies herself as 'Black', this term has also been used.

34. 'Writing *The Color Purple*', in Mari Evans (ed.), *Black Women Writers* (Pluto, London, 1985), pp. 453–7.

35. Michel Foucault, 'What is an author?', in J. V. Harari (ed.), *Textual Strategies: Perspectives in Post-structuralist Criticism* (Methuen, London, 1980); Roland Barthes, 'The death of the author', in *The Rustle of Language* (Blackwell, Oxford, 1986), pp. 49–55.

36. Patricia Waugh, *Practising Postmodernism/Reading Modernism: Gender and Autonomy Theory* (Edward Arnold, London, 1992).

37. Barbara Christian, 1988, cited by Elspeth Probyn: *Sexing the Self: Gendered Positions in Cultural Studies* (Routledge, London, 1993), p. 34.

38. This can clearly be seen from the controversy in the 1980s when it was discovered that a book to be published by Virago, which was supposedly written by an Indian woman, was in fact written by a white male. The book was withdrawn from sale.

39. In writings by men, love is often seen to be the preserve of women. Many feminist critics see this as one of the important aspects of pleasure in the romance. See, for example, Rosalind Coward, *Female Desire: Women's Sexuality Today* (Paladin, London, 1984). See also the collection of essays edited by Lynne Pearce and Jackie Stacey, *Romance Revisited* (Lawrence and Wishart, London, 1995).

40. Toril Moi, *Sexual/Textual Politics* (Methuen, London, 1985).

41. See Janet Radcliffe-Richards, *The Sceptical Feminist: A Philosophical*

Enquiry (Routledge and Kegan Paul, London, 1980), for a discussion of this problem.

42. Diana Fuss, *Essentially Speaking: Feminism Nature and Difference* (Routledge, London and New York, 1989); Judith Butler, *Gender Trouble: Feminism and the Subversion of Identity* (Routledge, London and New York, 1990).

43. See Lennard J. Davis, *Resisting Novels: Ideology and Fiction* (Methuen, London, 1987) for a fuller exploration of the manipulative effect of novels, and particularly the problems of an uncritical identification.

44. Frigga Haug (ed.), *Female Sexualization*, translated by Erica Carter (Verso, London, 1987).

45. Cora Kaplan, 'Keeping the color in *The Color Purple*', in *Sea Changes* (Verso, London, 1986), pp. 177–87.

46. Most of the interviewees in fact did this.

47. In Chapter 4, Elaine Millard writes about *The Color Purple* specifically as a text in relation to other texts.

48. See, for example, the work of Michel Foucault in *The Order of Things: An Archaeology of the Human Sciences* (Vintage/Random, New York, 1973).

49. For critical analyses of disenabling female characters and strategies for revising/rewriting them, see Deirdre Burton, 'Through glass darkly: through dark glasses', in Ron Carter (ed.), *Language and Literature: An Introductory Reader in Stylistics* (Allen and Unwin, London, 1982), pp. 195–217, and Sara Mills, *Feminist Stylistics* (Routledge, London, 1995).

50. Gayatri Spivak, 'Imperialism and sexual difference', in *Sexual Difference Conference Proceedings* (Oxford Literary Review, Southampton, 1986), pp. 225–40.

51. Gayatri Spivak, *In Other Worlds: Essays in Cultural Politics* (Methuen, London, 1987).

52. I am indebted to Zoe Wicombe for making this point to me. Peggy Kamuf also makes this clear in her article, 'Writing like a woman', in Sally McConnell-Ginet (ed.), *Women and Language in Literature and Society* (Praeger, New York, 1982), pp. 284–97.

53. Peggy Kamuf, 'Femmeninism', p. 96 in Jardine and Smith (see note 9 above).

54. Dorothy Smith's work on the way identity structures such as femininity are negotiated in a relational way demonstrates how the textual nature of identity may be used productively. See Dorothy Smith, *Texts, Facts and Femininity: Exploring the Relations of Ruling* (Routledge, London, 1990).

55. Jonathan Culler, 'Reading as a woman', in *On Deconstruction* (Routledge and Kegan Paul, London, 1983), pp. 43–64, p. 51.

56. Mary Crawford, 'Identity, "passing" and subversion', in Celia Kitzinger and Sue Wilkinson (eds), *Heterosexuality* (Sage, London, 1993), p. 44.

57. Elspeth Probyn's work is important in this respect. In the late 1990s moves are afoot to reclaim experience through a poststructuralist frame which regards its strategic importance in negotiating text/reader roles *without* assigning it the status of essence, origin or

authenticity. See Elspeth Probyn, *Sexing the Self* (Routledge, London, 1993).

58.   June Jordan, cited in Pratibha Parmar, 'Black feminism: the politics of articulation' in Jonathan Rutherford (ed.), *Identity: Community, Culture, Difference* (Lawrence and Wishart, London, 1990), p. 111.

3
Gynocriticism

Sue Spaull and Lynne Pearce

Elaine Showalter: 'Feminist criticism in the wilderness'
Jean Rhys: *Wide Sargasso Sea*
Margaret Atwood: *Surfacing*

I

In 1986, Dale Spender offered the following evaluation of her university education: 'A grossly inaccurate and distorted view of the history of letters.'[1] No doubt many women would now accept her statement as a just description of their own literary education, for her book *Mothers of the Novel* is a recent addition to a fairly well-established mode of feminist criticism. Spender identifies one hundred women novelists before Jane Austen and yet, she says, her first encounter to the literary 'greats' was an encounter with great men. 'I left university with the well-cultivated impression that men had created the novel and that there were no women novelists (or none of note) before Jane Austen' (p. 115). With so many women writing during the 1700s, and achieving recognition amongst contemporary audiences, Spender questions the disappearance of all but a few of these women since the eighteenth century. She concludes that 'in order to be great, one must be a man' (p. 119). In an attempt to redress the balance, Spender devotes her book to the examination of those, now 'obscure' eighteenth-century women novelists. She claims that it was women who 'mothered' the novel and, moreover, that their novels act as a 'record of women's consciousness, a documentation of women's experiences as subordinates in a male-dominated society'. She asks: 'what have the men done with all the women, and why?' (p. 3).

Spender is clearly not the first to address herself entirely to a female literary tradition, nor is she the first to question the validity of the canon of 'great' literature. Our aim in this chapter is, first, to trace the move to establish such a female literary tradition. In doing so, we will focus on those critics working in the 1970s who, noting the absence of a female perspective within the literary canon, sought to focus on women's writing and women's lives. Specifically, we will be examining critics whose aim was not only to read women's literature for its portrayal of women's experience (as in 'authentic realist' criticism – see Chapter 2) but who sought to identify an authentic female voice in women's writing: a style and genre which were distinctly female. We will draw on the work of Ellen Moers, Patricia Meyer Spacks and Nina Baym[2] but concentrate on the work of Elaine Showalter, who coined the phrase 'gynocritics' to describe what is commonly known as 'woman-centred' criticism.[3] We hope that my explication of the work of these women will then serve as a useful background for our own readings of *Wide Sargasso Sea* and *Surfacing*, which we will carry out using Showalter's gynocritical model.

Elaine Showalter describes gynocritics as 'the psychodynamics of the individual or collective female literary tradition' (p. 201). She assesses the task confronting feminist critics as identifying 'the unique difference of women's writing' (p. 186). And, indeed, this is how many feminist critics have structured their readings of women's writing. Their aim is to seek out a feminine aesthetic, or 'essence', which differentiates women's writing from men's. That feminine aesthetic is often identified with language: a language specific to women's writing, whose 'difference' is guaranteed by the 'femaleness' of the author. The critics further focus on other aspects of literature: its genre, style, themes, character portrayal or subject matter and so on. At each stage, they return to their original premise: that the language and textual strategies of women's writing are a result of the author's gender-specific experience of everyday life. Thus, their analyses of the qualitative 'difference' of women's writing are carried out with regard to the female author's biological, psychological and historical differences from men. But most importantly, that 'difference' is shown as a result of women's social and economic position within patriarchal society: a society so repressive that at times (as Dale Spender argues) it has barely allowed women a voice at all.[4]

Examining women's writing in the United States between 1820 and 1870, Nina Baym describes the fiction of the period as 'profoundly oriented toward women' (p. 11). She argues that women were writing specifically for female audiences following a story-line rarely used by men. Concentrating on plot as the common factor amongst the novels – 'The many novels all tell, with variations, a single tale' – Baym compares the various female protagonists' journeys towards self-fulfilment with Jungian rites of passage (p. 11).[5] She argues that 'the failure of the world to satisfy either reasonable or unreasonable expectations awakens the heroine to inner possibilities' (p. 19). Read in their context – as a response to nineteenth-century society – the novels express women's capacity for personal change and endeavour. They represent 'a moderate, or limited, or pragmatic feminism' (p. 18). Baym sees the form and content of these novels as a direct expression of their authors' positions within nineteenth-century American society. She reads them as a reflection of women's oppression under patriarchy, but also as a subtle and limited resistance to that patriarchy.

Similarly, most of the critics writing within gynocriticism offer an analysis of women's writing both as a response and as a challenge to patriarchy. Ellen Moers argues categorically that '[There] is no such thing as *the* female genius or *the* female sensibility'.[6] And further: 'there is no single female style in literature'. Yet in her readings of women writers from the eighteenth century onwards, she too identifies common factors in their work, examining those factors in relation to women writers' experience, their social setting and audiences, and importantly, their mutual influence upon one another. And she too sees much women's literature as a challenge to the male tradition and to the silencing of women effected by patriarchy:

> Each of these gifted writers had her distinctive style; none imitated the others. But their sense of encountering in another woman's voice what they believed was the sound of their own is, I think, something special in literary women – perhaps their sense of the surrounding silence, or the deaf ears, with which women spoke before there was such an echo as women's literature. (p. 66)

Moers sets out to establish 'the echo of women's literature', the female literary tradition which men have destroyed; to retrace the connections between women writers which were often so difficult for them to forge during their own lifetimes. She identifies common themes in the wealth of literature she examines, and frequently the common handling of those themes. Whilst throughout her book she relates her findings back to women's experience itself, she moves beyond 'authentic realist' criticism to assess why women's perspectives differ from that of their male contemporaries; to pinpoint those aspects of women's experience which generate the style and content of their writing; and to examine the means by which women offer some resistance to patriarchy through their writing.

Just as Nina Baym noticed the different portrayal of female characters by men and women writers respectively – '[men's] good women were far more passive than the female protagonists created by women themselves' (p. 13) – so Moers focuses on their different handling of similar subject matter. Moers is particularly interested in the strategies women have used to resist patriarchy. For example, she assesses women's handling of the subject of adultery (traditionally fertile ground for men's writing), describing it as 'part of a feminist outburst against the institution of marriage as created not in heaven but on earth by unjust, man-made laws' (p. 154). And she continues: 'The adultery novel after Rousseau became the woman writer's vehicle of attack on the economic and social-class realities that make a mockery of love; as well as a vehicle of demonstration that woman has a capacity to think, feel and act for herself.' Throughout *Literary Women*, Moers finds similar evidence of women's expression of their frustration at the constraints society has placed on them. Examining women's language, she focuses on their use of metaphors as one technique by which they encapsulate both their powerlessness and their resistance to patriarchy. Moers notices the frequency with which women use metaphors involving birds of various kinds, and in various situations. Examining their use in *Jane Eyre*, she asks: 'Is the bird merely a species of the littleness metaphor? Or are birds chosen because they are tortured, as little girls are tortured . . . Or because bird-victims can be ministered by girl-victims' (p. 245). Continuing her analysis, Moers suggests that '[The] more feminist the literary conception . . . the larger, wilder and crueller come the birds' (p. 246). She illustrates the point with an extract from Willa Cather's novel *The Song Of The Lark* (1915), where after the female protagonist has been made an unwanted offer of a 'cosy' marriage by her lover, a golden eagle appears overhead. Cather writes: 'O eagle of eagles! Endeavour achievement, desire, glorious striving of human art! From a cleft in the heart of the world she saluted it . . .'[7] Moers also observes the absence from women's writing of a bird metaphor frequently used by men – that of the nesting bird traditionally associated with motherhood. She notes that it 'seems striking by its absence from women's literature, or by the bitterness with which it is used to imply rejection of the maternal role' (p. 247).

Moers' analysis of the 'monstrous' also informs her discussion of the 'Female Gothic' – a phrase which she coined and which has been used to classify an important tradition in women's writing ever since. Her discussion begins with an assessment of Mary Shelley's *Frankenstein* in the light of Shelley's own experience of life. She compares the birth of the monster with Shelley's traumatic experience of the birth and death of her own child, thereby aligning women's writing with their biological and psychological experience. Taking this further, she examines the 'Female Gothic' tradition in relation to 'the savagery of girlhood . . . also the self-disgust, the self-hatred and the impetus to self-destruction that have been increasingly prominent themes in the writing of women in the twentieth century' (p. 107). Quoting Mary

Wollstonecraft, Moers equates the 'terrors, restraints and dangers' of the Gothic novel with 'the realities of a woman's life' (p. 134).

Like Moers' *Literary Women*, Patricia Meyer Spacks' book *The Female Imagination* (1975) is an examination of the similarities of experience and response of women writers across the centuries. Spacks endeavours to assess the feminine essence of women's writing: an aesthetic unchanging through time. She asks: 'What are the ways of female feeling, the modes of responding, that persist despite social change? Do any characteristic patterns of self-perception shape the creative expressions of women?'[8] Drawing on the reactions of her students to women's writing, she focuses on the similarities between the experiences of the woman reader and the woman writer even when divided by one hundred years or so. Spacks describes the 'difference' of women's writing as a 'delicate divergence' (p. 315). Like Moers, she examines women's handling of subject matter traditionally used by men. She identifies a female literary tradition working within a male tradition. 'The books do not destroy or even seriously challenge the old, man-created myths about women, but they shift the point of view' (p. 315). But although Spacks assumes that there is something in women's writing and female creativity which transcends historical boundaries – a female voice unaffected by differing social contexts – her study also identifies subtle changes in women's modes of expression from the eighteenth and nineteenth centuries to the twentieth century. Whilst in eighteenth- and nineteenth-century novels by women, Spacks argues that female protagonists sometimes offered 'at least subterranean challenges to the vision they appear to accept', she sees an increasing propensity amongst twentieth-century women writers to express feelings of powerlessness, of frustration and anger (p. 315). She says: '[they] dramatize the heroism of suffering, irony and self-pity' (p. 152). Even depictions of rebellion frequently end in madness or nervous breakdown. Spacks offers the 'female imagination' as the only possible outlet for women's true aspirations, the means by which they can 'affirm in far-reaching ways the significance of their inner freedom' (p. 316). An important 'difference' of women's writing is that for many women imagination remains a significant dimension of reality. As far as their writing is concerned, Spacks sees this as a positive result of women's social alienation, encouraging unique forms of expression. Spacks' description of the 'female imagination' bears a close resemblance to Elaine Showalter's notion of the 'wild zone' which is central to her attempt to establish the 'difference' of women's writing. Having examined the background to this project, we will devote the following section of this chapter to an analysis of Showalter's work itself.

Most of Elaine Showalter's own attempt to assess the 'unique difference of women's writing' is contained in two essays: 'Towards a feminist poetics' (1979) and 'Feminist criticism in the wilderness' (1981).[9] Since the second of these two essays contains – and expands on much of the material of the first, we will concentrate our discussion on the latter, which also incorporates Showalter's in-depth explanation of her 'gynocritics' theory.

Showalter begins her discussion by analyzing the position feminist literary criticism had reached before the 1970s. She argues that its main feature was its unwillingness to engage with any theoretical debate. This could be accounted for partly by the variety of theory with which it could potentially engage; but it was also due to many feminists' suspicion of the predominantly male critical schools, which were seen as 'arid and falsely objective' (p. 181). In contrast, feminist criticism was rooted in the subjective: 'the authority of experience' (p. 181). It should, however, be noted that in her earlier essay, 'Towards a feminist poetics', Showalter is herself vehemently opposed to alliances between male scholars and 'male' theory: a view which has since been tempered, but one still likely to erupt amongst feminist scholars who feel the appropriation of Freud, Lacan, Foucault *et al.* has been at the expense of alternative, female-authored theorizing (see Introduction).

In an attempt to offer some form of classification of the many diverse forms of feminist criticism that had nevertheless begun to emerge in the 1970s, Showalter divides them into two modes. The first she labels 'the feminist critique'. This involves the feminist as a reader, usually in re-reading male texts: offering different interpretations of the images of women found there, or questioning misconceptions about women in other forms of criticism (see Chapter 1). Showalter argues that the role of such criticism is limited. At best it can only compete with different readings of the same text and, further, it relies on the male critical theory it attempts to revise. It must always work within an androcentric model: one which begins from the premise of patriarchal cultural dominance. Feminist criticism is thus halted in its attempt to establish its own theoretical base. Showalter identifies the need for a form of criticism that is woman-centred, independent of men, and seeking 'to find answers to the questions that come from *our* [women's] experience' (p. 184). She argues that feminist criticism must find 'its own subject, its own system, its own theory and its own voice' (p. 184). This brings her to her second mode of criticism: the woman as a writer, or 'gynocritics'. By concentrating specifically on women's writing, Showalter argues that feminist critics immediately 'leap to a new conceptual vantage point' (p. 185). Their concern henceforth is to examine the *difference* of women's writing: to *begin* with the question 'Do women write differently [from men], and if so, how?' Drawing together a variety of gynocritical theories, Showalter classifies them into four specific groups or 'models of difference' – biological, linguistic, psychoanalytical and cultural – each of which she sees as a development from the one before. She evaluates them in turn, but concentrates on the fourth, the model of cultural difference, which incorporates elements of the other three and which, she argues, constitutes the most sophisticated analysis of women's difference. Below is a brief summary of each of the models.

Biological criticism This analyzes the difference between women's and men's writing as a result of the difference of their bodies. Showalter points to the allegiance between this form of criticism and Victorian theories about women's physiology, which justified women's inferior social status by describing the adverse effects of their physiology on the functioning of their brains. Although biological feminist criticism rejects these theories of inferiority, Showalter notes that some critics have accepted their 'metaphorical implications'. For example, Gilbert and Gubar in *The Madwoman in the Attic* claim that since creativity has been defined as a 'male' activity – 'the writer fathers his text' – there are enormous problems for female creativity.[10] Showalter argues that as well as metaphors of literary paternity, metaphors of literary maternity predominated in the eighteenth and nineteenth centuries (although often to describe the work of male authors). She describes attempts by feminist critics to reclaim these metaphors, to show how women's use of the body as a source of imagery is an assertion of the strength of her difference, not its weakness. Showalter therefore acknowledges the importance of the study of biological imagery in women's writing. But she concludes that biological criticism can only be effective in conjunction with the study of linguistic, social and literary theories, since 'there can be no expression of the body which is unmediated by [these] structures' (p. 189).

Linguistic criticism Showalter identifies the debate over language as 'one of the most exciting areas in gynocritics'. Language is seen as a system that structures and shapes our perception and understanding of reality. Furthermore, it is seen as a male-constructed classification system into which women must force their experience. Many French feminists (Showalter names Monique Wittig, Annie Leclerc and Chantal Chawaf) argue that this linguistic debate is central to the discussion of women's difference. They argue for the creation of a female language as an appropriate expression of female experience.[11] Within masculine discourse, woman is 'forced to speak in something like a foreign tongue, a language with which she may be personally uncomfortable'.[12] It is with the French feminists that Showalter locates the overlap between her 'biological' and 'linguistic' models of gynocritics. The creation of a feminine language, they claim, will involve creating a language system whose first allegiance will be to the natural rhythms of the female body. Showalter, however, disapproves of a theory that divorces feminist criticism from the intellectual and academic world, dispensing with academic or official discourse and thereby alienating itself. She claims that women will be forced to remain silent unless they can communicate with their male counterparts. In a similar way, Mary Jacobus argues for a women's writing that works within male discourse but works 'ceaselessly to deconstruct it: to write what cannot be written'.[13] But Showalter stresses the need to improve women's access to language, to remove the hidden censorship which denies women the 'full resources of language'. Until that is done, she claims, 'it ought not to be in language that we base our theory of difference' (p. 193).[14]

Psychological criticism   According to Showalter, much psychoanalytically oriented feminist criticism takes its lead from Freudian notions of the Oedipal phase and Lacan's application of that theory to the acquisition of language and entrance of the child to the 'Symbolic Order'.[15] Freudian theories concentrate on women's 'castration complex': their difference is centred on their lack of a penis and the psychological effects caused by that lack. Referring back to her analysis of biological criticism, Showalter demonstrates how a feminist criticism based on such a Freudian analysis is continually confronted by problems of women's disadvantage and consequent inferiority. Certainly Gilbert and Gubar argue that women's difference is characterized by their struggle to overcome the disadvantages inherent in their gendered psychology. Although, as will be discussed in Chapter 5 ('French feminisms'), Lacan's theory sees women's psychic 'disadvantage' as being linguistically rather than biologically determined (what they 'want' is not a penis *per se* but what it represents in terms of symbolic power), it is still a model predicated upon female 'lack'.

Showalter nevertheless identifies some feminists who have made positive use of psychoanalytic theory. She cites Nancy Chodorow's work *The Reproduction of Mothering: Psychoanalysis and the Sociology of Gender*.[16] Chodorow offers an alternative interpretation of Freud's theory. Concentrating on the pre-Oedipal phase, she suggests that it is in fact the female child who positively identifies with the mother, and the male child whose experience is negative – an experience of being 'not female'. After the Oedipal phase, women experience difficulties with feminine identity *vis-à-vis* the masculine Symbolic Order, but their unity with other women remains. Showalter finds instances of a similar analysis in other feminist critics (critics who include Ellen Moers, Nina Baym and Patricia Meyer Spacks). These women focus on relationships between female characters in women's novels, and on the relationships amongst women writers themselves.[17] She concludes that psychoanalytic feminist theory can offer some explanation of 'similarities between women writing in a variety of cultural circumstances' (p. 197), but that other factors are left unexamined. For a gynocritical theory that covers all aspects of women's writing, Showalter turns to an examination of theories of 'cultural' difference.

Cultural Criticism   By using a model of women's cultural difference, Showalter argues that feminist critics can also incorporate ideas about their language, bodies and psyche, but they will 'interpret them in relation to the social context in which they occur' (p. 197). She argues that a cultural theory identifies women's 'collective experience within the cultural whole', whilst simultaneously acknowledging important differences amongst women writers.

Showalter quotes Gerda Lerner in suggesting 'the possibility of the existence of a female culture *within* the general culture shared by men and women' (p. 198). She then goes on to examine a model for this female culture, devised by two anthropologists, Shirley and Edwin Ardener. The Ardeners analyze society in terms of 'muted' and 'dominant' groups. They argue that: 'Whilst every group in society generates its own ideas about reality at a deep level, not all of these can find expression at a surface level because the . . . communicative channel is under the control of the dominant group.'[18] Women are in this relatively inarticulate position; they constitute a 'muted group' whose reality does not get represented. The Ardeners stress that women are not 'silenced', however: 'The muted structures are "there" but cannot be "realized" in the language of the dominant structure. Where society is defined by men, some features of women do not fit that definition.'[19] The important issue is whether they [women] are able to say all they would wish to say, where and when they wish to say it' (p. 20).

The Ardeners suggest that muted groups almost have to 'translate' their thoughts into the dominant mode of communication; they require an 'extra step' after the thought is conceived before it can be realized in speech. They stress that this probably works at an unconscious level, and extremely rapidly. The Ardener's theory extends beyond a concern with language to more fundamental notions of culture and its relation to nature. The symbolic stress between the two was first observed by Lévi-Strauss:

> The contrast of nature and culture would be neither a primeval fact, nor a concrete aspect of universal order. Rather it should be seen as an artificial creation of culture, a protective rampart thrown up around it because it only felt able to assert its existence and uniqueness by destroying all the links that led back to its original association with the other manifestations of life.[20]

Likewise, the Ardeners argue that men have been in the position of having to define themselves in relation to women and to nature in order to accommodate 'the two logical sets which classify human beings by different bodily structures: male/female and the two sets: human/non-human' (Edwin Ardener, p. 5). Since the model for 'mankind' (i.e. 'humankind') is based on that for *man*, their opposites women and non-mankind – tend to be ambiguously placed. The Ardeners refer to the non-human as 'wild'. Consequently, those elements of female experience which fall outside the dominant structure, as defined by men, are also seen as features of the 'wild'.

Showalter goes on to discuss the conceptual potential of a 'wild-zone' for feminist critics. She writes:

> We can think of the 'wild-zone' of women's culture spatially, experientially, or metaphysically. Spatially it stands for an area which is literally no-man's-land, a place forbidden to men, which corresponds to the zone in X [reference to a diagram by the Ardeners] which is off limits to women. Experientially it stands for the aspects of the female life-style which are outside of and unlike those of men; again, there is a corresponding zone of male experience alien to women. But if we think of the wild zone metaphysically, or in terms of consciousness, it has no corresponding male space since all of male consciousness is within the circle of the dominant structure and thus accessible to or structured by language. (p. 262)[21]

In her essay, Showalter names a number of feminist critics (including Mary Daly, Hélène Cixous and Monique Wittig: see Chapter 5) for whom the 'wild zone', or something like it, has become a romantic and liberating mythology. Such visions of 'escape' are, however, seen by Showalter as problematically utopian. Because (going back to the Ardener model) women are inside two traditions simultaneously, feminist critics must address themselves to both the dominant and muted structures within texts. Women's writing should thus be seen, at all times, as a *'double-voiced discourse* [our italics], containing a dominant and muted story' (p. 204). What this means, in practice, is that readers and critics should never expect to discover a textual 'wild-zone' that does not, to some extent, intersect with the culture of the dominant group and through whose language it finds expression.

It is with this model in mind that we now proceed to our readings of Jean Rhys's *Wide Sargasso Sea* and Margaret Atwood's *Surfacing*.

II

By engaging with Showalter's cultural model of gynocritics for our reading of Jean Rhys's *Wide Sargasso Sea*, we will be examining the novel for Rhys's two different perceptions of reality corresponding to 'dominant' and 'muted' groups.[22] Within the text, it can be argued that Rhys creates these two axes in a variety of different forms. The most obvious is the male/female dichotomy. But there is also a racial divide, primarily between the British and Jamaican communities (obfuscated by Antoinette's 'creole' identity, i.e. one of mixed (white) European and (Black) Afro-Caribbean descent). There are frequent references to the differences between the naturally wild landscape of the Jamaican countryside, and memories of the cultivation and urbanization of England, representing the conflict between nature and culture. And, perhaps most importantly, there is the contrast Rhys draws between madness and sanity. Collating the 'negatives' from all the above oppositions, Rhys concentrates on a portrayal of 'Otherness', of cultural negativity as defined by Western civilization's system of signification: the 'muted' group. But she also challenges the classification system itself by depicting this cultural negativity as a source of power and strength for the 'native' population. *Wide Sargasso Sea* can be seen as Rhys's attempt to find a matriarchal and 'natural' discourse. Metaphorically, we can see the 'wild-zone' of the Jamaican landscape and culture as a platform for that discourse: a space within which the muted groups can speak. Yet the dominant culture is ever-present, embodied in the British imperialism personified by Rochester. Hence the importance of the concept of madness in the novel, which must immediately become a relative term in its position at the centre of the debate about alternative perceptions of reality.

Wide Sargasso Sea is based on Charlotte Brontë's novel *Jane Eyre*.[23] Using Brontë's depiction of Rochester's first wife, Rhys vividly portrays a young woman's struggle against male dominance (as well as her personal confrontation with British imperialism). Returning her to the lush Jamaican landscape of her childhood, Rhys traces the story of Antoinette Cosway (later renamed Bertha by her husband), through her marriage to Rochester, to 'madness' in the attic at Thornfield Hall. The novel is concerned to depict the gulf, due both to cultural and gender differences, between the experiences and lifestyle of its young Creole heiress – her perception of 'reality' – and that of Rochester: the male, British colonial. In their commentary on *Jane Eyre*, Gilbert and Gubar in *The Madwoman in the Attic* describe Bertha as Jane's 'hunger, rebellion and rage'. This too corresponds to Rhys's portrayal of Antoinette's madness: a madness that epitomizes her difference from Rochester, and her refusal to accept his perception and values as the norm. By displacing Brontë's Rochester into an alien culture, Rhys attempts an inversion of the dominant ideology in order that she may allow the muted group to speak.

Wide Sargasso Sea falls into three parts, the first of which is told by

Antoinette. In the second, Rochester describes his arrival in the West Indies, his marriage and its disastrous consequences. And the final part is again narrated by Antoinette, this time from her imprisonment in her husband's English attic. The novel is initially concerned with Antoinette's insecurity (and that of her whole family), due to their racial origin. Neither Antoinette nor her mother have either 'money or blackness to secure themselves an identity'.[24] It is largely through her use of sensuous imagery that Rhys vividly depicts the ambivalent relationship of the young Creole heiress with the landscape, in much the same way that Charlotte Brontë had done in *Jane Eyre* and Emily Brontë in *Wuthering Heights*. Due to her ambiguous identity, Antoinette suffers first at the hands of her own society – a 'white nigger', resented by the recently freed slaves – and, later, as Rochester's wife, subject to his Western, male desire for imperialist domination. Thus, Antoinette feels alternately secure and afraid, free and imprisoned; feelings powerfully evoked in her dreams, but also in the pervasive atmosphere of the whole novel.

In the first section of the novel, Rhys evokes, both dramatically and sensually, the cultural barriers between the English and Jamaican communities. The relationship between Antoinette's mother and her second (English) husband, Mason (as well as Antoinette's own relationship with her stepfather), reinforces this cultural divide, and prefigures the marriage between Antoinette and Rochester around which the novel is centred. Many of the themes introduced in the first section, together with the imagery and symbolism supporting them, form the background to the ensuing struggle of wills between the novel's Creole heiress and her domineering English husband. The struggle is as much about the conflict between two opposing 'realities', however, as about that between two incompatible personalities. And each reality is multi-faceted, increasing the complexity of the struggle. There is the obvious opposition between the recently freed slaves and the British community – who were once their masters (a position for which Rochester must accept responsibility, despite his more recent arrival in the country). But Rhys delves more deeply. Rochester clearly embodies the imperialism which brought his forefathers to the West Indies, and it is the attitudes that characterize this nationalist trait which seem to have become naturalized in him to form part of his 'maleness'.

From the first abrupt sentences of the novel, we are made aware of Antoinette's alienation, belonging neither to the white community of ex-slave owners, nor to the country's Black community: 'They say when trouble comes close ranks, and so the white people did. But we were not in their ranks' (p. 15). It is this lack of identity which constitutes the basis of Antoinette's insecurity. She longs to become part of the Jamaican culture epitomized by Christophine (the Cosway's Black Jamaican housekeeper, a powerful woman who possesses the magical powers of 'obeah'). But her desire is thwarted by her heritage, and by her mother's aspirations to become part of the middle-class white community. The disappearance of the old order – the collapse of the Coulibri Estate, once owned by Antoinette's father, with the release of the slaves – results in a threatening chaos verging on anarchy 'why should anybody work?' (p. 17): an anarchy threatening the security and stability of the whole white community. Rhys uses the family's garden as a powerful metaphor for the collapse of that old order:

> Our garden was large and beautiful as that garden in the Bible – the tree of life grew there. But it had gone wild. The paths were overgrown and a smell of dead flowers mixed with the fresh living smell. Underneath the tree ferns, the light was green. Orchids flourished out of reach or for some reason not to be touched. One was snaky looking, another like an octopus . . . (p. 16)

Instead of the beautiful, cultivated land of a wealthy estate, the garden has returned to its natural wildness. The metaphor is central to the novel as a whole, contrasting the 'unnatural' orderliness of the British community with the more natural, more relaxed community of Jamaica. It is important that the 'wildness' of the gardens should appear to have triumphed. But whilst the garden has retained its beauty, Rhys's imagery is mixed – the orchids are like snakes and octopuses, there is the smell of dead flowers mixed with that of the living. Rhys thus conveys the threat lurking in this beauty, a threat which is to remain an inherent part of Antoinette's experience of both her childhood and adult worlds.

Throughout Charlotte Brontë's *Jane Eyre*, we see Jane continually gathering strength from her friendships with other women: with the servant Bessie at Gateshead, with Helen Burns and Miss Temple at Lowood, and with Diana and Mary at the parsonage where she eventually seeks refuge, having fled Rochester and Thornfield Hall. So, too, Antoinette's greatest support is from the Black woman Christophine, but also from her faltering friendship with Tia.

Tia is Antoinette's closest (indeed, only) 'play-mate' during this period of her childhood, yet whilst the bonds linking them are obviously strong, there are marked differences between them. Tia is closely associated with the magical qualities of the 'native' Jamaican with the 'secret' which is to become central to Rochester's experience of an alien world. And it is this mysterious, sometimes inhuman, quality which simultaneously attracts Antoinette to Tia, and yet prevents the fruition of their friendship. 'Then Tia would light a fire (fires always lit for her, sharp stones did not hurt her bare feet, I never heard her cry)' (p. 20). Despite their mutual need for camaraderie and their apparent compatibility, the cultural and social barriers between them are so strong as to make any egalitarian, envy-free relationship impossible. Antoinette's fall in social status owing to the collapse of the Coulibri Estate, rather than breaking down the social divisions between them, allows Tia to give vent to her bitter resentment of the other girl's former position: to express her own recently gained superiority: 'Real white people, they got gold money. They didn't look at us nobody see them come near us. Old time white people nothing but white nigger now, and black nigger better than white nigger' (p. 21).

Antoinette's mother's second marriage to an Englishman marks their reinstatement in the white community. Or so it appears. The marriage foreshadows that between Rochester and Antoinette. Both matches are initially materialistic, and in both an attitude of British imperialism evolves – the need to conquer and control. Mason's inability to understand the Black people, or indeed the Creole community into which he has married, is also later reflected in Rochester's uneasiness amongst his wife's friends and servants, his ceaseless but fruitless attempt to unveil the 'secret' of the place and its natural inhabitants.

Antoinette is aware that Mason's arrival will have given rise to a renewed threat from the Jamaican people. Yet her feelings towards both races remain ambivalent. Whilst she recognizes Mr Mason's insensitivity and short-sightedness: 'my mother knows but she can't make him believe it. I wish I could tell him that out here is not at all like English people think it is. I wish . . .' (p. 29), she is drawn to the sense of comfort, security and solidity offered by his resolute 'Englishness'. The picture of the Miller's Daughter remains for her a symbol of all that is 'England' contrasted with the mystical, often threatening, strangeness of her Jamaican culture. She is comforted by the sense of being dominated and controlled, content not to have to question, not to have to work out her own identity, and not to have to think about her 'destiny' – a question answered more easily by the Christian, God-fearing English people than by the more 'realistic' (and fatalistic) Jamaicans:

> There are more ways than one of being happy, better perhaps to be peaceful and contented and protected, as I feel now, peaceful for years and long years, and afterwards I may be saved, whatever Myra says. (When I asked Christophine what happened when you died, she said, 'You want to know too much'.). (p. 31)

The climax of the first section of the novel is the burning of the Coulibri house, leading to Antoinette's brother's death and her mother's madness. In a fast-moving display of sensual impressions, the fire focuses many of the tensions and anxieties, insecurities and misunderstandings experienced by Antoinette and the whole Cosway family in relation to the native Black community. The incidents associated with the fire are to prove Antoinette's apparent peacefulness ill-judged. Against a mirage of sense-impressions – the noise of the crowd outside ('like animals howling'), smoke, the smell of Antoinette's burning hair, flames as the bamboo catches – Mason's words of comfort are hollow rhetoric: 'They will repent in the morning. I foresee gifts of tamarinds in syrup and ginger sweets tomorrow' (pp. 32–3). The horror and confusion is vividly evoked in the flurry of activity and emotions: Annette in hysterics, Pierre lifeless in her arms, Christophine, Mannie and Sass rushing to and fro with waterpitchers, the anonymous, menacing crowd staring up at them from the outside. And again, Mason's rhetorical prayer to God falls cold and insignificant, with the added irony that it appears initially to be responsible for subduing the crowd. But Jamaican 'superstition' is shown to be stronger than any Christian belief. The plunge of Coco, the parrot, to its death, wings clipped and aflame, finally disperses the hating Black people, poignantly prefiguring Antoinette's own fall to death – hair burning, figurative wings clipped – from the balcony of Thornfield Hall.

Antoinette's final clutch at the relative happiness of her Coulibri childhood re-emphasizes the divide between herself and the Jamaican identity she longs for. Seeing Tia after the chaos and terror of the fire, Antoinette reaches out to her as her only remaining link with the cultural community who have risen against her and her family. The final image of the scene freezes the impasse between the two girls in a static moment of attraction/repulsion, of like and unlike – perhaps the most powerful image in the novel:

> When I was close I saw the jagged stone in her hand but I did not see her throw it. I did not feel it either, only something wet running down my face. I looked at her and I saw her face crumple up as she began to cry. We stared at each other, blood on my face, tears on hers. It was as if I saw myself. Like in a looking-glass. (p. 38).

The search for self-identity is a theme common to much women's writing, and the mirror is constantly used to symbolize this search due to its ability to trap an image of the self. Yet that image is not always an obvious likeness. Showalter's analysis is again pertinent here. Her notion of the woman writer's 'double-voiced discourse' can usefully be transposed to portrayals of female characters in women's novels. Hence Antoinette is simultaneously inside and outside the Jamaican culture of her homeland. Again, Jean Rhys has extracted her symbolism from her source-text, *Jane Eyre*, where mirrors also play an important part. Jane is constantly confronting her 'truest and darkest double' in reflections of herself. Perhaps the most significant of these encounters is the first one, which occurs in the 'red room' after her conflict with her stepbrother, John Reed:

> Returning, I had to cross before the looking-glass; my fascinated glance involuntarily explored the depth it revealed. All looked colder and darker in that visionary hollow than in reality: and the strange little figure there gazing at me with a white face and arms speckling the gloom, and glittering eyes of fear moving where all else was still, had the effect of a real spirit . . . (p. 46)

And it is this 'real spirit' which is later released through its embodiment in Bertha, Rochester's mad first wife.

Jean Rhys, then, is using the looking-glass for similar purposes. At the end of *Wide Sargasso Sea*, Antoinette is deprived of a mirror, just as she has also had her name taken from her. Rochester has attempted to destroy her identity as completely as possible – and certainly to destroy her affinity with the 'muted group'. She says:

> Names matter, like when he wouldn't call me Antoinette, and I saw Antoinette drifting out of the window with her scents, her pretty clothes and her looking-glass.
> There is no looking-glass here and I don't know what I am like now. I remember watching myself brush my hair and how my eyes looked back at me. The girl I saw was myself yet not quite myself. (p. 147)

As I have suggested, Antoinette's is a constant search for her self-identity and her insecurity is carried through from her childhood. Her final confrontation with Tia is really the climax of her struggle to locate herself in the Jamaican 'order' where Tia already has a place. Antoinette's position *vis-à-vis* the two main opposing cultures, Jamaican and British, is to remain ambivalent. Her marriage to Rochester separates her still further from the Jamaican, yet at the same time, she finds herself still more in need of its strength and support. It is not until her suicidal jump into the flames at Thornfield Hall that she would seem to have finally found that strength herself – to have found her true identity which seems to consist, in some sense, of her union with Tia; perhaps her union with other women as suggested in Chapter 7: 'But when I looked over the edge I saw the pool of Coulibri. Tia was there. She beckoned to me and when I hesitated, she laughed. I heard her say, "You frightened?" And I heard a man's voice, "Bertha! Bertha!" . . . I called "Tia!" and jumped . . .' (p. 155)

Antoinette's ambivalent position between the two cultures or, to invoke the language of the 'wild zone', two 'consciousnesses', thus becomes one of the controlling structures of the novel. In the first section, for example, we have seen Mason's Englishness as it appears to Antoinette, carrying with it the apparent security of a stable father-figure. It is the longing for similar security and stability that would seem to underlie Antoinette's acquiescence in her arranged marriage with Rochester. Contrasted with this solidity and its accompanying insensitivity is the mystery and magic associated with Christophine and Tia: Christophine's powers of obeah, Tia's ability to light fires and her inability to feel pain. In her endless search for identity and security, Antoinette finds sympathy and innate understanding in these people, fulfilling the lack created by her rejection by her mother. Similarly, she shares their almost pantheistic relationship with the Jamaican countryside, although it is clearly no benevolent natural world: 'And if the razor grass cut my legs and arms I would think "It's better than people". Black ants and red ones, tall nests swarming with the white ants, rain that soaked me to the skin – once I saw a snake. All better than people. Better. Better, better than people' (p. 24). Through the Jamaican women's affinity with the natural world, Jean Rhys would seem to emphasize what Lévi-Strauss described as the symbolic stress between society and nature: the association of women with a more primitive, 'uncivilized' way of life – with all that is 'not man'. The idea is also central to Showalter's cultural model of gynocritics. Rhys shows this 'otherness' in a positive light. Just as the symbol of the mirror is carried over from *Jane Eyre*, so the recurring image of fire is extracted from the earlier novel. Jean Rhys's depiction of Jamaica is one of an intense, sensuous and emotional experience. Thus, fire is important for its destructive qualities, but also for the vivid colours and other qualities which link it with the lush Jamaican landscape. These colours can again be traced back to *Jane Eyre*, as can the importance of fire itself. And those elements of the novel which Gilbert and Gubar have described as Jane's own 'hunger, rebellion and rage' are transposed by Jean Rhys onto the passionate, powerful women of the Jamaican community. The destruction of the Coulibri house by fire confirms the power of the Jamaican world, symbolically acknowledging its triumph over British imperialism. The former association of Tia with fire and Antoinette's final act of defiance against Rochester in her suicidal destruction of Thornfield Hall could be seen to reinforce this enigmatic link between the magical powers of a 'primitive' cultural community and those of all women in their attempt to evade male repression.

The fire kills Pierre (Antoinette's 'idiot' brother), and sends Annette (her mother) 'mad', a madness which finally sets a seal on her rejection of her daughter and causes her husband to desert her. After a brief interval of refuge in a convent, Antoinette is forced back 'outside' into the dangerous insecurity of the real world. Her subsequent nightmare is ominously like a premonition. It is the same dream she had had on the eve of the changes leading to her mother's marriage – walking through a forest, followed by an enemy, paralyzed. This time she is clad in white, again followed by a hating man, and again terrified. Both dreams remain unexplained. Antoinette says, 'I dreamed I was in Hell' (p. 51). The disjointed stumbling sentences of the description evoke a nightmare world of powerlessness, and it is this world that is further evoked through the depiction of her marriage to Rochester.

The central section of Wide Sargasso Sea is narrated by Rochester, with a brief passage from Antoinette's viewpoint. The relationship between narrator, reader and characters, is, indeed, a complex one throughout the text as the focalization shifts between the two protagonists. Consequently, the reader is presented with two different versions of 'reality': those of the muted and dominant groups (although there are rarely two different accounts of the same event). Because of the way the novel is structured, because it is Antoinette's perception which frames the narrative and because of the setting of this narrative, the reader is directed to sympathize with Antoinette, not with Rochester. Indeed, it could be argued that Rhys uses irony to stage a critique of Rochester's version of 'reality' by allowing him to 'speak for himself'. And because of the style and setting, the acute and vivid evocation of the pervasive atmosphere of Jamaica – and particularly of its matriarchal community – the muted group can even be seen to make itself heard through Rochester's own confused incomprehension. It is Rochester's insecurity, his inability to make sense of his new life, that completes our disbelief in his perception. Thus, the novel is constructed around these two conflicting 'realities'. The conflict is presented both contiguously – through the juxtaposition of Antoinette's and Rochester's respective narratives – but also within each narrative itself; Antoinette experiences both British and Jamaican cultures (which may be seen to correspond to masculine and feminine discourses respectively), and Rochester's narrative is constantly at odds with the world he is portraying. His acknowledged inability to relate to that world reaffirms this disparity.

The conflict Rochester experiences in many respects resembles Antoinette's earlier feelings of beguilement and repulsion in her relationship with her Jamaican landscape and community. His fluctuating emotions are apparent from the wavering, divided opening sentence of his description: 'So it was all over, the advance and retreat, the doubts and hesitations. Everything finished, for better or for worse' (p. 55). The entire novel is centred on this movement between contraries, exchanges between primary images – light and darkness, day and night, sun and moon, heat and cold, fire and ice – all of which somehow coalesce on Antoinette's honeymoon island 'Desire, Hatred, Life, Death, came very close in the darkness. Better not know how close. Better not think, never for a moment' (p. 79). By collapsing these opposites together, Rhys is perhaps trying to 'express the inexpressible', to reach that point of female experience which is beyond the bounds of patriarchal discourse.[25] It is at these enigmatic, evocative moments that the writing is at its most poetic. And it is through this poetic writing that Rhys seems to 'work within "male" discourse' but 'work ceaselessly to deconstruct it' (Jacobus, p. 12). Whilst Rhys is clearly drawing sharp distinctions between male and female perceptions of reality, and hence expressing difference in male/female terms, the novel could be seen to be focused on female experience, and it is within this experience that notions of 'difference-as-opposite' are brought into question. (As I have suggested, this female world is the main subject of the narrative even when Rochester acts as narrator.) It is in this way that Rhys allows 'feminine values [to] penetrate and undermine the masculine structures which contain them' (Showalter, 1981, p. 28). Rochester is here the outsider in an alien culture and community, and it is his ideology and perception which are at odds with the dominant world-view.

Thus, whilst it is the blurring of boundaries and indistinct plurality of vision which characterize the whole atmosphere of Jamaica in the novel and enhance the beauty and magic of the honeymoon island, for Rochester this is 'unreal', and it is also distressing. He dislikes and distrusts Antoinette's ambiguous racial background. Unable to 'place' her within a race, he implies that she must be 'impure' in other ways: a criticism carrying heavy moral overtones including that of sexual promiscuity: 'her eyes . . . are dark and can be disconcerting. She never blinks at all it seems to me. Long, sad, dark alien eyes. Creole of pure English descent she may be, but they are not English or European either' (p. 56). From the outset, Rochester describes Antoinette in these terms: as an alien, a stranger, sometimes almost sub-human. Antoinette's world is not Rochester's world, her 'reality' is not his. Rochester says: 'But the feeling of something unknown and hostile was very strong. "I feel very much a stranger here" I said. "I feel that this place is my enemy and on your side" ' (p. 107). He cannot accept the disfunction between his previous experience and the 'reality' now confronting him. Consequently, he consistently attempts to impose his own views onto Antoinette: 'Reality might disconcert her, bewilder her, hurt her, but it would only be a mistake, a misfortune, a wrong path taken, her fixed ideas would never change. Nothing that I told her influenced her at all' (p. 78). The ironic treatment of Rochester is at its height here: clearly, this description could equally fit his attitude to Antoinette's 'reality'. For Antoinette, Rochester's reality is 'like a cold dark dream' (p. 67). He is associated with England, with London: the city, streets and houses full of people. Antoinette becomes one with the rivers, mountains and sea of her homeland, the intense colours and smells, and, above all, the intense emotions. Rochester is afraid of this intensity: afraid of an environ-ment and feelings he is unable to control. And he is even more afraid of a woman – indeed, what could be described as a whole matriarchal community – over whom he is seemingly powerless (see Chapter 7).

Rhys uses symbolic inversion to demonstrate the fallacy of a patriarchal mono-dimensional reality. The novel is indeed a 'cele-bration of the negative'.[26] Just as women have traditionally been associated with lack, with Freudian notions of castration, with silence and absence, so Rhys inverts this experience. It is Rochester who suffers this 'lack', this 'speechlessness': 'As for my confused impres-sions they will never be written. There are blanks in my mind that cannot be filled up' (p. 64). In so doing, Rhys exposes the logic of patriarchal discourse for what it is. As Dale Spender suggests: 'What we have confidently called logic and believe to be "uncontaminated" by human values, may indeed be culture-specific, arbitrary and inappropriate. We may need to change our ideas of what constitutes logic if we are to come closer to making sense of the world.'[27] Rhys inverts the patriarchal order, where women are classified as negative, as 'wrong', their reality invalid. Through *Wide Sargasso Sea*, she exposes the other side of the coin. Displaced from his own, male-dominated, 'orderly' society, Rochester comes face to face with the 'wild zone' of female experience: 'It was a beautiful place, wild, untouched, above all untouched, with an alien, disturbing, secret loneliness. And it kept its secret. I'd find myself thinking "What I see is nothing – I want what hides – that is not nothing." ' (p. 73). Rochester is simultaneously afraid and curious, torn between frustrated disbelief and the compulsion to discover the 'secret'. Yet he is also incapable of acknowledging the validity (even the superiority) of this 'other reality'. He is conscious of a terrible sense of lack – 'I want what hides' – but in order to acknowledge Antoinette's reality as valid, he must deny his own status and authority: the power of subscribing to, and controlling, the dominant world-view. The solution to Rochester's dilemma comes with the discovery of insanity in Antoinette's family, and his suggestion that Antoinette herself might have inherited that insanity. The labelling of the two opposing realities, those of dominant and muted, male and female groups, now moves into the realms of 'sanity' and 'insanity': a classification carrying with it the whole weight of Western 'scientific' judgement. Rochester's growing hatred of Antoinette, owing to his inability to understand or influence her, now finds justification in his discovery of her seemingly pathological mind. He thus redoubles his efforts to destroy Antoinette's already insecure identification with her adopted Jamaican culture: to destroy that reality in which he has no part. He calls her Bertha, after her 'mad' mother, instead of Antoinette – an act which Antoinette parallels with Christophine's magical powers, so strong is its effect on her self image, 'Bertha is not my name. You are trying to make me into someone else, calling me by another name. I know, that's obeah too' (p. 121). He taunts her as a 'marionette'. He refuses to make love to her, even to speak to her. Having once described her as 'alien', a stranger, Rochester now sees Antoinette as animal-like: savage, wild and unruly, very much like the description of Bertha in *Jane Eyre*. Thus the Rochester of *Wide Sargasso Sea* says:

> Then she cursed me comprehensively, my eyes, my mouth, every member of my body, and it was like a dream in the large unfurnished room with the candles flickering and this red-eyed wild-haired stranger who was my wife shouting obscenities at me. It was at this nightmare moment that I heard Christophine's calm voice. (p. 12)

whilst the description of Bertha in *Jane Eyre* runs: 'and my ears [Rochester's] were filled with the curses the maniac still shrieked out; wherein she momentarily mingled my name with such a tone of demon-hate, with such language! – no professed harlot ever had a fouler vocabulary than she . . .' (p. 335).

Rochester can only complete his suppression of Antoinette by returning with her to England, where he can regain the security of controlling the dominant world-view, where he will be 'sane', his 'reality' 'real', and Antoinette 'insane', living in a dream-world. Phrases like 'law and order' and 'justice' inevitably ring hollow in the Jamaican 'wild zone'. Even God – a symbol of the highest power in the patriarchal hierarchical 'order' – has no jurisdiction in Christophine's matriarchal community. She says: 'This is a free country and I am a free woman' (p. 131). Just before their return to England, however, Rochester has a moment of remorse through which he suddenly becomes more receptive: 'So I shall never understand why, suddenly, bewilderingly, I was certain that everything I had imagined to be truth was false. False. Only the magic and dream are true – all the rest's a lie. Let it go. Here is the secret. Here' (p. 138). His brief moment of revelation confirms the ironic treatment of his narrative for this section of the novel. His acknowledgement of the existence and validity of an alternative reality to his own confirms the positive depiction of this female experience throughout. Yet even here, Rochester's patriarchal discourse is imposed on the enigmatic contrasting reality, a reality which he can never grasp except in terms of 'magic' and 'the secret'. His description moves characteristically to talk of possession and domination: 'Not lost, I had found it in a hidden place and I'd keep it, hold it fast. As I'd hold her' (p. 138), and finally to an analogy with 'treasure' and reference to acquisitiveness: 'But they left their treasure, gold and more gold. Some of it is found – but the finders never tell, because you see they'd only get one third then: that's the law of treasure. They want it all, so never speak of it' (p. 139). Yet despite his continued need for domination, Rochester is finally receptive to the otherness which he has previously tried to dismiss; to the night and the darkness of which he was previously afraid, and perhaps even to Antoinette herself: 'Blot out the moon,/ Pull down the stars./ Love in the dark, for we're for the dark/ So soon, so soon' (p. 139). But it is too late, and when he is greeted by the hatred of Antoinette's eyes, the moment passes. His own hatred, humiliation and pride return with a vengeance and the battle of wills continues. But despite his apparently having the upper hand, Rochester can never achieve overall power. Antoinette retains a reserve of female power which Rochester can never destroy, and of which he will always feel the lack: 'Above all I hated her. For she belonged to the magic and the loveliness. She had left me thirsty and all my life would be thirst and longing for what I had lost before I found it' (p. 141). Again, Rhys has inverted one of the fundamental axes of patriarchal discourse. It is Rochester who experiences the lack or 'castration' traditionally associated with women.

The final section of the novel moves to England and Antoinette's imprisonment in Rochester's attic at Thornfield Hall. Here, the textual imagery – filtered through Antoinette's 'wild zone' consciousness – contrast the warmth and intensity of Jamaica with the coldness of England. Memories of Jamaica are invited by the flames of the fire, and by the single red dress Antoinette has retained from her previous life. The dress carries all the intense sensuous qualities of Jamaica: the colours, the smells, the spiritual and emotional experiences:

> As soon as I turned the key I saw it hanging, the colour of fire and sunset. The colour of flamboyant flowers. 'If you are buried under a flamboyant tree' I said, 'your soul is lifted up when it flowers. Everyone wants that . . .' The scent that comes from the dress was very faint at first, then it grew stronger. The smell of vetivert and frangi-panni, of cinnamon and dust and lime trees when they are flowering. The smell of sun and the smell of the rain. (p. 151)

Thornfield Hall seems to her like 'a cardboard house' – it is not 'reality'. Deprived of light and warmth, she no longer knows where she is. The darkness here is not like that of Jamaica, broken by moon and stars and moonflowers. Here she is imprisoned, denied any identity. She is no longer called Antoinette (Rochester has renamed her Bertha) and she does not possess a mirror in which to 'see herself'. Yet Antoinette retains some of her strength. Grace Poole describes the Hall as a refuge, a place where, as a woman, she is safe from the patriarchal world outside:

the house is big and safe, a shelter from the world outside which, say what you like, can be a black and cruel world to a woman. Past the lodge gate a long avenue of trees and inside the house the blazing fires and the crimson and white rooms. But above all the thick walls, keeping away all the things that you have fought till you can fight no more. (p. 146)

The Hall takes on almost womb-like qualities – protective and secure. But, like the red-room in *Jane Eyre*, it is also a prison. Antoinette alone does not feel the benefit of its 'security'. She is still fighting ('she hasn't lost her spirit'): 'living in her own darkness' she remains detached from Rochester's attempts to defeat the 'magic and loveliness' she possesses. The attic thus becomes a 'wild zone' itself, where, through her 'madness', Antoinette is able to defy Rochester's attempts to render her powerless. Her final act of defiance is to destroy Thornfield Hall in a fire whose flames contain an array of images from her Jamaican world.

Jean Rhys has skilfully rewritten Brontë's account of the fire at Thornfield Hall so as not to end her own novel with Antoinette's suicidal jump from the flames. The event is described as a premonition, and the novel closes as Antoinette wakes from her dream, steals the key to the attic from Grace Poole and carefully wends her way along the dark passages of Thornfield Hall, lighted by the single flame of the candle she carries. The narrative describing the fire itself is fast-moving and dream-like with its ever-changing scenario: a confusion of impressions of England and Jamaica. Antoinette calls on Christophine for help, deriving her final strength from the other woman's solidarity as well as her magical powers. As the fire gradually spreads, cinematic images of Antoinette's childhood flit one by one across her mind: the grandfather clock, Aunt Cora's patchwork, orchids, jasmine, tree-ferns, moss, the picture of the Miller's Daughter, the parrot, Rochester . . . Finally, she sees Tia, by the pool in Coulibri, and it is towards this image that she jumps to her death. It is not, ultimately, Rochester who 'breaks' Antoinette. Her self-destruction is a final act of her own will and strength; an escape from imprisonment. And the lighted candle in the culminating sentence would seem to be an image of the retention (or final acquisition) of this strength, Antoinette's independence, her consciousness and spirit which she will not allow Rochester to destroy or overpower.

Now at last I know why I was brought here and what I have to do. There must have been a draught for the flame flickered and I thought it was out. But I shielded it with my hand and it burned up again to light me along the dark passage . . . (pp. 155–6)

Jean Rhys thus establishes the strength of the 'muted group' or feminine discourse. In *Wide Sargasso Sea* that discourse is indeed a 'positive source of strength and solidarity', as Showalter has suggested.

Showalter's cultural model of gynocritics is also a useful structure for analysis of Margaret Atwood's *Surfacing*.[28] The novel takes the form of spiritual quest, in which the female protagonist returns to the natural world in search of mystical vision. Her quest could equally be interpreted as a search for a feminine discourse: her escape from, and challenge to, the patriarchal social order she has previously accepted as the 'norm'.

Following Showalter's model it becomes clear that this is a text in which the protagonist is the subject of 'double-voiced discourse'. Whilst pursuing her struggle towards self-identity and greater self-knowledge through a metaphysical 'wild-zone' experience, she must simultaneously continue to relate to her three companions (two males and one female) who are representatives of the dominant order. Such dialogue becomes increasingly difficult, however. On more than one occasion she is so immersed in her search for a 'feminine' vision that she can barely remember the language of her companions.[29] The two discourses can thus be seen to correspond to Showalter's structure of 'muted' and 'dominant' groups, with particular emphasis being placed on the fact that no matter how 'silenced' the protagonist feels herself, she is never *entirely* outside of the dominant culture. The novel is set on an island in one of the lakes of Northern Quebec, where the protagonist has returned in search of her father, a lone forester who disappeared about one month previously. She is accompanied by her partner and another married couple, all of them Canadian nationalists who abhor the 'Bloody fascist pig Yanks' (p. 9) for their excessive capitalism and encroachment on Canadian territory, and are yet ill at ease in the wilderness of the natural world. The narrative follows the protagonist's search for her missing father, which serves as a pretext for her search for her inner self: we observe her gradual submersion into nature and towards mystical vision. Her relationship with her lover and her two other companions (and theirs with one another) are played out alongside this search. Through her changing perception, we are gradually offered differing perspectives on those relationships. The third thread of the novel – and an important part of the protagonist's journey towards self-knowledge – is her attempt to come to terms with her abortion: an act which she now sees as murderous. As the novel progresses, she is increasingly able to confront her own memory of the event, but it is only as she completes her spiritual quest that she is finally able fully to accept her own responsibility for evil as well as good. Throughout the novel, Atwood emphasizes the contrast between the natural, 'primitive' world of the countryside and the cultured 'civilized' world of city life. Like Jean Rhys, she draws a parallel between these two worlds and female and male perceptions of reality respectively. By setting the novel in the Canadian wilderness, she is better able to question and challenge the values of the patriarchal social order, as Rhys did against the background of the Jamaican community. And like Rhys, Atwood builds on the two axes of the male/female, culture/nature dichotomy. Despite their abhorrence of all things American, the protagonist's male companions are increasingly associated with American values: the need to conquer and control, the need to destroy. By contrast, the female protagonist finds affinity with the innocent inhabitants of the natural world: the slaughtered heron they find hanging in the undergrowth.[30] As the novel progresses, she is further associated with the creativity and resourcefulness of that wilderness, while at the same time learning to bear responsibility for her own 'evil' and destruction.

It is, for the most part, the sexual relationships between the four main characters in the novel, together with the protagonist's memories of her relationship with her previous partner, that act as the arena for Atwood's examination of the patriarchal social order. Within these relationships, that social order is still apparent despite the different 'order' offered by the natural world. The male need to dominate is the prevailing feature of both relationships. This is especially true of David and Anna, the married couple who accompany the protagonist. She observes: 'Anna was more than sad, she was desperate, her body her only weapon and she was fighting for her life, he was her life, her life was the fight . . .' (p. 154). Their fight is vividly depicted when David forces Anna to pose naked whilst he and Joe film her: ' "Come on, we need a naked lady with big tits and a big ass", David said in the same tender voice; I recognized that menacing gentleness, at school it always went before the trick, the punchline' (p. 234). The image of Anna 'in the air, upside down over his shoulder, hair hanging in damp ropes' (p. 135) parallels the earlier image of the dead heron they find in the forest 'hanging upside down by a thin blue nylon rope tied round its feet and looped over a tree branch, its wings fallen open' (p. 115). Thus the women are associated with the innocent, natural world, incapable of combating the power of their male counterparts. Like the heron, their only 'defense was flight, invisibility' (p. 135).

The relationship between the protagonist and Joe, her lover, also offers an interesting insight into this male/female dichotomy. The protagonist's acceptance of the partnership is almost fatalistic She thinks of choosing a man 'like buying a goldfish or a potted cactus plant, not because you want one in advance but because you happen to be in the store and you see them lined up on the counter' (p. 42). She observes Joe's need for greater commitment on her part with a mixture of ironic indifference and dread:

Prove your love, they say. You really want to marry me, let me fuck you instead. You really want to fuck, let me marry you instead. As long as there's a victory, some flag I can wave, parade I can have in my head. (p. 87)

She refuses his offer of marriage, accepting that her refusal will only heighten his need. Despite her fear of the consequences, her search for her missing father and her search for self increasingly offer her the power to resist the oppression inherent in their relationship and to reassess her own needs.

Whilst the protagonist attempts to unravel the mystery behind the disappearance of her father, the reader struggles to make sense of the often conflicting strands of her story about her marriage, her husband and her child. At various points in the novel she relates incidents from her past. She remembers her inability to return home after her wedding and keeping her child hidden from her parents. The image of her brother as he nearly drowned recurs – although the incident took place before she was born. She remembers her husband treating her like an invalid instead of a bride after their wedding ceremony; she feels herself to have been betrayed by him. The incidents do not form a coherent whole because of course she never actually had a child and she is confusing the imagined wedding with the abortion of her child. It is only once the protagonist achieves greater self-knowledge that the picture finally falls into place. As her dual search – her search for her missing father and her search for self – gradually coalesce she acknowledges that it is not her father's death that concerns her as much as her. The protagonist observes her own 'death' – her inability to feel – with increasing anxiety:

In the night I had wanted rescue, if my body could be made to sense, respond, move strongly enough, some of the red light bulb synapses, blue neurons, incandescent molecules might seep into my head through the closed throat, neck, membrane . . . I rehearsed emotions naming them . . . what to feel was like what to wear, you watched others and memorized it. (p. 111)

Her lack of feeling is reflected in her cool analysis of her relationship with Joe, and with David and Anna. She observes them all with detached objectivity, distancing herself still further as she immerses herself in the natural world. The only emotion she feels is 'the fear that I wasn't alive' (p. 111). As we learn later, this fear is largely the result of her inability to confront the intense emotions surrounding her previous lover's betrayal of her and her acquiescence in the abortion of her child.

In her article, 'Margaret Atwood: the surfacing of women's spiritual quest and vision', Carol Christ traces the protagonist's journey in *Surfacing* from innocence and assumed powerlessness through the recognition of her complicity in evil to self-knowledge and the sense of power. Christ argues:

> Her association of power with evil and her dissociation of herself from both reflect a typical female delusion of innocence, which hides her complicity in *evil* and feeds her false belief that she can do nothing but witness her victimization. In order to regain her power the protagonist must realize that she does not live in a world where only others have power or do evil.[31]

Showalter's notion of a 'double-voiced discourse' in Atwood is perhaps evidenced in the protagonist's acceptance of her participation in the masculine world of such power and evil. Carol Christ identifies the sighting of the slaughtered heron as the incident which disillusions the protagonist of her childhood innocence. On seeing the dead heron, she says: 'I felt a sickening complicity, sticky as glue, blood on my hands, as though I had been there and watched without saying No or doing anything to stop it' (p. 130). Other incidents of childhood cruelty flash through her mind, completing her realization that, as Christ puts it, 'the path to redemption through childhood [was] closed' (p. 321). The protagonist's acknowledgement of some level of personal guilt leads her to the next stage in reclaiming her power to feel and act.

Redoubling her efforts to unravel the mystery of her father's disappearance, she concentrates on increasing her understanding of his obsession with the native Canadian drawings. In search of one such drawing, she dives deep into the lake. But instead of the drawing she is confronted with an image of her father's dead body, and thus a final acceptance of his death. The incident serves to release her own blocked senses. The image of her dead father corresponds to the memories of her nearly drowned brother, the latter of which she suddenly recognizes as a substitute for her memory of her aborted foetus. The protagonist can then recall the correct facts surrounding the other incidents. The man she remembers was her lover, not her husband, there was no wedding, no childbirth – only the abortion, which she had had on his instruction. Confronted with the correct version of events, the protagonist cannot deny her complicity in an act she sees as intensely evil: 'it was hiding in me as if in a burrow and instead of granting it sanctuary I let them catch it. I could have said no but I didn't; that made me one of them too, a killer' (p. 145). She interprets her newly acquired self-knowledge as a gift from the gods, pantheistic gods, who have succeeded for her where Christianity (centred in the myths and legends of patriarchy) had failed: 'I regretted the nickels I'd taken dutifully for the collection plate . . .

These gods, here on the shore or in the water, unacknowledged or forgotten, were the only ones who had ever given me anything I needed; and freely' (p. 145). Guided by her search for her father, the protagonist finds herself moving towards a 'wild zone' experience: the place where matriarchal values outweigh the powerful evil of patriarchy. She says of her father: 'He had discovered new places, new oracles, they were things he was seeing the way I had seen true vision: at the end, after the failure of logic' (p. 145). The notion of the 'failure of logic' is an important one. As the protagonist moves further into that 'wild zone', she becomes increasingly aware of her own inability to express her thoughts and feelings. The language system does not belong to her; does not address her perception of reality. When Joe asks her if she loves him, she says: 'It was the language again, I couldn't use it because it wasn't mine. He must have known what it meant but it was an imprecise word . . .' (p. 106). After her visionary experience in the lake, she is still more acutely aware of the obstructiveness of the supposed logic of language: 'Language divides us into fragments, I wanted to be whole' (p. 146). With her new-found vision, she is able to interpret things without the use of that language system, to differentiate objects by their very essence, their shape and form: 'Sight flowing ahead of me over the ground, eyes filtering the shapes, the names of things fading but their forms and uses remaining, the animals learned what to eat without nouns' (p. 150). The two discourses become increasingly detached from one another, so that the protagonist has to struggle to communicate with her companions: 'I had to concentrate in order to talk to him, the English words seemed imported, foreign . . .' (p. 150). And she is suddenly acutely aware of the facade created by the dominant discourse, the illusion of power created through words and ideology. Moreover, she recognizes the falseness of this image. She no longer feels threatened by the men's need for sexual domination. Her description of David from her position inside the 'wild zone' offers a perfect critique of Showalter's dominant group:

> The power flowed into my eyes, I could see into him, he was an imposter, a pastiche, layers of political handbills, pages from magazines, affiches, verbs and nouns glued on to him and shredding away . . . He was infested, garbled, and I couldn't help him, scrape down to where he was true. (p. 152)

Having been offered some guidance by her father, it is to another woman, her dead mother, that the protagonist must look for the completion of her vision. Sensing that this guidance will be found in an old scrap book she had made as a child, she opens it to find pictures she had drawn of 'a woman with a round moon stomach: the baby sitting up inside her gazing out' (p. 158). She decides to conceive a child. Having confronted her complicity in death, she now recognizes her potential for creativity. She sees that 'nothing has died, everything is alive, everything is waiting to become alive' (p. 159). Outside, under a full moon, she wills herself to conceive a child with Joe. She feels that the sexual power is all hers. And she envisages the birth, this time without the interference of male medical technology:

> This time I will do it by myself, squatting, on old newspapers in a corner alone; or on leaves, dry leaves, a heap of them, that's cleaner. The baby will slip out easily as an egg, a kitten, and I'll lick it off and bite the cord, the blood returning to the ground where it belongs; the moon will be full, pulling. In the morning I will be able to see it: it will be covered with shining fur, a god, I will never teach it any words. (p. 162)

Following her 'mating' with Joe, the protagonist becomes still further alienated from her friends. In order to pursue her quest to its final fulfilment, she chooses to stay on alone on the island after their departure. Casting rationality aside – 'there are no longer any rational points of view' – she undergoes a final transformation that enables her to be completely at one with the wilderness. She carries out a ritual destruction of the effects of the civilized world: pots and pans, clothing, books, etc. 'Everything from history must be eliminated, the circles and the arrogant square pages' (p. 176). She then sets out on her final journey into the 'wild zone', the place beyond language, beyond the Lacanian Symbolic Order (see Chapter 6), where boundaries cease to exist: 'they are against borders' (p. 180), and where, Christ suggests, 'she experiences mystical identification with all forms of life' (p. 324). Atwood's deliberate omission of full-stops in the subsequent sentences serves to reinforce the protagonist's sense of fluidity, her loss of personal identity: 'In one of the languages there are no nouns, only verbs held for a longer moment/ The animals have no need for speech, why talk when you are a word/ I lean against a tree, I am tree leaning' (p. 181).

Having achieved the sense of her own creativity and power through her affinity with the natural order, the protagonist returns to the cabin and opens a can of beans, symbolizing her return to the modern world. Joe returns once more to find her, and she decides to leave the island with him. But although this 'return' confirms Showalter's thesis that no woman can remain permanently outside the dominant culture and its discourses or ideologies, she nevertheless retains the wisdom she has gained from her sojourn in the 'wild-zone'. She will no longer accept a position of powerlessness within the patriarchal social order: 'This above all, to refuse to be a victim. Unless I can do that I can do nothing. I have to recant, give up the old belief that I am powerless and because of it nothing I can do will ever hurt anyone' (p. 191).

III

As we explained in the first section of this chapter, Showalter's attempt to find a theoretical basis for feminist criticism stems from her desire to analyze the 'difference' of women's writing. This 'difference', she goes on to argue, is the result of the different experience of female authors from that of male authors. Hence the inadequacy of male critical theory which constitutes 'a concept of creativity, literary history, or literary interpretation based entirely on male experience and put forward as universal' (p. 183). Showalter thus challenges the assumptions of patriarchal liberal humanism, which claims that universal truths are evidenced in literature through the privileged (predominantly male) texts which go to make up the canon of great literature. Showalter argues that such gender blindness inevitably fails to address women's experience. Gynocritics fulfils the need for a theory based on women's experience, women's perception of reality. However, in *Feminist Practice and Poststructuralist Theory*, Chris Weedon reminds us that:

> if women's experience is different from the experience of men, it is important to understand why. Either we can see women as essentially different from men or as socially constituted as different and subject to social relations and processes in different ways to men . . . Theory must be able to address women's experience by showing where it comes from and how it relates to material social practices and the power relations that structure them.[32]

The way in which experience is formulated is one of the mechanisms that Showalter herself fails to address. By arguing for a stable female aesthetic, unchanging across time, Showalter overlooks the means by which an individual experience is structured through language and thereby through the range of different discourses operative during any historical period. Whilst she acknowledges the importance of the linguistic debate within feminism, her theory does not take account of the vital role language plays in constructing our meanings and our experience. Because her model of dominant and muted groups rests on the notion of two different but unchanging perceptions of reality, Showalter fails to question patriarchy itself – the system whereby power is organized on the basis of biological sex. Instead, she accepts gender difference as having inherent meaning, unchanging across time and therefore 'natural'. The woman author's 'femaleness' can thus be identified as the source of her different writing strategies. Moreover, the meaning of the text can also be found through its author's 'femaleness' and her consequent experience of reality: its meaning can be found outside the text itself. As Chris Weedon argues, a theory such as Elaine Showalter's can only attempt to 'revaluate the feminine which patriarchy devalues' (p. 81). There is no questioning within gynocritics of the means by which certain values have become associated with femininity, or the muted group, and others with masculinity and the corresponding dominant group. Poststructuralist theory proposes a notion of gender as socially produced, through language and through the interaction of different discourses. Thus, no meaning is always already there. Similarly, 'masculinity' and 'femininity' do not pre-exist the discursive processes that give them meaning: they are constructed through these processes.

By refusing to address the problem of the production of meaning, Showalter poses serious difficulties for the feminist critic. Toril Moi points to the discrepancy between Showalter's notion of the 'feminist critique' and its approach to male writing and the notion of gynocritics with its analysis of female writing. Whilst the feminist critique is a 'historically grounded inquiry which probes the ideological assumptions of literary phenomena', Toril Moi notes that 'this sort of "suspicious" approach to the literary text seems . . . largely absent from Showalter's second category'.[33] She continues: 'if texts are seen as signifying processes, and both writing and reading grasped as textual production, it is likely that even texts written by women will be subjected to irreverent scrutiny by feminist critics' (p. 78). But instead of studying 'textual production', Showalter advocates that the feminist critic spend her time acquiring a 'close and extensive knowledge of women's texts' (p. 203), each of which will, as Toril Moi says, 'become the transparent medium through which experience can be seized' (p. 76).

It would be unfair, however, to accuse Showalter of total ignorance of the social construction of gender difference. As we explained, the reason for her choice of a cultural model of gynocritics is that it 'incorporates ideas about women's body, language and psyche but interprets them in relation to the social contexts in which they occur' (p. 197). Her theory also incorporates an awareness of the existence of a variety of discourses at work at any one time: 'women's writing is a "double-voiced" discourse that always embodies the social, literary and cultural heritages of both the muted and dominant' (p. 201). However, the problem with the theory is that it fails to examine these notions further. Showalter would seem to assume that gender difference was culturally produced at some unspecified point in history and has continued to be produced in exactly the same way ever since: a theoretical blindspot which has come to be known as *cultural essentialism* (see Glossary). Whilst acknowledging the existence of different discourses, she insists on their division into groups – the dominant and the muted, or masculine and feminine. She does not question the means by which these categories are constructed. As Chris Weedon suggests: 'the meanings of feminine and masculine vary from culture to culture and language to language. They even vary between discourses within a particular language, between different feminist discourses for instance, and are subject to historical change' (p. 22). Without acknowledging such historical change, the task of identifying a 'female aesthetic' becomes an extremely difficult one.

An additional problem arises from Showalter's tendency to prioritize gender over other differences: class differences, racial differences and differences in sexuality (see Chapters 7 and 8). Her system of binary oppositions – dominant and muted groups – does not provide a forum in which to examine these variations within feminist discourse. In our reading of *Surfacing*, for example, some of the characteristics which Atwood ascribes to the *nationality* of the Americans are adopted as features of the dominant group by extending the binary oppositions: dominant/muted, masculine/feminine, culture/nature, American/Canadian. Our reading of *Wide Sargasso Sea* contains an even more glaring 'oversight' by conflating British imperialism with masculinity and the dominant group, whilst assigning Antoinette, Christophine and Tia to the muted group regardless of racial difference.[34] Gayatri Spivak stresses the dangers inherent in much Anglo-American feminist criticism of '[reproducing] the axioms of imperialism'. She states:

> A basically isolationist admiration for the literature of the female subject in Europe and Anglo-American establishes the high feminist norm. It is supported and operated by an information-retrieval approach to 'Third World' literature which often employs a deliberately 'non-theoretical' methodology with self-conscious rectitude.[35]

In her own reading of *Wide Sargasso Sea*, she focuses on the distinction between the interests of the 'white Creole', Antoinette, and those of the 'native', Christophine. Whilst we have located the 'wild zone' of Rhys's novel as the areas of 'female' experience which cannot be expressed, Spivak suggests that is in the native, Christophine, that *Wide Sargasso Sea* marks with uncanny clarity 'the limits of its own discourse' (p. 271). Our gynocritical reading thus subsumes Christophine's difference into the wider arena of *feminine* difference with little reference to her oppression as a Black woman. (See Chapter 8 for a full problematization of this.)

It is clear, then, that Showalter's model of gynocriticism is severely flawed by its concentration on gender difference alone; and to the extent that it could even be argued to encourage 'distorted' readings of women's writing. Nevertheless, Showalter does provide the reader with a set of tools with which to produce a feminist reading of novels by women. As we hope to have demonstrated in our readings of *Wide Sargasso Sea* and *Surfacing*, the theory facilitates a different approach to a novel than that allowed for by, for example, either traditional liberal humanist criticism, or indeed, by authentic realist feminist criticism. There is no doubt that Showalter's model helped initiate debate into many of the problems central to women writers and to feminist critics and, despite its blindspots, offered one of the first serious challenges to the male-dominated schools of literary criticism.

Notes

1. Dale Spender, *Mothers of the Novel* (Pandora, London, 1986), p. 115.
2. Ellen Moers, *Literary Women* (The Women's Press, London, 1977); Patricia Meyer Spacks, *The Female Imagination: A Literary and Psychological Investigation of Women's Writing* (Allen and Unwin, London, 1976); Nina Baym, *Women's Fiction: A Guide to Novels by and about Women in America 1820–1970* (Cornell University Press, London, 1978).
3. Elaine Showalter, 'Feminist criticism in the wilderness' in Elaine Showalter (ed.), *The New Feminist Criticism: Essays on Women, Literature and Theory* (Virago, London, f. pub. 1981). All further references are given after quotations in the text.
4. The reader should note the relationship between this notion and Kate Millet's sexual politics (see Chapter 1).
5. Amongst others, Baym examines the work of Catherine Sedgwick, Maria McIntosh, Susan Warner and Maria Cummins.
6. Moers (see note 2 above).
7. Willa Cather, *The Song of the Lark* (1915), cited in Moers (see note 2 above).
8. Spacks (see note 2 above).
9. In Mary Jacobus (ed.), *Women Writing and Writing About Women* (Croom Helm, London, 1979) pp. 22–42; and *Critical Inquiry*, Winter 1981. Also *The New Feminist Criticism*, ed. Elaine Showalter (London, Virago, 1986), pp. 125–43 and pp. 243–70.
10. Sandra Gilbert and Susan Gubar, *The Madwoman in the Attic* (Yale University Press, New Haven, 1979). See Chapter 4.
11. See Chapter 5 for an examination of the importance of language in dicussions of gender.
12. Carolyn Burke, 'Report from Paris', p. 844, cited in Showalter (see note 3 above).
13. Mary Jacobus, 'The difference of view', pp. 10–22 in Jacobus (see note 9 above), pp. 12–13.
14. Although it might now seem that Showalter's 'reading' of the work of the French feminists is rather superficial and dismissive, it should be remembered that at the time this essay was first published (1978) these writings were still relatively unknown amongst Anglo-American scholars.
15. See discussion of Lacanian psychoanalysis in Chapters 5 and 6 and Glossary for explanation.
16. Nancy Chodorow, *The Reproduction of Mothering* (University of

California Press, Berkeley, 1978), cited in Showalter (see note 3 above).

17. Literary and cultural criticism based on Chodorow's theory has become increasingly popular with feminist critics since this chapter was first published. See, for example, Patricia Waugh's reading of Virginia Woolf's *To the Lighthouse* in *Feminine Fictions* (Routledge, London and New York, 1989).

18. Edwin Ardener, 'Belief and the problem of women', in Shirley Ardener (ed.), *Perceiving Women* (Malaby Press, London, 1975).

19. Shirley Ardener, *Defining Females: The Nature of Women in Society* (Croom Helm, London, 1978).

20. Claude Lévi-Strauss, *Les Structures Elementaire de la Parente* (Mouton, Paris, 1967), cited in Ardener (see note 18 above), p. 5.

21. Showalter's notion of the 'wild zone' clearly bears a close resemblance to Kristeva's 'semiotic' (see Chapter 5), but care should be taken not to confuse the two vocabularies since Showalter's 'metaphysical' space is not a psychoanalytic one.

22. Jean Rhys, *Wide Sargasso Sea* (Penguin, Harmondsworth, 1968). All further references are given after quotations in the text.

23. Charlotte Brontë, *Jane Eyre* (Penguin, Harmondsworth, 1982).

24. Louis James, *Jean Rhys* (Longman, London, 1978), p. 51.

25. See the discussion in Chapter 5 of Luce Irigaray's directive that in order to 'access' the feminine it is necessary to disrupt the simple oppositions on which the theoretical oppositions are founded.

26. Barbara Babcock, *The Reversible World: Symbolic Inversion in Art and Society* (Cornell University Press, London, 1978), p. 14.

27. Dale Spender, *Man Made Language* (Routledge and Kegan Paul, London, 1980), p. 97.

28. Margaret Atwood, *Surfacing* (Virago, London, 1979 f. pub 1972). All further references are given after quotations in the text.

29. The protagonist's relation to language and discourse is also discussed from a Marxist-feminist perspective in Chapter 6.

30. Atwood's use of the natural world and images of birds to represent women further illustrates Ellen Moers' suggestion that these are themes common to much women's writing.

31. Carol Christ, 'Margaret Atwood: the surfacing of women's spiritual quest and vision', in *Signs*, Winter 1976, p. 320.

32. Chris Weedon, *Feminist Practice and Poststructuralist* Theory (Blackwell, Oxford, 1987), p. 8.

33. Toril Moi, *Sexual/Textual Politics* (Methuen, London, 1985), p. 76.

34. See Chapter 7 for discussion of the similarly problematic conflation of racial and sexual identity.

35. Gayatri Chakravorty Spivak, 'Three women's texts and a critique of imperialism', in Henry Louis Gates (ed.), *'Race', Writing and Difference'* (University of Chicago Press, Chicago, 1985).

4
The anxiety of authorship

Sue Spaull, Elaine Millard and Lynne Pearce

Sandra Gilbert and Susan Gubar:
The Madwoman in the Attic
Susan Gubar: ' "The blank page" and female creativity'
Angela Carter: *The Magic Toyshop*
Alice Walker: *The Color Purple*

I

Sandra Gilbert and Susan Gubar's study *The Madwoman in the Attic* was first published in 1979.[1] Alongside Ellen Moers' *Literary Women* (1976) and Elaine Showalter's *A Literature of their Own* (1977), it was one of the first major studies of women writers which set the course for Anglo-American feminist criticism, whose main thrust was to be its concern to identify a distinct *female* literary tradition. All three works examine the ways in which society shapes women's perspective of the world, together with the style and subject matter of their writing. Yet despite the similarities between these works and with Showalter's later theoretical writing, the theorists' respective approaches to this female literary tradition show many clear divergences and differences from one another.[2] Whilst they all address themselves to the problem of identifying the 'difference' of women's writing, and the social reasons for that difference, the conclusions they reach, or rather, the emphasis within those conclusions, are surprisingly different.

As well as examining Gilbert and Gubar's *The Madwoman in the Attic* in this chapter, we shall be discussing a second article by Susan Gubar called ' "The blank page" and the issues of female creativity'.[3] In both these works, the critics begin by addressing themselves to a society and culture which are essentially patriarchal. Within this context, their examination of Western literary history and of men's and women's respective positions in relation to that literary history takes Freudian psychoanalysis as its starting-point.[4]

The Madwoman in the Attic opens with the question: 'Is a pen a

metaphorical penis?' (p. 3). The question is central to Gilbert and
Gubar's discussion of feminist poetics. In order to establish the
existence of a female literary tradition, the authors first address
themselves to the position of women writers *vis-à-vis* their male
counterparts. An essential part of this discussion centres on the idea
that creativity is inextricably linked with male sexuality. Gilbert and
Gubar stress that 'the patriarchal notion that the writer "fathers" his
text just as God fathered the world is and has been all-pervasive in
Western literary civilization' (p. 4). With supporting evidence from a
wealth of male writers and theorists over the centuries, the authors
then elaborate the pen/penis metaphor still further. They quote
Edward Said's suggestion 'that the unity or integrity of the text is
maintained by a series of genealogical connections: author–text,
beginning–middle–end, text–meaning, reader–interpretation and so
on. Underneath all these is the imagery of succession, of paternity or
hierarchy' (p. 5).[5] They argue that the power of a man's pen 'like his
penis's power, is not just the ability to generate life but the power to
create a posterity to which he lays claim' (p. 6). So the writer, through
writing, has a stake in the literary future. And further, as the 'owner'
of his text, he is, by extension, the owner of the 'subjects' of the text:
the characters, scenes and events that he has created.[6] These notions
of paternity, authority and ownership form an essential background to
Gilbert and Gubar's ensuing discussion of female creativity.

Extending their original question, they ask: 'If the pen is a
metaphorical penis, with what organ can females generate texts?'
(p. 7). They argue that it has been no accident that the pen has been
defined as a male tool, encouraging, and even perhaps establishing
the notion that it is both *physiologically* and sociologically impossible
for women to write. If creativity is an extension of male sexuality, then
clearly women do not possess the power to write. Gilbert and Gubar
argue that women have been forced into a position where they must
remain passive. They 'exist only to be acted on by men' (p. 8).
Returning to notions of ownership and authority, Gilbert and Gubar
stress the power of language and the printed word: '[The male
author's] literary creations are his possessions, his property. Having
defined them in language and thus generated them, he owns them,
controls them, encloses them on the printed page' (p. 12). Other men
can challenge this 'authority' by generating their own fictions – by
'talking back' with a different version of 'reality'. Gilbert and Gubar
accept Harold Bloom's psychoanalytic theory as a useful model of this
process.[7] Bloom compares the relationship between the male author
and his precursors with the father–son relationship as defined by
Freud. Every writer must take part in a literary Oedipal struggle in
order to overcome the power of his forefathers: 'a man can only

become a poet by somehow invalidating his poetic father' (p. 47). But women, it has been argued, lack the power – the pen/penis – to challenge the fictions of their male precursors. There is no place for women in this Freudian power struggle. Hence the images of women created by male writers have taken on greater 'authority', their female successors unwilling or unable to challenge them.

Reworking Harold Bloom's ideas still further, Gilbert and Gubar identify Milton as the poet who has the supreme power in this patriarchal literary order. They suggest that: 'In an extraordinarily distinctive way, therefore, Milton is for women what Harold Bloom . . . calls "the great Inhibitor, the Sphinx who strangles even strong imaginations in their cradles" ' (p. 191). It is Milton, then, in *Paradise Lost*, who 'most notably tells to woman . . . the story of [her] secondness, her otherness, and how that otherness leads inexorably to her demonic anger, her sin . . .' (p. 191).

Gilbert and Gubar argue that 'women in patriarchal societies have historically been reduced to mere properties, to characters and images imprisoned in male texts because generated solely . . . by male expectations and designs' (p. 12). Male writers have thus 'enclosed' women on the printed page. Elaborating this metaphor, Gilbert and Gubar continue:

> As a creation 'penned' by man . . . woman has been 'penned up' or 'penned in'. As a sort of 'sentence' man has spoken, she has herself been 'sentenced', fated, jailed for he has both 'indited' her and 'indicted' her. As a thought he has 'framed', she has been both 'framed' (enclosed) in his texts, glyphs, graphics, and 'framed-up' (found guilty, found wanting) in his cosmologies. (p. 13)[8]

This notion that women are forced into a position of passivity in the process of literary production is also the theme of Susan Gubar's article ' "The blank page" and issues of female creativity'. She argues that 'female sexuality is often identified with textuality' (p. 294) and further that:

> [The] model of the pen-penis writing on the virgin page participates in a long tradition identifying the author as a male who is primary and the female as his passive creation – a secondary object lacking autonomy endowed with often contradictory meaning but denied intentionality. Clearly this tradition excludes women from the creation of culture, even as it reifies her as an artifact within culture. (p. 295)

In both *The Madwoman in the Attic* and ' "The blank page" and issues of female creativity', Gilbert and Gubar compare the male act of imprisoning the female in his writing with the act of killing. He both silences the female, and 'stills' her – in essence, he 'kills' her (MW, p. 14). Gilbert and Gubar suggest that this proves a further link between the pen and 'maleness', just as the human male's superiority over the female has traditionally been linked to his ability to hunt and kill. They further suggest that woman has been 'killed into a "perfect" image of herself' by successive male authors (p. 15). That perfect image is, in effect, a male dream of female perfection. As such, Gilbert and Gubar argue, it represents 'the most pernicious image male authors have ever imposed upon literary women' (p. 20). It is the image of the Angel which Gilbert and Gubar find proliferating in male writing, together with its 'necessary opposite and double' – the image of the monstrous woman (p. 17). Both images, it will be shown, are used to a similar end by male writers. And the profound effects of these images on women and their writing are central to Gilbert and Gubar's analysis of the female literary tradition.

The images of Angel and Monster have both been used, Gilbert and Gubar argue, to further the male writer's attempts to control the female subjects of his texts, and, by conclusion, women themselves (including women writers). Many feminists and anthropologists have shown that the male need to control women arises from his fear of her 'Otherness'.[9] Denied a position within the social order, denied the autonomy and the subjectivity represented by the pen, Gilbert and Gubar stress that woman inevitably achieves a position of symbolic ambiguity. She is excluded from culture and because of her consequent 'difference', she

> becomes herself an embodiment of just those extremes of mysterious and intransigent Otherness which culture confronts with worship or fear, love or loathing. As 'Ghost, fiend, and angel, fairy, witch and sprite, she mediates between the male artist and the Unknown . . .' (pp. 19–20).[10]

Gilbert and Gubar trace the image of the Angel from the Middle Ages through Dante, Milton and Goethe. As the Angel, woman is wholly passive and essentially self-less: a complement and comfort to man. The image reaches its most extreme form in nineteenth-century literature, where the association between man's writing and the act of killing is particularly appropriate: 'in the severity of her selflessness, as well as in the extremity of her alienation from ordinary fleshly life, this nineteenth-century angel-woman becomes not just a memento of otherness but actually a memento mori . . . an "Angel of Death" ' (p. 24).[11] At the opposite extreme is the image of the Monster. Frequently, the two images may exist within one character: 'the monster may not only be concealed *behind* the angel, she may actually turn out to reside *within* (or in the lower half of) the angel' (p. 29). These contradictory images of woman created by man encapsulate his ambivalence towards female sexuality. They represent the 'mythic masks' he has 'fastened over [woman's] human face to lessen [his] dread of her "inconstancy" ' (p. 17). The images also represent man's ambivalence towards his own physicality, and Gilbert and Gubar reiterate Simone de Beauvoir's suggestion that:

> woman has been made to represent all of man's ambivalent feelings about his inability to control his own physical existence, his own birth and death. As the Other, woman comes to represent the contingency of life that is made to be destroyed. (p. 34)[12]

Just as the passivity of the image of the Angel, devoid of generative power, must inevitably act as a deterrent for women wishing to write, so too the image of the Monstrous woman, incorporating as it does the male dread of female *autonomy*, serves to reinforce the notion that creativity is the domain of men: 'as a representative of otherness, [woman] incarnates the damning otherness of the flesh rather than the inspiring otherness of the spirit, expressing what . . . men consider the angelic humility and "dullness" for which she was designed' (p. 28). Thus, the female freak becomes a 'powerfully monitory' image for any woman wishing to write.

It is against this background that women have attempted to find their position in the literary order. Returning to Harold Bloom's Freudian model of literary paternity, it becomes clear that women's position *vis-à-vis* literary history is very different from that of their male counterparts. From a feminist perspective, Bloom's model raises more questions than it answers. The question Gilbert and Gubar confront is 'where does a woman writer "fit in" to the overwhelmingly and essentially male literary history Bloom describes?' (p. 48). The answer, of course, is that women do not 'fit in'. And it is this problem which forms the centre of Gilbert and Gubar's discussion of feminist poetics. How do women negotiate their position within (or outside) the male literary tradition? And what is their relationship with their female precursors?

Having established that a woman writer's position in relation to her male precursors is a very different one from that of her male counterpart, Gilbert and Gubar go on to examine the nature of that difference. They describe a man's reaction to his forefathers as an 'anxiety of influence': in order to establish his own position as a writer, he must first do battle with his literary fathers; he must assert his 'authority' over their achievements; his style and subject matter over theirs. They then describe a woman writer's reaction to literary history not as an 'anxiety of influence' but as an 'anxiety of authorship'. Because she has been 'enclosed' by male definitions of herself and her own potential, the woman writer doubts not only what she writes, but her ability to write at all. For twentieth-century women writers, the position is somewhat easier. Gilbert and Gubar suggest that contemporary writers will usually seek out a female precursor in order to overcome the worst effects of the patriarchal literary tradition against which they are defined. However, even in doing so, twentieth-century women must come to terms with the 'anxiety of authorship' imbibed in the writing of their 'motherly precursors'. Gilbert and Gubar argue, therefore, that before any woman can write, she must first come to terms with these male images of herself: 'Before the woman writer can journey through the looking glass toward literary autonomy . . . she must come to terms with the images on the surface of the glass' (p. 16). A woman must therefore struggle against her own socialization, she must 'battle not against her [male] precursor's reading of the world but against his reading of her' (p. 49). Because of this struggle, the 'anxiety of authorship' is, Gilbert and Gubar argue, one of the hallmarks of female creativity. In our reading of *The Color Purple*, we will examine Alice Walker's work in relation to Harriet Beecher Stowe's novel, *Uncle Tom's Cabin*, in an attempt to demonstrate Walker's use of her female precursors, because, as Gilbert and Gubar argue, women will frequently find a female precursor in order to validate their own artistic endeavours. Yet, despite this, Gilbert and Gubar suggest that all women writers are likely to have a negative experience of their own gender, experiencing it as a 'painful obstacle, or even a debilitating inadequacy' (p. 50). Gilbert and Gubar's theory of the 'difference' of women's writing – their 'feminist poetics' – centres on the 'inferiorization' shared by all women writers. Women's creativity is profoundly affected by a variety of factors: their alienation from their male precursors, their need to find their female precursors, their 'dread of the patriarchal authority of art', and inherently 'unfeminine' nature of creativity (p. 50). Gilbert and Gubar stress that whilst positive role models may have helped many contemporary women writers, their eighteenth- and nineteenth-century predecessors had to undertake an enormous struggle in order to overcome their anxiety of authorship. Hence, 'women writers participate in a quite different literary subculture from that inhabited by male writers' (p. 50).

In examining the female literary subculture further, Gilbert and Gubar make a number of observations. Virginia Woolf argued that before women could write they must 'kill' the 'angel in the house' – and, by extension, the angel's opposite – the monster.[13] For, 'whether she is a passive angel or an active monster . . . the woman writer feels herself to be literally or figuratively crippled by the debilitating alternatives her culture offers her' (p. 57). But what Gilbert and Gubar observe is the way in which women frequently 'use and misuse' male literary traditions (p. 80). Far from destroying the male images of themselves, those images of angels and monsters proliferate in writing by women too. Yet the important difference lies in the messages conveyed by their texts:

> Women from Jane Austen and Mary Shelley to Emily Brontë and Emily Dickinson produced literary works that are in some sense palimpsestic, works whose surface designs conceal or obscure deeper, less accessible (and less socially acceptable) levels of meaning. Thus these authors managed the difficult task of achieving true female literary authority by simultaneously conforming to and subverting patriarchal literary standards. (p. 73)

It was in this way women were to overcome their 'anxiety of authorship'. But a further characteristic of their writing has been their obsessive interest in the limited options offered them by society. Gilbert and Gubar thus describe the 'oddity' of women's writing as the result of their struggle to transcend the anxiety of authorship. By working within a male literary tradition, yet working to subvert it, Gilbert and Gubar argue that women are 'enacting a uniquely female process of revision and redefinition that necessarily caused them to seem "odd" ' (p. 73).[14]

One of the most important assertions of Gilbert and Gubar's feminist poetics is that most women's writing contains a hidden story, and that that hidden story represents 'woman's quest for self-definition' (p. 76). They argue that 'in publicly presenting acceptable facades for private and dangerous visions, women writers have long used a wide range of tactics to obscure but not obliterate their most subversive impulses' (p. 74). In ' "The blank page" and the issues of female creativity', Susan Gubar examines one such story. Gubar's article is centred around a discussion of Isak Dinesen's short story, 'The Blank Page'. Gubar summarizes the story thus: a Carmelite order of nuns grow flax to manufacture the most exquisite linen in Portugal. The linen is so fine it is used for bridal sheets in neighbouring royal houses. After the wedding night, the sheet is publicly displayed to attest to the virginity of the princess. It is then reclaimed by the convent where the central piece of stained sheet 'which bore witness to the honour of a royal bride' is mounted, framed and hung in a long gallery with a plate identifying the name of the princess. Female pilgrims who journey to the convent view these sheets. But they are especially interested by one blank, snow white sheet with a nameless plate. Commenting on this story, Gubar makes several points which are pertinent to the ideas behind the feminist poetics she and Gilbert develop in *The Madwoman in the Attic*. One of the most important is the link between female sexuality and textuality. Just as women are imprisoned by male images of themselves in men's writing, so here there is little distinction between the woman and her text: although apparently defiant, this woman, also, has been forced to use her own body in the creation of her 'text' (the 'blank' sheet). Gubar argues that the framed, bloodied sheets in the gallery illustrate two important points about the links between the female anatomy and creativity. The first is that many women experience their own bodies as the only available medium for their art, inheriting that part of a male literary tradition which has focused on women as its primary subject matter.[15] The second is that 'one of the primary and most resonant metaphors provided by the female body is blood' (p. 296). The rationale behind Dinesen's story, then, is that because women have for so long been the passive 'subjects' of texts (figuratively 'killed' into art by male producers) it has been extremely difficult for them to conceptualize their own relationship to creativity in terms other than through their own bodies. The anonymous 'princess' of Dinesen's story, however, like the women writers and artists of former generations has, at least, found a way of writing her body into her text in a newly subversive way. Exploiting the metaphorical pun connecting the bridal sheet with the 'sheet' of paper, Gubar argues that: 'in terms of the patriarchal identification of women with blankness and passivity . . . Dinesen's blank page becomes radically subversive . . . Not a sign of innocence or purity or passivity, this blank page is a mysterious but potent act of resistance' (p. 305). She suggests that the fact that the sheet has been displayed means that the anonymous princess has forced some sort of acknowledgement of her act, of her autonomy. Significantly, the absence of any blood on that sheet on a literal level 'may mean any number of alternative scripts for women' (p. 305). Within Dinesen's story it raises the questions: Was the princess not a virgin? Did she run away and retain her virginity? Was her husband impotent? and so on. Hence, 'the interpretation of the sheet seems as impenetrable as the anonymous princess herself' (p. 305). The story thus becomes a powerful metaphor for all the subversive female-authored texts which have resisted explanation and 'enclosure'.

If we return to *The Madwoman in the Attic*, we can see that there too Gilbert and Gubar focus on women's 'refusal to certify purity' as an essential feature of the female literary tradition. In *The Madwoman in the Attic*, the authors continue to stress the way in which women writers 'have been especially concerned with assaulting and revising, deconstructing and reconstructing those images of [themselves] inherited from male literature . . .' (p. 76). The dual images of angel and monster thus become important as an analogy for the contradiction between the 'publicly acceptable facade' presented by women and their 'private dangerous visions' (p. 74). Through their writing, women express their frustration at the limited roles assigned them by society. Gilbert and Gubar argue that they 'almost obsessively create characters who enact their own, covert authorial anger' (p. 77). By rewriting the monstrous image of themselves created by their male precursors, women thus give expression to feelings central to the female experience.

> It is significant, then, that when the speaker of 'The Other Side of a Mirror' looks into her glass the woman that she sees is a madwoman, 'wild with more than womanly despair', the monster that she fears she really is rather than the angel she has pretended to be. (p. 77).

One story particularly illustrative of Gilbert and Gubar's theory of feminist poetics is Charlotte Perkins Gilman's short story 'The Yellow Wallpaper'.[16] Gilbert and Gubar claim that Gilman's story 'seems to tell *the* story that all literary women would tell if they could speak their "speechless woe" ' (p. 89). The story, written in 1890, describes the experiences of a woman suffering from a 'severe postpartum psychosis', or nervous breakdown. Her husband, who is also her physician, is treating her with methods used by the famous nervous-disorder specialist, S. Weir Mitchell, in treating Gilman herself. He has confined her to a large garret room in an 'ancestral hall' he has rented and forbidden her to read or write until she recovers. The cure worse than the disease, the protagonist's condition can only decline. She comments that she feels it would help her to write something, but locked away in a room that was once a nursery 'she is literally locked away from creativity' (MW, p. 90).

The most important feature of the nursery room is its wallpaper: sickly yellow paper with an asymmetric pattern which both disgusts and fascinates the woman. Gilbert and Gubar suggest that the paper 'surrounds the narrator like an inexplicable text, censorious and overwhelming as her physician husband, haunting as the "hereditary estate" in which she is trying to survive' (p. 90). Underneath the pattern there lies a further formation: the wall-paper is barred, and trapped behind these bars is a woman desperate to escape. Gilbert and Gubar suggest that the figure is 'concealed behind what corresponds . . . to the facade of the patriarchal text'. They argue that as the narrator 'sinks more deeply into what the world calls madness', the 'terrifying implications' of both the figure and the wallpaper begin to haunt the ancestral mansion. The 'yellow smell' of the paper begins to permeate the whole house and so too the trapped woman begins to creep through the house into the garden and along the road (p. 90). Gilbert and Gubar then propose that the figure creeping behind the wallpaper 'is both the narrator and the narrator's double' (p. 91). By the end of the story, the narrator facilitates the figure's escape from behind the wallpaper – her escape from her 'textual/architectural confinement'. And Gilbert and Gubar stress that there is clearly more to the tale than mere madness. 'More significant are the madwoman's own imagining and creations, mirages of health and freedom with which her author endows her like a fairy godmother showering gold on a sleeping heroine' (p. 91). The figure from behind the wallpaper creeps away to freedom. The protagonist notes 'I have watched her sometimes a way off in the open country creeping as fast as a cloud shadow in a high wind'. Gilbert and Gubar compare the movement of that cloud with 'the progress of nineteenth-century literary women out of the texts defined by patriarchal poetics into the open spaces of their own authority' (p. 91). For the woman writer, and for Gilman in particular, it represents the 'flight from disease into health' (p. 91).[17]

According to Gilbert and Gubar, Gilman's story exemplifies the spirit of rebellion that may be found linking author and character in much women's writing. Just as Gilman's protagonist and her trapped double express Gilman's own frustration and anger at the ways in which patriarchy stifles women's creativity, so, too, do many other women writers 'reflect the literal reality of their own confinement. Recording their own distinctively female experience, they are secretly working through and within the conventions of literary texts to define their own lives' (p. 87). This somewhat problematic conflation of author and character, then, together with a focus on the way women writers have rewritten the traditional female stereotypes of English literature, are Gilbert and Gubar's primary means of arguing for the 'difference' of women's writing. Although positioned at an even greater disadvantage than their male contemporaries, women writers can be seen to have fought – and won – their own battles with the patriarchal authority of the 'precursor text' and, in so doing, established their own, alternative female literary tradition. One final feature of Gilbert and Gubar's textual practice that readers should be alerted to is their rhetorical mode. Like Millett, both writers are great stylists, and summarizing their arguments as we do here cannot do justice to the energy and flamboyance with which they present their material. Despite their great length (and *The Madwoman in the Attic* is, itself, a text of epic proportions!) the chapters on the work of the Brontës, Elizabeth Barrett Browning and Mary Shelley are compulsive reading, often rivalling the original texts in their narrative suspense.

II

Sandra Gilbert and Susan Gubar focus their attention on nineteenth-century women writers, for whom, they suggest, the 'anxiety of authorship' is particularly acute. *The Madwoman in the Attic* contains a number of readings of nineteenth-century novels by women. In each reading, they demonstrate the way in which the female author has 'used and misused' male literary traditions. If we turn to Angela Carter's novel, *The Magic Toyshop*, it is quite possible to work a similar analysis, despite the fact that the novel, whose first publication date was 1967, falls outside the period studied by Gilbert and Gubar.[18] Angela Carter almost certainly uses male writing strategies more self-consciously than her nineteenth-century precursors. She writes:

> Reading is just as creative an activity as writing and most intellectual development depends on new readings of old texts. I am all for putting new wine in old bottles, especially if the pressure of the new wine makes the old bottles explode.[19]

The notion of 'putting new wine in old bottles' is clearly analogous with Gilbert and Gubar's idea that women enact 'a uniquely female process of revision and redefinition' (MW, p. 73) and that they are 'especially concerned with assaulting and revising, deconstructing and reconstructing those images of women inherited from male literature' (MW, p. 76).

Angela Carter has described herself as being in the 'demythologizing business' (NFL, p. 70). Many of her novels, especially her early novels, including *The Magic Toyshop*, are steeped in mythology, and have a strong psychoanalytic bent. Carter has suggested that 'the literary past, the myth and folklore and so on, are a vast repository of outmoded lies' (p. 74). In other words, they serve to reinforce existing patriarchal structures. Paulina Palmer argues that Carter, in *The Magic Toyshop*, uses mythology and psychoanalytic materials to 'represent the self-perpetuating and closed nature of patriarchal structures and institutions'.[20] To a large extent, then, Carter is using the tools of a male literary tradition in order to represent woman's imprisonment within that patriarchal structure. She attempts to subvert traditional patriarchal themes and imagery in fairly subtle and covert ways.[21]

The novel can be compared in a variety of ways with the nineteenth-century stories of 'enclosure and escape' discussed by Gilbert and Gubar. The setting itself resembles the confines of Bluebeard's castle, an impression reinforced when Melanie discovers a severed hand in the kitchen drawer. The 15-year-old girl's first sighting of the house and shop places it firmly in a nightmare world of myth and folklore.

> Between a failed, boarded-up jewellers and a grocer's . . . was a dark cavern of a shop, so dimly lit one did not at first notice it as it bowed its head under the tenement above. In the cave could be seen the vague outlines of a rocking horse and the sharper scarlet of its flaming nostrils . . . (p. 39)

Here Melanie, like her Aunt Margaret, is to remain trapped, notching off the weeks by the appearance of the green banded china each Sunday, and on Monday wishing she could use the little bridge on her willow-patterned plate to 'run away from her Uncle Philip's house to where the flowering trees were' (p. 74). And not only are Melanie and Margaret physically trapped: they are also spiritually trapped into conventional female roles.

The most significant image in *The Magic Toyshop* is that of the puppet, an image especially pertinent to a feminist analysis of the novel. Within the power structure of the toyshop, women's position is equal to that of the puppets. Uncle Philip, the toymaker, takes on the role of a particularly despotic patriarch, whilst Melanie, his orphaned niece, and Margaret, his wife, are reduced to positions of terrified powerlessness whenever he is present (and usually when he is not). In addition, throughout the novel visual images of the women are particularly important. In the opening section, before the death of her parents, Melanie spends hours posing in front of the mirror:

> She also posed in attitudes, holding things. Pre-Raphaelite, she combed out her long, black hair . . . *A la* Toulouse Lautrec, she dragged her hair sluttishly across her face . . . she contrived a pale smug Cranach Venus with a bit of net curtain . . . After she read *Lady Chatterley's Lover*, she secretly picked forget-me-nots and stuck them in her pubic hair. (p. 2)

Significantly, the poses she takes up are derived from male images of women. Her subjectivity has been shaped by those images. The novel traces Melanie's awakening sexuality along with her adolescent yearnings: 'Since she was 13 when her periods began, she felt she was pregnant with herself bearing the slowing ripening embryo of Melanie-grown-up inside herself for a gestation time the length of which she was precisely not aware' (p. 20). Although her quest for self-definition is at the centre of the novel, it may thus be seen that it is strictly limited by the roles and potential assigned to her by her cultural heritage, her socialization and the overbearingly patriarchal world she inhabits. Looking into the mirror, the images she sees are those previously inscribed there by male authors, painters and women's magazine writers. The boundaries of Melanie's adolescent imaginings are thus marked by thoughts of her future roles as lover, wife and mother.

Immediately she enters the confines of her uncle's house, Melanie's loss of autonomy becomes apparent. Recognizing her powerlessness, she feels herself to be like one of her uncle's puppets: 'She was a wind-up putting-away doll, clicking through its programmed movements. Uncle Philip might have made her over, already. She was without volition of her own' (p. 76). Her feelings of powerlessness intensify, in relation to both her Uncle Philip and her cousin Finn. She no longer has a mirror in which to see herself, a further factor contributing to her loss of subjectivity: 'She was seized with panic, remembering that she had not seen her own face for so long' (p. 103). Control of her identity is taken over by Finn and Uncle Philip. She begins to see herself as she is seen by others. Discovering the spy-hole into her room from Finn's, she realizes that 'all the time, someone was watching her' (p. 109). Later, she sees the picture Finn has painted of her through the spy-hole, undressing: an image of an idealized, pale, pure virginal girl, which is how he sees her and 'not precisely as she saw herself' (p. 154). She recognizes herself, uncannily, in one of her uncle's toys on her first day in the shop: 'a sylphide in a fountain of white tulle. She had long, black hair down to the waist of her tight bodice' (p. 67). Finally, she must literally fit the image Uncle Philip has of her, forced to take part in one of his puppet shows alongside his puppets. He complains: ' "I wanted my Leda to be a little girl. Your tits are too big" ' (p. 143). Melanie is thus denied her own sexuality. She must take on the role of angel: passive and virginal.

Examining the 'cultural production of femininity', Palmer states that Carter focuses on 'one of the roles conventionally allocated to woman in a patriarchal culture – object of exchange' (p. 183). Within the patriarchal social order, women become tokens in the battle for power between men. The patriarchal world of the toy-shop is essentially violent. Uncle Philip himself exudes violence: 'His authority was stifling', 'His size shocked her . . .', 'How could she, Melanie, have ever guessed that her Uncle would be a monster with a voice so loud she was afraid it would bring the roof down and bury them all?' (p. 77). Carter's analysis of the struggle for power between the younger male, Finn, and the older patriarch is clearly Freudian: Finn undertakes an Oedipal struggle in an attempt to displace Uncle Philip's authority. The struggle is inherently violent, culminating in Philip angrily sending Finn crashing down onto the stage from the heights of the puppet theatre during one of his performances. But the most important manifestation of male violence is in relation to women and particularly in acts of sexual violence.

Melanie becomes the 'object of exchange' in the power struggle between Philip and Finn. Throughout the novel, there are a number of 'rape' scenes and violent sexual acts. One of Melanie's first encounters with Finn is heavy with sexual overtones. 'She could see the pointed tip of his tongue between his teeth' (p. 45), and she is immediately aware of the predatory threat encapsulated in his maleness: 'He was a tawny lion poised for the kill – and was she the prey?' On both this occasion and later in the pleasure garden when Finn first kisses her, Melanie's romantic notions of heterosexual love rapidly vanish in the face of the harsh reality of the inherently destructive nature of male sexual desire: 'She remembered the lover made up out of books and poems she had dreamed of all summer; he crumpled like the paper he was made of before this insolent, off-hand, terrifying maleness, filling the room with its reek' (p. 45).

The scene in the pleasure garden is indeed a 'rape' scene, during which Finn's sexual desire is clearly part and parcel of his desire to submit Melanie entirely to his will. Her reaction, far from sexual arousal, is one of disgust and horror:

> Finn inserted his tongue between her lips, searching tentatively for her own tongue inside her mouth. The moment consumed her. She choked and struggled, beating her fists against him, convulsed with horror at this sensual and intimate connection, this rude encroachment on her physical privacy, this humiliation. (p. 106)

The final, and most outrageous, 'rape' occurs in Uncle Philip's performance of 'Leda and the Swan'. This is preceded by the 'rehearsal' which Philip suggests Finn should carry out with Melanie. Carter's use of the 'Leda and the Swan' story once again demonstrates her awareness of mythology's role in reinforcing patriarchal structures and the conventional relationship between the sexes. In accordance with the female literary tradition outlined by Gilbert and Gubar, Carter reworks patriarchal mythology in order to illustrate her female character's repression. In the two Leda scenes – the rehearsal and the final performance – both the men participate in attempts to 'rape' Melanie. During the first of these, where Finn takes the part of the swan, Melanie awaits Finn's action passively, with bated breath, emotionless and utterly subdued: 'They lay together on the bare, splintered boards. There was no time any more. And no Melanie, either' (p. 149). It is Finn who prevents intercourse taking place; significantly not out of consideration for Melanie, but because of his realization that Uncle Philip has orchestrated the whole situation: it is his will that he, Finn, should rape Melanie. 'He's pulled our strings as if we were his puppets, and there I was, all ready to touch you up just as he wanted' (p. 152). The sexual act is thus even further removed from Melanie's wild romantic imaginings. She is once again forced to shift her level of consciousness to acknowledge that Finn's act would have been one of power and violence, not one of love and tenderness. She is forced to accept his displacement of her notion of 'making love' with the aggressive act of 'fucking'.

The second 'Leda' scene is even more violent, symbolizing Uncle Philip's continuing position as the supreme patriarch. The swan he has created, whilst absurd and cumbersome, is also terrifyingly phallic with its 'long neck made of rubber' which 'bent and swayed with an unnerving life of its own' (p. 167). Melanie is indeed subsumed by the huge swan which 'made a lumpish jump forward and settled on her loins . . . The gilded beak dug deeply into the soft flesh . . . The obscene swan had mounted her' (p. 167). In further defiance of Philip,

Finn destroys the swan during the night. Melanie's position is thus a contradictory one. Whilst she feels superior to Finn and repulsed by him, she is also grateful for the protection he offers her from her uncle. As Paulina Palmer points out: 'As is typical of woman in patriarchal society, she is pressured to seek refuge from one man in the arms of another' (p. 187). Melanie thus gradually resigns herself to the prospect of sex and marriage with Finn; she accepts the roles of lover, wife and mother assigned her by society. Melanie's enclosure within patriarchal structures is thus complete, and Finn has finally 'won' her from his Uncle Philip. In Carter's vision of this patriarchal nightmare world, it would appear that there is no escape.

> She knew they would get married one day and live together all their lives and there would always be pervasive squalor and dirt and mess and shabbiness, always, forever and forever. And babies crying and washing to be done and toast burning all the rest of her life. And never any glamour or romance or charm. (p. 177)

But finally, we must turn our attention to the second woman in the novel: Philip's wife, Margaret. Margaret's position is an important one in Carter's analysis of women's submissiveness in the face of men's assertive power. The metaphor of the puppet as a representation of women's powerlessness is at its height in Margaret, for she – like Philip's puppets – is dumb. Margaret thus epitomizes woman's position in the patriarchal social order. In Susan Gubar's words, she is 'a tabula, a rasa, a lack, a negation, an absence' (p. 306). To an even greater extent than Melanie, it would appear that Margaret lost her subjectivity and her autonomy the day she entered her life with Philip, at which point she also lost her voice. More completely than Melanie, she appears to submit to Philip's authority. Dressed in the 'ultimately dejected and miserable grey dress' which Melanie decides Philip must have chosen for her, Margaret is crushed by his presence, 'frail as a pressed flower' she 'seemed too cowed by his presence even to look at him' (p. 73). His only communication with Margaret is 'to bark brusque commands' (p. 124) and his satisfaction in her submissiveness reaches its height when, on Sundays, she wears the stiff, silver collar he has made for her. 'The necklace was a collar of dull silver, two hinged silver pieces knobbed with moonstones which snapped into place around her lean neck and rose up almost to her chin so that she could hardly move her head' (p. 112). The collar makes it difficult for Margaret to eat, but increases Philip's appetite as he '[gazes] at her with expressionless satisfaction' (p. 113). Just as he expresses displeasure at Melanie's sexual being – her periods and her breasts – so too he does his utmost to stifle Margaret's sexuality and physicality, reducing her literally to the state of her replica in his puppet theatre.

Yet Margaret's silence represents more than her submission to patriarchal authority. Following the Gilbert and Gubar model, it is in Margaret that we should perhaps identify Carter's 'double', her 'covert authorial rage'. Like Bertha, the madwoman in the attic in *Jane Eyre*, it is Margaret who finally challenges the patriarchal order depicted in the novel. And, like Bertha, it is Margaret who is responsible for the fire which destroys the toy shop in the closing scene. Just as in Susan Gubar's analysis of Dinesen's story 'The Blank Page', blankness was shown as 'an act of defiance', so Margaret's silence hides her secret and her ultimate defiance of Philip's authority. From her first night at the toy shop, when she discovers Margaret and her two brothers playing Irish music and dancing in the kitchen, Melanie recognizes the vitality of her Irish relatives which seems to survive even the oppressive atmosphere of her uncle's house. They are 'the red people' who, through their magical qualities, are able to ward off the pervasive evil spirits of the patriarchal world. 'Not four but three angels . . . All the red people lighting a bonfire for her, to frighten away the wolves and tigers of this dreadful forest in which she lived' (p. 112). The spirit they uphold represents a challenge to Uncle Philip's patriarchal control. Through their secret music-making, they retain their own autonomy and creativity. But the 'red people' also have demonic qualities, exactly those qualities which Gilbert and Gubar suggest that men associate with women's 'otherness', and which are linked to women's 'speech': 'in patriarchal culture, female speech and female presumption – that is angry revolt against male domination – are inextricably linked and inevitably daemonic' (MW, p. 35). So Carter, too, links Margaret's defiance of her husband with the male literary images of female anger. Finn's picture of Uncle Philip represents him burning in hell. And the final scene of the novel is of the flames of the burning toyshop as Margaret and her brother Francie are shown about to murder Philip with an iron bar. But before this final scene, the secret behind Margaret's silence is revealed as Melanie and the reader are told of her incestuous relationship with Francie. The relationship is her ultimate defiance of her husband's authority and the rigid, patriarchal structures he upholds; her greatest act of autonomy. Just as 'the blank page contains all story in no story', so Margaret's silence 'contains all potential sound' (BP, p. 305). And at the point when Philip finds her in her lover's arms and discovers her secret, Margaret's voice returns, together with the will to destroy the ogre who has ruled her life: 'Struck dumb on her wedding day, she found her old voice again the day she was freed' (Carter/*The Magic Toyshop*, p. 197). Whilst Melanie's escape from the burning house throws her conclusively into her future life with Finn and the implied roles of wife and mother, the novel leaves us guessing as to Margaret's future. What is certain, however, is that she escapes from Philip's despotic rule, either through death in the fire which also destroys him, or into unhindered future autonomy and the choice to live openly with the man she loves.

Like her nineteenth-century predecessors, then, Angela Carter's novel is 'marked not only by an obsessive interest in [the] limited options' available to women – writers included – but also by the 'obsessive imagery of confinement' used by many female artists, revealing the ways in which they 'feel trapped and sickened both by suffocating alternatives and by the culture that created them' (MW, p. 64). Carter, too, analyzes women's position by revising male genres, including material from mythology and psychoanalysis. In many respects, *The Magic Toyshop* conforms to patriarchal literary standards. Significantly, Carter uses her female character's silence – a characteristic traditionally identified with women by patriarchy – to subvert those literary standards. This technique is echoed in the French feminist critics who take up the Lacanian concept of the 'lack' as the most significant feature of female creativity.[22] Like Dinesen's blank page, Carter's use of Margaret's silence is 'not a sign of innocence or purity or passivity: it is 'a mysterious but potent act of resistance' (BP, p. 305). Thus, in a subtle and covert way, Carter challenges the patriarchal social order she has represented.

In *The Madwoman in the Attic* Gilbert and Gubar suggest that Milton's *Paradise Lost* is the dominant literary precursor of nineteenth-century fiction and Milton, himself, a literary father figure from which, like Satan, the daughter must rebel. This view informs their reading of *Wuthering Heights*:

> The sum of this [*Wuthering Heights*] novel's visionary parts is an almost shocking revisionary whole. Heaven (or its rejection), hell, Satan, a fall, mystical politics, metaphysical romance, orphanhood and the question of origins – disparate as some of these matters may seem, they all cohere in a rebelliously topsy-turvy retelling of Milton's and Western Culture's central tale of the fall of woman and her shadow self, Satan. (p. 255)[23]

In attempting now to use their strategies of detecting the female process of revision and redefinition of woman's self-image in nineteenth-century literature, and applying it to a reading of a twentieth-century Black woman's novel, *The Color Purple*, it seems important to locate a similarly powerful cultural precursor for Alice Walker.[24]

We have shown how Gilbert and Gubar's central argument is that a female tradition of writing developed in the nineteenth century, largely in response to a patriarchal literary order. However, we have further argued that by the 1980s a more autonomous women's tradition has to be taken into account. Important too, as Cora Kaplan has argued in her essay, 'Keeping the color in *The Color Purple*', is to acknowledge that American literature is the product of a very different culture with an independent literary tradition and markedly different history of racial conflict. Kaplan suggests that Walker must be considered a writer 'explicitly in resistance to existing fictions and politics', particularly white and Black Southern fictions, in order to understand how 'her critique and reconstruction of "family", "community" and "femininity" has been made'.[25] Gilbert and Gubar identify Milton as the most powerful mythologizer of patriarchal values from which nineteenth-century writers seek emancipation. In considering the literary precursors of Alice Walker's story of Black family relationships, Harriet Beecher Stowe's *Uncle Tom's Cabin* (1852) will be the text we shall take as of central importance as a precursor. It is a text which James Baldwin has described as a 'cornerstone of American protest fiction'.[26] The story concerns a noble-hearted and deeply religious slave who is sold by the kindly Shelby family when they experience financial setbacks. He is separated from his wife and children and though at first is bought by an idealistic master, indebted to him for saving the life of his little daughter, Eva, he is forced by their deaths into the hands of a brutal plantation owner, Simon Legree, who beats him to death for concealing the whereabouts of two female runaway slaves. Particularly in its emphasis on the interdependence of family and religious values which are embedded in a glorification of passive suffering and self-sacrificing domesticity, it provides themes which are taken up and transformed in Walker's revisionary work.

In their essay on George Eliot, Gilbert and Gubar identify Stowe as an important, if marginalized, alternative to the central female tradition, emphasizing the strategy of 'feminine receptivity and nurturance', that enabled her to solve the 'anxiety of authorship' by 'excluding any portrait of herself from the fictional world she created' (MW, p. 483). Later critics, however, have seen an image of self in the central character of Tom, who shares all the characteristics of the vapid, self-abnegating, Victorian heroine. Stowe's novel, as Baldwin stresses, is as concerned as Milton's epic with questions of heaven and hell, damnation and salvation. Stowe's narrative of Black slaves, he suggests, is not a story of individuals, but of symbols or touchstones by which to measure the white community's humanity. In order to win our sympathies, Baldwin continues, the Black characters, George and Eliza, are 'as white as she can make them', bleached to an acceptable 'coloured' appearance or, if outwardly Black or woolly-haired like Tom, so 'phenomenally forbearing' that he is 'robbed of his humanity and divested of his sex' (p. 12). Tom's case is permitted to wring the hearts of white readers because, though Black, he earns redemption through suffering. Blackness, Baldwin argues, is construed as the shadow that lies athwart (American) national life. If, as Gilbert and Gubar claim, Milton's misogyny is a mythology that nineteenth-century writers 'covertly reappraise and repudiate by misreading and revising the story of woman's fall' (p. 80), it is the far more overwhelming equation of Black with suffering and damnation that is at the heart of *Uncle Tom's Cabin*. For Stowe the slaves, like souls in hell, have been damned in order that they might be saved and to point others the way to salvation. Significantly, after the self-sacrificing death of Tom, the other slaves escape to Africa to become missionaries, redeeming themselves by converting others to the white man's God, an irony that is picked up and reversed in Nettie's account of the missionary worker she encounters on her journey back from Africa in *The Color Purple* (p. 195).

The reader's 'love' of Uncle Tom is dependent on his protection of both the saintly Little Eva and the runaway female slaves, Cassie and Emmeline, which involves a total abnegation of self. The obverse of this saintliness is, suggests Baldwin, figured in the demonical figure of Biggar Thomas, Richard Wright's rapist and murderer, who, in his acceptance of his own dehumanization, is Uncle Tom's mirror image, a way of expressing the author's rage.[27] The image of the 'nigger' in white American literature has undergone the same polarization into saint and monster that Gilbert and Gubar uncovered in the male images of women. Just as a masculine fear of female procreation spawned the monstrous breeding goddesses of 'Death', 'Errour' and 'Sin' in Spenser's *The Faerie Queene* (MW, pp. 33–6), so white male fear of Black male sexuality has created the emasculated Tom or sub-human Biggar. Toni Morrison has also shown the results of the internalization of this process of dehumanization vividly in her acclaimed novel, *Beloved*.[28] Here, a runaway slave has butchered her own small daughter rather than have her recaptured and grow up in slavery. Witness to the horror of her desperate act, the slavemaster's thoughts run on the animal nature of the slaves:

> See what happened when you overbeat creatures God had given you responsibility of – the trouble it was and the loss. He could claim the baby but who would tend her? Because the woman – something was wrong with her. She was looking at him now, and if his nephew (who was responsible for the beating) could see that look he would learn that lesson for sure: you can't just mishandle creatures and expect success. (Morrison/*Beloved*, p. 150)

His last dismissive thought completes the denial of a common humanity to Black people: 'All testimony to the results of a little so-called freedom imposed on people who needed every care and guidance in the world to keep them from the cannibal life they preferred' (Morrison/*Beloved*, p. 151).

The Color Purple can be read in terms of Gilbert and Gubar's definition of women as revisers of traditional themes, as well as an interrogation of the damaging images imposed on Black family relationships by white Americans which have been reinforced by the evangelical fervour of *Uncle Tom's Cabin*. If the Black women in Stowe's domestic economy are protected from the worst excesses of white exploitation by the interventions of the kindly patriarch, Tom, the obverse is the case in *The Color Purple*. White characters feature in the story and have the power to do enormous damage, as in the oppression of Sophia by the mayor and his wife, but it is, as Celie points out, the fault of Harpo, her husband, that she is trapped into service: 'Oh hold on, hell, I say. If you [Harpo] hadn't tried to rule over Sophia, the white folks would never have caught her. Sophia is so surprised to hear me speak up she aint chewed for ten minutes./ That's a lie, say Harpo./ A little truth in it, says Sophia' (p. 170). In the event, the white characters' ineffectual dependence on the competent domesticity of their Black servants is set against Sophia's suffering. The myth of the happy house slave willingly dedicating herself to the care of the young master or mistress is ironically mocked in Sophia's final rejection of Miss Eleanor Jane: ' "I love children", say Sophia. "But all the colored women that say they love yours is lying. They don't love Reynolds Stanley anymore than I do . . . some colored folk so scared of white-folks they claim to love the cotton gin" ' (p. 225).

Rather than protect the women from white oppression, it is the Black men in the novel who exploit and abuse them, whether they are fathers, brothers, husbands or lovers. Celie, whose story is confided in letters to God, has been raped at 14 by the man she supposes to be her father and passed on, as damaged goods, to Mr —, whose sole concern is to find a drudge for the house and a 'mother' for his children. Pa recommends her usefulness to him: 'She ugly, Don't even look like she kin to Nettie but she make the better wife. She ain't smart either and you better watch her or she give away everything you own. But she can work like a man' (p. 9). Celie is the author's embodiment of a worthless female self: made monstrous through both her ugliness and the horror of her circumstances. Both the incestuous conception and loss of her children is the source of crushing guilt and loss of self-esteem. She accepts her oppression by her father and her husband because she is convinced she is worthless. She is unable to confide the horrors of her situation to anyone except God, whom she describes later in the novel to Shug Avery as 'big and old and graybearded and white. He wear white robes and go barefooted' (p. 168). Celie's self-denial, dutiful forbearance and domestic virtue are every bit as striking and angelic as those of Uncle Tom. These traits leave her defenceless because her anger has been suppressed as part of her learned Christian dutifulness:

> I can't even remember the last time I felt mad, I say. I used to get mad at my mama cause she put a lot of work on me. Then I see how sick she is. Couldn't stay mad at her. Couldn't be mad at my daddy cause he my daddy. Bible say, Honor father and mother no matter what. Then after a while every time I got mad, or start to feel mad, I got sick. Felt like throwing up. Then I start feeling nothing at all. (p. 39)

In every aspect of her life she is at the mercy of Mr —. Imprisoned in domesticity she is powerless to protect herself even from his children:

> Mr — children all bright but they mean. They say Celie, I want dis and Celie, I want dat. Our Mama let us have it. They try to get his attention he hide behind a puff of smoke./ Don't let them run over you, Nettie say. You got to let them know who got the upper hand./ They got it, I say./ But she keep on. You got to fight. But I don't know how to fight. All I know to do is to stay alive. (p. 17)

In her passivity Celie is the ideal housewife, married to the home (a feature brought out most strikingly in the Steven Spielberg film adaptation, where Celie's very presence in the house converts it from chaos to harmonious cleanliness and domestic comfort). She is compared favourably by Mr —'s sisters with their brother's first wife who neglected all such domestic duties. The latter, described by one sister as a slattern, is the reverse image of Celie's goodness: the monstrous projection of Alice Walker's suppressed rage directed at domesticity. She makes it very clear who is to blame for the state of the hovel in Mr —'s sisters' antithetical scoldings:

> And cook, she wouldn't cook. She act like she never seen a kitchen./ She hadn't never seen his./ Was a scandal, say Carrie./ He sure was, say Kate./ What you mean, say Carrie./ I mean he just brought her here, dropped her, and kept on running after Shug Avery. That what mean. Nobody to talk to, nobody to visit. He be gone for days. Then she start having babies and she young and pretty. (p. 19)

Child-bearing is, for the monstrous female horrors (Errour and Sin) created by Spenser and Milton and cited by Gilbert and Gubar as fearful images of the mother, either a curse or cause of suffering which none of the female characters can control (p. 33). To be the 'angel in the house' under these circumstances is shown to be truly monstrous, the projection of self-loathing in response to powerlessness in which the victim acquiesces. In its scornful treatment of Celie's dutiful housekeeping, *The Color Purple* revises the domestic road to salvation that is the 'message' of *Uncle Tom's Cabin*, where, as Gilbert and Gubar point out, 'Christian love resides especially in the powerless' and the female traits of domesticity and self-sacrifice bring eternal life (p. 482). The passive virtues of domesticity are rejected in the novel as a self-inflicted burden, reinforced by the laws of an unsympathetic white man's god who shows no signs of responding to Celie's outpourings despite her uncomplaining goodness. For Alice Walker, the oppressive nature of domesticity is located in the Black woman's subservience to men: a state which is far more crushing than Sophia's relationship with the white racists, because it is less identifiable as oppression. Left to themselves and free to come and go as they please, Shug and Celie transform the suffocating nature of 'woman's work and woman's world' into something more creative:

> Us talk about houses a lot. How they built, what kind of wood people use. Talk about how to make the outside of your house something you can use. I sit down on the bed and draw a kind of concrete skirt. You can sit on this I say, when you get tired of sitting in the house. (p. 178)

In a further process of self-definition, Alice Walker has revised the traditional roles of monster/slattern, and angel/housekeeper to create a new perspective. If, for white culture, the binary division of whore and madonna casts a baleful influence on how women imagine themselves, the split is far more insistent in the contrast of pious downtrodden motherhood embodied in the Black 'mammy' figure, familiar to us, if not from fiction, then from numerous Bette Davis films (where doting Black servants alternately coax and scold recalcitrant Southern belles) and the scandalous figure of the sexually available Black female blues singer who, it is implied, can only make her way by whoring as well as singing. In Stowe's 'protest novel', the route traced for emancipation is through self-denial and submission; in *The Color Purple* the liberated, non-conformist Shug Avery embodies the transgressive qualities associated with the female siren. She is, however, at one and the same time Albert's mistress and Celie's mother/lover and in her polymorphous ambiguous sexuality is made to embody all that might be accounted 'demonic' in the asexual evangelical world of *Uncle Tom's Cabin*.

Shug is emblematic of the sexual identity repressed in Celie whose experiences of marriage is of a degrading and loveless 'fucking'. However, Shug is very unlike the madwomen and ghost figures that Gilbert and Gubar have identified as the repressed sexual psyches of nineteenth-century heroines. In fact, she is a reversal of the whole angel/monster dichotomy. For Celie, domesticity brings disappointment and suffering, but Shug transforms everything, including housekeeping, through her warm, sweet sexuality that is both sensuous and maternal at the same time. She is the Queen Honeybee of her nickname even though the good women of the community find her scandalous: 'Her mammy say she told her so. Her pappy say, Tramp . . . the preacher . . . talk about slut, hussy, heifer and street cleaner' (p. 40). Celie and Shug's well-being seem interdependent. Neglect of domestic virtue brings Shug to Mr — on the point of death. Celie's submissive repression of her sexual needs deny her any life of her own. Celie's domesticity rehabilitates both Albert and Shug, while Shug's warm sensuality transforms each of the married pair. In the final pages of the story the three are shown living as a single unit: Shug as a kind of benign Heathcliff figure, taken into the home, rather as if Edgar Linton had consented to share Catherine Earnshaw with his rival. Alice Walker has worked to reconcile the opposition between mistress as sexual object and wife as domestic chattel through the enactment of sexual awakening in which polymorphous perversity (a non-focused, pre-genital sexuality) reactivates Celie's childhood longings, enabling her to reconnect her sexuality with comfort and pleasure and allowing the catharsis of all past abuses:

> My mama die, I tell Shug. My sister run away. Mr — come git me to take care of his rotten children. He never ast me nothing about myself. He clam on top of me and fuck and fuck, even when my head bandaged. Nobody ever love me I say. She say I love you Miss Celie. And then she haul off and kiss me on the mouth . . . Then I feel something real soft and wet on my breast, feel like one of my little lost babies mouth./ Way after a while I act like a little lost baby too. (p. 97)

Apart from Celie and Shug, there are, of course, other women in the story who challenge and subvert the traditional polarization of female characters into angels or monsters. Sophia's quest for independence is to confront her oppressor directly: 'You ought to bash Mr — head open, she say. Think about heaven later' (p. 39). Yet Sophia's physical resistance, however awe-inspiring, results only in separation and loss. Celie's sister, Nettie, meanwhile, provides a full-blown evangelical alternative to domestic submission. Her letters from Africa offer a further challenge to the version of salvation that has been handed to the Black races by a European church, and they question the easy assumption of an African identity's power to liberate. The movement out of Africa that is the solution to Harriet Beecher Stowe's story is reversed in the homecoming of Nettie, her children and Tashi, the Olinka girl.

In conclusion, then, it is quite possible to argue that Alice Walker has turned the abolitionist's novel on its head, finding an evangelical celebration of self that denies the necessity for sacrifice and locates salvation in sisterhood and co-operation; husband, wife and their common lover stitching pants together. This is sentimental perhaps – even utopian – but it is nevertheless a text which widens the possibility for change in the representation of Black women.

Like the nineteenth-century novels examined by Gilbert and Gubar,

Alice Walker's interrogation of a split female subject uses the dichotomy of angel and monster, archetypes of male Western culture, in a quest for an emancipated self. Unlike the nineteenth-century novel, however, Walker makes fewer concessions to convention in the final resolution of her story and the rebellion is an overt, rather than a covert one. 'Black women write against the erosion and repression of female sexuality as it is channelled by male desire', writes Susan Willis in her discussion of Black women writers.[29] They also write against the double constraints of race and gender and a criticism that concentrates on locating a *female* tradition can only obscure the former.

Gilbert and Gubar's criticism locates recurrent themes and images in the writing of women, noting how they were surprised by the coherence of theme and imagery that they encountered in the works of writers who were often geographically, historically and psychologically distant from each other. They use this unity to identify a distinctive female literary tradition, and in reading *The Color Purple* from such a perspective it is possible to concentrate attention on images of passivity, imprisonment, silence and disenfranchisement – together with the radical inversion of these images – as an expression of the author's own covert rage and revenge. This focus on the representation of individual characters nevertheless obscures the Black *community's* experience of memories of slavery and disenfranchisement; and this 'transhistorical and essentialist' reading may, as Cora Kaplan has indicated, lead us to 'teaching and thinking about these texts through an unintentionally imperialist lens, conflating their progressive politics with our own agendas, interpreting their versions of humanism through the historical evolution of our own' (p. 177). It is to this and other problems that we now turn in the concluding section.

III

The main limitation, then, with Gilbert and Gubar's mode of analysis is that it appears to assume a universal archetypal female subject which ignores the changing modes of femininity which become possible at particular historical moments. Thus, Angela Carter, a white English woman writing fiction set in the late 1950s/early 1960s, is made to share the same female literary tradition as Alice Walker – a Black American writer dealing with post-slavery in the American South. Not only this: they would be assumed to be placed in relation to the same literary precursors. This is obviously such a preposterous undertaking that in order to facilitate our own reading of Alice Walker we chose to substitute Beecher Stowe for Milton as Walker's 'authority of influence' because American literature clearly partakes of a different tradition from English literature. We were able to focus on the features in *The Color Purple* that seemed specific to the writing of a Black American only by shifting ground and finding a suitable precursor text. Gilbert and Gubar's prioritization of Milton in the writing of women makes a watertight argument for oppressive patriarchy, but in effect it imposes a specific frame that moves into a metaphysics of heaven and hell and removes them from a specific historical context. For example, reading Celie's 'ugliness' as a dramatic reversal of the image of the angel in the house, we ignore the specificity of Western social conditioning which works to deny Black women a self-image of physical attractiveness.

Following Gilbert and Gubar's theory of how female authors have sublimated their creative frustrations in the characters of 'monstrous women', the conflation of author with character can at first be seen as superficially attractive: Angela Carter has equated Melanie's adolescent yearnings with her own and Alice Walker claims to be the 'medium' through which Celie and the other characters speak.[30] It would also be possible to argue for the authors' (secret) doubles in the characters of silent Aunt Margaret and sexually liberated Shug Avery. This stance nevertheless reinforces the male critics' assumption of a qualitative difference in the writing of men and women and reduces women's stories to a single narrative of anger and entrapment. Further, there is a contradiction in setting up the female author as the transcendental signified of her text whilst attempting to take a stand against patriarchal authority.[31] In our own reading we were forced to discard the simple analogy of author and character. We were able to adopt a psychoanalytical framework to position these women writers against a male literary tradition, and to seek out the common themes which might place them in a female tradition. But what was omitted was any attempt to use these themes to discuss the psychological states of the authors.

In their discussion of the psychodynamics of female creativity, Gilbert and Gubar make no distinction between female nature and the process that determines the social nature of female subjectivity. They stress the individual psyche at the expense of the community and reinforce the negative conceptualization of femininity as something dark and self-lacerating, rather than as structured in response to specific contexts. Particularly when reading *The Color Purple*, to search for archetypal representation in the novel is to ignore much of what is important to Black readers. Cora Kaplan has suggested specific ways in which new writing from Black women: 'dialogises the languages, black and white, in which race, class and gender have been discussed in America' (p. 182). Gilbert and Gubar rarely take account of the fictional nature of the literary text or the specific material conditions under which writers work. In order to facilitate our reading, we have drawn analogies between Angela Carter's self-conscious challenge to patriarchal structures and Gilbert and Gubar's idea that all women's writing is inherently revisionary. In fact, Gilbert and Gubar suggest that the revisionary process is an essential feature of the woman writer's femaleness and not a conscious political stance.

As we noted at the end of Part I, the feature of *The Madwoman in the Attic* that is most difficult for another critic to reproduce is the particularities of the writers' style. Gilbert and Gubar themselves are engaged in the revisionary process they describe: large sections of the text are given up to restructuring the plots of the novels under discussion to bring them in line with their stories of entrapment and escape. In doing so, their criticism becomes inextricably bound up in the metaphysical imagery of the master text whose influence they seek to define. For example, the story of the Fall taken from Milton is re-enacted over and over again to the point of tedium, as in the following passage, this time with reference to George Eliot's *Middlemarch*:

> Behind the dream-Casaubon, however, lurks the real Casaubon, a point Eliot's irony stresses from the scholar's first appearance in *Middlemarch*, just as – the Miltonic parallels continually invite us to make this connection – the 'real' Milton dwelt behind the carefully constructed dream image of the celestial bard. Indeed, Eliot's real Casaubon, as opposed to Dorothea's idealized Casaubon, is in certain respects closer to the real author of *Paradise Lost* than his dream image is to the Miltonic epic speaker. Like Milton, after all, Casaubon is a master of the classics and theology, those provinces of masculine knowledge . . . from which all truth could be seen more truly. (p. 217)

The effect is to reduce each new text to a logic of the same: Milton as Satan, woman writer as Eve. These of course are serious criticisms, but we must not lose sight of the positive contribution made by Gilbert and Gubar to women's studies. *The Madwoman in the Attic* is a pioneering work that provides a framework within which to study the major contribution made by women writers to nineteenth-century literature, contrary to their usual positioning as marginal figures in the male 'great tradition'.

Notes

1. Sandra Gilbert and Susan Gubar, *The Madwoman in the Attic* (Yale University Press, New Haven, 1979); referred to as MW in further references.
2. See discussion of Showalter's work in Chapter 3.

3. Susan Gubar, ' "The blank page" and the issues of female creativity', *Critical Inquiry*, vol. 8, Winter 1981; referred to as BP in further references.

4. Gilbert and Gubar's use of psychoanalysis is very different from the French feminists (see Chapter 5) and the two should not be confused. Gilbert and Gubar borrow a variety of concepts and theories from Freudian psychoanalysis and use them as a background for their own theory of feminist poetics.

5. Edward W. Said, *Beginnings: Intention and Method* (Basic Books, New York, 1975), p. 83.

6. Thomas Szasz has pointed to the power involved in any classification or naming process, by which wo/man can attempt to impose an order on things or people; to control them:

> Classification is not reserved for science or the scientists. It is a fundamental human act. To name something is to classify it. But why do men name things? The answer often is: to gain control over the thing named, and, more generally, over one's power to act in the world . . . The act of naming or classifying is intimately related to the human need for control or mastery. (Thomas Szasz, *Ideology and Insanity* (Calder and Boyars, London, 1973), p. 196)

7. Harold Bloom, *The Anxiety of Influence* (Oxford University Press, New York, 1973).

8. Susan Penfold and Gillian Walker argue that certain images of woman recur across time, race and culture and that the consistency of these myths and symbols has led to the belief that they are a universal part of a collective consciousness (or unconsciousness), representing deep and universal truths about the nature of women. See *Women and the Psychiatric Paradox* (Oxford University Press, Oxford, 1984), p. vii.

9. See, for example, Susan Griffin, *Woman and Nature* (The Women's Press, London, 1984); Mary Daly, *Gyn/Ecology* (The Women's Press, London, 1978); Barbara Ehrenreich and Deirdre English, *For Her Own Good* (Pluto, London, 1979).

10. We would suggest that Gilbert and Gubar's use of the term 'Otherness' in relation to women differs from Showalter's use of it in her discussion of the 'wild zone' (see Chapter 3). Showalter recuperates the concept to make positive reference to woman's subjective position, whilst Gilbert and Gubar refer to man's negative classification of woman.

11. For a discussion of women's position in the nineteenth century, with particular reference to the restraints inflicted on upper- and middle-class women, see Ehrenreich and English (note 9 above).

12. Simone de Beauvoir, *The Second Sex* (Knopf, New York, 1953).

13. Virginia Woolf, 'Professions for women', in *The Death of the Moth and Other Stories* (Harcourt, New York, 1942), pp. 236–8.

14. Mary Jacobus has also suggested that women's writing works within male discourse but works 'ceaselessly to deconstruct it'. See 'The difference of view', in Mary Jacobus (ed.), *Women Writing and Writing about Women* (Croom Helm, London, 1979), p. 13.

15. For further discussion of the relationship between woman's body and

her creativity, see Chapter 5 on French feminists, whose attitude towards that relationship is far more positive and entirely different from Gilbert and Gubar's.

16. Charlotte Perkins Gilman, *The Yellow Wallpaper* (Virago, London, 1973).
17. For a contrasting reading of 'The Yellow Wallpaper' see Chapter 6.
18. Angela Carter, *The Magic Toyshop* (Virago, London, 1982). It should also be noted that Gilbert and Gubar have since published two large books on women's writing in the twentieth century: see Sandra Gilbert and Susan Gubar, *No man's land: the place of the woman writer in the twentieth century*, 2 vols (Yale University Press, New Haven, 1988).
19. Angela Carter, 'Notes from the front line', in Micheline Wandor (ed.), *On Gender and Writing* (Pandora, London, 1983), p. 69, referred to as NFL in further references.
20. Paulina Palmer, 'From "coded mannequin" to bird woman: Angela Carter's magic flight', in Sue Roe (ed.), *Women Reading Women's Writing* (Harvester Wheatsheaf, Hemel Hempstead, 1987), p. 183.
21. This is the most significant difference between Gilbert and Gubar and the French feminists, whose concern is with the gendered structure of language rather than with representation.
22. See Chapter 5.
23. For comments on Gilbert and Gubar's reading of *Wuthering Heights* see Chapter 5.
24. Alice Walker, *The Color Purple* (The Women's Press, London, 1983).
25. Cora Kaplan, 'Keeping the color in *The Color Purple*', in *Sea Changes* (Verso, London, 1986), pp. 176–87.
26. James Baldwin, 'Everybody's protest novel', in *Notes of a Native Son* (Corgi, London, 1964); Harriet Beecher Stowe, *Uncle Tom's Cabin* (1852), authoritative text ed. Elizabeth Ammons (New York, Norton, 1994).
27. Richard Wright, *Native Son* (1940), cited by Baldwin (note 26 above) as 'Uncle Tom's descendant, flesh of his flesh, so exactly opposite a portrait when the books are put together'.
28. Toni Morrison, *Beloved* (Chatto and Windus, London, 1987).
29. Susan Willis, 'Black women writers: taking a critical perspective', in Gayle Greene and Coppelia Kahn (eds), *Making a Difference: Feminist Literary Criticism* (Methuen, London, 1986), pp. 211–37.
30. The celebratory conflation of author and character is, of course, being put to entirely opposite ends to Kate Millett's defamatory association of D. H. Lawrence and his misogynist *male* characters in *Sexual Politics* (see discussion in Chapter 1).
31. A more detailed discussion of this blind spot in Gilbert and Gubar's work can be found in *Sexual/Textual Politics* (Methuen, London, 1985), pp. 57–69, where Toril Moi discusses the 'radical contradictions' revealed between 'feminist politics and patriarchal aesthetics'.

5
French feminisms

Elaine Millard, Sara Mills and Lynne Pearce

Julia Kristeva: *The Kristeva Reader*
Luce Irigaray: *Speculum of the Other Woman*
Emily Brontë: *Wuthering Heights*
Angela Carter: *The Magic Toyshop*

I

Twenty years on from its first engagement with the discourses of Anglo-American feminism, it is interesting to reflect upon our changing relationship to the body of theory known somewhat problematically as 'French Feminism'. This term has been used to characterize a style of engagement with literary theory itself, as much as to denote specific theorists. French feminism caused a productive crisis in Anglo-American feminist theory (broadly speaking, 'images of women criticism', authentic realism, sexual politics). French feminism, like structuralist and post-structuralist criticism more generally in France, grew out of two closely connected, but quite different disciplines: linguistics and psychoanalysis. While Anglo-American critics were busy rebelling against the canon of English literature and the choice of reading lists, and setting up their own presses, the French feminists were part of an equally bold enterprise that set out to put in question, through an engagement with Saussurean linguistics and Lacanian psychoanalysis, the whole philosophical basis of language. Their target, rather than raising questions about the representation of women in writing, was an interrogation of gendered subjectivity and its relationship to aesthetic practice. 'Woman' as sign, for them, is a fictional construct of patriarchal discourse. One of the major points of difference from Anglo-American criticism is their emphasis on the impossibility of locating a place outside patriarchy from which 'woman' could be articulated. The names of certain French feminist theorists were in the 1980s the index of a desirable, but perhaps utopian, quest for a feminist critical practice that would liberate the theorist from competing ideologies of establishment versus feminist practices, moving in the direction of a subjectivity that would no longer be dependent on a specific sexual identity: one that transcends the gender principle.

As Elaine Millard noted in the first version of this chapter, there has always been a problem in grouping Hélène Cixous, Luce Irigaray and Julia Kristeva, together with other, less well-known theorists, under the term 'French feminists'; changes and developments in the writings of the individual group members make any such alignment even more problematic today.[1] In the past ten years, for example, Kristeva's work has shifted away from a theorization of subjectivity and gendered creativity (which is our principal focus of interest in this chapter) to a more purely psychoanalytic (i.e. non-literary) interrogation of melancholia and 'the abject'.[2] Irigaray's latest publication, meanwhile, *I Love You: Sketch of a Possible Felicity in History* (1995) moves on from her earlier critique of patriarchally defined psychoanalytic discourse as a 'logic of the same' (see discussion below) to an 'exploration of the grounds for a possible inter-subjectivity between the two sexes'.[3] With this development it would seem that she is also rejecting the 'logic of lesbianism' present in her earliest work, together with her former celebration of the conjunction between female sexuality and feminine writing (*parler femme*). Although the work of both these theorists remains grounded in post-Lacanian psychoanalytic theory, therefore, their movement away from an interrogation of gendered subjectivity and (women's) writing *per se*, means that they can no longer be yoked together under the same umbrella as far as feminist literary criticism is concerned.

It is also fair to say that interest in such attempts to specify the 'difference' of women's writing has dwindled amongst feminist critics as we have moved through the 1990s, although there are still a considerable number of studies which engage the work of Kristeva in their readings of literary and other texts.[4] Needless to say, it was the charges of 'essentialism' (see Glossary) that attended the early work of the group that caused many readers to shy away from the early theories of 'writing the body', attractive as these might have been in granting a much-needed specificity to female textual production. For those wishing to defend the writing of Cixous and Irigaray, such critique has demanded a strenuous re-explication of the theories concerned, with critics like Elizabeth Grosz and Margaret Whitford making strong arguments for why the accusations of many Anglo-American commentators have been blinkered and misplaced.[5] As a result of these developments, then (both within the writings of the feminists themselves, and in their critical and theoretical *reception*), the identity, profile and reputation of the French feminists (taken either singly, or as a group) is assuredly not what it was in 1989, when this chapter on French feminism first appeared.

In terms of changed perceptions, we must also take into account the erosion of difference between Anglo-American and European feminist thought: the rigorous attack on 'identity politics' being practised by Judith Butler and other 'Queer' theorists (see Chapter 7) has taken up, and significantly advanced, the destabilizing of identity initiated by Kristeva, Irigaray, Cixous *et al.*[6] What has happened, therefore, is that the principle of interrogating gendered and sexual identities by focusing on their inscription by/through language has become part of a much larger, and often less psychoanalytically specific project, and one in which the 'utopian' desire to constitute a female/feminine identity 'outside' a phallocentric economy has been emphatically rejected. The early writings of the French feminists, then, can be seen to survive in this legacy of sexual/textual deconstruction, but *not* as a revolutionary vision of female 'difference' (which, as will be seen below, was the somewhat paradoxical other side of the project).

It may be considered fortuitous that the readings of *Wuthering Heights* and *The Magic Toyshop* which follow focus principally on the deconstructive tools of Kristeva's and Irigaray's work that *have* survived. For most feminist critics today, Kristeva's concept of the 'semiotic' (as an aspect of both subject and text) has become almost as commonplace as that of the unconscious itself. In this respect, the reading of *Wuthering Heights* which is offered here, which employs the discourse of the semiotic to identify a large number of literary subversions in the text, may thus be seen to exemplify the way in which feminist critics have become used to rethinking the 'unconscious' of a text in these gendered terms. As far as Irigaray is concerned, meanwhile, a clear connection can be made between her work on masquerade cited here and the way in which that concept has been employed by American theorists like Eve Kosofsky Sedgwick to explore further the social and psychic constructedness of gendered and sexual identity within heterosexual culture.[7] Before moving on to the readings themselves, however, we are aware that readers new to the work of the French theorists will still require some explication and problematization of their early writings on which the readings are based. We therefore proceed with a short summary of what the early French feminist theories offered literary criticism, a brief explication of the Lacanian model of the constitution of the subject on which much of that theory was based, and finally, an account of those aspects of Kristeva's and Irigaray's theory with which the readings themselves engage.

Although, as we have already indicated, the work of Cixous,

Irigaray and Kristeva should not be unproblematically conflated, their early writing does share a common concern for the connection between *language, gender* and *subjectivity* which has its roots in Lacanian theory. And whilst Lacan's own theory of the constitution of the subject was, as we shall see, 'gender-aware', it was these French feminists who first read his account of the female subject's ambiguous relation to the Symbolic Order (see below) in terms of an explicitly feminist agenda. Accepting that patriarchal culture *did* work to exclude women from the Symbolic Order, all three theorists focused their attention, instead, on the pre-Oedipal stages of subject development and how the female subject's relationship to this phase might be positively redefined. In these writings great emphasis is placed on the *ungendered* and *pre-linguistic* nature of the Lacanian Imaginary (see below), and it was basically an assumption that female subjects preserve a special relationship to this stage of development that led to a theorization of Cixous's *écriture féminine* and Irigaray's *parler femme*: terms marking the linguistic and syntactical 'difference' of women's writing. Despite the paradox inherent in this idea of *'the feminine'* deriving from an *ungendered* stage of subject development (a connection that, as we shall see, has sometimes been resisted by Kristeva), this is the narrative that explains the French feminists' appeal to theorists seeking to prove the existence of a distinctly female aesthetic. As Rita Felski has observed,

> Some feminist theorists appear to suggest that there is indeed a specific connection between the semiotic and the 'feminine', insofar as the former is closely associated with the mother's body before the child's entry into a male-defined symbolic order. Alice Jardine writes in her explication of Kristeva, 'This space before the sign, the *semiotic*, has been and continues to be coded in our culture as feminine: the space of privileged contact with the mother's (female) body'. [8]

Before looking more closely at how the work of Kristeva and Irigaray has fed into this narrative of a female aesthetic, however (including how aspects of their work have been effectively misappropriated towards this end), we first offer a short account of the Lacanian model of subject development on which the principle of *écriture féminine* is based. In Lacan's readjustment of Freud, patriarchy is shown to be inscribed in the very language through which the child learns to define itself and in which it is confirmed in its gender. According to Lacanians, the child, prior to its entry into the sphere of language, experiences itself as diffused and undifferentiated from the world. It is an 'hommelette', a 'little man', which, like a broken egg, spills over and spreads itself with no fixed (ego) boundaries. It experiences its being in the world as a flux and is dominated by ever-changing drives (these drives Kristeva calls pulsions). Lacan terms this pre-Oedipal zone the Imaginary. An important transition stage in the process of identity formation occurs when, either at a literal or a metaphorical level, the child sees its image in a mirror and recognizes that it has boundaries and limits.[9] This bounded self is of course imaginary, since it is a projection of an image: the 'I' cannot be located there. Furthermore, because there is a disparity between the child's experience of itself as fragmented and boundless and this image of itself, the child relates to this image of itself as if to another. Thus, the mirror stage, as Lacan terms it, signifies a moment when the child recognizes the boundaries of its self at the very moment when it also recognizes the instability of that fictive self.

It is not, however, until the acquisition of language, when the child can make its desires explicit to another and enter into social exchanges, that this self becomes formulated, that is, named and defined by its entry into the Symbolic Order. The Symbolic is marked by the law of structuration of meanings which Lacan calls the *nom-du-père*: the Law of the Father. In order to enter the Symbolic Order, some elements of the Imaginary that cannot be expressed within the Symbolic's formulations are repressed, and effectively silenced. At the point of entry into this realm of the Symbolic, i.e. the acquisition of language, the subject splits, and what of the Imaginary cannot find expression in words is repressed in the unconscious. This repressed 'experience' is a key to understanding what Kristeva terms the 'semiotic' (or the zone of the unconscious on which conscious speech depends).[10] It is at the level of the Imaginary that French feminists locate the feminine. As the child says 'I', it constructs a fiction of selfhood that depends on the syntax of the language it has been born into; as Ragland-Sullivan suggests: 'the Symbolic dimension imposes language as a mask on the body, weaving it as a text.'[11] The 'I' position carries the authority and self-possession which Lacan designates as male. This, for French feminists rereading Lacan, is the crux of the matter (indeed, what effectively *is* the matter), that the child's sense of identity is filtered through external views of itself formulated in a language where the 'I' position is male. It is Lacan's view that language, shaped through the patriarchal *nom-du-pere* with which only the boy child can identify himself, reserves the 'I' position for one gender, placing the other in a negative position, always having to negotiate a mediated identity. In the Lacanian account of language acquisition, the phallus is the master signifier, in the face of which the feminine can be defined only as lack. Woman is a gap, a silence, invisible and unheard, repressed in the unconscious. Kristeva argues that this 'feminine' remains at the level of the 'semiotic', accessible in

patriarchal discourse only at the point of contradiction, meaninglessness and silence.

Unlike Anglo-American feminist accounts of women's oppression
within language, Lacan's scheme suggests it is a determined psychological cause: a necessary stage in socialization.[12] Lacan writes of the
subject's relation to language, making its role seem a dominant and
inescapable one:

> Thus the subject too if he appears to be the slave of the language is
> all the more so of a discourse in the universal movement in which
> his place is already inscribed at birth, if only by virtue of his proper
> name. Reference to the experience of the community, or to the
> substance of this discourse, settles nothing. For this experience
> assumes its essential dimension in the tradition that this discourse
> itself establishes. This tradition, long before the drama of history is
> inscribed in it, lays down the elementary structures of culture. And
> these very structures reveal an ordering of possible exchanges
> which, even if unconscious, is inconceivable outside the permuta-
> tions offered it by language.[13]

The subject then is processed by the linguistic categories which
structure experience. There can be no possible socialization outside
this structuration so that, in Lacan's schema, a woman who 'refused'
to enter the Symbolic Order through language would remain
unsocialized, psychotic and autistic. The French feminists whose work
is drawn on here challenge the basic determinism of this Lacanian
model, while employing its interrogation of subjectivity to locate the
feminine, which has been lost or suppressed in the system.[14] Whilst
the French feminists retain Lacan's psycho-linguistic categories of
Symbolic and Imaginary, and do not suggest that any subject, male or
female, could live permanently 'outside' the Symbolic, all have sought
to positively redefine our relationship to the pre-Oedipal stages of
subject development: that which has been 'repressed' in the Imaginary
might periodically erupt as a distinctive and liberating form of creative
expression.

We move on now to outline briefly those aspects of Kristeva and
Irigaray's theory which will be of particular significance in the readings
which follow. As will have begun to emerge from the preceding
discussion, Julia Kristeva's rewriting of the Lacanian model of subject
development is a suggestive, but somewhat teasing one, for feminists.
It is suggestive because her description of the pre-Oedipal psyche as a
space/place marked by the rhythms and patterns of sounds that are
the basic 'pulsions' of the oral and anal drives provides an explanation
for how the Symbolic Order is sometimes disrupted in linguistic and
textual performance (the 'semiotic' erupts into the speech/text). But it

is problematic because, although associated with what Kristeva has herself named 'feminine' writing, the semiotic is not, in itself, gender-specific since what it represents is a pre-gendered, pre-linguistic stage of development. In her later writings and interviews, Kristeva has sought to clarify her position on this point, realizing how crucial it is for feminists seeking evidence of a female aesthetic. Asked by Susan Sellers in an interview, if women have a 'privileged relationship to the semiotic . . . through their own real or potential experience of maternity' she replies:

> As far as [literary] style is concerned – the actual dynamics of language, this recourse to the semiotic, the inscription in the archaic relation to the mother in language – it isn't the monopoly of women. Men writers such as Joyce, Mallarmé or Artaud are proof of this. It's a question of subjectivity. It's possible that in aesthetic creation we occupy several positions. Any creator necessarily moves through an identification with the maternal, which is why the resurgence of this semiotic dynamic is important in every act of creation.[15]

Although she subsequently undermines the force of this statement by implying that women are more likely to get stuck in the 'hell' of the semiotic because of their problems of differentiating from another female ('one who is the same'), her pronouncement as far as language and creativity is clear: even if the semiotic is characterized as a period of mother–infant bonding, it is a phase of development in which the child *experiences itself as gender-less*, and the psychic expressions associated with this phase may erupt in both male and female adults in later life.

If we now move on to *how* the semiotic expresses itself in linguistic and literary production, we find an emphasis on *textual incoherence* and the presence of linguistic items that are in some way reminiscent of 'infant babble': portions of text in which sound becomes detached from meaning, or where – as in certain avant-garde works – sound *becomes* the meaning:

> This heterogeneousness to signification operates through, despite, and in excess of it and produces in poetic language 'musical' but also nonsense effects that destroy not only accepted beliefs and significations, but, in radical experiments, syntax itself . . . for example, carnivalesque discourse, Artaud, a number of texts by Mallarmé, certain Dadaist and Surrealist experiments.[16]

What is immediately puzzling about this description is of course the degree to which the semiotic features of a given text are part of the *conscious* project of the artist concerned. Although its psychic characterization as part of the subject's 'repressed unconscious' would suggest that such eruptions ought to occur *involuntarily* in speech/ writing, Kristeva's own literary examples are all of modernist texts in which the various 'incoherences' are part of a self-conscious, aesthetic experiment. The same sense of a 'manufactured semiotic' is also present in the writings of Cixous and Irigaray.[17]

As far as its practical application within literary criticism is concerned, meanwhile, it could be argued that the semiotic can be engaged in three main ways: first, in an account of authorial production (as part of a demonstration of how authors lose conscious control of their texts); second, via a (metaphoric?) model of the text as psyche with its own conscious and unconscious, and in which certain disruptive elements can be seen as analogous to the semiotic (even if their presence has been consciously contrived by the author); and third, in readings of literary characters in whom the semiotic periodically erupts. The reading of *Wuthering Heights* which follows concentrates on the last two of these categories.[18]

It is to Luce Irigaray that we shall now turn for her interrogation of the sign 'woman' and the nature of female sexuality. Luce Irigaray has aroused considerable hostility both from her (male) psychoanalytical colleagues and from feminists. Her challenge to the orthodoxies of Freudian and Lacanian theories (or rather non-theories) of femininity in her doctoral thesis, *Speculum de l'autre femme*, resulted in her expulsion from Lacan's Ecole Freudienne. In this playful, but ultimately complex, theoretical analysis, she demonstrates how the privileging of what is visible and therefore deemed positive (i.e. the penis elevated to the status of phallus, the master signifier) relegates 'woman' to absence in existing structures of psychoanalytical and philosophical discourse. She describes the feminine as 'interdit' (literally 'forbidden', but also 'spoken in between'), located in between signs, between the realized meanings, between the lines:

> Therefore the feminine must be deciphered as interdict; within the signs or between them, between the realised meanings, between the lines . . . and as a function of the reproductive necessities of an intentionally phallic currency, which, for the lack of the collaboration of a (potentially female) other, can immediately be assumed to need its other, a sort of negative or inverted alter ego.[19]

Irigaray proceeds to demonstrate how, in psychoanalytic theory, woman is man's 'specularized Other', her function to reflect back man's meaning to himself, becoming the negative of this reflection. Woman is thereby forced into a subjectless position by the patriarchal 'logic of the same'. In reading Freud, she shows, by skilful quotation from his analysis and theorizing, that he has modelled his account of the little girl's development on that of the little boy, so that female sexuality is perceived not as something particular to women, but constructed as the negative response to the male's desire. Irigaray questions Freud's account of the seemingly total repression of a little girl's sexual instincts which Freud suggests follows from her acknowledgement of her inferiority to the boy's far superior penis. What Freud has ignored, Irigaray shows, is the nature of the girl's first love directed towards the mother. His solution, penis-envy, however, can be seen to have been made in the interests of his own sex:

> When Freud solves this problem by insisting that the girl has always been a boy, and that her femininity is characterized by 'penis-envy', he is obviously defending his male point of view and his wish to perpetuate sexual homogeneity; a non-sex organ, a castrated sex organ or 'penis-envy', does not constitute a sexual heterogene but rather represents a type of negativity that sustains and confirms the homogeneity of masculine desire. (p. 63)

In reading Freud, she highlights his neglect of pre-Oedipal experience that relegates the girl-child's relationship to the Imaginary, and which therefore can find no expression in the realm of the Symbolic. In this respect a woman, silenced in discourse, is as Irigaray has described elsewhere, in the position of the psychotic: 'Spoken more than speaking, enunciated more than enunciating, the demented person is therefore no longer an active subject of the enunciation . . . he is only a possible mouthpiece for previously pronounced enunciations.'[20] Irigaray succeeds in her readings in undermining the neutrality of philosophical/psychoanalytical discourse, revealing the process by which the philosopher/psychoanalyst has talked about himself from the security of his subject position. In order to attempt to access the primordial experience of femininity, she suggests it is necessary to work to disrupt the simple foundational oppositions on which theoretical systems are based:

> We have to reject all the great systems of opposition on which our culture is constructed. Reject, for instance, the oppositions fiction/ truth, sensible/intelligible, empirical/transcendental, materialist/ idealist. All these opposing pairs function as an exploitation and negation at the beginning and of a certain mode of connection between the body and the word for which we have paid everything.[21]

Having uncovered the impossibility of articulating the feminine in the existing structure of language, she has initiated the search for another form of expression that might claim to be a feminine language. She suggests that 'writing women' will create that which as yet is inexpressible; a female subject with the potential to create its own meanings rather than be caught in the 'masquerade' of femininity. This is, of course, a utopian quest. Because women are both inside and outside a discourse that gives no space to the feminine, the primary task is to disrupt the settled order rather than to define what form another order might take. It is the possibility of there being something that can be defined, except by reference to the masculine, that is the central concern of Irigaray's psychoanalytical concepts:

> Woman remains that nothing at all, or this all at nothing, in which each (male) one seeks to find the means to replenish the resemblance to self (as) to same. Thus she moves from place to place, yet, up to the present it was never she that was displaced. She must continue to hold the place she constitutes for the subject, a place to which no eternal value can be assigned lest the subject remain paralysed forever by the irreplaceableness of his cathected investments. Therefore she has to wait for him to move her in accordance with his needs and desires.[22]

To write the body or 'parler femme', then, is to confront and displace this masculine 'movement', to escape its definitions and confines, to attempt a reformation of the Symbolic. Irigaray does not claim that either to write or 'parler femme' is easily definable or achievable. She does, however, *attempt* it. In the (infamous) *This Sex Which is not One* she offers women a manifesto for 'writing the body', arguing for the existence of an explicit relationship between women's polymorphously perverse sexuality ('Woman has sex organs virtually everywhere') and the 'non-linear', non-logical nature of women's speech and writing. She uses the form of women's sexual organs as a metaphor or analogy of this textual difference:

> woman's autoeroticism is very different from man's. He needs an instrument to touch himself: his hand, woman's genitals, language . . . But a woman touches herself by and within herself directly, without mediation, and before any distinction between activity and passivity is possible. A woman 'touches herself' constantly without anyone being able to forbid her to do so, for her sex is composed of two lips which embrace continually. Thus, within herself she is already two – but not divisible into ones – who stimulate each other.[23]

Like Cixous, Irigaray's early writings thus hinge on this contradictory project of deconstructing the masculine/feminine binarism of existing psychoanalytic theory (in which the feminine is always presented as the negative term or 'lack') and producing an alternative (and newly positive) concept of femininity and female sexuality. Whilst the latter has become increasingly problematic to feminists aware of its essentializing potential, her assault on phallocentric psychoanalytic discourse still remains useful. Included in the latter is her advocacy of *mimicry* and *masquerade*: a model of feminine/feminist resistance that – as was observed earlier – has since been annexed by much 'Queer' theory. As will become evident in the reading of *The Magic Toyshop* which follows, the purpose of masquerade is to emphasize the fact that far from being 'natural' or 'innate', femininity is a culturally produced identity which has to be 'worked at' and performed. By performing this role 'to excess' women can thus make visible, and implicitly subvert, feminine and heterosexual norms. In Carter's text, as we shall see, Melanie is made the agent of just such subversions, whilst in terms of contemporary culture the pop star Madonna is usually cited as the one of the most successful icons of a feminine masquerade.

II

We proceed now with our readings of *Wuthering Heights* and *The Magic Toyshop* which engage Kristeva's concept of the semiotic and Irigaray's of mimicry and masquerade respectively. Emily Brontë's *Wuthering Heights* has already attracted the attention of critics of many different persuasions.[24] It is a central text in Sandra Gilbert and Susan Gubar's *The Madwoman in the Attic*, whose work is discussed in detail in Chapter 3, and it is by way of contrast with French feminist work that we would like to begin this section with a discussion of their reading of the novel. Gilbert and Gubar, through a 'mythic' interpretation rather than close analysis, retell the story of the women they designate as Cathy I and II and her lovers, wresting the tale from the grasp of its fictive narrators, Lockwood and Nelly Dean, whose limited perspectives cease to be an issue in the new narrative. In the process, they represent the author, Emily Brontë, to their own readers as a proto-feminist literary scholar, who was writing against both a literary patriarch, Milton, and her own father. This revision of the novel is quite deliberate on their part as the following passage shows:

> Having arrived at the novel's conclusion we can now go back to its beginning and try to summarize the basic story that *Wuthering Heights* tells. Though this may not be the book's only story, it is surely a crucial one. As the names on the window-sill indicate, *Wuthering Heights* begins and ends with Catherine and her various avatars. More specifically, it studies the evolution of 'Catherine Earnshaw into Catherine Heathcliff and Catherine Linton, and then her return through Catherine Linton II and Catherine Heathcliff II and to her "proper" role as Catherine Earnshaw. More generally, what this evolution and devolution conveys is . . . a parodic anti-Miltonic myth.'[25]

Gilbert and Gubar, by restructuring the narrative, have imaged for their history of women's literature, a model of the ideal literary woman, specifically engaged with a thematic structuring device located outside her text.

Given the fact that Brontë never mentions either Milton or *Paradise Lost* in *Wuthering Heights*, any identification of her as Milton's daughter may at first seem eccentric or perverse. Shelley, after all provided an overtly Miltonic framework in *Frankenstein* to reinforce our sense of her literary intentions. But despite the absence of Milton reference, it eventually becomes plain that *Wuthering Heights* is also a novel haunted by Milton's bogey. We may speculate indeed that Milton's absence is itself a presence, so painfully does Brontë's story dwell on the places and persons of his imagination. (p. 252)

The persuasive power of the rhetorical frame of this essay and its obsessive reshaping of each story to fit a new gynocritical canon of women's writing, demonstrates how the gaps, the unspoken elements of this text, encourage the reader to rush in with her own desires. For Gilbert and Gubar, Milton's is this text's 'unspoken', but many other critics have noted an aporia or uncertainty within the text's central logic and have glossed it in different ways. *Wuthering Heights* seems to invite this onrush of interpretation, and this is also testified, both by its recurrent fascination for adolescent readers, and by the multiplicity of competing readings available to fill the space which seems to have opened up in the fabric of the Symbolic codes.[26] Hillis Miller catalogues the variety of interpretations at hand:

There have been interpretations of *Wuthering Heights* in terms of the fair-haired girl and the dark-haired boy in the Gondal poems or by way of the motifs of doors and windows in the novel (Dorothy van Ghent); or in terms of the symmetry of the family relations in the novel or Brontë's accurate knowledge of the laws of private property in Yorkshire (C. P. Sanger); or as in more or less orthodox and schematic Freudian terms as a thinly disguised sexual drama displaced and condensed (Thomas Moser); or as a dramatisation of a conflict between two cosmological forces, calm and storm (Lord David Cecil); or as a moral story of the futility of grand passion (Mark Schorer) . . . or as the expression of a multitude of incompatible partial selves breaking down the concept of a unitary self (Leo Bersani), or in more or less sophisticated Marxist terms (David Wilson, Arnold Kettle, Terry Eagleton).[27]

Miller accounts for this plethora of interpretation as an effect of the reading required by the text. He illustrates the way in which it:

is made up of repetitions of the same in the other which permanently resist rational reduction to some satisfying principle of explanation. The reader has the experience, in struggling to understand the novel that a certain number of the elements which present themselves for explanation can be reduced to order. This act of interpretation always leaves something over, something just at the edge of the circle of theoretical vision which the vision does not encompass. This something left out is clearly a significant detail. There are always in fact a group of such significant details which have been left out of any reductions to order. The text is over rich. (p. 52)

There is evidence that this sense of something 'missed out' as a key to understanding has always been the experience of reading the novel. Charlotte Brontë has described its first reviewers as: 'Astrologers, Chaldeans and Soothsayers, gathered before the "writing on the wall" and being unable to read the characters or make known the interpretations'[28] Competing readings find themselves suspended in the gaps between Nelly and Lockwood's perceptions, searching for clues in words, 'detached sentences' and 'faded hieroglyphics', scribbled on the margins of biblical texts, inscribed on lintels and scratched into window-sills, together with confessions whispered into the pillow by Catherine in a fevered delirium. Miller sums up the undecidability neatly thus: 'each appearance is the sign of something absent, something earlier or later or further in' (p. 60).

Much psychoanalytic criticism has shown us that we produce texts by reading them and that the texts we produce repeat the stories that obsess us. In all the cited readings of *Wuthering Heights*, reader, text and language are caught up in an endless displacement of desire. It is not our intention to add to these competing readings by writing yet another version of the novel to set alongside the rest. Our purpose is to draw attention to the fragmentation of narration and the mingling of genre, whereby the fantastic and uncanny erupt into the hard realism of the story of a family's struggle over inheritance. The text refuses a simple resolution, however much the match between the younger Cathy and Hareton Earnshaw is foregrounded. This elusiveness of meaning is such that the novel conforms to the following description of the Kristevan model of textuality: '[the text] presses the linguistic sign to its limits, the semiotic is fluid and plural, a kind of pleasurable creative excess over precise meaning and it takes sadistic delight in destroying or negating such signs'.[29] As we mentioned in Part I of this chapter, Kristeva's thesis is that these 'meanings' remain as the semiotic, inscribed inside the symbolic as part of the condition of its coherence. It is essential to grasp that the semiotic cannot be separated out from the symbolic but remains as a pressure on language as contradictions, meaninglessness, silence and absence. It works from within signification, indicating what is lacking in codified representation. Tensions between the symbolic surface and its semiotic undercurrents connect the obsessive interest that readers find in this novel with Kristeva's concept of an unconscious present in a text. This unconscious communicates to the reader some idea of a pre-Oedipal oneness, an unnameable unity of being that can only be expressed as a lack in the present or at the time of reading. 'Woman', Kristeva has argued, does not exist except as constituted in opposition to the male, that which is other than, rather than a thing in itself. 'In "woman", I see something that cannot be represented, something that cannot be said, something above and beyond nomenclature and ideologies.'[30] And she also says:

> If logical unity is paranoid and homosexual (directed by men to men) the feminine demand . . . will never find a proper symbolic, will be at best enacted as a moment inherent in rejection, in the process of ruptures, of rhythmic breaks. In so far as she has a specificity of her own, a woman finds it in asociality, in the violation of communal conventions, in a sort of symbolic singularity.[31]

Although in her own literary criticism, such as in her discussion of the semiotic and symbolist poetics, Kristeva works at the level of sounds, repetitions and disruptions of grammar, that is, with writing which interrogates small units of language, rather than larger units of signification, the theoretical basis of her methodology is a productive way in to *Wuthering Heights*. Instead of repetition of sound and description at sentence level, what is at work in this narrative is a disruption of all the 'macro elements' of classic realism. Time is dislocated, narration is fragmented, its narrators presented ironically and shown to be limited in their point of view, genre is disrupted; but above all, the smooth working of binary oppositions is transgressed. These neat dispositions of difference into antithesis are what Roland Barthes has described as 'the very spectacle of meaning' which saturate the classic realist text.[32]

In texts figuring romance, reader expectation anticipates an antagonistic opposition of male sexual rivalry, in this case between the legitimized, patriarchal choice, landowner Edgar Linton, and the dark Byronic outsider, Heathcliff. However, neat oppositions break down as the simple divide between true and false lover is negated by Edgar Linton's harshness and Heathcliff's asexual indifference. Oppositions of natural versus civilized, duty set against desire, landowner versus servant, the present with the past, spirituality and materialism, are all productive of meaning. It is, however, around the transgressive figure of Heathcliff that the interpretation of the symbolic codes cluster and meanings proliferate. The reader is as uncertain as the internal narrator, Lockwood, of how to dispose her sympathies. Heathcliff, arriving from nowhere, from no named parentage and bearing no Christian name, 'from the very beginning he bred bad feeling in the house' (p. 49) which pervades the story until he dies, similarly alone, leaving nothing: no child, only a single name and the date of his death recorded on his headstone, soon to be covered over in lichen and moss.

The character of Heathcliff created a scandal in its time, prompting this admission from Charlotte Brontë, supposedly writing to defend her sister's work from its critics, in the 1850 Preface to the novel: 'whether it is right or advisable to create beings like Heathcliff I do not know, I scarce think it is' (p. 40). In every sense Heathcliff's presence in the text is a transgressive and disruptive one and can be seen as an element from the semiotic clothed in the language of the symbolic.

Similarly, representations of Catherine multiply within the text in a process of dispersal and fragmentation that is marked by a similar fragmentation of signifiers. Her presence cannot be pinned down to a single signifier and her name remains oscillating in the reader's perception no less than that of Lockwood, the narrator:

> The ledge where I placed my candle, had a few mildewed books piled up in one corner; and it was covered with writing scratched on the paint. This writing was nothing but a name repeated in kinds of characters, large and small – Catherine Earnshaw, here and there varied Catherine Heathcliff and again to Catherine Linton. In vapid listlessness I leant my head against the window and continued spelling over. Catherine Earnshaw-Heathcliff-Linton, till my eyes closed; but they had not rested five minutes when a glare of white letters started free from the dark as vivid as spectre – the air swarmed with Catherines. (p. 61).

The attempt to spell out the name results only in further disintegration and displacements. The eruption of the semiotic into the symbolic is figured at this moment, so that the 'sense' of the names is lost and instead there is simply the anarchic free-play of the signifier. Many commentators have noted that the ghost that haunts the narrative is not that of the young woman, dead in childbirth, but of the adolescent Cathy, lost at the point where she chooses/is compelled, to enter into womanhood, as culturally defined by the society in which she lives and which is symbolized by the constricting clothes she wears on her return to the Heights from Thrushcross Grange:

> instead of a wild, hatless little savage jumping into the house and rushing to squeeze us all breathless, there lighted from a handsome black pony a very dignified person with brown ringlets falling from the cover of a feathered beaver, and a long cloth habit which she was obliged to hold up with both hands that she might sail in. (p. 93)

It is the 'girl half savage and hardy and free' to whom Catherine longs to return in her illness and who tries to find her way back into the Heights, who appears in Lockwood's uncannily prophetic dream. Yet the name given is that of the married woman:

> 'Who are you?' I asked, struggling meanwhile to disengage myself. 'Catherine Linton' it replied shiveringly (why did I think of Linton? I had read Earnshaw twenty times for Linton) 'I'm come home: I'd lost my way on the moor!' As I looked I discerned a child's face looking through the window. (p. 67)

A similar misrecognition, or displacement of signifiers, occurs in Chapter XIII when Isabella is brought to Wuthering Heights as

Heathcliff's bride. It might be supposed that this would have been the role reserved for Cathy in any conventional romantic plot. In a letter to Nelly, Isabella gives an account of her cold reception, including a detailed description of how Joseph greets a tantrum in which she dashed a bowl of gruel to the ground with the name of her friend and rival: ' "Ech, ech", exclaimed Joseph, "Weel done Miss Cathy! weel done, Miss Cathy. Howsiver t'maister shall tum'le oer them broken pots; un then we's hear summat; we hears how it's to be" ' (p. 180). Thus Isabella at the very moment when she is asserting herself in a separate identity to Cathy, as Heathcliff's wife, is taken for Cathy herself.[33]

A further confusion of identities is created by the confusion of selves experienced by the central characters, given expression by Catherine before her separation from Heathcliff in the statement: 'Nelly, I am Heathcliff', and his equally emphatic: 'Oh, God, it is unutterable. I cannot live without my soul' (p. 180). Particular readers may choose to invest the ambiguity thus created with a particular meaning, as Mary Daly does in *Pure Lust*. She writes: 'It is clear enough to viragos from these words that Heathcliff is the disguise of the female Friend of Emily Brontë's dream. "He" feels an identity with Catherine that only another female friend could feel.'[34] For Gilbert and Gubar, the key to understanding the passage and with finding the key to the whole novel is to read the pair as halves of an androgynous whole: 'together they . . . [Cathy and Heathcliff] constitute an autonomous androgynous (or more accurately gyandrous) whole: as a woman's man and a woman for herself in Sartre's sense, making up one complete woman' (p. 295). What however, seems more important than establishing a particular interpretation is a recognition of the disruption of certainty that has been engendered by these semiotic elements which surface at key moments of the text.

Julia Kristeva's poetics, in its emphasis on textuality rather than the intentions of the author or the experience of the characters as reflections of an external reality, has allowed us as feminist readers to identify those areas of disjunction, silence or contradiction, which may count as evidence for a suppressed feminine within the text, unable to make itself fully heard, because it cannot be contained within the symbolic order which it threatens to disrupt. Toril Moi's reading of Kristeva's work emphasizes its revolutionary potential.[35] She is the theorist with whom Moi chooses to end her own quest for a theoretical position that liberates the critic from humanist and essentialist suppositions. Moi admires, in particular, Kristeva's ability to open up language to the free-play of the signifier: 'Applied to the field of sexual identity and difference, this becomes a feminist vision in which the sexual signifier would be free to move; where the fact of being male or female no longer would determine the subject's position in relation to power, and where, therefore, the very nature of power would be transformed' (p. 172).

We would like now to make use of the more defiantly feminist approach to psychoanalysis and women's sexuality provided by Luce Irigaray; in particular, to make use of her ideas on 'masquerade' of male-defined femininity and the disruptive potential of 'mimicry' as a feminist strategy. By mimicry, we mean Irigaray's method of reproducing the discourse of others in such a way as to undermine the authority of the original. She sees it as an interim strategy for dealing with patriarchal discourses in which the woman deliberately reveals the mechanisms by which she is exploited. Similarly, a masquerade is a deliberate assumption of the roles assigned to woman in the name of femininity. By adopting a masquerade a woman is able to experience herself as she is positioned by the desire of the masculine. In both cases, mimicry and masquerade involve a degree of exaggeration and excess, so that the female constructs a limit-case scenario, which will highlight the weaknesses and indeed the fragility of structures used to oppress her.

Angela Carter's first novel *The Magic Toyshop* will seem, to many readers, a far cry from the kind of disruption of language and symbolic representation which characterizes the semiotic.[36] The structure and features of style are disconcertingly conventional and the content of the story, an adolescent girl's rite of passage to womanhood, a staple of romantic fiction. However, rather than a simple realist narrative, it can be viewed as calling into question conventional masculine and feminine roles. The concepts of mimicry and masquerade can aid the reader in describing this process whereby roles are destabilized.

Many women's texts like this one have been read as simply autobiographical (see Chapter 2). Indeed, Angela Carter herself has in fact hinted, in an interview given to *The Observer* prior to the filming of this novel, at an 'autobiographical' origin for the writing:

> When the book came out in 1967 it was reviewed as a kind of fairy story. But when I read it again I was struck with the intense sense of adolescent longing in an extraordinary sexual yearning. What it reminded me of was endless afternoons alone in a room smelling of sun-warmed carpet, stuck in the Sargasso Sea of adolescence when it seems you are never going to grow up.[37]

This story of female adolescence, however, is caught up in patterns of narrative that undo the simplicity of reflected experience by refracting the characters through the convex mirrors of fantasy and myth. The writing does not however approach the fluidity or disruptive power of the semiotic. However, just as Jacques Lacan recast Edgar Allan Poe's *The Purloined Letter* as an allegory of the signifier, this story can be read as an acting out of the crisis of the female subject described by French feminist psychoanalytic models.[38] The crisis is itself figured in the generic form of a fable. Indeed, the reader is confronted by a curious clash of discourses, where fable seems to be the dominant, but where this stability is undercut by its juxtaposition with other discourses. Here, textuality announces itself in terms of fable. Place is left undefined: an Edwardian house somewhere in the country gives place to a toyshop somewhere in the seedier parts of London, while time schemes are sketchy; things take place 'one night', time is marked out by the changing of seasons and the bizarre stuffed bird cuckoo clock created by the puppet-master, Uncle Philip. The latter is designated as the villain of the piece, and he is delineated in the simple terms of a fairy tale ogre: 'Uncle Philip never talked to his wife except to bark brusque commands. He gave a necklace that choked her. He beat her younger brother. He chilled the air through which he moved. His towering, blank-eyed presence at the head of the table drew the savour from the good food she cooked' (p. 124). This vision of masculinity taken to its ultimate excess is further reinforced by allusions to Bluebeard and to the puppet-maker of the Hoffman story.

If Uncle Philip patterns out every feminist's concept of the patriarch, Aunt Margaret's situation most particularly demonstrates the silencing that the imposition of a male symbolic order forces on the feminine. Dumbness marks Aunt Margaret's entry into the patriarchal home and is broken only when this is threatened with destruction and the spell is broken (p. 197). In this sense, Uncle Philip and Aunt Margaret are not so much characters as they are ciphers pushing the roles of masculinity and femininity to their limits – so that rather than being representations of gender roles, they are mimicking them to the point of absurdity.

The text throws into question those elements of storytelling that have become accepted as literary norms. Like the French feminists under discussion, Carter chooses myth as the site of entry into a new Imaginary. Alicia Ostriker has described this feature of women's writing as a process of revisionary myth-making that plunders sanctuaries of existing language where our meanings of 'male' and 'female' have been preserved.[39] Carter similarly perceives that some stories carry meanings that threaten but which can be revised for feminism. She claims to be in the 'demythologising business' and is 'interested in myths – though I'm much more interested in folklore – just because they are extraordinary lies designed to make people unfree . . . I used bits and pieces from various mythologies quite casually because they were to hand'.[40] For example, central to *The Magic Toyshop* is a revisionary exploration of the myth of Leda and the Swan, which poets such as Yeats have employed as a symbol of a phallic potency which sees rape as the prerogative of male power. This myth involves the mapping out of a passive position onto Melanie, the central character, and it is in the playing out of this myth when excesses of masculinity and femininity are put on display; it is at this moment when mimicry of the myth takes place that these roles are most destabilized.

Melanie is shown to be in quest of a female self which is elusive: 'Since she was thirteen, when her periods began, she felt she was pregnant with herself, bearing the slowly ripening embryo of Melanie-grown-up inside herself for a gestation time the length of which she was precisely not aware' (p. 20). At 13, the security of girlhood has to be disrupted for entry into an adult role that involves coming to terms with her sexuality. The continuing quest for self is shown refracted through a literary and cultural ragbag of images that have created ready-made expectations and possibilities for being. The novel is set in a literary frame by the opening that associates Melanie's awakening adolescent sense of self with the new-found land that is John Donne's 'America', 'safest when by one man, manned'. Melanie's role models have been shaped not only by the metaphysics of love but also by pre-Raphaelite and Romantic imagination. In these discourses, the image of woman is eternally the model, muse and idealized mistress, simultaneously feared and desired; her role is to be the passive, reflecting Other of the male. This position is represented in Irigaray's writing as a protean ability to shape-shift:

> Woman is neither open nor closed. She is indefinite, in-finite, form is never complete in her. She is not infinite but neither is she a unit(y), such as letter, number, figure in series, proper noun, unique object (in a) world of the senses, simple ideality in an intelligible whole, entity of a foundation etc. This incompleteness in her form, allows her continually to become something else, though this not to say that she is ever univocally nothing. No metaphor completes her.[41]

In many ways this description resembles the Monster/Angel dichotomy that is at the heart of Gilbert and Gubar's analysis of women writers' ambivalence to images of self (see Chapter 4). In Melanie's musing about the sexual activity of her parents, mimicked fragments of D. H. Lawrence ('sacrificed to the dark gods') jostle with parodies of scraps from letters to women's magazines, and each fragment of disparate discourse reinforces and plays to excess the image of a passive femininity.

Luce Irigaray's challenge to Freud is based on her contention that in considering female sexuality Freud took as his basis the visible difference between the male and female sexual organ. His differentiation depends on speculation: to look at woman is to see nothing that proclaims her sexual difference other than an absence. Using the man as the norm, femininity is then its negation: the sex which does not have a penis. Because the definition always takes as its starting-point the masculine, woman is therefore outside representation. Because for Lacan the function of language is not to communicate but to give the subject a place from which to speak, woman is constantly placed in the male view, as forever the object of the male subject, so that there is no place from which she can reflect herself. Toril Moi gives a neat summary of Irigaray's position:

> The woman for Freud as for other Western philosophers becomes a mirror for his own masculinity. Irigaray concludes that in our society representation and therefore also social and cultural structures are products of what she sees as a fundamental hom(m)osexualité. The pun in French is on homo (same) and homme (man): the male desire for the same. (p. 135)

Woman, Irigaray argues, is conceived only as the mirror image of man. As if to exemplify the process whereby this self-definition is effected, in *The Magic Toyshop*, Melanie 'pregnant with herself', poses before the bedroom mirror in roles carefully selected from men's paintings and poetry. These images, the formulations of the masculine Imaginary, serve only to restrict women developing psychic traject-ories which accord more with their own needs. Irigaray has described this process of assumed but superficial desires thus:

> Is it necessary to add, or repeat that woman's improper access to representation, her entry into a specular and speculative economy that affords her instincts no signs, no symbols or emblems or methods of writing that could figure her instincts, make it impossible for her to work out or transpose specific representations of her instinctual object-goals? The latter are in fact, subjected to a particularly peremptory repression and will only be translated into a *script of body language*. Silent and cryptic. Replacing the fantasies she cannot have – or can have only when her amputated desires turn back on her masochistically, or when she is obliged to lend a hand with 'penis-envy'. (p. 124)

It is Melanie's 'improper access to representation', particularly to the allure of images of femininity, which makes her vulnerable to the manipulation of her Uncle Philip. She comes to view herself as the object of his attention, the heroine of his stories: 'She was a wind-up putting-away doll clicking through its programmed movements. Uncle Philip might have made her over, already. She was without volition of her own' (p. 76). Her passage to womanhood seems, in this patriarchal system, to demand a symbolic loss of virginity to an all-powerful phallic male. Rape is sanctioned in the patriarchal structur-ing of things, where woman is delivered, gift-wrapped in flimsy vestments, both to the male gaze and a castrating power. Melanie's acquiescence in the ritual is prefigured in the first scene of the novel where the fantasies acted out in the wedding dress leave her 'hobbled in yards of satin which would rip and tear and tangle irreparably' (p. 20). Her body is swamped by the wedding garment which chills and constrains her, 'she sweltered and rolled in white satin'. Her surrender to the romantic image suggested by her mother's dress prepares her for the Leda role and submission to the phallic swan: 'Melanie was forever grey, a shadow. It was the fault of the wedding dress-night, when she married the shadows and the world ended' (p. 77). To be swathed in a similar material is a pre-requisite for the Leda role: just as in the return from Thrushcross Grange of a newly grown-up Cathy in *Wuthering Heights*, becoming a woman for Melanie involves disguise. Melanie is drawn into another masquerade of femininity:

> One night, Aunt Margaret drew a length of white chiffon out of a paper bag . . . She gestured Melanie over to her and draped the material around her shoulders. All at once Melanie was back home and swathing herself in diaphanous veiling before a mirror. But the cuckoo clock poked out its head and called nine o'clock and there she was in Uncle Philip's house.
> 'Your costume', wrote Aunt Margaret on a pad to save herself getting up. 'For the show.'
> 'What am I?' asked Melanie.
> 'Leda, He is making a swan . . . That is how he sees you. White chiffon and flowers in your hair. A very young girl' . . . Melanie would be a nymph crowned with daisies once again; he saw her as once she had seen herself. In spite of everything she was flattered. (p. 141)

The acting out of the Leda story parodies the cultural sanctioning of phallic supremacy, an ideology that is internalized by both the male subject and woman as object of desire. In the event, this set piece in the novel is turned into ridiculous *mimicry* both in rehearsal and its final performance. Unlike the awesome bird in the W. B. Yeats' poem whose 'shuddering' loins engender the history of Troy, Uncle Philip's marionette is obviously constructed, and badly constructed. It is a 'mocked up swan', 'made of hollow wood'. Instead of the grace and power of the assumed shape of the 'heavenly visitant' whose 'beauty and majesty' bear its victim to the ground, it is 'a grotesque parody of a swan; Lewis Carroll might have created it.' It approaches 'dumpy and homely and eccentric', making 'lumbering progress, its feet going splat, splat, splat' (p. 165).

The text mocks the reverence granted the phallic signifier by juxtaposing Melanie's perception of its clumsiness with the inflated rhetoric of Uncle Philip's narrative. 'Almighty Jove in the form of a swan wreaks his will' is followed by the phrase 'the swan made a lumpish jump forward'. The ultimate mockery of the patriarchal exaltation of penis to phallus occurs in Finn's comic account of his disposal of the swan in the remnants of the 'pleasure gardens':

> 'And I took this spade with me, to dig a grave for the swan, and I kept dropping the spade. And the swan's neck refused to be chopped up; the axe bounced off it. It kept sticking itself out of my raincoat when I buttoned it up to hide it and it kept peering round while I was carrying it, along with all the other bits of swan and the spade as well. I had my arms full, I can tell you. It must have looked to a passer-by as if I were indecently exposing myself, when the swan's neck stuck out. I was embarrassed with myself and kept feeling to see if my fly was done up.' (p. 173)

This technique of quoting from the male ordering of things in order to reveal its flaws is exactly the mode adopted by Irigaray in re-examining the ideas of Greek philosophers, in particular Plotinus, in 'Une mère de glace'.[42] By mimicking the voice of those she analyzes in such a way as to deflate it, her text can challenge the assumptions on which it rests. In this final section of Angela Carter's novel, masculine fantasy of the phallus has been cut down from the dignity of powerful deity to the squalid exhibitionism of a dirty old man in a raincoat. Mimicry has been used, as Irigaray suggests, to destabilize an accepted order.

The mythic framework of the novel is juxtaposed with elements of popular fiction, Gothic romance and fairy story, so that the reader is propelled into a world that is a repository of vague, unnameable fears and ever-present threats projected on to otherwise mundane elements. Melanie's uncle's shop is Bluebeard's castle, where the severed hands of small girls can be found in the knife drawer (p. 118) and the strewn limbs of dismembered puppets are found in the workroom (p. 170). It is both a fox's den, dirty and malodorous, and the puppet master's workshop where male fantasies are put on stage. Running through this dream work, the search for a female identity is repeated and transformed. The women of the story lack wholeness (are all castrated): from Melanie's recollections of a mother whom she cannot imagine naked (her clothed body seems to hide a lack); her aunt struck dumb in the house of the archetypal patriarch; and Mrs Rundle, whose married title is an assumed one and whose unmarried state is a sign of incompleteness. Only the small child, Victoria, has a simple wholeness which comes partly from ignorance, partly from her continuing unity with a substituted mother figure. 'Victoria, happy Victoria who still lived in the land of Beulah, where milk and honey flow, an Eden where the snake still slumbers in futurity, mindless Victoria slept like a top' (p. 169). This text thus points to a potential femininity which could speak in its own voice rather than simply masquerading as a mirror to male aggrandizement.[43]

The story then can be read as a fable of the absence of what can be written of female desire. The pleasure garden to which Finn introduces Melanie is defunct: a wasteland whose queen, slimy and fungus-streaked, has lost her consort. Though Melanie escapes intact from struggles with both the grotesque swan and defloration by Finn, planned by her wicked Uncle, it is still in the economy of male desires that she must shape her future. At the climax of the adolescent sexual encounter, it is Finn who withdraws himself from the act, not she who rebuffs him. Although by such abstinence he is challenging Uncle Philip's patriarchal ordering of things, as male, he denies Melanie her own sexuality. As Finn, enacting the part of the swan in rehearsal, topples her 'in slow motion' to the floor, Melanie waits 'tensely for it to happen' but it is Finn who controls the sexual encounter: ' "No", said Finn aloud. "No!" again. The tension between them was destroyed with such wanton savagery that Melanie fell limply back and struggled with tears' (p. 150). She has been delivered from the older patriarch into the arms of a younger one, who is just as much in control. Her own destiny is a passive acceptance of the inevitability of the female role – female sexuality remains within the norms of the phallocentric. Melanie has a prophetic vision as Finn sits beside her:

> in his outrageous jacket, unclean in the clean sheets, yawning so that she saw the ribbed red cathedral of his mouth and all the yellow teeth like choir boys. She knew that they would get married one day and live together all their lives in dirt and mess and shabbiness, always forever and forever. And babies crying and washing to be done and toast burning all the rest of her life. And never any glamour or romance or charm. Nothing fancy. Only mess and babies with red hair. (p. 177)

If, on the one hand, the novel's main thrust is against the falsification of the romantic bridegroom, there remains the expectation that marriage is an inevitability. No alternative exists. Woman's desire is as yet unnameable and it is into the keeping of another male that Melanie's escape from the older patriarch leads. She is mirrored in Finn's eyes (p. 193) as she is shaped by his painting into an 'asexual pin-up' which is not how she sees herself (p. 154). Finn's refusal of Melanie's desire mirrors the emptiness which Irigaray detects at the centre of masculine discourse:

> a person who is in a position of mastery does not let go of it easily, does not even imagine any other position that would amount to getting out of it. The masculine is not prepared to share the initiative of discourse. It prefers to experiment with speaking, writing, enjoying 'woman' rather than leaving to that 'other' any right to intervene, to 'act' in her own interests. What remains most completely prohibited is that she should express something of her own sexual pleasure.[44]

Melanie's hopeful quest for a new world of womanhood in *The Magic Toyshop*, suggested by the introductory analogy of the discovery of America, is thrown in doubt by the final line of the novel. Having burned the infernal desiring machine of the puppet master to the ground, the couple 'gaze at each other in a wild surmise'. The connotations of the speculation which promises a new beginning for male and female relationships are taken from a John Keats poem, where the phrase 'wild surmise' refers to the wonder which the adventurer Cortez might have felt when surveying the New World.[45] The new world 'imagined' is now even less of a material reality than that promised by John Donne's America of the opening. It remains a utopian possibility, multiply displaced through literary images, whose origin is not located in experience but in textual encounter.

The novel offers other possibilities for an alternative form of socialization in the transgressive incestuous subculture of the toyshop's kitchen, where Aunt Margaret and her brothers communicate in music and dance, modes of expression that may, by their closeness to what Kristeva describes as the rhythmic pulsions of the semiotic, escape the realms of the symbolic ruled by the *nom/non du pere*, or in this case Uncle Philip.[46] These possibilities are, however, undeveloped and half rejected by an ending that leaves the survival of Aunt Margaret, her surrogate child, Victoria, and her brother/lover in doubt. By ending with a quotation that resounds enigmatically, Carter defers the closure of a romance, whilst always leaving this as a possibility, so that the text itself becomes a staging point in a feminist interrogation of the nature of 'woman'.

It is important to recognize that the interrogation of 'woman' at the cornerstone of Irigaray's work does not translate into either a complete theory of gendered identity, or, indeed, a mode of textual criticism. Irigaray is at pains to stress that her work is tentative and questioning. In the Questions section of *This Sex Which is Not One*, she describes her work in terms of exploration and process:

> To come back to my work: I am trying, as I have already indicated, to go back through the masculine imaginary, to interpret the way it has reduced us to silence, to muteness or mimicry, and I am attempting from that starting point and at the same time to (re)discover a possible space for the feminine imaginary. (p. 164)

Similarly, in this reading, neither the novelist nor the philosopher/psychoanalyst move towards a more positive description of what this new imaginary might be and in this sense each lays herself open to charges of mystification and ahistorical romanticism. However, both novelist and theorist can be seen in their writing practice to be actively engaged in a process of revisionary questioning of the categories and signs that have constructed what passes under the name of woman.

Irigaray's strategies of disclosing masquerades and mimicking masculine discourse provide useful tools in opening out Carter's novel, to
reveal a complex, self-consciously feminist text.

III

It is clear from this necessarily brief engagement with the writing of
French feminist theorists that no single position can be assigned to
them. In the 1980s their work appeared more intellectually daunting
than the work of early Anglo-American writers because of the breadth
of the reading that informed their discussions of psychoanalysis and
philosophy and the referencing of their work to an alien corpus of
writing. This corpus of work has now been widely appropriated by
Anglo-American feminist theory and put to work for feminist
purposes; for example in lesbian feminist criticism and post-colonial
feminist criticism, as we demonstrate in Chapters 7 and 8.

There are obviously difficulties in attempting to make a dense and
allusive form of theorizing work in the explication of literary texts and
it is to these problems which we would now like to turn. One of the
first problems we encountered with using French feminist work is
simply one of being caught in an endless process of displacement,
whereby the origin of significance might always be located elsewhere
anterior to the text being read, sometimes in male-authored texts, such
as Lacan or Freud, sometimes to a female exegete like Jane Gallop or
Jacqueline Rose.[47] Jane Gallop has written precisely on this process of
deferral of meaning in the search for origin, suggesting that it is ever a
deferment of desire:

> If the subject's desire comes from the Other, the subject does not
> know what she desires but must learn it from the Other. The desire
> to know what the Other knows, so as to know what one desires so
> as to satisfy that desire, is the desire behind all quests for
> knowledge.[48]

Jane Gallop links reading with desire, the urge to control, to gain
mastery. The overwhelming question which informed our reading of
French feminist theory was, what might we be able to appropriate
from feminist revision of French psychoanalytic theory. We chose to
focus on those elements which presented themselves as accessible
concepts which establish ways of reading and/or writing in the face of
male authority.

In reading *Wuthering Heights*, we used Kristeva's category of the
semiotic to undercut cohesive 'interpretations' of meaning in the novel
and point up its indeterminacy as a central feature of a feminist
reading. Kristeva's psycho-linguistics allowed a way into locating

repressed elements of the text that work to undermine the authority of the symbolic codes in operation. In suggesting an anarchic disturbance working beneath the surface logic of the narrative, we were able to demonstrate the way in which Emily Brontë's novel had inscribed within its signs a problem as yet without a name. In some of Kristeva's early writing, the semiotic is located as a zone of revolutionary potential. The difficulty, however, of associating this 'problem' with Kristeva's 'semiotic' is that it quickly translates into a model of the text which conflates the repressed with the feminine, and the feminine with madness. Kristeva's own writings, indeed, paint a 'dark' picture of the semiotic as the site of adult psychosis. In the section, 'I who want not to be', in *About Chinese Women*, Kristeva discusses the emergence of the semiotic in women's writing as the call of the mother:

> For a woman, the call of the mother is not only a call from beyond time, or beyond the socio-political battle . . . this call troubles the word: it generates hallucinations, voices, 'madness'. After the super-ego, the ego founders and sinks. It is a fragile envelope, incapable of staving off the irruption of this conflict, of this love which had bound the little girl to her mother, and which then, like a black lava, had lain in wait for her all along the path of her desperate attempts to identify with the symbolic paternal order. Once the moorings of the word, the ego, the super-ego, begin to slip, life itself can't hang on: death immediately moves in.[49]

She characterizes Sylvia Plath as 'one of the women disillusioned with meanings and words' and sees in the rhythms of *Ariel* for 'those who know how to read her, her silent departure from life'. The implicit message seems to be: accommodate to the symbolic, be content with small disruptions or die. Indeed, the end result of a theoretical bid to establish the 'feminine' as coterminous with dissidence and marginality results in a view of female artists that assumes pain, suffering and imprisonment of hope which can only be escaped through madness or death, both rather self-defeating strategies.

In Kristeva's work, this notion of the elision of the feminine and the semiotic appears problematic. Although Kristeva suggests that it is a sphere which is closer to the maternal and to which women have a special access because of their particular resolution of the Oedipal crisis, there is little to suggest that she sees the feminine as being restricted to females. Indeed, having determined to her own satisfaction that woman 'does not exist' and that speaking as a woman is an impossibility, she then focuses most of her attention on the language of male writers, seeking in them a repressed feminine that is asexual, the badge of marginality and exclusion. Women's writing is neglected except where it is discussed rather conventionally, as in the case of

Sylvia Plath's *Ariel*, to demonstrate madness and disadvantage. In setting up 'aesthetic practices' as her major concern, her theory often privileges the textual over the sexual, relegating women and their texts to the silence and obscurity of indifference. This is obviously a difficult and negative feature for this chapter, since we wish to situate our readings firmly within a feminist frame and foreground woman as the producer rather than the product of writing. Whilst it is clear that Kristeva's work has been used effectively by feminists striving to analyze the feminine, it is not a concept which helps us to describe a female aesthetic, nor a feminine aesthetic which women can appropriate.[50]

There is also a problem with the 'authority' with which Kristeva's writing dismisses other feminists' work. Kristeva, as Jane Gallop has pointed out, presumes to know: '[her] assertive style and her mastery of several difficult jargons give the appearance of "knowledge" and authority. Kristeva presumes the right to assert, to speak as if she "knows" '.[51] We are not asserting that knowing itself is problematic for women; rather that her style seems to be overly dense and the readings that she herself produces of some of Mallarmé's poetry are rather disappointing and verging on the banal. As Anne Rosalind Jones states:

> Focusing on sound, repetition and disruptions of grammar, [Kristeva] relates [Mallarmé's] written texts to archaic psychosomatic processes. Mallarmé himself had an elaborate theory of the expressive potential of various letters, 'p' suggests a piling up or holding onto riches, 'r' suggests a pushing away, 't' has a stabilizing, stopping effect. Such onomatopoeic essentialism is not surprising in a poet, but it is surprising that a post-Saussurean linguist accepts it, given the structuralist insistence on the arbitrariness of sound/ meaning links in language.[52]

Furthermore, as we noted earlier, this tendency to focus solely on male writers for revolutionary poetics is striking in a theorist who has been identified as a feminist.[53]

Irigaray is equally 'authoritative' in her skilful deconstruction of those elements of Western thought that have 'framed' women as a mirror image of the male. Her revision of psychoanalytical theories of sexuality are presented far more tentatively and interrogatively than those of Julia Kristeva. She, too, has a theory of the subject-in-process but concentrates her efforts on an attempt to push towards what 'woman' might be if she were able to follow the movement of a different desire. We have used her work to demythologize the objectification of woman as the 'specular other' of the male and to suggest utopian possibilities. However, whilst these critical manoeuvres have led to a productive vision of the possibilities untapped within femininity, many critics of Irigaray's writing, who include Chris Weedon, have strongly objected to what they read as Irigaray's argument for an integral relationship between sexuality and language.[54] This would seem to be viewing Irigaray's metaphors of fluidity and contiguity as essentialism, an acceptance of biology as the most powerful determinant of subjectivity; however, it could be argued that this is to take literally what is offered as analogy, to interpret utopian longings for a description of external reality. Nevertheless, many feminists continue to reject what they see as a new form of biological essentialism that reduces accounts of women's language to an inarticulate babbling, and women themselves to the eternally feminine. Luce Irigaray, in particular, has aroused the kind of hostility voiced by Monique Plaza: 'Luce Irigaray closes us in the shroud of our own sex, reduces us to the state of child woman: illogical, mad, prattling, fanciful . . . thus is woman.'[55] As we move into the late 1990s, therefore, the legacy of French feminism is in dispute. Whilst its defenders, like Elizabeth Grosz and Margaret Whitford (see note 5) are working hard to explicate Kristeva, Irigaray *et al.*, in a way that will make them acceptable and intelligible to the feminist community at large, other theorists have now taken up the challenge posed by this psychoanalytic work to make explicit the tension between the subject and her insertion in language within a historical framework and to effect a reconciliation between theories of the structure of the psyche and material existence.[56] Even in this revisioning of psychoanalytic theory, however, the presence of this early French feminist theory is felt. Whatever the problems and limitations of its utopian vision, their re-writing of Freud and Lacan's work has been integral to the feminist appropriation of psycho-analysis.

Notes

1. Other French feminists include Monique Wittig, Catherine Clément, Annie Leclerc, Christine Delphy, Michèle LeDoeuff and Sarah Kofman, whose work can be sampled in an anthology edited by Toril Moi, *French Feminist Thought* (Blackwell, Oxford, 1987) and in Elaine Marks and Isabelle DeCourtivron's edition, *New French Feminisms* (Harvester, Brighton, 1980). See also Monique Wittig's *The Straight Mind and other Essays* (Harvester Wheatsheaf, Hemel Hempstead, 1992). But as this chapter will go on to show, there are many feminists who do similar theoretical work, some of which is based on theories developed in France, who are not themselves French, for example Gayatri Chakravorty Spivak, whose work we consider in Chapter 8.

2. Julia Kristeva, *Powers of Horror: An Essay on Abjection*, trans. Leon S. Roudiez (Columbia University Press, New York, 1982).

3. Luce Irigaray, *I Love You: Sketch of a Possible Felicity in History* (Routledge, London, 1995); see also Luce Irigaray, *Je, Tu, Nous: Towards a Culture of Difference* (Routledge, London, 1993).

4. See, for example, Gerardine Meaney, *(Un)Like Subjects: Women/Theory and Fiction* (Routledge, London, 1993) who examines Cixous, Irigaray and Kristeva in relation to women's writing. Other critics such as Rita Felski in *Beyond Feminist Aesthetics* (Hutchinson Radius, London, 1989) have challenged this quest for a female or feminist aesthetic as an effective red herring.

5. Elizabeth Grosz, *Jacques Lacan: A Feminist Introduction* (Routledge, London, 1990) and Margaret Whitford, *Luce Irigaray: Philosophy in the Feminine* (Routledge, London, 1991).

6. Judith Butler, *Gender Trouble: Feminism and the Subversion of Identity* (Routledge, London and New York, 1990).

7. Eve Kosofsky Sedgwick, *Between Men: English Literature and Homosocial Desire* (Columbia University Press, New York, 1985); and *The Epistemology of the Closet* (Harvester Wheatsheaf, Hemel Hempstead, 1991).

8. Felski (note 4 above) p. 35.

9. Lacan himself locates this phase at 6 months and thus considers it as a literal experience that children undergo; however other theorists have seen this as a metaphorical stage of identity formation where the image in the mirror is more indicative of the difficulty of recognizing a sense of self in relation to others. As Ellie Ragland-Sullivan puts it: 'Each of us tries to become whole and ideal in the eyes of others on the basis of a desire to be thought of in certain ways, which others can never validate as fully true.' (Ragland-Sullivan, 'The imaginary' in E. Wright (ed.), *Feminism and Psychoanalysis* (Blackwell, Oxford, 1993), p. 174.

10. For a discussion of the relation between the semiotic and the Symbolic, see Sara Mills: 'No poetry for ladies: Gertrude Stein, Julia Kristeva and modernism', pp 85–107, in Dave Murray (ed.), *Literary Theory and Poetry: Extending the Canon* (Batsford, London, 1989).

11. Ragland-Sullivan (see note 9 above), pp. 173–6; p. 174.

12. Consider, for example, Dale Spender's critical work on 'man-made' language, with its suggestion of a patriarchal conspiracy against the feminine. Spender makes the problem a social difficulty which can be overcome through a variety of social and legal means (Spender, 1980).

13. Jacques Lacan, 'The agency of the letter in the unconscious or reason since Freud', *Écrits: A Selection*, translated by A. Sheridan (Tavistock, London, 1980), p. 148. This essay, which has been of powerful significance in theorizing the relation of the subject to the Symbolic Order, poses enormous difficulties for the reader. A useful introduction to Lacan's work is provided by Malcolm Bowie in 'Jacques Lacan' in John Sturrock (ed.), *Structuralism and Since* (Oxford University Press, Oxford, 1979), pp. 116–53.

14. These French feminists are not concerned with literary criticism.

Instead of literary texts, their writing most frequently engages with the major works of Western philosophical thought, from Plato to Freud. These are not explications, but major reworkings of ideas that go unchallenged in the writings of their male colleagues, illustrating the historical processes whereby the feminine has been defined and debased in men's texts. Where literary texts are the object of study, for example, in the criticism of Julia Kristeva, they are examined in terms of a politics of style that reveals the suppressed feminine in male writing, particularly in those whose sexuality places them outside the mainstream of literary conventions, for example, Marcel Proust and Jean Genet. Rather than concerning themselves with the representation of women's 'experience', their texts take issue with a dominant masculine tradition of psychoanalytical analysis that, through the concepts of the Oedipal and castration complexes, locates femininity as lack and a convention of philosophy that is locked into male patterns of discourse. For a collection of essays which attempts to use Hélène Cixous' work for the analysis of literary texts, see Helen Wilcox, Keith McWatters, Ann Thompson and Linda Williams (eds), *The Body and the Text: Hélène Cixous, Reading and Teaching* (Harvester Wheatsheaf, Hemel Hempstead, 1990).

15. Julia Kristeva, 'A question of subjectivity – an interview' in P. Rice and P. Waugh (eds), *Modern Literary Theory: A Reader* (Edward Arnold, London, 1989), p. 131.

16. Julia Kristeva, *Desire in Language: A Semiotic Approach to Literature and Art*, ed. Leon S. Roudiez, translated by Thomas Gorg *et al.* (Blackwell, Oxford, 1980), p. 133, quoted in Felski (note 4 above), p. 34.

17. Luce Irigaray, *This Sex Which is Not One*, translated by Catherine Porter with Carolyn Burke (Cornell University Press, Ithaca, 1985 f. pub. 1977); Hélène Cixous and Catherine Clément, *The Newly Born Woman*, translated by Betsy Wing (Manchester University Press, Manchester, 1986 f. pub. 1975).

18. In this sense, Kristeva does not offer a theory of femininity or take up issues which are consciously feminist. When, however, the semiotic and the symbolic are employed by the Marxist-feminist critics discussed in Chapter 6, these terms are placed within a framework that allows the politics of how subjects are engendered to be articulated.

19. Luce Irigaray, *Speculum of the Other Woman*, trans. Gillian C. Gill (Cornell University Press, Ithaca, 1985), p. 22. All further references are given after quotations in the text.

20. Luce Irigaray, *Le Langage des Dèments* (Mouton, Paris), quoted by Toril Moi 'Patriarchal reflections: Luce Irigaray's looking glass' in *Sexual/ Textual Politics* (Methuen, London, 1985).

21. From an interview given to L. Serrana and E. Hoffman in Holmes and Meier (eds), *Women Writers Talking*, pp. 238–9, quoted in Jan Montefiore, *Feminism and Poetry* (Pandora, London, 1987), pp. 141–3.

22. *Speculum of the Other Woman* (see note 19 above), p. 227.

23. Irigaray, *This Sex Which is Not One* (see note 17 above), extract included in Elaine Marks and Isabelle de Courtivron (eds), *New*

French Feminisms (Harvester Wheatsheaf, Hemel Hempstead, 1981), pp. 99–106; p. 100.

24. Emily Brontë, *Wuthering Heights* (Penguin, Harmondsworth, 1965).

25. Sandra Gilbert and Susan Gubar, *The Madwoman in the Attic* (Yale University Press, New Haven, 1979), p. 803. All further references are given after quotations in the text.

26. This fascination is exemplified in Rachel Brownstein's account of a high-school student's classroom response: 'Gloria has read *Wuthering Heights* sixteen times . . . It was the first thing she ever said to me without raising her hand' (Brownstein, *Becoming a Heroine: Reading about women in novels* (Penguin, Harmondsworth, 1982), p. 137.

27. J. H. Miller, *Fiction and Repetition* (Blackwell, Oxford, 1982), p. 50. All subsequent references appear after quotations.

28. Currer Bell (Charlotte Brontë), 'Biographical notice of Acton and Ellis Bell 1850', reproduced in the Penguin edition of *Wuthering Heights* (see note 24 above), pp. 30–65.

29. Terry Eagleton's account of Kristeva's model which appears in *Literary Theory: An Introduction* (Blackwell, Oxford, 1983). This is an excellent general introduction to new theories of the text although it does not give sufficient attention to the development of a feminist critique within mainstream male theory or to feminist theory itself. This is the province of Toril Moi's *Sexual/Textual Politics*, which along with many other surveys of feminist theory can be read as a much-needed supplement.

30. Julia Kristeva, 'La femme ce n'est jamais ça', *Tel Quel*, vol. 59, Autumn 1979, pp. 19–24, quoted by Toril Moi in *Sexual/Textual Politics* (see note 20 above), p. 163.

31. Julia Kristeva, ' A Partie de polylogue', interview with Françoise van Rossum Guyon in *Revue des Sciences Humaines*, December 1979, pp. 495–501.

32. *Roland Barthes by Roland Barthes*, translated by Richard Howard (Hill and Wang, New York, 1977), p. 138.

33. In many ways Isabella acts out the romantic aspirations of the young Cathy in her relationship with Heathcliff, and is another aspect of the possibilities for the lost child. This kind of reading finds not unified characters but fragments of the sign 'woman', and thus contrasts markedly with an authentic realist viewpoint, that might begin to discuss Isabella in terms of a critique of domestic violence. See Chapter 2.

34. Mary Daly, *Pure Lust: Elemental Female Philosophy* (The Women's Press, London, 1984), p. 382.

35. Toril Moi, 'Marginality and subversions: Julia Kristeva', in *Sexual/ Textual Politics* (see note 20 above), pp. 150–73.

36. Angela Carter, *The Magic Toyshop* (Virago, London, 1982).

37. From an interview given by Carter to Moira Paterson, 'Flights of fancy in Balham', pp. 42–5, in *The Observer*, November 1986.

38. Jacques Lacan, 'Seminar on *The Purloined Letter*', translated by Jeffrey Mehlman, *Yale French Studies*, vol. 48, 1972, pp. 38–72.

39. Alicia Ostriker, 'The thieves of language: women poets and revisionist mythmakers', *Signs*, vol. 8, no. 1, Spring 1982, pp. 66–78.

40. Angela Carter, 'Notes from the front line', in Micheline Wandor (ed.), *On Gender and Writing* (Pandora, London, 1983), pp. 69–77.

41. Luce Irigaray, *Speculum of the Other Woman* (see note 9 above), p. 229.

42. Luce Irigaray, 'Une mère de glace', in *This Sex Which is Not One* (see note 17 above), pp. 168–79.

43. Although obviously there are problems in seeing Victoria's femininity as a utopian vision of what the feminine could be like, since it is femininity at an infantile stage of development. Perhaps the image simply holds open a vision of a different type of femininity which could develop, if it did not follow the trajectory of current patriarchal frameworks.

44. Luce Irigaray, *This Sex Which is Not One* (see note 17 above), p. 157.

45. John Keats, 'On first looking into Chapman's Homer', in H. W. Garrad (ed.), *The Poetical Works of John Keats* (Ansen House, Oxford Standard Authors, Oxford, 1956), p. 38.

46. This pun in French works on the fact that the authority manifested in the Father is essentially a negative one; authority within this patriarchal model is about denying others and saying 'no'.

47. Jane Gallop, *Reading Lacan* (Cornell University Press, Ithaca, 1985); Jacqueline Rose, *Sexuality in the Field of Vision* (Verso, London, 1986).

48. Jane Gallop, *Feminism and Psychoanalysis: The Daughter's Seduction* (Macmillan, Basingstoke, 1982).

49. Julia Kristeva, 'On Chinese women' in Toril Moi (ed.), *The Kristeva Reader* (Blackwell, Oxford, 1986), pp. 138–60.

50. See especially the section entitled 'Another generation is another space', in 'Woman's time', pp. 209–11 in *The Kristeva Reader* (see note 49 above).

51. Jane Gallop, *Reading Lacan* (see note 47 above), p. 185.

52. Anne Rosalind Jones, 'Julia Kristeva on femininity: the limits of a semiotic politics', *Feminist Review*, no. 18, November 1984, pp. 56–78 (p. 59).

53. Although feminist is not a label that Kristeva herself has ever unproblematically used to describe her work.

54. Chris Weedon, *Feminist Practice and Post-structuralist Theory* (Blackwell, Oxford, 1987).

55. Monique Plaza, 'Phallomorphic power and the psychology of women', translated by M. David and J. Hodges, in *Ideology and Consciousness*, vol. 4, Autumn 1978, pp. 5–36. Plaza is anxious to stress the material nature of women's oppression against the purely philosophical and ideological categories employed by Irigaray.

56. For feminist theorists who attempt to develop a materialist feminist psychoanalytical analysis of the subject, see, amongst others, Jackie Stacey, *Star Gazing: Hollywood Cinema and Female Spectatorship* (Routledge, London, 1994) and Anne McClintock, *Imperial Leather: Race, Gender and Sexuality in the Imperial Contest* (Routledge, London, 1995).

6
Marxist-feminism

Lynne Pearce and Sara Mills

The Marxist-Feminist Literature Collective:
'Women's writing'
Margaret Atwood: *Surfacing*
Charlotte Perkins Gilman: 'The Yellow Wallpaper'

I

The relationship between Marxism and feminism has been described as an 'unhappy marriage', but the liaison between Marxist-feminism and literary criticism has proved an even more problematic 'affair', resisting and subsuming all the normal categories of kinship.[1] Since one of the partners in this relationship has recently been pronounced 'dead', as we noted in the Introduction, some argument against divorce is necessary, particularly in the light of recent rumours about an 'affair' with a new partner (materialism).

Some recent feminist critics, such as Donna Landry and Gerald Maclean, and Rosemary Hennessy have argued that Marxist-feminism should more appropriately be termed materialist feminism.[2] This change of terminology signals for these critics not so much a coming to a theoretical dead-end with Marxism, but a move towards seeing the relationship between feminism and Marxism as 'unfinished business', as something which still needs working through.[3] For Landry and Maclean, however, it seems as if Marxist theory alone is not to be the primary focus of attention, and Hennessy makes this quite explicit in her decision to try to infuse some vitality into materialist feminism by inflecting it with discourse theory (see Glossary). The work of these critics is important in forcing Marxism in general to move towards new theoretical positions which are more able to account for current socio-economic and cultural situations, as Landry and Maclean state: 'Socialism must be re-invented from within feminism and other new social movements, such as those which contest racism and heterosexism' (p. 1). However, we would argue that those reinventions can continue, based within the realms of Marxist theory rather than within a more amorphous materialism.[4] There are a number of reasons for this: first, Marxist theories are theoretical frameworks, which, through constant engagement and interrogation, have been developed to more adequately address current issues; materialism does not have this sense of explicitly formulated theories. Secondly, Marxist theories are the only ones which have so far been developed which consistently and systematically concern themselves with economic relations and with historical and contextual information; materialism does concern itself with these factors but not as systematically. Thirdly, Marxist theories have been developed to explain and, more importantly, combat oppression and injustice; whilst materialist critics may also be engaged in this type of action, there is no comparable sense in which opposition to oppression is written in at a theoretical level. Finally, whilst it is clear that political events within the Eastern bloc and elsewhere have brought about the demise of communism as a state system, and these changes have themselves precipitated a crisis within Marxism as whole, it is necessary to recognize that Marxism itself, when separated from vulgar Marxism, still holds immense explanatory power and resonance.[5]

We will attempt here to summarize the trajectory of Marxist-feminist theory, and our summary will be in constant dialogue with this more recent move towards a change of terminology to materialism. The problem of offering any adequate summary of Marxist-feminist criticism resides first in the fact that its practice has been developed more consciously in the social sciences and cultural studies arena than in literary criticism *per se*.[6] Secondly, and in paradoxical relation to this first point, there are few feminist literary studies that have not, to a greater or lesser extent, been informed by Marxist/socialist perceptions of the social construction of women and gender. The latter fact obviously relates directly to the 'origins' of the modern Women's Movement in the various New Left campaigns of the 1960s (see Chapters 1 and 2). Indeed, looking back to the chapter on 'Sexual politics', the reader will recall that Kate Millett's definition of politics as 'power-structured relationships, arrangements where one group of persons is controlled by another' is potentially Marxist in its articulation, although, as was also explained, her prioritization of patriarchy over capitalism as the nexus of oppression has since been rejected as a rather crude attempt to 'stand Marxist theory on its head'.[7] A further problem that is inherent in the notion of 'Marxist-feminism' is the very fact that it is a hyphenated concept, continually reminding its practitioners of the uneasy relationship of the one part to the other; is feminism merely an addition to Marxism or vice versa?

This, of course, relates to the larger political argument (again touched upon in Chapter 1) of the respective claims of capitalism and patriarchy as the fundamental categories of oppression; the one reducing the other to a constituent sub-category.[8] This difficult, and often bitter, debate, which had very practical ramifications for various left-wing organizations in the 1970s, has been replaced by a concern to move forward from ranking oppressions or assuming that one institutional factor has primacy in determining inequality.[9] Post-structuralist and post-modernist theories have enabled literary critics to work with contradictions of this kind far more easily, and to see the relationship between the two institutions as mutable, shifting and tangential. As Maggie Humm writes on the subject: 'Neither Marxism nor feminism can totally incorporate each other.'[10] It is true, however (as Humm's subsequent remarks tacitly admit) that much Marxist-feminist literary criticism has taken the form of a simple modification of the Marxist paradigms of analysis, which are feminist only because they address issues of gender as well as/instead of class. This is a problem we shall return to in the concluding section, but it is proper to introduce it here since it is an issue that relates particularly to our chosen theoretical texts and to our subsequent readings.

This tentative problematization of the concept of Marxist-feminism should already have suggested to the reader that its practice, in literary criticism especially, will be far from monolithic. Here, more than with any of the other theories introduced in this book, we are dealing with an approach which has as many qualities as the contexts in which it has been used. There is no simple answer to questions such as 'What is Marxist-feminism?' or 'What issues will a Marxist-feminist reading address?' Beyond an obvious commitment to the questions facing women in the 'real world' (understood broadly in the term 'materialism'), literary Marxist-feminism will manifest itself in a wide range of readings, all defining their particular commitment rather differently. Thus, critical writings as far apart in their theses as Penny Boumelha's *Thomas Hardy and Women*, Rosemary Hennessy and Rajeswari Mohan's 'The construction of women in three popular texts of empire' and Terry Lovell's *Consuming Fiction* may all be held up as examples of texts which may be described as 'Marxist-feminist', although the first is concerned with the relation of sexual ideology to narrative form, the second with problematizing materialist feminist theory when confronted with the analysis of imperial texts, and the third with the conditions surrounding the *production* of the novel and the role of women therein.[11] In addition, there are many other feminist theories, including those introduced in this book, which, as indicated above, were born out of a modern Women's Movement which was itself intimately related to a new socialist consciousness.[12]

Yet while all the theories put into practice in this book may be seen to have their own particular relation to a materialist feminism (in so far as 'Marxism and feminism are both theories about the power of the "real" world and its impact on literary imagination'), none is *systematic* in its application of any particular methodology devised by Marxist-feminists.[13] This is why we have chosen to use an example of an avowedly Marxist-feminist literary criticism and sought to engage with it in our own readings of Margaret Atwood's *Surfacing*, and Charlotte Perkins Gilman's 'The Yellow Wallpaper'. The critical text in question is an article by the Marxist-Feminist Literature Collective (MFLC) of 1978, now regarded as breaking new ground in its practical application of a new synthesis of Marxism, feminism and psychoanalysis.[14] This article, entitled 'Women's writing: Jane Eyre, Shirley, Villette, Aurora Leigh' performs readings of each of the listed texts in turn, concentrating on how their 'not-saids' (explained below) represent the destabilizing of the prevailing ideologies inscribed in literary texts and (since the article is specifically concerned with ideologies relating to gender) constitute their feminism. Although concrete in its application, the theoretical assumptions behind these readings are not made clear in the article and need to be inferred through prior knowledge of Marxist theory. What we shall now do here, therefore, is offer a brief summary of the principles that lie behind the Collective's readings, simultaneously illustrating their application in the article itself. Our own readings that follow will consequently be themselves based on a working through of the theoretical assumptions of the article rather than a simple repetition of the readings it performs.

Since the late 1970s, the type of Marxism that has been favoured by feminist literary critics is that which has primarily developed from the work of Marxist theorists such as Louis Althusser and Pierre Macherey.[15] The attraction of these theorists is that they suggest methods of reading texts which are compatible with the poststructuralist realization that literature is not simply the reflection of the world outside the text. This is in opposition to the type of critical practice offered by earlier Marxist critics like Georg Lukács and Christopher Caudwell, with their preference for socialist-realist texts.[16] Although Lukács actually argued for the importance of form in determining a work's radical potential ('the truly social element in literature is the form'), this was only the case if that form, in some way, exposed or reflected the structure of society itself.[17] Thus, the realist novel was seen as a 'bourgeois epic', whose three-part form reflected the profile of a society torn apart by capitalism while straining towards a new resolution or synthesis: Lukács described such a novel which 'mirrors, in microcosmic form, the complex totality of society itself. In doing this, great art combats the alienation and fragmentation of capitalist society, projecting a rich, many-sided image of human wholeness.'[18] This model was itself based on what is now popularly known as 'the Marxist dialectic', although the programme of Thesis–Antithesis–Synthesis, as we explained above (see note 7), actually derived from Hegel. While it is consequently debatable whether the dialectic is an appropriate model for the Marxist literary critic to make use of, we have employed it as a structural device in the reading of *Surfacing* which follows; as an index of transformation against which the changing relationships of the characters to their material circumstances is plotted.

Another way of understanding Lukács' approach and, at the same time, recognizing the attractions of Althusser and Macherey for feminist critics, is to consider their contrasting attitudes to the role of 'ideology' in the literary work. While Lukács saw the representation of degenerate late-capitalist ideology as reactionary and unproductive, Althusser's formulation of the complex relationship between 'base and superstructure' lent a new interest to literary texts precisely because of their ideological content. In the MFLC article, the writers use Althusser's own definition of ideology as 'a representation of the imaginary relationship of individuals to their real conditions of existence' to define the role of the text itself:[19] 'Literary texts are assumed to be ideological in the sense that they cannot give us a knowledge of the social formation; but they do give us something of equal importance in analysing culture, an imaginary representation of real relations' (p. 27). Texts, in other words, reveal to us the workings of the ideologies that they themselves are inscribed by. It will be seen at once that this is a much more satisfactory and enabling view of the text than Lukács' prescription that it simplistically mirror the 'Truth' of reality itself.

But to understand how the MFLC use Althusser's radical restatement of the relationship between ideology and the economic base, it is first necessary to say a little about the Althusserian source itself. The key text here is Althusser's 'Ideology and ideological state apparatuses' of 1971.[20] This article is concerned with the way that ideological practices inform the actions and thinking of individuals. Althusser set himself to understand the difficult question of why some groups of individuals believe certain ideas which are not in their interest; he suggested that ideological knowledge (that is, knowledge which masks the reality of the relations between groups of individuals and institutions) is supported by having an institutional base. This is quite important and concretizes ideology, making it more of a material practice, rather than simply a form of 'false consciousness'.[21] The essence of the hypothesis of the article is summed up by Chris Weedon in *Feminist Practice and Post-Structuralist Theory*:

Louis Althusser argues . . . that the reproduction of the relations of production, which is central to the maintenance of capitalist social relations, is secured by ideological state apparatuses such as schools, the church, the family, the law, the political system, trade unionism, the media and culture, backed by the repressive apparatuses of the police and the armed forces. Each ideological state apparatus contributes to the reproduction of capitalist relations of exploitation in the 'way proper to it' and the means by which it determines dominant meanings is language.[22]

What is revolutionary about Althusser's formulation is that it gives the 'superstructure' a role equal to that of the 'base' in the perpetration of capitalism. He also provides the literary critic with the extremely useful, related concept of interpellation, used to explain how the individual is governed by these 'ideological state apparatuses' (ISAs). Interpellation also is a concept which helps to explain how it is that individuals feel that ideological knowledge is in fact their own, or that it is common sense. Althusser states:

I shall . . . suggest that ideology 'acts' or 'functions' in such a way that it 'recruits' subjects among the individuals (it recruits them all), or 'transforms' the individuals into subjects (it transforms them all) by the very precise operation which I have called interpellation or hailing, and which may be imagined along the lines of the most common everyday police (or other) hailing: 'Hey, you there'. (p. 48)

Althusser here suggests that individuals are constituted as subjects through the process of being called upon to recognize themselves by a range of ideological knowledges.[23]

Interpellation is central to both of the readings performed in this chapter. In the section on *Surfacing* it is related specifically to the heroine's own interpellation by the ideological state apparatus of the family and its attendant agencies (gender difference and romantic love), while the reading of 'The Yellow Wallpaper' is concerned both with the interpellation of the protagonist and ourselves as women readers of the text into a particular role: that of the mad woman.

In their readings of Brontë and Barrett Browning, the Collective shows how the texts concerned 'evade and interrogate' Althusser's ISAs in the areas of class structure, kinship and Oedipal socialization. Just how they 'evade and interrogate' these ideologies necessitates introducing another Marxist concept: the Machereyan 'not-said' or 'unsaid'. Pierre Macherey has been of especial importance to literary critics since, unlike Althusser, his writings practise criticism of particular literary texts.[24] The 'not-said' of a text might be thought of as an 'unspoken sub-text', which, by its very telling silence, interrogates and undermines what is represented by the dominant message of the text. Ideology within this model is posited as a contradictory assemblage of ideas straining for an impossible coherence; the silences and gaps are in fact symptomatic of the 'papering-over' of difficult questions and issues. In other words, a Machereyan reading, like a deconstructive one, is concerned with identifying the 'gaps' in a given text and speculating on what they reveal: as Terry Eagleton puts it, 'criticism, then, does not site itself in the same space as the text itself, allowing it to speak or completing what it leaves unsaid. On the contrary, it installs itself in the text's very incompleteness in order to theorize the lack of plenitude – to explain the necessity.'[25] To take just one example of such a practice, the MFLC posit that *Jane Eyre* in its very exclusion of kinship relations, is effectively challenging their legitimate existence. Thus, although the dominant message of the text might be seen to be working towards a reactionary conclusion, by restoring the dominant kinship structures (Jane finds her lost family and is married to Rochester), its 'not-said' covertly challenges this status quo: MFLC state '*Jane Eyre* does not attempt to rupture the dominant kinship structures.' The ending of the novel ('Reader, I married him') affirms those very structures. The feminism of the text resides in its 'not-said', its attempt to inscribe women as sexual subjects within this system (p. 35). Such a reading makes explicit connections between this type of Marxist-feminism and a more general poststructuralist resistance to closure and 'inherent' or singular meanings within a text. In the reading of 'The Yellow Wallpaper' which follows we argue that it is the text's very refusal to offer a conclusive ending that constitutes its problematization of madness in materialist terms.

It is necessary to consider finally the way in which the MFLC combine this feminist utilization of Althusser and Macherey with the psychoanalysis of Jacques Lacan and Julia Kristeva. Althusser, like Valentin Voloshinov, grafted a model of the psyche developed within psychoanalysis onto a Marxist model of social structures, in order to come to a description of the individual subject constituted out of a complex negotiation with social forces.[26] The most obvious point of intersection, and the one we shall ourselves be using in our readings, is that which inheres around the notion of the imaginary.[27] Althusser's definition of ideology, as we have already seen, is as the 'representa-tion of the imaginary relationship of individuals to their real conditions of existence'. The 'imaginary' here constitutes the failure of individuals to recognize that the ideological forces by which they are interpellated are neither real nor inevitable. They are thus the victims of social relations that they perceive to be natural and determinate, but which are imposed upon them by a variety of social institutions or ISAs.

The 'misrecognition' of an imaginary relationship is also at the heart of Lacanian theories of subjectivity. As has already been explained in Chapter 5, the Lacanian Imaginary refers specifically to the pre-

Oedipal identification of a child with its mirror-image before it has acquired an autonomous sense of self. This is followed by a second split which occurs when the child, in Lacanian terms, enters language (the Symbolic Order): 'just as the infant of the mirror phase misrecognises itself as unified and in physical control of itself, so the speaking subject in the symbolic order misrecognises itself and its utterance as one and assumes that it is the author of meaning.'[28] It will be seen that this second 'misrecognition' is conceptually similar to Althusser's notion of the Imaginary as it pertains to the interpellation of the individual by ideologies. In both instances, the subject believes that s/he is in control of a situation which is, in fact, determined by structures within the dominant culture. It is just this 'delusion' that allows, on the one hand, for our existence as social beings (without such a misrecognition we could not function effectively in the world), yet on the other, for our manipulation by the forces of the State.[29]

The MFLC exploit the possibility of deliberately 'confusing' these two uses of the imaginary in their reading of Charlotte Brontë's *Villette* (1853) in which it is postulated that the nun who appears to Lucy Snowe 'banishes the Lacanian "Imaginary" and reinstates the "Symbolic" realm' (p. 41). In Marxist terms, this full entry into the Symbolic Order may be thought of as analogous with the heroine's realignment with the Ideological State Apparatuses by which she has been interpellated.[30] Thus, while until the appearance of the nun, Lucy Snowe's delayed alignment with the Symbolic means that she resists the prevailing ideologies of kinship, class and Oedipal socialization, the three 'visitations' (all simultaneous with her declarations of love for the male) announce her subsequent interpellation by them. While this conflation of Lacan and Althusser leads to a radical rereading of this particular text, it should nevertheless be remembered that Lacan's Symbolic Order is a universal psychic category and not at all ideological and/or socially articulated. One of the problems with the MFLC reading, indeed, is that it makes it appear as though the Symbolic Order is roughly equivalent to some sort of 'dominant discourse' and *not* a psychic formation. This has implications for possible modes of resistance since whilst the Althusserian subject is problematically 'trapped' in a particular ideological mind-set until something (i.e. another oppositional or alternative ideology) enables her to recognize the nature of her oppression, the Lacanian subject's potential resistance is part and parcel of her imperfect psychic transition to the patriarchally inscribed Symbolic Order. Once these differences of 'origin' are noted however – one social and cultural, the other psychic – the dialogue between the two 'imaginarys' *can* be put to productive use.

To summarize then, it is the Marxist-Feminist Literature Collective's engagement with the following that we shall be particularly concerned with in the readings:

1. The Althusserian formulation of Ideological State Apparatuses and their interpellation of subjects (fictional characters and readers).
2. The Machereyan 'not-said'.
3. The integration of materialist with psychoanalytic models.
4. The relation of all these theories to issues of gender.

By coincidence, the literary texts we have chosen have in common 'nameless' heroines who are alienated from the social context that has been prescribed for them as women. The two readings, nevertheless, approach the materialist implications of this with two very different sets of hypotheses, and will therefore demonstrate the range of possible Marxist-feminist critical positions.[31]

II

Margaret Atwood's *Surfacing*, like the nineteenth-century 'realist' novel that Georg Lukács saw as profiling the rise and fall of capitalist society, is divided into three parts.[32] In order to explore the hypothesis that such a structure may be thought of as analogous to the Marxist dialectic, we have organized the reading under the subheadings of Thesis, Antithesis and Synthesis, with each 'phase' roughly corresponding to a section of the novel. Within these subdivisions, we practise readings which derive from the Althusserian and Machereyan theories outlined in Part I. As in the Marxist-Feminist Literature Collective's readings of Brontë and Barrett Browning, we have looked for ways in which the text both reflects and interrogates Althusser's Ideological State Apparatuses (ISAs), through the interpellation of the heroine and the other characters.[33] In this analysis, our principal focus is on the family, together with its attendant ideologies of gender difference and romantic love. However, because *Surfacing* must be regarded as a self-consciously political or interrogative text, we do not, like the MFLC, attempt to 'discover' its feminist subversion in its 'not-said', except in our closing comments on the problems surrounding its ending.[34] In crude terms, the story is about the heroine making these discoveries herself: coming face to face with her own 'not-said' in the form of the ideologies by which she has been interpellated.

Thus, instead of analyzing the 'not-said', which would simply constitute a repetition of the narrator's ideological questionings, we have chosen to perform a reading which explains this process of self-discovery in terms of the heroine's changing relation to the Lacanian

Symbolic Order. Our contention is that it is the very dislocation between her ideological interpellation and her psychological subjectivity (see Part I above) that enables her to challenge 'her imaginary relationship' to her 'real conditions of existence'. Thus, as the narrative moves through the dialectic of Thesis–Antithesis–Synthesis, the heroine's changing position *vis-à-vis* the Symbolic Order may be seen to culminate in a 'revolution' through which she eventually arrives at a 'synthesis' of the different 'stories' she has told from within the ideological structures by which she has been interpellated.

Thesis

In Part One of the novel, it is gradually revealed that the heroine is caught up in what Althusser describes as 'the imaginary distortion of the ideological representation of the real world' (p. 154). 'Distortion' is a key term here, since it describes well the false narratives she uses to tell the story of her life: her 'marriage', her 'child', the 'drowning' of her brother. In these stories, she mixes together elements of what 'really happened' with what she believed happened, or what might have happened. At various points, she even draws attention to the treachery of 'memory': the discrepancy between what one experiences, and what one learns afterwards. For example, about her childhood in the war, the heroine states:

> Anna was right, I had a good childhood; it was the middle of the war, flecked grey newsreels I never saw, bombs and concentration camps, the leaders roaring at the crowds from inside their uniforms, pain and endless death, flags rippling in time to the anthems. But I didn't know about that till later, when my brother found out and told me. At the time it felt like peace. (p. 18)

This compares to the story she tells, on the very first page of the novel, of an incident that happened to her brother in a restaurant before she herself was born (p. 7); and it also relates to her constant checking and correcting of elements within the narrative: 'That won't work, I can't call them "they" as if they were someone's family: I have to keep from telling that story' (p. 14) and 'The old priest was gone. What I mean is dead' (p. 18). Then, at the very end of Part One, she brings her propensity for distortion to full consciousness, thus preparing for the process of antithesis that occurs in Part Two:

> I have to be more careful about my memories, I have to be sure that they're my own and not the memories of other people telling me what I felt, how I acted, what I said: if the events are wrong the feelings I remember about them will be wrong too, I'll start inventing them and there will be no way of correcting it, the ones who could help are gone. I run quickly over my version of it, my life, checking it like an alibi; it fits, it's all there till the time I left. Then static, like a

jumped track, for a moment I've lost it, wiped clean; my exact age
even, I shut my eyes, what is it? To have the past but not the
present, that means you're going senile. (p. 73)

What we need to consider here is the reason the heroine tells the
stories she does. A clue resides in the last quotation in which she
refers to 'the memories of other people telling me what I felt'. This, of
course, is an excellent paradigm for a description of the functioning of
Althusser's ISAs. The stories the heroine tells are the ones her
interpellated self deems she should tell. Let us consider some examples.

In Part One of the novel, the heroine may be seen to be conditioned
by not one, but two, ideologies of the family. The first of these is
represented by the pre-war nuclear family, whose traditions and
beliefs were largely shared by both French- and English-speaking
Canadians. In the heroine's own story, these two social groups are
symbolized respectively by her parents, and by Paul and his wife. The
other view of the family by which she has been interpellated is its
partial disestablishment by the 'new permissiveness' of the 1960s. This
is the 'revolution' represented by the heroine's contemporaries: her
'ex-husband', Anna, David and Joe. It is important to note, however,
that these factors only represent a partial overthrow of the system. All
of them have 'disowned their parents long ago, the way you are
supposed to' (p. 17), but they still believe in marriage for themselves
(Anna and David have been married for several years; Joe wants to
marry). Their real difference from their parents is that they no longer
believe in the sanctity or exclusivity of marriage; all claim the right to
have heterosexual affairs and to get divorced.

Around these two models of the family, the heroine constructs two
different stories of her past life. In the first of these stories (the one that
her parents would have understood), she has been married and had a
baby which she subsequently left with her husband when the
marriage failed. In the second (the story of her 'own generation'), she
has been married, had a baby, but has also been divorced. Neither of
these stories, as we find out later, is the 'true' one: she was a mistress,
not a wife; and instead of a baby, she had an abortion. For much of the
narrative, the difference between the telling of these two stories is very
subtle. In the following quotation, however, we witness the sort of
linguistic slippage characteristic of her awkward transition from one
ideology to another:

My status is a problem, they obviously think I'm married. But I'm
safe, wearing my ring, I never threw it out, it's useful for landladies.
I sent my parents a postcard after the wedding, they must have
mentioned it to Paul; that, but not the divorce. It isn't part of the
vocabulary here, there's no reason to upset them. I'm waiting for
Madame to ask me about the baby, I'm prepared, alerted, I'll tell her

> I left him in the city; that would be perfectly true, only it was a
> different city, he's better off with my husband, former husband. (p. 23)

Between 'husband' and 'former husband' is the fine difference
between the two ideologies by which the heroine has been interpellated.

The functioning of Althusser's Ideological State Apparatuses,
including the family, depends on the perpetration of a number of
constituent ideologies. The ones we have chosen to consider here are
those relating to gender difference and romantic love. As with the
family, the heroine's interpellation by gender is a mixture of pre-war
and 1960s ideology. Having rejected the 'crinolines and tulle' (p. 108)
femininity cultivated by her Canadian childhood, she, like Anna, is
now a product of 1960s permissiveness. Although, in Part One of the
novel, she reports the sexual politics of the group with an objectivity
which might be seen as critical, her passive acceptance of David and
Joe's sexist authority reveals that she is not in a position to challenge
her interpellation. Moreover, her accounts of her own past relationships with men show that she was very much the victim of crude
power games. If we construct a profile of the heroine's gender
development we can see that her transition from Old Canada to
Modern America did nothing to alter her status as feminized sexual
object: inferior to and dependent upon the male. In childhood she, like
Anna, fed upon the latter-day 'princess in the tower' stories that she
now illustrates: 'ladies in exotic costumes, sausage rolls of hair across
their foreheads, with puffed red mouths and eye-lashes like tooth-
brush bristles; when I was ten I believed in glamour, it was a kind of
religion and these were my icons' (p. 42).

Yet, the 'liberated' femininity she assumed as an art student was no
less the product of patriarchal exploitation. When her tutor became
her lover, she surrendered her potential career to his authoritative
dismissal of her sex:

> For a while I was going to be a real artist; he thought that was cute
> but misguided, he said I should study something I'd be able to use
> because there never have been any important women artists. That
> was before we were married and I still listened to what he said, so I
> went into Design and did fabric patterns. But he was right, there
> never have been any. (p. 52)

The final rejoinder here, 'but he was right' also acts as an indicator that
in Part One of the novel the heroine is still largely unable to grasp the
extent to which she has been manipulated in sexual-political terms.
This is reflected both in the way she and Anna perform all the
domestic tasks and silently submit to crude sexist remarks, and, more
subtly, in her 'subconscious' compliance to Joe's wishes: 'He feels me
watching him and lets go of my hand. Then he takes his gum out,
bundling it in the silver wrapper, and sticks it in the ashtray and

crosses his arms. That means I'm not supposed to observe him; I face front' (p. 8).

Where the sexual politics of gender difference relate more specifically to the ideology of romantic love, however, the heroine may already be seen to have assumed an ambivalent position when the novel opens. Her 'divorce' has alienated her from the concept of romantic love, so that she no longer 'believes' in it:

> We begin to climb and my husband catches up with me again, making one of the brief appearances, framed memories he specializes in: crystal clear image enclosed by a blank wall. He's writing his initials on a fence, graceful scrolls to show me how, lettering was one of the things he taught. There are other initials on the fence but he's making his bigger, leaving his mark. I can't identify the date or the place, it was a city, before we were married; I lean beside him, admiring the fall of winter sunlight over his cheekbone and engraved nose, noble and shaped like a Roman coin profile; that was when everything he did was perfect. On his left hand is a leather glove. He said he loved me, the magic word, it was supposed to make everything light up, I'll never trust that word again. (p. 47)

A little earlier, she uses this fact of her 'divorce' to explain her inability to 'love' Joe:

> I'm trying to decide whether or not I love him. It shouldn't matter, but there's always a moment when curiosity becomes more important to them than peace and they need to ask; though he hasn't yet . . . I'm fond of him, I'd rather have him round than not; though it would be nice if he meant something more to me. The fact that he doesn't makes me sad: no one has since my husband. A divorce is like an amputation, you survive but there's less of you. (p. 42)

As we shall see in the next section, this 'disbelief' in romantic love is linked explicitly to the heroine's alienation from language. It is, indeed, her first point of dislocation from her interpellation as a feminine subject: her first resistance to the ideologies into which she has been born.[35]

Antithesis

In accordance with the dialectical model, Part Two of the novel sees the heroine moving towards a position in which all the ideologies by which she has been interpellated are problematized and finally overthrown by an epiphany analogous to revolution: the discovery of her father's dead body. We will consider this transformation with respect to the triad of family, gender difference and romantic love considered in the first section, and suggest ways in which it is the heroine's changing relation to the Symbolic Order that has enabled this revolution.

We begin with the family itself. While still telling the same stories as in Part One, the heroine now militantly rejects the traditional family structure. She consistently presents herself as the 'divorced woman', and names her husband as the guilty party. In the present, she resists and rejects a 'second marriage' with Joe, and exposes the hypocrisy and degeneracy of Anna and David's relationship. Yet this cannot be considered a fully feminist consciousness, because she is still unable to liberate herself from the lie that she was once married. Her growing cynicism, however, which is ultimately related to her disaffection with romantic love, enables her to perceive the institution of marriage as infinitely corrupt:

> I remembered what Anna had said about emotional commitments: they've made one, I thought, they hate each other; that must be almost as absorbing as love. The barometer couple in their wooden house, enshrined in their niche on Paul's front porch, my ideal; except they were glued there, condemned to oscillate back and forth, sun and rain, without escape. (p. 138)

Similarly, in her perception of the power politics associated explicitly with gender difference, the heroine presents a new, ironic awareness. The sexual harassment to which she and Anna are subjected throughout the text is now reported with a grim sense of its potential brutality. During this section of the novel we are presented with three 'surrogate' rapes: of Anna by David when he wants to film her naked; of herself by David; and of herself (after the discovery of the body) by Joe. Here is a quotation from the latter:

> I didn't want him in me, sacrilege, he was one of the killers, the clay victims damaged and strewed about him, and he hadn't seen, he didn't know about himself, his own capacity for death . . . 'What's wrong with you?' he said, angry; then he was pinning me, hands manacles, teeth against my lips, censoring me, he was shoving against me, his body insistent as one side of an argument. (p. 147)

As with her rejection of the ideology of romantic love, moreover, this new consciousness is part and parcel of the heroine's new awareness of language. Reporting on David's 'rape' of Anna, she reflects: ' "Come on, we need a naked lady with big tits and a big ass", David said in the same tender voice; I recognised that menacing gentleness, at school it always went before the trick, the punchline' (p. 147). Even before she discovers her father's body, the heroine has become aware of the 'double-speak' that separates her own linguistic field from that of the others. She continuously talks at cross-purposes with them, in words they fail to understand: 'I said, "I think men ought to be superior." But neither of them heard the actual words; Anna looked at me as though I'd betrayed her and said, "Wow, are you ever brainwashed," and David said "Want a job?" and to Joe,

"Hear that, you're superior" ' (p. 111). By failing to hear the 'ought' that qualifies the heroine's statement, Anna and David display their respective inscription by discourses that she herself now stands outside of.[36]

To understand more clearly how the heroine arrives at this antithetical relation to these dominant ideologies, we shall now focus again on the institution of romantic love. The linguistic alienation that we have witnessed operating in her relation to the other ideologies may be seen to stem from this fundamental dislocation. Indeed, Part Two of the novel is full of instances of her antagonism to the dominant ideologies. The crisis of her relationship with Joe, for example, hinges on their communication problem in this area of 'love':

> It was the language again. I could not use it because it wasn't mine. He must have known what he meant but it was an imprecise word; the Eskimos have fifty-two words for snow because it is important to them, there ought to be as many for love. 'I want to' I said. 'I do in a way.' I hunted through my brain for any emotion that would coincide with what I'd said. I did want to, but it was like thinking God should exist and not being able to believe. (pp. 106–7)

In Lacanian terms, this alienation from the dominant ideologies may be read as the heroine's regression from the Symbolic Order in which, as a woman, she had only ever been imperfectly integrated. At the beginning of Part Two she records significantly:

> I was seeing poorly, translating badly, a dialect problem, I should have used my own. In the experiments they did with children, shutting them up with deaf and dumb nurses, locking them in closets, depriving them of words, they found that after a certain age the mind is incapable of absorbing any language; but how could you tell that the child hadn't invented one, unrecognisable to everyone but itself? (p. 76)

The allusion here to the heroine using a 'dialect' of her own prepares the way for her full reappropriation of the 'semiotic' in Part Three.[37] In Part Two, her 'translation problem' is further evidenced by her misrecognition of her father's scientific papers. Instead of his cave drawings, she sees images of her own aborted child; instead of him being mad (estranged from the conventions of 'normal society'), it is herself. Throughout this section, however, delusion and illumination mix, and she understands the dislocation of her language even as she sinks deeper into it: 'The secret had come clear, it had never been a secret, I'd made it one, that was easier. My eyes came open, I began to arrange' (p. 103).

According to the Lacanian analogy, meanwhile, the discovery of her father's body may be read as the heroine coming literally face to face with the Symbolic (The-Law-of-the-Father); that is, recognizing it for what it is, while situating herself outside of it.[38] In the final pages of Part Two, we see the semiotic consciousness repossess the heroine to the point where she can barely understand the language of those about her, and yet she sees through the 'ideology' of their language as though instinctively: 'I had to concentrate in order to talk to him, the English words seemed imported, foreign; it was like trying to listen to two separate conversations, each interrupting the other' (p. 150). This psychological dislocation, moreover, is concomitant with the heroine's realization of the fraudulent ideologies espoused both by herself and those around her. Of David, she remarks:

> The power flowed into my eyes, I could see into him, he was an imposter, a pastiche, layers of political handbills, pages from magazines, affiches, verbs and nouns glued onto him and shredding away, the original surface littered with fragments and tatters . . . Second-hand American was spreading over him in patches, like mange or lichen. He was infested, garbled, and I couldn't help him: it would take such time to heal, unearth him, scrape down to where he was true. (p. 152)

With this new 'meta-consciousness' she begins to see through the distortions of her past stories and to correct them: she had never been married, she had an abortion instead of a wedding, she had never had a brother.

Synthesis

Part Three of *Surfacing* follows the heroine's complete repossession by the semiotic through to her realignment with the Symbolic following her identification with the ghost of her dead father. In terms of the Hegelian dialectic, they may be seen as the passage from antithesis, through revolution, to a new 'transcendent' synthesis. But before drawing some conclusions from these final transactions, it is worth first considering their implications in terms of the heroine's ideological interpellation that we have followed throughout this reading.

The reader will probably have noticed already that in the movement from 'thesis' to 'antithesis' there was a visible conflation of the three ideologies identified at the outset of the novel, with the heroine's alienation from the discourse of romantic love gradually infecting her relation to the sexual politics of gender difference, and simultaneously undermining both 'versions' of the family as Ideological State Apparatus. Similarly, in the 'semiotic' phase of Part Three, to reject one of these ideologies is to reject them all: a summation which links with the more anthropological readings of the text (see Chapter 3), which interpret this phase of the novel simply as a rejection of 'culture' *per se*. In so far as culture may be seen to relate to industrial capitalism, this wholesale rejection of the trappings of civilization is certainly of interest for a Marxist-feminist reading: the point at which capitalism can be seen to subsume patriarchy as the greater evil.[39] Indeed, the heroine herself generalizes, by subsuming her previous problematization of gender difference in her larger rejection of the capitalist forces: 'But then I realised it wasn't the men I hated, it was the Americans, men and women both. They'd had their chance but they'd turned against the gods' (p. 154).

Specifically in terms of her relation to the ideology of the family, Part Three sees the heroine pass through a symbolic 'total rejection' to an equally symbolic 'compromise'. The former is achieved in the context of her ritual destruction of the signifiers of industrial capitalism: her exorcizing of all things metal:

> I slip the ring from my left hand, non-husband, he is the next thing I must discard finally, and drop it into the fire, altar, it may not melt but it will at least be purified, and blood will burn off. Everything from history must be eliminated, the circles and the arrogant square pages. I rummage under the mattress and bring out the scrapbooks, ripping them up, the ladies, dress forms and decorated china heads, the suns and the moons, the rabbits and their archaic eggs, my false peace, his wars, aeroplanes and tanks and the helmeted explorers. (p. 176)

This symbolic overthrow of the State Apparatus then gives way, after her realignment with the Symbolic Order, to a rationalization of both her former positions. Both the stories she had previously told she now recognizes to be false. Neither married nor divorced, she realizes that her former lover had never been part of any family institution, either conventional or permissive; neither had be been exceptionally good, or exceptionally evil:

> I can remember him, fake husband, more clearly though, and now I feel nothing for him but sorrow. He was neither of the things I believed, he was only a normal man, middle-aged, second-rate, selfish and kind in the average proportions; but I was not prepared for the average, its needless cruelties and lies. (p. 188)

In terms of the heroine's final synthesis of the ideologies surrounding gender differences, meanwhile, it is important to note that her own active revolution begins with her symbolic 'drowning' of 'Random Samples':

> The film coils onto the sand under the water, weighted down by its containers; the invisible captured images are swimming away into the lake like tadpoles, Joe and David beside their deflated log, axemen, arms folded, Anna with no clothes on jumping off the edge of the dock, finger up, hundreds of tiny Annas no longer bottled and shelved. (p. 166)

Besides its obvious revenge for her own abortion (the image of the bottled foetus recurs throughout the text), the heroine's gesture is an attempt finally to dissolve the iniquities of gender difference. In their watery grave, the macho axemen and the pornographic female body are no more. Similarly, her own journey back to the semiotic pre-Oedipal stage releases the heroine from her own interpellation as female subject. During her time in the forest, she completely loses sense of herself as 'feminine': she is merely female. Upon her return to civilization, she regards this ungendered self ironically:

> That is the real danger now, the hospital or the zoo, where we are put, species and individual, when we can no longer cope. They can never believe it is only a natural woman, state of nature, they think of that as a tanned body on a beach with washed hair waving like scarves; not this, dirt-caked and streaked, skin grimed and scabby, hair like a frayed bath-mat stuck with leaves and twigs. A new kind of centrefold. (p. 190)

After the discovery of her father's body, the heroine is also able fully to perceive her earlier interpellation by the ideology of romantic love. Correcting the earlier story of her 'husband's' declaration of love as he inscribed his name on a fence, she confesses that he never even wrote letters: 'All I had was the criticisms in red pencil he paperclipped to my drawings' (p. 148). Moreover, he declared his love for her only by way of an apology:

> He did say he loved me though, that part was true; I didn't make it up. It was the night I locked myself in and turned on the water in the bathtub and he cried on the other side of the door. When I gave up and came out he showed me snapshots of his wife and children, his reasons, his stuffed and mounted family, they had names, he said I should be mature. (p. 149)

The climax of the heroine's realignment with the semiotic occurs in Chapter 24 when, forbidden contact with all things civilized and reduced to a naked, 'animal' state, the heroine also loses all consciousness of language. Not merely does she speak a different language to that of humans: she has no necessity to speak at all. She has re-entered a world where the signifier is continuous with the signified, and being exists only as a context:

> In one of the languages there are no nouns, only verbs held for a longer moment.
> The animals have no need for speech, why talk when you are a word
> I lean against a tree, I am a tree leaning
> I break out again into the bright sun and crumple, head against the ground I am not an animal or a tree, I am the thing in which the trees and animals move and grow, I am a place (p. 181)

From this primal state, the language of 'the Americans' is only a senseless noise. The voice of Reason has been rumbled; the Derridean non-referentiality of the sign that first surfaced in the heroine's response to various road signs in Chapter 1, here culminates in a vicariousness that is also a scathing indictment of capitalism itself: 'Behind me they crash, their boats crash, language ululating, electronic signals thrown back and forth between them, hooo, hooo, they talk in numbers, the voice of reason. They clank, heavy with weapons and iron plating' (p. 185). Yet from this fantasy existence, in which she imagines herself to be outside of language and outside of ideology, the heroine is forced to return to what is literally 'the material world'. Having conceived her child on her own terms in a symbolic attempt to win back the means of reproduction, she has recognized the need to take possession of the conditions of production.[40] This achieved, she passes through two encounters with the ghosts of her dead parents which act as her re-entry to the material world, 'to the city and its pervasive menace' (p. 189). But while the forces which drive her back may be regarded as ultimately material ('I can't stay here forever, there isn't enough food'), it is important to recognize the prior necessity of the heroine's psychic realignment with the Symbolic. This is effected by her act of identification with the Father. She takes her place in the world again by literally 'seeing through her father's eyes': 'I say Father. He turns towards me and it's not my father. It is what my father saw, the thing you meet when you've stayed here too long alone.' (p. 187) This movement is then completed in the final paragraph of the chapter when the heroine recognizes that her father's footsteps are, in fact, her own.

This is a similar realignment to the Symbolic that the Marxist-Feminist Literature Collective identify at the end of *Jane Eyre* and *Villette*. In one sense it, too, reads like a reactionary conclusion. Atwood's heroine, like Brontë's, takes her place again within the standard kinship relations. Yet, in so far as the text is to satisfy a Marxist-feminist commitment to the material conditions of our existence, such reintegration must be seen as necessary. The state of revolution, like the semiotic itself, cannot endure forever, and we are, unless maintaining a false ahistoricity, forced to resume/assume our positions as social beings within the Symbolic Order, whilst of course never being able to truly resume those same positions:

> No gods to help me now, they're questionable once more, theoretical as Jesus. They've receded, back to the past, inside the skull, is it the same place. They'll never appear to me again, I can't afford it; from now I'll live in the usual way, defining them by their absence; and love by its failures, power by its losses, its renunciation. I regret them; but they give only one kind of truth, one hand. (p. 189)

This recognition of the text's final commitment to a historical and social solution is of vital importance to the Marxist-feminist critic, if she is to postulate an effective alternative to the ahistorical, 'mythological' readings of *Surfacing* which abound. The Introduction to the Virago edition by Francine du Plessix Gray is typical of this type of reading, regarding the climax of the text as a mystical and religious experience:

> But Atwood's genius rises above these debates. For her naturalistic epiphanies are of a strictly mythic nature and never tend to stereotyping or separatism. The female religious vision that she presents in her utterly remarkable book also marks the surfacing, I believe, of a future tradition of religious quest in women's novels. (p. 6)[41]

Without this final synthesis which sees the heroine preparing to take her place again amongst the 'cities and factories', the Marxist critic would be justified in regarding the text as an anarchic sell-out. The fact that the 'revolution' effected is itself individual rather than social will, even so, be regarded by many Marxists as one of its failures. Such a problematic amalgam of concerns with the material and the psychic within the text of course relates to the larger problem to be addressed in Part III, of whether the ahistoricity of psychoanalytic method can ever be successfully incorporated into a materialist account of subjectivity.

Yet if we suspend these difficulties temporarily, it will be seen that within the argument we have been developing here, the heroine's re-entry into the Symbolic Order may be seen to effectively complete the dialectical movement of the text as a whole. Marxist and psychoanalytic models would appear to close together in a powerful alliance of their explanations of subjectivity. But what of feminism? As in the Marxist-Feminist Literature Collective article, the feminism of this reading has not resided in the theoretical models themselves, as much as the gender issues they have been used to uncover. Yet embedded in the last page of Atwood's remarkable text are two sentences in which all of the issues raised by this reading are brought to a conclusion that is its synthesis; that does acknowledge the heroine's renegotiation of the Symbolic Order; but which also admits for feminists in the material world the possibility of change. Beneath its cynicism and probability of failure resides hope. The family – complete with its satellites of gender difference and romantic love – is not what it was, but it is now the subject of potential discussion and negotiation: 'If I go with him we will have to talk, wooden houses are obsolete, we can no longer live in spurious peace by avoiding each other, the way it was before, we will have to begin. For us it's necessary, the intercession of words; and we will probably fail, sooner or later, more or less painfully' (p. 192).

Charlotte Perkins Gilman's 'The Yellow Wallpaper' has become increasingly important for many Anglo-American feminists, and it is a text which has already been interpreted from various feminist critical positions.[42] Most critics read it as a simple story of a woman being driven mad because of her virtual imprisonment by her husband. Because she is forced into inactivity by him, madness is her only escape. Gilman's text is thus often read as radical, which indeed it is, but it is often misrecognized as a simple reflection of women's experience in the world. One of the most important readings, in this context, is that by Sandra Gilbert and Susan Gubar which is summarized in Chapter 4.[43]

There are several ways in which a Marxist-feminist reading would take issue with Gilbert and Gubar's essentialist reading of the short story, and this reaction forms the basis of the following discussion. First, there is the fact that Gilbert and Gubar assume that the author of the text is the protagonist. Perkins Gilman and the narrator are often run together as if they constituted a single identity, and the text is therefore read as a straightforwardly autobiographical account of Gilman's experience of madness. This is clearly problematic, since, although a Marxist-feminist position is concerned with the conditions of production of the text, it is in terms of how social forces impinge upon the individual constructing the text, and not in terms of unproblematic relations between that subject and the text. As we show later in this section, an autobiographical reading is imposed on the text to resolve it, to give it closure; it is this notion of resolution which a Marxist-feminist reading refuses, preferring to concentrate on the gaps and inconsistencies within the text in order to highlight the workings of ideology. Secondly, Gilbert and Gubar call this text 'a paradigmatic tale which . . . seems to tell the story that all literary women would tell if they could speak their "speechless woe" ' (p. 89). Without denying the importance of the text in feminist literary history, and within the history of consciousness-raising, a Marxist-feminist reading would question the fact that a text about a woman's madness, and therefore madness itself, is central to women's literary expression. This is surely accepting the limitations imposed upon women writers by notions of masculine rationality and its polar opposite female sensitivity, intuitiveness and, ultimately, female madness. For Gilbert and Gubar, this woman character's experience can be read as standing for all women's experience under patriarchy, with madness as a potential escape from such oppression. Texts such as Marge Piercy's *Woman on the Edge of Time*, Jean Rhys's *Wide Sargasso Sea*, Toni Morrison's *Beloved* and *Sula*, and Margaret Atwood's *Surfacing* as we showed earlier, tend to be interpreted as posing descent into madness as a potential source of escape: as a haven from which to flee patriarchal oppression. However, feminists such as Monique Wittig, Judith Butler, Diana Fuss, Laura Donaldson and Gayatri Chakravorty

Spivak have worked hard to dismantle the notion of a unitary female experience – especially one represented by a white middle-class woman – and it now seems possible to argue for a rereading of these 'women and madness' texts to highlight the problems of asserting that madness is liberatory.[44] Gilbert and Gubar attempt to deny that this is indeed madness, because they term it 'what the world calls madness' (p. 90), implying that there is some 'sense' in this choice by the narrator. Indeed, after Michel Foucault's work on madness and civilization, and Dorothy Smith's work on femininity and mental illness, it is necessary to be rightly sceptical of the division between insanity and sanity, particularly as it relates to women.[45] However, even within the terms of the text, it is difficult to see what happens to the narrator as empowering, except by relying on radical feminist conventions of reading madness as a form of self-expression and power. Finally, Gilbert and Gubar assume that in some way the woman confined to the house is the same as the women who creep outside since they say: 'And the woman creeps too (like the yellow smell) through the house, in the house, and out of the house, in the garden and "on that long road under the trees" ' (p. 90) whereas, in the text, these 'women' are posed as separate from the narrator herself. Yet despite the fact that the narrator explicitly states that 'I think there are a great many women' and she also says, 'Sometimes I think there are a great many women behind [the wallpaper], and sometimes only one' (p. 15), Gilbert and Gubar insist on seeing these numerous women as the narrator: 'Eventually it becomes obvious to both the reader and the narrator that the figure creeping through and behind the wallpaper is both the narrator and the narrator's double' (p. 91). It is true that the narrator later confuses herself with the women in the wallpaper, but for a Marxist-feminist reading, it is important that this is read as a misrecognition, as an acceptance of madness, rather than as an act of solidarity with other women. Even for the narrator, this identification is not viewed positively: 'Most women do not creep by daylight . . . I don't blame her a bit. It must be very humiliating to be caught creeping by daylight! . . . I always lock the door when I creep by daylight' (p. 16). This statement of identification by Gilbert and Gubar is analogous to their insistence on reading the narrator as Charlotte Perkins Gilman herself, and to reading the narrator as Everywoman, which is helped by the fact that the narrator alone is not named (as in *Surfacing*), and can therefore be presumed to have a fairly open reference to females in general (see Chapter 2 on Authentic realism). This reading is encouraged by the fact that Jenny/Jane, the narrator's sister-in-law, is also caught staring at and touching the wallpaper, thus suggesting a special relationship between women in general and madness. What a Marxist-feminist reading retains is the notion of specificity, both historical and social. This open reference of the text is to be resisted, as we show later.

It is interesting to consider how Gilbert and Gubar interpret the end of the story, where the narrator's husband swoons with horror (or as Gilbert and Gubar put it, with 'surprise') at what she has done to the room:

> But John's masculine swoon of surprise is the least of the *triumphs* Gilman imagines for her madwoman. More significant are the madwoman's own imaginings and creations, mirages of health and freedom with which her author endows her like a fairy godmother showering gold on a sleeping heroine. The woman from behind the wallpaper creeps away, for instance, creeps fast and far on the long road, in broad daylight. 'I have watched her sometimes away off in the open country,' says the narrator, 'creeping as fast as a cloud shadow in a high wind.' Indistinct and yet rapid, barely perceptible but inexorable, the progress of that cloud shadow is not unlike the progress of nineteenth-century literary women out of the texts defined by patriarchal poetics into the open spaces of their own authority. (p. 91) [emphasis added]

We have quoted this passage in full as there are several points to be made in the context of a Marxist-feminist reading. Because of the radical feminist and liberal-humanist insistence on closure, Gilbert and Gubar are forced to interpret the narrator crawling over her husband as a triumph, and to view the creeping women positively; otherwise the text would be incoherent. This implies that once the reader has decided that this is a text which has one meaning, then the rest of the text is read to accord with that meaning. However, from a Marxist-feminist position, it is precisely this 'incoherence', this lack of closure which needs to be investigated; analyzing the text itself reveals first that the woman's action of creeping over her husband is posed as both a triumph and as a defeat; and secondly, that although these 'women' are rather negatively portrayed they are nevertheless something with which the narrator identifies.

Let us consider the ending of the story in some detail to provide evidence for these two claims. The narrator has peeled off most of the wallpaper, she has locked herself in the room and thrown the key out of the window, she has tried to bite the bed because she is so angry, and she has tied herself with a long rope so that she will not be taken outside. Her husband has tried to break down the door, and eventually she tells him that she has thrown the key outside the window. When he enters she reports:

> ' "What is the matter?" he cried. "For God's sake, what are you doing?" I kept on creeping just the same but I looked at him over my shoulder. "I've got out at last," said I, "in spite of you and Jane. And I've pulled off most of the paper, so you can't put me back!" Now

why should that man have fainted? But he did, and right across my path by the wall so that I had to creep over him every time!' (p. 19)

As we mentioned earlier, most readings of the text interpret the ending as a triumph of the narrator over her husband, since she creeps over him, and she explicitly states, 'I've got out at last'. However, the position mapped out for the reader to adopt in this last section is not a comfortable one; the reader cannot necessarily assume that the narrator is in a position of 'truth', that the information given her is unmediated, nor that she is to view the narrator crawling around the room positively. In some sense at least, although the reader is not expected to take John's position unproblematically either, his fainting leads us to question the notion that this is a scene of triumph. The central figure is left crawling round the room, one imagines interminably, until her husband recovers. There is no suggestion that she has any escape from this crawling, for she says, 'I had to creep over him *every time*' (p. 19). Thus, she may have 'got out' of the wallpaper but she certainly has not got out of the room; the bars of the wallpaper no longer restrain her, but the bars of the room do. She has 'escaped', but the reader is not sure what exactly she has escaped into. Thus, although the ending of the story only 'makes sense' in a liberal-humanist reading if we read it as a triumph, in a Marxist-feminist reading, it is this 'making sense' which is to be resisted; instead it is the contradictions, which are ignored in other readings, which are concentrated upon.

Similarly, with the 'women' outside and behind the wallpaper, the fact that the 'women' creep (not a particularly positive term), should be enough to signal to the reader that they are not creatures to be admired. The reader is left unsure as to the exact nature of these 'mirages of health and freedom' which the 'women' offer. Consider, for example, the end of the story where the narrator says, 'I don't like to look out of the windows even, there are so many of those creeping women, and they creep so fast' (p. 18), and later, when she says, 'I don't want to go outside . . . For outside you have to creep on the ground, and everything is green instead of yellow' (p. 18). Clearly, here, creeping is portrayed negatively and not as a positive escape route. However, the narrator does identify with the women finally, and is not able to distinguish herself from them, nor from the 'woman' behind the wallpaper; first, because she herself begins to creep, and secondly, because she states that John and Jane 'can't put me back' behind the wallpaper (p. 19), which suggests that she thinks she is the 'woman' she discovered in the wallpaper. However, the portrayal of this identification is full of contradictions and cannot be read as straightforwardly positive; for example, she describes the figure behind the wallpaper as a 'strange, formless sort of figure that seems to skulk about behind that silly and conspicuous front design' (p. 8).

As we noted in the introduction to this chapter, a Marxist-feminist reading is concerned with the gaps and contradictions of a text; the places where ideology is attempting to bring the story to a neat close, but where because of the nature of ideology, closure can only be partially or superficially achieved. It is in analyzing the ending of this story that we see where other readings are forced to attempt to recuperate the protagonist's final surrender to madness as triumph. For example, Gilbert and Gubar state: 'That such an escape from the numb world behind the patterned walls of the text was a flight from disease into health was quite clear to Gilman herself' (p. 91). However, even within the terms of the text it is unclear whether the final fall into madness is such a positive one. Clearly, the life behind the wallpaper is negatively portrayed, as is the life that the central figure leads, confined in isolation. Yet can the so-called escape ('a flight from disease into health') really be regarded as positive? It would seem that there are few grounds in the text for imagining that the narrator escapes into the haven of insanity from the hell of patriarchal oppression. This is essentially the major problem of the ideological relation between women and madness which this text highlights. It is precisely because it is impossible to resolve a text which poses madness as a form of escape that the ending is contradictory or confusing. What can the woman who is now mad go on to do? What exactly has she escaped into? There are very few strategies for resolving this type of text. Once madness has been posed as an escape, little detail can be given of the exact nature of the escape; in Marge Piercy's *Woman on the Edge of Time*, the heroine escapes into a utopia of her own imaginings, but it is difficult to articulate such an alternative 'reality' given the constraints on madness within Western society. What Perkins Gilman has done here is to leave the text unresolved, and we should not see this as a failure in the plot, but rather indicative of the problems with the ideologies concerning women and madness.

However, the text has been resolved, in the Virago edition at least, by placing after it a text by Gilman called 'Why I wrote "The Yellow Wallpaper" '. It should be remembered that this short text was not included with the short story until 15 years after its first publication. Gilman calls it 'the story of the story' (p. 19), and most critics read it as a 'key' to the story – a way of relating the story to the life of Gilman herself, and to women in general. However, it can be read as another story about the story, a further attempt to make an incoherent text make sense. In this 'afterword', Gilman states that she herself suffered from 'a severe and continuous nervous breakdown tending to melancholia – and beyond' (p. 19) and the way that she recovered sanity was by refusing the rest cure and plunging into 'work, the normal life of every human being' (p. 20). The difference between the two texts is often blurred, so that we assume that the protagonist of the first text overcomes madness just as Gilman did.[46] This blurring of the difference between 'real life' and 'story' is also encouraged because of the reference to Weir Mitchell in the story, who was the major proponent for the infamous rest cure which Perkins Gilman reports that she escaped from. However, although this information is pertinent, it does not allow us to achieve resolution for 'The Yellow Wallpaper'. Thus, we can only assume that, rather than being an escape, this type of madness presented here can be read as a symptom and effect of oppression, and can in turn become oppression in its own right. Although it is important to revalue those things which women have created as alternatives to 'male' behaviour, it is dangerous to revalue the very chains which bind us. Madness may equal resistance to and refusal of oppressive ideologies, but it does not indicate escape. Madness itself is heavily ideologically determined.

A further contradiction in the text is the nature of the narrator's voice: the way in which this text is related to us. At first, the reader feels that it is being kept as a diary, since there are entries such as: 'There comes John, and I must put this away – he hates to have me write a word' (p. 5) and 'We have been here two weeks, and I haven't felt like writing before, since that first day' (p. 6). However, throughout the process of developing madness, the style does not vary greatly; the narrator is lucid, and uses well-connected sentences – not at all the conventions which are generally used for representing madness. Perhaps the only element which shows that the narrator is suffering from incipient insanity is the rapid changes of subject, signalled by very short, one-sentence paragraphs. However, it is interesting that some of her most lucid paragraphs are those in which she is describing the growths and changes in the wallpaper, for example: 'The outside pattern is a florid arabesque, reminding one of a fungus. You can imagine a toadstool in joints, an interminable string of toadstools, budding and sprouting in endless convolutions – why, that is something like it' (p. 12). The narrator's lucidity and self-reflexiveness remain with her even when she is crawling round the room interminably, and performing strange actions, such as biting the bed, and tying a rope around her. This very control and clarity of the narrator seems at odds with the actions of the character, and with the conventions for the representations of madness; this makes the reader ask where this voice is coming from and question its supposedly straightforwardly biographical reference.

A Marxist-feminist reading is concerned to show that this is a very specific depiction of madness, and that the nature of this type of madness is constructed by patriarchal pressure and by social conventions. Madness is extremely heterogeneous and overdetermined, arising from, and caused by, a variety of sources.[47] Yet the type of madness portrayed here is socially constructed, and can clearly be overcome, rather than being accepted triumphantly as a form of feminist liberation. Using psychoanalysis in this context also shows us that this is not liberation: the physician/husband/father figure of John is portrayed as an embodiment of 'the Law of the Father' (see Chapter 5 and Glossary). Indeed, all of the male figures in the text are merged: discussing Weir Mitchell, the narrator quotes a friend who had observed, 'He is just like John and my brother only more so' (p. 9). Within this patriarchal setting, the female figure has transgressed the Law, and lapsed into the Imaginary: the pre-Oedipal phase where difference is not as important as sameness. However, as emerged in our reading of *Surfacing*, the Imaginary is only a temporary stage in the child's development, and as a permanent choice, it is essentially a psychotic position: a rejection of the Symbolic Order, and hence of language and meaning.

This regression into the pre-Oedipal stage is reinforced by the fact that throughout the text, the narrator is reduced to the status of a baby or child: she is petted by her husband: 'He is very careful and loving, and hardly lets me stir without special direction' (p. 5) and 'Dear John gathered me up in his arms and just carried me upstairs and laid me on the bed' (p. 10). He calls her 'little girl' (p. 11) and says to her 'Bless her little heart! . . . She shall be as sick as she pleases!' (p. 12). Also, she is kept in a room which used to be a nursery and she is forced, like a child, to have an afternoon nap. A flight into childhood dependence, or into the Imaginary, is one which the reader is left to feel ambivalent about: the flight into the Imaginary/Wallpaper, where anything and nothing can be seen/read, is to be welcomed and/or rejected as psychotic. Regression into the pre-Oedipal gives the illusion of coherent identity (identification with the other 'women'), but this is not a form of feminist solidarity; it is an illusion. This is clearly a misrecognition by the central figure of the way that ideological forces have interpellated her. She has been called upon by her husband to misrecognize herself as a child, but this interpellation is not real or inevitable and can be resisted. By the end of the text, this confused position is polarized still further, as I have shown above, since the reader has either to align herself with the Symbolic Order (and John), or with the Imaginary (and the madwoman). Many feminist readers align themselves with the madwoman, but the text does not necessarily offer such an option, since to align with her is to align with the Imaginary. Yet is it possible to do so, since this 'madness' is related to us in the calm voice of the Symbolic Order?

It is this process of interpellation which is most worrying about this text. The text interpellates women readers into a position of sympathy with the narrator, and thus leads them to recognize within themselves the elements of madness which the protagonist is undergoing. Thus, in reading the text, the connection between madness and womanhood is restated, in the same way as patriarchal texts run together these notions of femininity, frailty and madness. It is this false recognition which needs to be challenged and resisted.[48] Centring on the contradictions in the text leads the reader to formulate a position from which to resist this reading. This text is, of course, an imaginary representation of the real relations in society, and it would therefore be erroneous to assume, as we are led to believe, that all women are potentially capable of going insane. Yet this is how the text addresses its women readers on the surface at least (but not, it must be noted, its male readers, who have insisted on reading it as 'Gothic horror').[49] There is no inherent link between femaleness and insanity, but, since the nineteenth century, a causal relation has been constructed, as Phyllis Chesler and Elaine Showalter have shown.[50] This link needs to be subjected to a radical critique.

Let us consider how the text goes about getting the reader to collude in this false identification process: the text takes as its motif something which most readers can recognize, which presents itself as banal and common sense: that is, staring vacantly at wallpaper and following the patterns. This initial recognition is then carried through to a recognition of this as a pre-condition for madness. The story is, after all, called 'The Yellow Wallpaper', as if it were the wallpaper which were the cause of the madness. The diary form and the use of the first person pronoun 'I' makes the reader feel that she is reading a private, personal account, which is reinforced by the fact that on several occasions the reader is directly addressed: for example, 'I think that woman gets out in the daytime! And I'll tell you why – privately – I've seen her!' (p. 15). Thus, the reader is positioned as a confidante to the narrator, and her sympathy is sought. Also, as we noted above, the narrator is not, unlike the other characters in the text, given a name, and this encourages a reading of the character as Everywoman (all women), and therefore as potentially having reference to the individual reader herself. However, we need to interrogate the usefulness of a reading strategy that leads the woman reader to assume that the madwoman referred to in the text is none other than herself. Although, as has been shown in Chapter 2, there are occasions when an authentic realist reading is strategically useful, it does not seem useful to recognize madness within oneself, unless it is to question the origin of that madness.

'The Yellow Wallpaper' can be read as a historically specific account of what can induce madness, without being a text which offers coherent solutions to that condition. What needs to be focused on is the specificity of the conditions which produce madness as described in the text (remembering that all of Freud's female patients suffering from hysteria were from the middle class), rather than assuming that it has universal reference for all women. Indeed, John describes her condition as 'a slight hysterical tendency' (p. 4). The narrator of the text is clearly from the upper middle class: her husband is a doctor, and they are staying in an 'ancestral hall . . . a colonial mansion, a hereditary estate' (p. 3) for the summer. Are we to assume, from the repetitions and rephrasing of this, that the protagonist is trying to make some point about her position in society? She points out that the house is 'quite alone, standing well back from the road . . . and there are . . . lots of separate little houses for the gardeners and people' (p. 4). From the house, 'I get a lovely view of the bay and a little private wharf belonging to the estate' (p. 7). She is also at pains to point out that, 'My brother is also a physician, and also of high standing' (p. 4); thus, we are not to assume that she has simply married into the upper middle class. The wife is forced to stay at home, without occupying herself with work of any kind; the paradigm of the middle-class housewife during the nineteenth and early twentieth centuries. Whilst this ideological vision of the confined housewife presents itself as natural, it is in fact very historically specific and is directly determined by external economic factors, as Barrett shows: 'It has yet to be proved that capitalism could not survive without the present form of domestic labour. On the other hand it is equally difficult to regard the development of the family as unrelated to the changing needs of capitalist production.'[51] Unlike the working-class women of the time, the middle-class housewife does not concern herself with the cleaning and cooking of the household, but rather its management by other women. The protagonist's madness is a logical progression or an amplification of this alienation from labour, for eventually, she can no longer act at all: 'I don't feel as if it was worthwhile to turn my hand over for anything' (p. 9). This madness is an intensification of the alienation inherent in the condition of idleness enforced on the bourgeois female at this time, by their husbands and the male workforce.

The cure she is offered is more inactivity: that is, greater alienation. The only cure that the protagonist can offer for her 'illness' is 'more society and stimulus' (p. 4) and to be allowed to write. Her husband does not agree that writing is a cure for her, and even the narrator can see that even though occasionally she feels that 'if I were only well enough to write a little it would relieve the press of ideas and rest me', she can still see that 'I find I get pretty tired when I try' (p. 7). Simply being allowed to write is not the cure, since this constitutes a repetition of the symptoms; writing only cures when it leads to a form of critique of the condition described.[52] She goes on to say: 'I don't know why I should write this. I don't want to. I don't feel able. And I know John would think it absurd. But I must say what I feel and think in some way – it is such a relief! But the effort is getting to be greater than the relief' (p. 10). This 'expression' of her problem in a diary is not perhaps a cure, because it simply describes the symptoms and aggravates them. This obviously does not constitute writing as work. In 'Why I wrote "The Yellow Wallpaper" ', Gilman notes that what cured her was: 'work, the normal life of every human being; work, in which is joy and growth and service, without which one is a pauper and a parasite' (p. 20). We are not drawing on the Afterword to resolve 'The Yellow Wallpaper' but simply to note that Gilman did not complete the text in the way that she completed the story of her own madness. Thus, the juxtaposition of the Afterword seems to undercut and contradict the readings of 'The Yellow Wallpaper' as a text about escape into madness. However, neither the protagonist nor John can see the structural reason for the protagonist's madness, and that is the fact that she is deprived of involvement with productive work of any sort. Different participants in the reading process assume different reasons for the narrator's madness; the protagonist herself does not give an explanation for it, except to allude to 'nervousness' (p. 6); her husband is content to assume that there is 'no reason to suffer' (p. 6). The reader is led to assume that the reason the woman goes mad is because of her oppressive relation with her husband; however, there is a further reason, and that is her confinement and inactivity which is indicative of a larger social phenomenon, the exclusion of middle-class women from productive work in this period.

In conclusion, a Marxist-feminist reading of 'The Yellow Wallpaper' enables the reader to be critically aware of the type of reading which she has been led to believe is 'natural', and also the way the text 'calls upon' her. Within this type of reading practice, she can centre on the contradictions in the text, rather than having to force the information in the text into a coherent whole, resulting in closure. She can also question the way she is positioned by the text, and become in Judith Fetterley's terms a 'resisting reader'.[53]

III

Several potential problems in the practice of an effective Marxist-feminist criticism were raised in Part I of this chapter, and others will have been seen to emerge in the course of the readings themselves. The principal difficulties that we have decided to discuss may be listed under the following headings:

1. Marxist-feminism's lack of a homogeneous critical model.
2. The tendency for Marxist-feminism to be the simple adaptation of Marxist models to gender issues.
3. The dependence on models that are not primarily literary-critical.
4. The uneasy relationship between Marxist-feminism and psycho-analysis.
5. The place of Marxist-feminism within a more general feminist poststructuralist enterprise.

For the new student or reader coming to a theoretical literary practice for the first time, we recognize that it is the very amorphous nature of the Marxist-feminist model that may well constitute the greatest obstacle. Indeed, the central problem is that there is no one model, text, or even group of texts, that can be referred to. As with the French feminisms discussed in the preceding chapter, readings performed under the general auspices of a Marxist-feminist model may be as esoteric as the contexts in which they appear, and without the nominal author-identification of, say, 'Kristeva' or 'Cixous'. Without simple 'primary texts', as such, Marxist-feminism offers no easy access to the new reader, and the individual must be prepared for a long struggle before she finally works out where she stands politically *vis-à-vis* many diverse theories, and which of those she feels it most useful to appropriate.[54]

This lack of a homogeneous model also relates directly to the second problem we need to consider; that is, the ambiguous relationship of feminism to Marxism. As was indicated in Part I, there is the tendency for Marxist-feminist practice to become the simple adaptation of Marxist models to gender issues. This, essentially, is what the Marxist-Feminist Literature Collective's practice was: using the concepts of Althusser and the reading strategies of Macherey to address female-centred issues in their chosen texts. The reading of *Surfacing* that we performed here may be considered an even more blatant exercise of this sort of approach, with the Hegelian and Althusserian theses built into the very structure of the reading. The reading was Marxist-feminist only because we chose to address the text in relation to the heroine's interpellation by gender-oriented ideological apparatuses. We can understand that some feminists might be justifiably anxious in adopting a methodology in which the feminist interest is apparently secondary. It returns us, too, to the central dilemma of the materialist feminist of how to negotiate and prioritize the competing claims of capitalism and patriarchy. The reading of *Surfacing*, for example, demonstrated a shift between the two, as the heroine's oppression was presented sometimes as her position as a woman, sometimes as a subject of American capitalism. While theoretically we might well choose to argue that an effective Marxist-feminism must recognize the inseparability of the one from the other, the conclusion of dual-systems theory, actual readings often do reveal precedence of the one over the other. Yet it could also be argued that this is the simple cost we have to pay if we are to make readings of texts that are genuinely historically specific. To the extent that women's oppression is related to wider economic practices (even if we resist the Marxist inference that it is primarily dominated by them) we have to surrender the idea of patriarchy as the primal grievance that Kate Millett postulated it was. The agencies of sexual politics are diverse and variable, and, as we saw in 'The Yellow Wallpaper', the oppression of each subject is bound to be a complex mixture of sex, economic dependence, race and class. The reading of 'The Yellow Wallpaper' argued strongly that without taking the full materialist circumstances of the protagonist's position into account, madness (à la Gilbert and Gubar) might be read as a good thing, forgetful of the fact that it constitutes physical and economic imprisonment. In conclusion, then, we would argue that, for all the difficulty in negotiating its competing demands, feminism cannot afford to dispense with Marxist analyses.

Yet even if the feminist reader makes this political commitment to a materialist criticism, there is the further problem that the Marxist models that she is most interested in are not necessarily literary ones. Moreover, their adaptation to critical practice is likely to be problematic, and she will run the risk of producing readings that provoke and/or irritate both Marxists and literary critics. The biggest danger from a poststructuralist position is the realization that a model such as Althusser's formulation of the Ideological State Apparatuses as an analysis of relations in 'the real world', cannot be directly applied to situations within a text without returning to the Lukácsian hypothesis that literature is in some way a 'reflection of the real world'. Such dangerous over-simplification can, we think, be overcome if the reading continues to remind the reader of its own ideological status throughout (cf. MFLC article, p. 27). While materialist criticism may thus be said to have its *raison d'être* in the fact that it is directed to readings that acknowledge the politics of 'the real world', it does not mean that we can regard the text as the real world.

But by far the most contentious aspect of the type of Marxist-feminism that we practised here is its theoretical relation to psycho-analysis. It is important to note that the early dating of the Marxist-Feminist Literature Collective article (1978) means that these connections were forged relatively early in the development of recent feminist literary criticism, and as such (despite the superficial incongruity) cannot be dismissed as marginal or esoteric. Indeed, it could be argued that Marxist-feminism has been informed by psychoanalysis from the start and that this intimate relation is one of the crucial ways in which Marxist-feminism, as such, can be distinguished from straightforward Marxist criticism. For critics like Cora Kaplan, the interest in both Marxism and psychoanalysis has been precisely in the way in which they can be related to one another on the issues surrounding gender and subjectivity.[55] The differences between Marxist and psychoanalytic critics are perceived by the former to be fundamentally ethical. The problem with Freudian and Lacanian models of human development is that they are individualistic and ahistorical, dealing with factors which are seen to be permanent and 'universal'. Thus according to Lacan, every human subject will have gone through the 'mirror-stage' on their way to the Symbolic, and this is a process that occurs regardless of historical or social context. The real dangers for such an assumption in a reading of a particular text will be that the behaviour of the characters concerned can be 'explained' regardless of their attendant social circumstances, and, even more problematically, resolved. Thus, a fully psychoanalytic reading of *Surfacing* might regard the heroine's individual revolution as in some way sufficient and exemplary: through a good bracing dip in the primal waters a woman can come to a new and improved relationship with herself and the world in which she lives. For Marxists, this injudiciously ignores the material conditions of her oppression, and suggests that we all possess within us the means of ameliorating our positions as individual agents, without attending to the social and political forces controlling us or relating our condition to that of others. Whilst our reading of *Surfacing* thus attempted to combine a psychoanalytical model of resistance and liberation with a materialist consciousness by following the MFLC and equating the Lacanian Symbolic Order with a Marxist conception of 'domestic ideology', a more satisfactory Marxist reading would have located the protagonist's means of liberation in her interpellation by contradictory ideologies (see note 19 above) rather than in the highly individualistic revolt of her psyche. However, psychoanalysis and Marxism have had a long and productive dialogue within feminist theory and in some ways the struggle between the personal and the social in the process of interpellation has helped to clarify the tensions between the personal and the social in the construction of the (textual) subject.

   This brings us finally to the practice of Marxist-feminism within a more general poststructuralism. Here we would make the point that it is the poststructuralist critic's ability to work with contradictions and differences that has enabled her to successfully negotiate the tensions inherent in a Marxist-feminist practice. The lack of resolution of the competing claims of patriarchy and capitalism mentioned above are a case in point, as are the potentially antagonistic positions of Marxism and psychoanalysis. Central to the practice of the poststructuralist reader is the notion of mutability and dialogue; Marxist-feminism's purpose, like that of deconstruction, is to read texts 'against the grain', so that the various ideologies which they inscribe (and are themselves inscribed by) are routed out and exposed. This 'sub-text' might be an unwitting testimony of patriarchy or the latent feminism unearthed in the Marxist-Feminist Literature Collective's readings of Brontë and Barrett Browning. Yet while born of contradictions and intent on revealing them, it should not be thought that Marxist-feminism is part of the often indulgent relativism that has given much American Deconstruction such a bad name amongst Marxist critics. Behind our 'guerrilla' activities, there is a commitment to the reading of literature as a means of understanding more clearly both the ideologies that have attempted to keep women 'in their place', and also the complicity and resistance of women themselves. This should be seen not merely as a negative critical activity, moreover, but also as a productive one. As Terry Eagleton has recommended that the time has come for us to reread texts so that they 'work for socialism', so should we make them work for feminism.[56] With such a wealth of existing theory and criticism available to be adapted to a more materially conscious criticism, we feel that the Marxist-feminist criticism of the 1990s is in a position to adapt, develop and refine the best of what has been practised, and to move towards a new level of feminist criticism in which 'pluralism' and 'commitment' are not mutually exclusive terms.

Notes

1.   Heidi Hartmann, 'The unhappy marriage of Marxism and feminism: towards a more progressive union', in Lydia Sargent (ed.), *The Unhappy Marriage of Marxism and Feminism: A Debate on Class and Patriarchy* (Pluto, London, 1981). Cora Kaplan uses Hartmann's metaphor to introduce her own problematization of the relationship in 'Pandora's box: subjectivity, class and sexuality in socialist-feminist criticism', in Gayle Greene and Coppelia Kahn (eds), *Making a Difference* (Methuen, London, 1985).
2.   Donna Landry and Gerald Maclean, *Materialist Feminisms* (Blackwell,

Oxford, 1993); Rosemary Hennessy, *Materialist Feminism and the Politics of Discourse* (Routledge, London, 1993).

3. Landry and Maclean (see note 2 above), p. viii.

4. The authors should be quite explicit here that they recognize the fact that their position is one which is not fashionable currently. The move towards materialist-feminism is general, and the term Marxism is itself one which has become extremely difficult to use, in both teaching and in research. However, for the reasons which have been sketched out in the Introduction and which we will detail in this chapter, we feel that there are good theoretical reasons for maintaining the term Marxism.

5. Vulgar Marxism is that stereotype of Marxism which reduces a complex set of theoretical frameworks to an obsession with class and economic relations. Whilst the present Prime Minister, John Major, is confident that simply calling for a classless society is enough to bring it about, we are very aware of the inequalities within society which are still due to class position and poverty; however, only a vulgar Marxism would assume that these are the only factors which determine inequality. We hope in this chapter to point in the direction of some of these more complex readings of Marxism. A more detailed account can be gained from exploring recent publications on Marxist theory, for example, Francis Mulhern's edited collection of essays, *Contemporary Marxist Literary Criticism* (Longman, Harlow, 1992); section 4 on Marxism in Douglas Tallack's edited collection, *Critical Theory: A Reader* (Harvester Wheatsheaf, Hemel Hempstead, 1995), and Terry Eagleton's *Ideology: An Introduction* (Verso, London, 1991). Of interest in this connection is Patrick Joyce's edited collection, *Class* (Oxford University Press, Oxford, 1995). The wealth of publications in this area is a heartening contrast to assertions of the death of Marxism.

6. See, for example, Michèle Barrett, *Women's Oppression Today* (Verso, London, 1985).

7. 'Stand Marxist theory on its head': this metaphor of taking a theory and subverting it to one's own purpose is the one Marx himself used in his appropriation of Hegel's 'dialectic'. Since the notion of the dialectic is used in the following reading of *Surfacing*, we offer here a brief summary of the Hegelian model as presented by A. J. P. Taylor in the Introduction to *The Communist Manifesto*: like other philosophers, Hegel sought for a world system and claimed to have done better than his predecessors. They had been baffled by the problem that the world would not stand still. No sooner did they devise a universal system than the world changed into something else. Hegel made change itself the heart of his system. Moreover, he laid down how change came about. A principle or idea – the thesis – was challenged by its opposite: the antithesis. From their conflict there emerged not the victory of one side or the other, but a combination of the two: the synthesis. In time this new thesis was challenged by a new antithesis. A new synthesis emerged, and thus history continued through this process of conflict. This was the Hegelian description of the process of dialectic.

Hegel's model, however, was a formulation of the dialectical movement of ideas, and failed to offer an account of the external forces which were their motivation. Marx is now understood to have stood the paradigm on its head by postulating that the movement of ideas depended on the changes that took place first on an economic level. Millett's subsequent replacement of capitalism with patriarchy as the fundamental motivating principle of society may thus be regarded as an inversion similar to Marx's own.

8. More recent feminist critics have attempted to grapple with the problem, not by asserting the primacy of patriarchy over capitalism, but by developing a dual systems model, that is, one which sees the oppression of women as due to a complex interplay of both institutions, together with other institutional forces. See Landry and Maclean (note 2 above) and Michèle Barrett, *The Politics of Truth: From Marx to Foucault* (Polity Press, Cambridge, 1991) and 'Ethnocentrism and socialist-feminist theory', *Feminist Review*, no. 20, 1985, pp. 23–47.

9. For a survey of these changes in focus within Marxist and socialist feminist theory, see for example the special issues of *Feminist Review*, no. 23: *Socialist Feminism: Out of the Blue*, and no. 31: *The Past Before Us: 20 Years of Feminisms*. Issue 31 is especially important in stressing the ways in which feminists can form alliances across differences, rather than concentrating on the specificity of oppression suffered by our identity-politics group.

10. Maggie Humm, *Feminist Criticism* (Harvester Wheatsheaf, Hemel Hempstead, 1987), Chapter 4, p. 73.

11. Penny Boumelha, *Thomas Hardy and Women: Sexual Ideology and Narrative Form* (Harvester Wheatsheaf, Hemel Hempstead, 1982); Terry Lovell, *Consuming Fiction* (Verso, London, 1987) and Rosemary Hennessy and Rajeswari Mohan, 'The construction of woman in three popular texts of empire: towards a critique of materialist feminism', *Textual Practice*, 3/3/Winter 1989, pp. 323–57

12. This trend has been particularly apparent in Britain; for a survey of some of the feminist theorists who have worked within Marxist-feminism and socialist-feminism see Terry Lovell (ed.), *British Feminist Thought: A Reader* (Blackwell, Oxford, 1990). See also Roberta Hamilton and Michèle Barrett's edited collection: *The Politics of Diversity* (Verso, London, 1986) for a discussion of Marxist-feminism within the context of Canada.

13. Humm (see note 10 above), p. 73.

14. Marxist-Feminist Literature Collective (MFLC), 'Women's writing: Jane Eyre, Shirley, Villette, Aurora Leigh', *Ideology and Consciousness*, vol. 1, no. 3, Spring, pp. 27–48.

15. See Alison Assiter, *Althusser and Feminism* (Pluto, London, 1990). Althusser's work is not particularly fashionable at present, partly because of the simplicity of his model of the relation between ideology and interpellation. However, this can be modified to enable the model to represent the complexity of the process of interpellation (see Sara Mills, 'Knowing y/our place', in M. Toolan (ed.), *Language, Text and Context: Essays in Stylistics* (Routledge, London, 1992), pp. 182–208).

16. For a Marxist discussion of these issues of representation and avant-garde literary practice, see Eugene Lunn, *Marxism and Modernism* (Verso, London, 1985).

17. Georg Lukács, *The Evolution of Modern Drama* (1909), cited by Terry Eagleton, *Marxism and Literary Criticism* (Methuen, London, 1976), p. 20.

18. Lukács cited by Eagleton (see note 17 above), p. 28.

19. For example, Christian churches, particularly the Church of England, preach a doctrine of brotherly (*sic*) love, yet they amass capital in the face of real poverty and show little tolerance for other religions and other lifestyles than those of the white heterosexuals who constitute their 'ideal' constituents. The Church of England, whilst accepting some women priests, is split in its attitude to women. Brotherly love is here an ideological representation of the real relations between the institution of the Church and its parishioners.

20. Louis Althusser, 'Ideology and ideological state apparatuses' (often referred to simply as the ISAs article), in *Lenin and Philosophy and Other Essays*, translated by Ben Brewster (New Left Books, London, 1971).

21. See Terry Eagleton's discussion of ideology in *Ideology: An Introduction* (see note 5 above).

22. Chris Weedon, *Feminist Practice and Post-structuralist Theory* (Blackwell, Oxford, 1987), p. 29.

23. For a Marxist-feminist analysis of interpellation see Sara Mills, 'Knowing y/our place' (see note 15 above), pp. 182–208 and also the debates between contributors in Sara Mills (ed.), *Gendering the Reader* (Harvester Wheatsheaf, Hemel Hempstead, 1994).

24. See, in particular, Macherey, *A Theory of Literary Production* (Routledge and Kegan Paul, London, 1978).

25. Terry Eagleton, 'Pierre Macherey and Marxist literary criticism', in G. H. R Parkinson (ed.), *Marx and Marxisms* (Cambridge University Press, Cambridge, 1982), p. 150.

26. Valentin Voloshinov, *Marxism and the Philosophy of Language*, translated by L. Matejka and I. R. Titunik (Harvard University Press, Cambridge, Mass, 1986 f. pub. 1929). For a feminist analysis of Voloshinov's work, see Lynne Pearce's *Reading Dialogics* (Edward Arnold, London, 1994).

27. Although this intersection of the Althusserian 'imaginary' with Lacan's Imaginary is tremendously suggestive, it is not altogether unproblematic, and care should be taken not to conflate the two out of context. In their respective sources, the Althusserian imaginary and the Lacanian Imaginary possess a whole range of attendant implications which do not relate to one another. However, to the extent that both are concerned with the subject's position within society, the cross-reference is germane. For further discussion of these terms, see Chapter 5 and the Glossary.

28. Weedon (see note 22 above), p. 52.

29. Perhaps this notion of the State as an agent is one of the many areas where Marxist theories have been substantially modified in recent years. In the light of Michel Foucault's work on the nature of power, particularly in *History of Sexuality*, vol. I, there has been a reassess-

ment of the nature of State power. This is not to suggest that there has been a re-evaluation of the power of the State as such, since it is clear that the Repressive State Apparatuses, to use Althusser's terms, are very much in the hands of the State; however, the operating of power by the State has begun to be seen as a much more complex process, often exceeding or falling short of the intentions of those involved in maintaining the status quo.

30. As well as being a stage in the development of the child, the Imaginary/Symbolic choice is an ongoing one throughout the subject's life.

31. A vulgar Marxist-feminist reading would simply analyze a text at the level of content for the representation of class and gender relations; for example arguing that *Wuthering Heights* is 'about' the exchange of property, or that *Tess of the d'Urbervilles* is 'about' women's negotiation of their limited access to wealth, rather than being simple stories of romantic love. Whilst that type of content analysis can be very useful, what we are trying to demonstrate here is that a concern with the 'not-said' of a text, or with the way that the text interpellates its readers, forces the critic into more productive analyses of the text.

32. Margaret Atwood, *Surfacing* (Virago, London, 1979).

33. It should be noted that for this reading we have used the term 'heroine' to identify the unnamed central female character. While the connotations of this term are not unproblematic (Anais Pratt uses 'hero' in her reading: see note 41 below), it does nevertheless distinguish the central role she plays among the other protagonists.

34. Catherine Belsey uses the notion of the *interrogative text* in *Critical Practice* (Methuen, London, 1980) to describe a text which is self-consciously aware of problems of its own construction and which, unlike 'seamless' realist texts, seems to invite analysis, because of the way in which it displays its gaps and inconsistencies.

35. For a fuller analysis of the ideologies of romantic love see Lynne Pearce and Jackie Stacey's edited collection, *Romance Revisited* (Lawrence and Wishart, London, 1995).

36. This is not however to assume that the heroine is not still inscribed within these patriarchal ideologies of gender difference, since the assumption that men *ought* to be superior still accords with stereotypical beliefs.

37. For a full explanation of 'Symbolic' and 'semiotic' see Chapter 5 and also the Glossary. Kristeva's notion of the semiotic has an advantage over Lacan's Imaginary for feminists, in so far as it does not necessarily constitute a regression or a *lack of language*, but rather the assumption of a certain kind of disruptive language. However, in so far as this reading is specifically linking psychological to materialist 'interpellation' we have reserved the Lacanian model to understand the full measure of the heroine's dislocation.

38. For a definition of Lacan's 'Law-of-the-Father', see Chapter 5 and the Glossary.

39. See Chapter 8 for a postcolonial reading of *Surfacing* which details this aspect further.

40. Althusser describes the relation between the means of reproduction,

that is, the process whereby societies recreate the conditions under which they developed, thus maintaining the status quo, and the conditions of production on page 1 of the ISAs article.

41. Another 'myth' reading of *Surfacing* is performed by Anais Pratt in 'Surfacing and the rebirth journey', in Arnold E. Davidson and Cathy N. Davidson (eds), *The Art of Margaret Atwood: Essays in Criticism* (Anansi, Toronto, 1981), pp. 139–57.

42. Charlotte Perkins Gilman, 'The Yellow Wallpaper' in Ann Lane (ed.), *The Charlotte Perkins Gilman Reader* (The Women's Press, London, 1981), pp. 3–20.

43. Sandra Gilbert and Susan Gubar, *The Madwoman in the Attic: The Woman Writer and the Nineteenth-Century Literary Imagination* (Yale University Press, New Haven, 1979).

44. Diana Fuss, *Essentially Speaking: Feminism, Nature and Difference* (Routledge, London and New York, 1989); Judith Butler, *Gender Trouble: Feminism and the Subversion of Identity* (Routledge, London and New York, 1990); Monique Wittig, *The Straight Mind and Other Essays* (Harvester Wheatsheaf, Hemel Hempstead, 1992); Laura Donaldson, *Decolonizing Feminism: Race, Gender and Empire-Building* (Routledge, London, 1992); Gayatri Chakravorty Spivak, *In Other Worlds: Essays in Cultural Politics* (Methuen, London, 1987).

45. Michel Foucault, *Madness and Civilisation: A History of Insanity in the Age of Reason* (Tavistock, London, 1981); Dorothy Smith, *Texts, Facts and Femininity: Exploring the Relations of Ruling* (Routledge, London, 1990), especially Chapter 2: 'K is mentally ill: the anatomy of a factual account', pp. 12–53.

46. Although even this assumption is difficult, since Gilman is said never to have fully recovered from her nervous breakdown (Ann Lane (see note 42 above), p. ix).

47. See Dorothy Smith (see note 45 above).

48. See Lennard Davis' *Resisting Novels: Ideology and Fiction* (Methuen, London, 1987), for an account of the general need for critique of some of the ideologies presented by novels.

49. Ann Lane (see note 42 above) notes that the story was described by H. P. Lovecraft as one of the great 'spectral tales' in American literature (p. xvii).

50. Elaine Showalter, *The Female Malady: Women, Madness, and English Culture 1830–1980* (Virago, London, 1987); Phyllis Chesler, *Women and Madness* (Allen Lane, London, 1974).

51. Michèle Barrett, *Women's Oppression Today: Problems in Marxist Feminist Analysis* (Verso, London, 1980), pp. 180–1.

52. See Michel Foucault's discussion of the confessional mode in *Discipline and Punish: The Birth of the Prison*, translated by Alan Sheridan (Vintage/Random House, New York, 1979); where the confessional simply accords with disciplinary frameworks it can only work to the benefit of those to whom the confession is made. Only where counter-identification occurs can the confessional work to critique these power relations.

53. Judith Fetterley, *The Resisting Reader: A Feminist Approach to American Fiction* (Indiana University Press, Bloomington, 1988); see also Sara

Mills (ed.), *Gendering the Reader* (Harvester Wheatsheaf, Hemel Hempstead, 1994).

54. However, critical texts such as Landry and Maclean, and Hennessy (see note 2 above) now offer introductions to the subject, and Terry Lovell's anthology *British Feminist Thought* (see note 12 above) enables the reader to become acquainted with many of the primary texts.

55. Cora Kaplan, *Sea Changes* (Verso, London, 1986).

56. Terry Eagleton, quoted by Raman Selden in *A Reader's Guide to Contemporary Literary Theory*, (Harvester Wheatsheaf, Hemel Hempstead, 1985), p. 45.

7

Lesbian criticism

Lynne Pearce

Karla Jay and Joanne Glasgow (eds): *Lesbian Texts and Contexts*
Alice Walker: *The Color Purple*
Jean Rhys: *Wide Sargasso Sea*

I

As we begin our preparations for the second edition of *Feminist Readings* in the summer of 1994 I am ironically aware that my commission to contribute a new chapter on 'Lesbian criticism' could well serve to date, rather than update, the volume.

Without wishing to appear millennial, there is little question that all areas of lesbian studies – not least lesbian literary criticism – are at a crossroads moment. This is largely the result of the rigorous attack on 'identity politics' spearheaded by American theorists like Judith Butler, Teresa de Lauretis, Eve Sedgwick and Diana Fuss, and the associated theoretical/political movement known as 'Queer'.[1] Although, as I shall indicate below, there have already been some persuasive attempts to argue for the *strategic* preservation of the category 'lesbian', I have little doubt that the radical de-centring of the term will make it increasingly difficult to identify a body of literature and/or criticism under that heading. What feminism has achieved since the mid-1980s is the insertion of gender-awareness into the critical mainstream, with the result that *all* gender identifications and sexualities are now being placed under rigorous scrutiny. What has been lost, as a result of the de-essentializing of key foundational terms ('woman', 'lesbian', 'Black'), has been the permission to organize our critical analyses and/or politics around such identities. I therefore predict that by the time the second edition of *Feminist Readings* is in circulation 'lesbian criticism' is even less likely to have a place on literature syllabuses than it has now, although – as one of my friends

225

has commented – ' "Queer" will be everywhere', with the (positive) implication that interrogations of sexuality as well as gender will have taken up permanent residence in the critical mainstream.[2]

The origins and development of lesbian criticism

Before assessing in greater detail the political and theoretical implications of this sea-change in gender studies we need first, however, to review the history of lesbian literary criticism.

Perhaps the first point to note here is that the study of homosexual literature has been *inadvertently* part of literary scholarship for many years for the simple reason, as Joseph Bristow has observed, that 'so many of the literary works within the canon have homosexuality if not as their central, then as their displaced, theme'.[3] This is to say that within the critical tradition of liberal humanism many scholars will have been aware of the homoeroticism present in the writings of authors like Virginia Woolf or Emily Dickinson, and will (albeit occasionally) have brought this information to bear upon their textual analyses. The incidental study of homosexual themes in literary texts is not the same, however, as criticism which is practised as part of a gay and lesbian politics, and it was only with the rise of feminist criticism in the 1970s that the 'recovery' and, indeed, celebration of such authors and texts became part of an orchestrated campaign.

Writing from the perspective of the 1990s, however, it is also clear that early lesbian criticism and early feminist criticism stood in somewhat strained relationship to one another. By the mid-1980s a cry had gone up about the white, heterosexual bias of feminist scholarship and there were complaints that the early feminist literary histories (such as Ellen Moers' *Literary Women* and Elaine Showalter's *A Literature of their Own*) were both racist and homophobic in their failure to deal with these so-called 'minority' groups.[4] Indeed, until the 1980s, lesbian criticism can be seen to have been subsumed within a wider 'gynocritical' project (see Chapter 3); lesbian authors and texts were being 'recovered' and reassessed, but as part of a much larger project to render visible all those women writers who had been 'hidden from history'. It is significant in this respect that as late as 1980 Bonnie Zimmerman was able to title her 'overview' of lesbian feminist criticism 'What has never been'.[5] And there is, of course, a covert politics to this 'closeting': much 1970s feminism worked hard to deliberately disassociate itself from lesbianism in its attempt to convince the population (academic and otherwise) that 'you don't have to be a lesbian [i.e. 'man-hater'] to be a feminist', with the result that women's visibility was at the expense of lesbians' *invisibility*.

This delay in disentangling from the feminist literary critical mainstream means that lesbian criticism has subsequently been forced to play 'catch up'. While general bibliographical surveys and 'images of women' criticism are now increasingly rare in feminist scholarship generally, these tasks are still being performed by lesbian critics. At the same time (and I will attend to the problematic irony of this later) that the term 'lesbian' is being radically de-centred, books like Bonnie Zimmerman's *The Safe Sea of Women: Lesbian Fiction 1969–1989* (1982) and Gabriele Griffin's *Heavenly Love? Lesbian Images in Twentieth-century Women's Writing* (1993) are being written and published.[6] Lesbian writing is being 'reconstructed' even as it is being 'deconstructed': while critics like Butler have succeeded in putting the category 'woman' into complete epistemological freefall, a great many literary critics are still committed to putting lesbians (as historical subjects/ identities) on the map. 'Visibility' and 'celebration' are, indeed, the undisguised objectives of a great deal of lesbian criticism still being produced. It is for this reason, clearly, that Elaine Hobby and Chris White see fit to publish an annotated bibliography of black women's poetry in Britain as a chapter (by Dorothea Smartt) in their volume *What Lesbians Do in Books* (1991), and why, in the same volume, Liz Yorke discusses Adrienne Rich's poetry in the following, celebratory, terms: 'Rich not only makes available what was previously "unspeakable", censored, unwritten, and named only in patriarchal terms – but also transforms the codes in which this relation is signified, as part of her revisionary poetic' (p. 43).[7] The rationale for both writer and critic is clear: a question of making oneself heard and of making oneself seen.

For those working within this general remit of revelation and celebration, textual analysis has remained dominated by the principles and practices of 'authentic realism' (see Chapter 1). From the 1970s to the present, a large number of lesbian literary critics have continued to analyze lesbian texts with the purpose of (a) testing their 'authenticity' against their own experience of 'lesbian existence' and (b) assessing their contribution in terms of positive lesbian role models.[8] Examples of this type of critical practice are widespread amongst even the most recent volumes. We have already seen, for example, the 'approval' granted to Adrienne Rich for producing an authentic and celebratory representation of 'lesbian existence' while, at the other end of the spectrum, Paulina Palmer criticizes the lesbian-feminist crime-writer, Val McDermid, for her 'simplistic and unconvincing' representation of lesbian characters.[9]

Viewed from the perspective of poststructuralist literary scholarship, this type of criticism at first seems hopelessly dated and naive. The question we need to ask, however, is *why* it has persisted? Bonnie Zimmerman goes some way to providing an answer in her remark:

> Like many contemporary critics, I am sceptical about applying the standards of 'verisimilitude' and 'authenticity' to literary texts, but I

also recognise this is exactly what my friends and students *do* expect from literature. I am uneasy about setting up the critic as a superior, expert reader, wielding highly specialized language, whose role is to educate the masses.[10]

The key term in Zimmerman's analysis is, of course, 'the reader', and even a cursory survey of the books and readers focused on lesbian literature will reveal the enormous investment lesbian readers have had in literature which is affirmative of their emotional experience and/or lifestyle. In the Jay and Glasgow collection, for example, Valerie Miner, Lee Lynch and Maureen Brady all refer to the central importance of literature in enabling lesbians to discover and legitimate their lesbian identities: identities whose 'deviancy' society has coped with largely by rendering them invisible.[11] In 'Cruising the libraries', Lynch graphically describes the hunger for sexual/textual affirmation: the evidence that one is 'not alone':

> For the next several years . . . I continued the activity I came to call 'cruising the libraries'. Identifying variant books was as subtle, frustrating, and exciting a process as spotting lesbians on the street. Success depended on a vigilant desperation. I *had* to find reflections of myself to be assured that I was a valuable human being and not alone in the world. (pp. 41–2)

With stakes this high it is hardly surprising that 'authentic realism' has persisted so long as the dominant reading-frame in lesbian literary criticism. It also explains why a good deal of the criticism produced in recent years has focused on contemporary lesbian-feminist fiction: the genre which most directly met the need for 'positive' and 'authentic' role models (although, as we observed in Chapter 2, the terms 'positive' and 'authentic' sit problematically alongside one another in this kind of criticism).

It is interesting to observe, however, that those engaged in producing literary histories of lesbian writing (see Zimmerman (1992), Griffin (1993) both cited above) admit that the days of this kind of lesbian reading/writing practice could be coming to an end. And the 'end', significantly, is being brought about by the novelists, dramatists and poets themselves who – under the apparent influence of the theoretical/political debates to be discussed below – are failing to deliver as many heroic, upbeat, fully coherent lesbian subjects with which the reader may 'identify'. Bonnie Zimmerman ends *The Safe Sea of Women* (1992) with the following overview and prognosis:

> Lesbian fiction of the 1970s and 1980s created a 'mythography', an imaginative representation of what lesbian feminists believed to be true about lesbian identity, relationships, culture and community. The fiction was idealistic, visionary, and closely connected to the

community whose views it reflected and influenced . . . But that community has profoundly changed during the 1980s. Although vestiges of Lesbian Nation can still be found, it is a far less powerful and cohesive idea than it was a decade ago. The influence of feminism is weaker, or more diffuse, as in society at large. Consequently lesbian fiction is less visionary and mythic, its voice less communal and more individual, even idiosyncratic. (pp. 207–8)

While I would argue that there are more factors that have influenced the representation of lesbians in fictional texts than the 'failure of community', it is clear that what Zimmerman sees as the new 'individualism', and others would prefer to think of as the post-modernist shattering of communal *and* individual 'identity', has undermined the principles of expressive-realist fiction.[12] Equally, at the popular end of the market (Sarah Schulman's novels, for example), the lesbian hero is no longer a figure that can be unproblematically embraced, and the 'lesbian existence' she occupies is no longer one which we may wish to imitate.[13]

It is equally clear, however, that lesbians will continue to search out representations of themselves in literature and that authentic realist reading practices – although questioned and frustrated – are likely to persist even in the most postmodernist of futures. Within the realm of *literary criticism*, however, it could well be the days of this kind of descriptive and evaluative analysis are over. Now that the biblio-graphies and surveys have finally made it to the shelves (nearly twenty years late!), it would be surprising if the majority of academics did not feel compelled to approach the representation of the lesbian subject in a more 'poststructuralist' way, even whilst continuing to read more 'naively' off-the-record.

What is a lesbian?

Unlike most of the other theoretical or critical approaches discussed in this volume, our understanding of lesbian criticism depends upon an a priori definition of the leading term which 'feminist criticism' *per se* has long put behind it (because few of us now believe in the possibility of there existing one type of feminist/feminist criticism). The implications of this difference for literary critics is well illustrated by the case of my own students. While few feel compelled to begin an essay on some other aspect of 'feminist criticism' with a discussion of 'what is feminism', the *majority* of those engaging with lesbian texts/critics feel compelled to ask 'what is a lesbian?' before engaging with the texts. Indeed, it is common for such students to spend the whole essay agonizing over this question whilst never getting round to a discussion of the texts! And the same problem is encountered in virtually every volume of lesbian literature/criticism: 'what is a lesbian' and, indeed, 'what is a lesbian text' (the question I will move on to next) have to be resolved before the associated textual practices can even be considered.

It would be fair to say that even in the heyday of what, in the United States, was known as 'Lesbian Nation', there were many contradictory definitions of lesbian identity.[14] Over the years, these have tended to polarize into two main groups that Eve Sedgwick has identified by the 'trope of inversion' and the 'trope of gender separatism'.[15] The first group understands same-sex desire as a displacement of the hetero-sexual dynamic onto two persons of the same sex. Two women may fall in love with one another but only if they maintain a masculine–feminine dynamic through the adoption of 'butch' and 'femme' roles. (The question of whether these roles are voluntary or 'innate' has, of course, been another heated area of sexology.) It is the 'inversion' of traditional gender roles that is the key to desire here with, it must be said, a particular onus on the 'butch' (who bears the mark of *visible difference*) to establish a lesbian identity not only for herself but for her 'passing' femme partner. *Vis-à-vis* the 'gender separatists', meanwhile, Sedgwick writes:

> Under this latter view, far from its being the essence of desire to cross boundaries of gender it is instead the most natural thing in the world that people of the same gender, people grouped together under the single most determinative critical mark of social organiza-tion . . . should bond together also on the axis of sexual desire. (pp. 57–8)

If, for the 'inversion' theorists, the key to homosexual desire is (sexual) *difference*, then for the 'gender separatists' (as characterized by Sedgwick) it is (sexual) *sameness*: 'identification' rather than the 'attraction of opposites' explains why women fall in love with one another.[16]

Whilst many lesbian theorists (see note 16) would dispute Sedg-wick's description of both these groups, and whilst the more recent 'Queer theory' has worked to dismantle such binarisms (even if it has created new ones), the lesbian-feminism of the 1970s and 1980s was much inclined towards Sedgwick's 'gender separatist' model (though readers should take care not to confuse this terminology with the notion of 'lesbian separatism': see Glossary). In both lesbian literature and theory the notion of a lesbian sexuality predicated upon 'sameness' and 'identification' held enormous sway. Adrienne Rich's essay, 'Compulsory heterosexuality and lesbian existence' (see note 9) became, in this context, a definitive document. Although critical of the heterosexist bias of the theory, Rich draws upon Nancy Chodorow's work in *The Reproduction of Mothering* to celebrate the devalued bond between mothers and daughters to argue:

> If women are the earliest sources of emotional caring and nurture for both female and male children, it would seem logical, from a feminist perspective at least, to pose the following questions: whether the search for love and tenderness in both sexes does not originally lead toward women; *why in fact women would ever redirect that search . . .*[17]

Lesbian desire is thus explained as a logical re-enactment of a woman's primary bond based upon the recognition of sexual sameness, although adult relationships are not necessarily experienced as a re-enactment of the mother–daughter relationship.

The examples of literary and other art forms that have explained/ celebrated lesbian romance and sexuality in these terms are extensive. From the nineteenth century through to the present, the tropes of 'sisterhood' and 'narcissism' have been invoked to explain the eroticism associated with a self/body so 'like' one's own (see Simone de Beauvoir, *The Second Sex* (1949), and a wide assortment of novels including H.D.'s high-modernist *Her* (1984), Katherine V. Forrest's popular romance *Curious Wine* (1983), and Jeanette Winterson's *Oranges are not the only fruit* (1985)).[18] Significantly, many of the above texts focus on adolescent or 'first' relationships with a strong emphasis on the 'innocence' and 'naturalness' of the attraction: the extratextual referent here is, of course, Plato's explanation of 'true love' as the discovery of the 'missing twin'. In other texts, like Jane Rule's *Desert of the Heart* (first pub. 1964) or Patricia Highsmith's *Carol* (first pub. 1952), the desire of the protagonists is still defined through the trope of identification/'sameness', but within the context of a surrogate mother–daughter relationship.[19] Meanwhile, although all those texts I have just mentioned feature explicitly erotic relationships, theories of lesbian sexuality predicated on 'sameness' have also been criticized for devaluing the specifically 'sexual' component in lesbian desire. This is seen as especially true of those theories deriving from Rich's purported definition of lesbianism as an emotional rather than an explicitly sexual bonding between women, and of her concept of a 'lesbian continuum' which has been seen to render *all* 'women-identified women' lesbian. While Rich's subsequent dialogues reveal that her 'Compulsory heterosexuality' essay was rather reductively misread by many of her followers, it was instrumental in establishing a school of theory that rendered the *majority* of women 'lesbian' whether or not their 'love' for one another was explicitly sexual.[20]

The recent work of Eve Sedgwick (1991), Judith Butler (1990 and 1993), and Diana Fuss (1991) now makes it impossible to define a lesbian as simply (they would say 'simplistically') a 'woman-identified-woman'.[21] Indeed, the whole thrust of Butler's enormously influential work has been (with a few caveats that allow, on certain occasions, a 'strategic' use of the term 'lesbian') to jettison identity-politics altogether. In *Bodies that Matter* (1993) she writes:

> As much as identity terms must be used, as much as 'outness' is to be affirmed, these same notions must be subject to a critique of the exclusionary operations of their own production . . . For whom is outness a historically available and affordable option? Is there an unmarked class character to the demand of universal 'outness'? Who is represented by *which* use of the term, and who is excluded? For whom does the term present an impossible conflict between racial, ethnic, or religious affiliation and sexual politics? What kinds of policies are enabled by what kinds of usages, and what are backgrounded or erased from view? (p. 227)

Like a number of Black feminist theorists before her, the grounds upon which Butler objects to identity categories like 'lesbian', then, is that although they may be useful terms around which to organize both personally and politically, it is only at the expense of other identities (like class, race and national identity) which become marginalized or excluded. This raises enormous problems for individuals (and this means all of us) who are *multiply identified*. By privileging one 'aspect' of our identity we do violence (Butler herself uses the emotive term 'cruelty') to another: in the act of accepting one part of our 'construction' we must inevitably 'reject' another. And even allowing for the fact that the gay community has traditionally made alliances with other 'minority' groups, there is the problem of which one of these 'coalitions' is dominant at any one time, which others excluded. Rather than getting embroiled in the earlier debates about whether lesbianism is to be defined as an emotional, sexual, or political preference, Butler is therefore challenging the legitimacy of all claims to 'coherent' identity (or, indeed, to *any* identities, even when constituted as multiple and/or plural). The question 'What is a lesbian?' is answered by the provocatively cynical 'Why do we need to know?'

And yet, despite the ethical angst about the exclusionary practices of identity politics, Butler's work is obsessed with the way in which the discourses of sexuality work to make us what we are. In this respect it must be said, however, that homosexuality is understood primarily through the 'pressure' it puts on heterosexuality. Queer politics (especially its 'street' manifestation in the form of drag, mime and *masquerade*: see also Chapter 5) works to challenge and de-legitimate the orthodoxy of heterosexual desire which is predicated upon the complex codes of gender difference. Through exposing the arbitrariness of those codes by arguing that all gender is *performative* (and 'secured' only through constant 'reiteration'), Butler and others have exposed the supposed 'naturalness' of heterosexuality.[22] Her work emphasizes just how hard women, in particular, have to work to produce and sustain the *femininity* which makes them an object of desire in a heterosexual economy. Without all this immense labour, she asks, would heterosexuality survive?

One immediate problem with this reasoning is that it has been understood, by some, to imply that the construction of our sexual identities is a matter of choice and free will: that we are both aware of our 'labours' and enact them willingly. This is clearly not the case, and in *Bodies that Matter* Butler goes some way to countering the impression by arguing that if identity is constituted through *repetition* it is also constituted by what she refers to as *citation*: the performativity of gender 'cannot be theorized apart from the forcible and reiterative practice of regulatory sexual regimes' (p. 10). Which is to say that 'the law', in the form of Lacan's 'Symbolic Order' (see Glossary), is instrumental in the (re)production of our gendered selves.

While the challenge of the 'Queer theory' lobby to heterosexuality is clear to see, its usefulness for gays and lesbians is (ironically) sometimes less obvious. In the act of radically de-stabilizing *all* sexual identities by exposing the precariousness of the gender differences/ similarities upon which desire is based, it inevitably asks as many questions about why any one of us should [wish to] be gay or lesbian as we should be heterosexual! The same deconstruction of gender and sexuality which renders male–female desire as 'nothing natural' renders female–female desire as 'nothing special', and there is an unwritten subtext to much of this theory which could easily return us to the (Freudian) model of all subjects as being *potentially* bisexual or 'polymorphously perverse' (see Glossary). But the question remains as to how helpful such a hypothesis is in our daily lives. For reasons that Butler herself acknowledges through her invocation of 'citationality', gender orthodoxies will continue to be reiterated at the same time that they are being deconstructed. Individuals will continue to 'present' and live their lives as heterosexual or homosexual, and *both groups* will continue to define themselves through or against the norms of gender difference and each other. Queer theory, it could be argued, offers a trenchant critique of identity politics by exposing the arbitrariness of our desires without paying sufficient attention to the desires themselves. Even if we accept the arbitrariness and fabrication of our construction as homosexual/heterosexual, it does not mean that we will stop *wanting* to identify with one or other group, or indeed, with some other identity ('Queer' included). For as I will now go on to argue, a provisional identity remains an identity nevertheless.

Strategic identity

As I made clear at the beginning of this chapter, I believe the challenges to identity-politics that are currently being mounted are so far-reaching that the future of academic study – including literary criticism – organized around categories like 'lesbian' is problematic. In the same way that 'women's studies' is gradually being supplemented/displaced by 'gender studies', I envisage that gay and lesbian studies (without, of course, ever having established themselves as legitimate epistemologies) will give rise to teaching and research that interrogates sexuality more generally. Whether or not this proves to be the case, the political implications will surely provide an interesting discussion point for readers of this chapter in the years to come.

In the present, meanwhile, there are a number of lesbian-feminists who are arguing for the strategic preservation of a lesbian identity. While allowing that, theoretically, the term may already be consigned to permanent quotation marks (according to Butler *et al.* you can never 'be' a lesbian: the best you can achieve is a perpetual state of 'becoming'!) they argue that such identities are personally and politically desirable and *necessary*. Many lesbians who support this view offer personal testaments to their continued investment in the problematic term. Biddy Martin, for example, in her study of lesbian autobiography, reflects on the way in which many of her authors need a sense of identity, even if it means negotiating two competing identities like sexuality and race:

> At the same time that such autobiographical writing enacts a critique of both sexuality and race as 'essential' and totalising identifications, it also acknowledges the political and psychological importance, indeed, the pleasures, too, of at least partial or provisional identifications, homes and communities.[23]

Similarly, Sally Munt, in her introduction to *New Lesbian Criticism*, candidly confirms her own contradictory position thus:

> In the main I agree with [Diana] Fuss that 'lesbian' is an historical construction of comparatively recent date, and that there is no eternal lesbian essence outside the frame of cultural change and historical determination. However, this strictly intellectual definition wouldn't stop me *feeling*, and sometimes behaving, as though the total opposite were true. We need our dream of a lesbian nation, even as we recognise its fictionality.[24]

Recognizing the importance of the 'dream' while also recognizing its fictionality seems to me a vital piece of common sense to hold onto in this debate. Although *we know* that there can be no one, monolithic definition of 'lesbian' which will hold together all the identificatory and sexual practices that cluster together under the term, our exclusions from other (dominant) group identities (such as heterosexual) will doubtless sustain the desire for an alternative collective identity.

I would also suggest that it is in literature, if not in literary *criticism*, that the dream is likely to be most visibly sustained. In market terms, if not in theoretical ones, lesbian texts and lesbian readers are (statistically) alive and well. No matter how spurious or provisional their classification, increasingly large numbers of women readers recognize that they are being 'addressed' *as lesbians* and it is surely through such interpellation (see Glossary) that 'imaginary communities', at least, will be sustained.[25] This is certainly the situation in the present when the popularity of lesbian genre fiction (crime and romance in particular) has risen to unprecedented heights. As Zimmerman has rightly observed, however (see above), the lesbian reading community is no longer the homogeneous group it was, and it remains to be seen if we will see the market further splinter into special interest groups (determined by coalitions with other identities, for instance) or whether the demand will be met by representation within a radicalized mainstream. (Witness, for example, the increasing numbers of books, films and TV programmes that feature gay and lesbian characters.)[26] In the circumstances, it would seem to me that it is likely to be publishers and the media, as much as academics, who will determine whether the category 'lesbian' is to survive as a legitimate textual/existential category.

The lesbian text

For those readers and critics who are able to convince themselves of the (at least, strategic) existence of a lesbian identity, the next challenge is to define a lesbian text. The problem, as I commonly pose it to my own students, is this: is a lesbian text a text written by a lesbian, about lesbians, or for lesbians? (Which they answer, as I've already indicated, by posing the a priori issue we have just considered: what, anyway, is a lesbian?) After following through the angst-ridden dilemmas of the latter debate, my readers here will be pleased to know that lesbian criticism has been moving towards a consensus in respect to the first question. While some publishers and publications still argue that for a text to be 'lesbian' it has to be written by a self-declared lesbian *author*, and while critics wishing to deal with explicit representations of lesbian sexuality and lifestyle might insist on lesbian subject matter, most of the more recent commentators prefer to locate the lesbianism of their texts in the complex relationship between *text and reader*.[27] This formula has the advantage of including the *many* texts whose authors (male and female) are not (officially, at least) lesbian-identified, and the equally large body of literature in which lesbianism is a hidden or marginalized subtext rather than its ostensible focus. The text–reader nexus allows us to think about both the way in which texts identify and position lesbian audiences, and of the way in which readers can read silent or recalcitrant texts 'against the grain' of their dominant reader-positioning in order to produce a lesbian reading. In their introduction to *Lesbian Texts and Contexts* (1990, see note 11) Jay and Glasgow, who themselves favour the text-reader formula, declare the advantages thus:

> We believe that one can read as a lesbian even if one is not thus self-identified . . . Reading, thus, is an exercise in interpretive strategies and is not, nor should it be, bound to specific, shared life experiences . . . We know experientially that it is, indeed, possible to 'read as a lesbian', to 'read with fresh eyes', whether one is lesbian or straight, male or female. Otherwise all reading is solipsistic and all texts hermetically inaccessible except to those already within the closed circle. (pp. 4–5)

It will be seen that this model of lesbian readership is significantly different from the 'authentic realist' approach I described at the beginning of this chapter. Jay and Glasgow's 'ideal readers' are not reading for confirmation/validation of their own 'life experiences', but to 'see with fresh eyes'. While I believe that, at some level, our existential identities can and do impinge upon our reading experiences (making us feel excluded from certain texts, for example, even whilst we might be able to 'understand' them), this location of the lesbian text as an active interface between text and reader seems to me the most useful form of definition. It also goes some way to enabling us to define what, if anything, is a 'lesbian aesthetic'.

The lesbian aesthetic

Because of the enormous (and continued) investment lesbian readers have had in authentic realism, it is only comparatively recently that critics have started to move beyond thematic and imagistic evaluations of lesbian texts and to ask more demanding questions such as: do lesbians write differently? Are there linguistic and stylistic features that are specific to lesbian texts? Is there, indeed, a lesbian aesthetic?

To some extent this theoretical 'change of gear' mirrors, belatedly, the route taken by mainstream feminist criticism. Once writers like Elaine Showalter and Ellen Moers had begun work establishing an alternative canon of women writers previously 'hidden from history', feminist literary critics recognized that it was time to establish the aesthetic and political grounds for the separation. Showalter herself responded to the challenge with her invention of the term 'gynocriticism' (see Chapter 3) and her proposal, in the essay 'Feminist criticism in the wilderness', that the 'difference' of women's writing could be expressed in four main ways: biological, psychological, linguistic and cultural.[28] The problems and limitations of Showalter's favouring of the cultural model are discussed in Chapter 3, but it would be fair to say that a good number of lesbian critics would probably argue a similar line *vis-à-vis* the way in which the specificity of lesbian cultural experience is bound to translate into a particular set of thematic preoccupations. The problem remains, however, of whether we can talk about a lesbian aesthetic in terms other than the thematic. Do lesbian texts demonstrate recognizably different stylistic and syntactical formulas to other women writers? Do lesbian texts employ special tactics to identify their audiences?

Apart from the important work of the French feminists such as Luce Irigaray on female language use (much of which is specifically lesbian in its attempt to link textuality with sexuality: see Chapter 5), there has been some extremely good recent work by British and American feminist scholars which has begun to identify a lesbian aesthetic in terms of structure, syntax and intertextuality. This work, it seems to me, has taken lesbian literary criticism into a new theoretical league by moving analysis away from the necessary but limited 'descriptive' analysis previously described. To illustrate the sort of work that has already been done at this level I would like to turn now to two essays included in Jay and Glasgow's *Lesbian Texts and Contexts*.

Marilyn R. Farwell's 'Heterosexual plots and lesbian subtexts' (pp. 91–103) is a useful example of the way in which the lesbianism of a text can be located in its structures as much as in its thematic content. Although her chosen text, Marion Zimmer Bradley's *The Mists of Avalon* (1982), has only a relatively small lesbian textual component, Farwell argues that it nevertheless works as an extremely disruptive force on the text's total narrative space denying a heterosexual orthodoxy. In this way the erotic exchange between Raven and Morgaine in Bradley's novel 'ask[s] to restructure that neat dependence on dualism that orders the rest of the novelistic landscape' (p. 100). The aesthetic implications of this, for Bradley, are that we define the lesbianism of a text not simply in terms of lesbian representation but according to the pressure it puts on the heterosexual 'dominant'. Following Teresa de Lauretis, she argues that: 'This distinction allows us to avoid calling a text feminist which in fact reinforces the structurally gendered spaces [and she cites Shakespeare's *As You Like It* and Ridley Scott's film, *Aliens*, as examples of this], or naming a space about lesbians transgressive that merely replicates gendered ideas' (p. 95). What Farwell is arguing in the last part of this statement is that we should question the supposed 'lesbianism' of texts in which the relationships between women simply mimic heterosexual norms. 'Authentic' lesbian texts should be required to offer us alternative models of gender relations and reflect this in plots which are substantially different from the heterosexual romance narratives. While many lesbian critics would doubtless find Farwell's own position suspiciously reactionary in this respect (the argument suggests that she would be prejudiced against texts focusing on butch–femme relationships seen to be imitating heterosexual norms, for instance), her demonstration of the way in which female–female relationships can severely disrupt the prototypical linear 'romance' plot (the triangle of two men competing for one woman ending with resolution in marriage, for example) is instructive.

Jane Marcus's essay, 'Sapphistory: the Woolf and the well' (pp. 164–179), meanwhile, locates the lesbianism of her chosen text – Virginia Woolf's *A Room of One's Own* (1929) – not in its structure but in its *syntax*. In what I believe to be one of the most exciting and ground-breaking essays in lesbian criticism yet to be published, Marcus reveals Woolf's text to covertly interpellate (see Glossary) a lesbian audience through a coded system of 'naming' (disguised references to con-temporary figures associated with Radcliffe Hall's trial) and *ellipsis*: literally the 'gaps' which may be filled with a lesbian *double entendre*. Together these devices amount to a strategy of sexual/textual *seduction* which may, indeed, be thought of as a lesbian aesthetic. Marcus writes:

> What, then, will we call it when the woman writer seduces the woman reader? I have suggested *sapphistory* as a suitable term for this rhetorical seduction . . . An earnest feminist appeal to political solidarity would not be half so effective as shameless flirtation, Woolf seems to feel. Not only narration but even punctuation is enlisted in her seductive plot: 'Chloe liked Olivia. They share a . . .' Dot dot dot is a female code for lesbian love. (pp. 167–8)

Apart from shifting our location of lesbianism of a text from thematic to stylistic features, the real strength of Marcus's aesthetic, it seems to me, is the way in which it emphasizes the interactive relationship between *text and reader* in the production of meaning. As I have argued elsewhere, it is the way in which texts position their readers (as male/female, straight/gay, feminist/non-feminist)) that is surely the best clue to their political and aesthetic status.[29] A text can only very problematically be defined as 'lesbian' on account either of its authorship or its lesbian content (think of the many male-authored texts which have voyeuristically featured representations of lesbian sex, for example), but the interpellation of a lesbian audience (either overt or, as here, covert) seems to be a legitimate claim to a lesbian identity. It also has the virtue, as here, of bringing a great many texts not primarily thought of as 'lesbian' into the field of lesbian textual analysis for the very reason that so much literature in the past could only communicate transgressive sexuality in a coded form. In the deployment of such 'gaps and silences' we may, indeed, come close to being able to define an aesthetic practice which may be thought of as characteristically lesbian. Diana Collecott comes to this conclusion in her essay 'What is not said: a study in textual inversion' where she claims that 'concealment and suppression' represent the majority of lesbians' continued experience of both living and writing.[30] While it could also be argued that a good deal of post-1970s lesbian-feminist literature is very definitely *not* aesthetically characterized by this sort of closeting, the special positioning ('seducing') of the ('lesbian') reader by the text holds true and accounts for a good deal of the *pleasure* that we derive from such reading practices.

My conclusion, then, is that it is in the dialogic relationship between text and reader – the way the text positions (seduces) the reader, and equally the way in which the reader can make claims upon closeted or otherwise resistant texts – that we can best locate a lesbian aesthetic. It is clear that authorship and thematic content alone cannot be the basis of a text's claim to a lesbian identity, but text and reader together can, I think, produce that legitimation. In the readings that follow I will test out this rationale by exploring the way in which two texts, one that has been widely received as a lesbian text (*The Color Purple*) and one that has not (*Wide Sargasso Sea*), position their readers in terms of sexual identity.[31] My hypothesis is that although carrying very little thematic content that may be thought of as ostensibly 'lesbian', the plot and structure of *Wide Sargasso Sea* make it, in some respects, *more* subversive of heterosexual orthodoxy than Walker's text in which the relationship between Celie and Shug is (a) subsumed in a discourse of liberal humanism and (b) effectively marginalizes its lesbian audience.

II

The Color Purple

Since its first publication almost ten years ago, Alice Walker's *The Color Purple* has acquired the status of a 'classic text'. Whilst, at first, its reputation was confined to feminist circles, it has since been more extensively 'canonized' and is now a favourite course text both at university and high school level. Many of my own undergraduates in Britain have studied this text for their 'A' level examinations, for example.

Although it might perhaps seem surprising that a book featuring an explicit lesbian relationship (between the principal narrator, Celie, and her husband's long-term 'mistress', Shug Avery) should be given such widespread 'approval' (to the extent that it is now read by 'schoolchildren'!), I hope to show how it is also a text whose subversive potential is easily subsumed within a liberal humanist (see Glossary) reading which neutralizes its representation of both sexual and racial politics. What is difficult to assess, and what perhaps becomes more difficult when one has become as 'overfamiliar' with a text as I have in this case, is the extent to which this 'liberal tendency' is a feature of the text or of the 'reading method' with which it is most commonly approached. The interesting point here, of course, is that whilst a 'classic realist' response to the novel will necessarily involve 'identification' with 'lesbian' characters (Celie and Shug), this does not mean that the majority of readers will feel themselves positioned as 'lesbian' (even on a temporary basis) or will ultimately classify *The Color Purple* as a lesbian text. This is clearly because the reader is offered so many other identifications and positionings in the narrative that lesbian sexuality is quickly swallowed up in the novel's ideological as well as spiritual 'pantheism'.[32] The implication here is that a lesbian reading of the text based on traditional, authentic realist practices will have to struggle hard to sustain its lesbian specificity. Because *The Color Purple* is a book which deals in other, equally urgent political affirmations (i.e. racial identity), and which also represents many other (more traditional) social and religious values (in particular, 'family values'), any reading based on reader–character 'involvement'/'evaluation' will find it hard to focus exclusively on the dissident sexuality represented by just two of its many characters. As Hilary Hinds has argued, it was this subsumption of subversive sexuality within other 'human rights' discourses (i.e. religious tolerance) that made the TV adaptation of Jeanette Winterson's *Oranges are not the only fruit* such an acceptable (indeed, such a highly successful) cultural product.[33]

What these opening comments are suggesting, then, is that a lesbian reading of Walker's novel based on the authentic realist practices that have dominated lesbian criticism for so long (see Part I) are likely to be unsuccessful in promoting it as a (radical) lesbian text. For it to acquire and sustain that status, a wholly different relationship between text and reader needs to be discovered: one that more effectively privileges lesbian sexuality over the other moral and political values dealt with in the text. Despite a number of (unsuccessful!) attempts of my own, however, I would suggest that such an 'oppositional' reading is extremely hard to produce in the case of this particular text. The liberal text–reader positioning is so strong and so pervasive that there is little opportunity for the lesbian reader to gain an alternative foothold. There are no spaces, as it were, where 'she' is addressed in private: even the most intimate scenes between Celie and Shug seem to me to be simultaneously broadcast to the non-lesbian (and white, middle-class) audience that the text is attempting to educate.[34]

According to Eve Sedgwick's distinction (see Part I), there can be little doubt either that Walker's novel is a representative of the 'gender-separatist' (or 'woman identified') version of lesbianism. The relationship between Celie and Shug is predicated upon a model of female/feminine 'sameness' and 'merger', which has its psychological and cultural referents in rather idealized visions of 'sisterhood' and 'mother–daughter' relationships. This is a text, indeed, in which all the adult relationships are seen as variants of familial prototypes, both good and bad. The fact that such relationships reproduce the experiences of early childhood both explains and emphasizes the theme of 'incest' at the text's core, but also implies that 'healthy' adult relationships depend upon a positive reworking of these parent–child relations. In line with Adrienne Rich's appropriation of Chodorow *et al.* (see Part I), this correction is centred primarily on the beneficent effects of loving and supportive mother–daughter relationships, but there are also hints that relationships between men (and between men and women) will improve only when the father–son bond has also been revised, as it is between Mr — and Harpo towards the end of the novel ('Well, one night I walked up to tell Harpo something – and the two of them was just laying there on the bed fast asleep. Harpo holding his daddy in his arms' (p. 191)).

It will be obvious to most readers, psychoanalytically trained or not, that Celie's lesbianism is 'caused', explained (and, perhaps, morally condoned?) by her lack of a (good) mother. Abused by her (step)-father, Celie is the subject of her own mother's fear and anger, and is brutally separated from her by her father's insatiable sexual appetite – which leaves her mother dead (in childbirth) and herself, pregnant. The implication is that, as a child and a young woman, Celie is without a positive female role model; which is presumably why the first sight of Shug Avery makes such an impression on her:

> I ast our new mammy bout Shug Avery. What it is? I ast. She don't know but she say she gon fine out.
> She do more than that. She git a picture. The first one of a real person I ever seen. She say Mr — was taking somethin out of his billfold to show Pa an it fell out an slid under the table. Shug Avery was a woman. The most beautiful woman I ever saw. She more pretty than my mama. She bout ten thousand times more prettier than me. I see her there in furs. Her face rouge. Her hair like somethin tail. She grinning with her foot up on somebody motorcar. Her eyes serious though. Sad some.
> I ast her to give me the picture. An all night long I stare at it. And now when I dream, I dream of Shug Avery. She be dress to kill, whirling an laughing. (p. 8)

Although this first (photographic) description of Shug compares her directly with Celie's mother, the portrait is not in itself 'maternal'. What Shug would seem to represent to Celie at this point is simply 'femininity' itself: a quality that she recognizes as beauty and as something that is absent both in herself and in her life. Despite the fact that much of the novel hinges on the contrast between Shug's beauty and Celie's 'ugliness', however, this is not 'difference' in terms of Sedgwick's 'inversion'. Whilst Shug's attraction to Celie is undoubtedly cast as feminine glamour, Celie, despite her 'ugliness' is not positioned as 'masculine'. Even in this first 'encounter', we see Celie staring at Shug's photograph as into a mirror. From the start, Celie not only wants Shug: she wants to *be* her – and, through her, to be '(re)incorporated' into the body of the 'good mother'.[35]

This 'gender separatist' dynamic of 'desire for' eliding into 'identification with' also characterizes the subsequent sexual relations between Celie and Shug. Although there is some 'tension of difference' in Celie's initial scrutiny of Shug's body ('First time I got the full sight of Shug Avery long black body with it plum nipples, look like her mouth, I thought I had turned into a man', p. 45), it is quickly circumscribed by references to the more motherly/sisterly affections which are experienced by both women:

> I work on her like she a doll or like she Olivia [Celie's own child] – or like she mama. I comb and pat, comb and pat. First she say, hurry up and git finish. Then she melt down a little and lean back against my knees. That feel just right, she say. That feel like mama used to do. Or maybe not mama. Maybe grandma. She reach for another cigarette. Start hum a little tune. (p. 48)

For readers relating to the text through an authentic realist practice of identification and evaluation (see Part I) this is, I would suggest, a very non-threatening form of lesbianism: an image of intimacy between women in which sexuality *per se* is subsumed in quasi-maternal intimacy and merger. Whilst some theorists might still argue, in line with Adrienne Rich's 'lesbian continuum' (see Part I), that the fact that *all* woman-woman relationships are implicitly lesbian is in itself hugely subversive, others will (and have) insisted that such a vision effectively takes the sexuality out of lesbianism. In this respect, Walker's text may be seen as a prime culprit, since even the 'sex scene' itself (the occasion when Celie and Shug first make love) is swamped in Oedipal imagery:

> My mama die, I tell Shug. My sister Nettie run away. Mr — come git me to take care his rotten children. He never ast me nothing bout myself. He clam on top of me and fuck and fuck, even when my head bandaged. Nobody ever love me, I say.

> She say, I love you, Miss Celie. And then she haul off and kiss me on the mouth.
>
> *Um*, she say, like she surprise. I kiss her back, say, *um*, too. Us kiss and kiss till us can't hardly kiss no more. Then us touch each other.
>
> I don't know nothing bout it, I say to Shug. I don't know much, she say.
>
> Then I feels something soft and wet on my breast, feel like one of my little lost babies mouth.
>
> Way after while, I act a little lost baby too. (p. 97)

It is, I would suggest, the explicit humanism of the sentiment expressed here (we all know what it is to feel like a 'little lost baby') that makes this description of lesbian love-making so accessible and acceptable to heterosexual readers: a theory that is certainly borne out in Chapter 2 where the self-identified heterosexual respondents of Sara Mills' questionnaire regard the text's representation of sexuality far more favourably than Linda who finds it 'whimsical' and 'irritating' (i.e. 'non-authentic' according to her own lesbian experience). What the heterosexual readers seem most impressed by, moreover, is the demonstration of equality and mutual (sexual) pleasure in Celie and Shug's relationship which they read as being somehow synonymous with non-penetrative sex. The (false) implication is, of course, that the abusive power dynamics of (some) heterosexual relations (brutally caricatured in Celie's relationship with Mr —) is magically absent in (all) lesbian relationships. Walker's text could thus be accused of winning the 'respect' of a heterosexual audience through an idealization of lesbian sexual practice: an idealization so complete that (at some level) it doesn't look like sex at all.[36]

This de-sexualization of sexuality is certainly reinforced by the way in which the relationship between Celie and Shug is seen to develop. Although we can infer that the two remain lovers for a good part of the narrative action, there are few explicit references to this fact, and this aspect of the relationship is easily side-lined as the reader becomes absorbed in the next stage of the drama which focuses on Celie's recovery of Nettie's letters. At different points we are made aware, also, of Shug's own undiminished heterosexual drives: both in her relationship with Mr — and latterly in her relationships with Grady and Germaine. In this context, the Shug–Celie relationship is quickly recast (or 'understood') as primarily a 'friendship', and what might be construed as subversive in the 'normalization' of a lesbian relationship (the image of Celie and Shug lying together in bed, listening to music, for example, see p. 178) becomes 'incidental' in a negative way.

In terms of her own growth and development, moreover, it could be argued that Celie's lesbian experience is devalued by being represented as a 'means' rather than an 'end in itself'. What it is a means to is, of course, her own sense of identity and self-respect, though at the end of the novel this translates into an 'autonomy' so consummate that she can do without the woman who enabled her to achieve it:

> Shug write me she coming home.
> Now. Is this life or not?
> *I be so calm.*
> If she come, I be happy. If she don't, I be content.
> And then I figure this the lesson I was suppose to learn. (p. 240)

While I would not wish to imply moral criticism of this 'independence', I think it can easily be seen how such a resolution reduces Celie's lesbian experience to simply *one factor* in her general humanist education. Shug's role was no more and no less than to show Celie how to 'love herself'; and then, to love and forgive others (including men). It was not about her discovering her sexuality *per se*.

As I suggested at the beginning of this section, to produce a reading of Walker's text which is more 'positively' lesbian is thwarted by its 'universalist' reader-positioning. Although Walker's novel was described as 'man-hating' in some of its early reviews (a criticism which also attended the launching of Steven Spielberg's film which was seen as especially offensive to Black men), it seems to me a text which is 'in league' with the white, male/female, heterosexual, liberal-minded audience which it hopes to educate further. This is not to deny that the representations of sexual violence depict Black masculinity in a poor light, but the book's narratives of progress and development (both Harpo and Albert become 'new men'), combined with contextualizing circumstances which indicate that all men are not (or need not) be like this, suggest that plenty of men (Black and white) could read the novel sympathetically and *not* feel included in its 'target' group. In this respect, the novel can, perhaps, be likened to some of the nineteenth-century slave narratives (such as Harriet Jacob's story of 'Linda Brent') in which the author's principal audience was the white, middle-class women of the south who might be enlisted in the fight for emancipation.[37] Whilst Walker's novel is clearly not this narrow in its reader target zone in as much as it addresses a Black, female audience *at the same time* as it appeals to a more 'universal' readership, I feel that Black female and/or lesbian readers are never especially *privileged*, or that other readers are seriously challenged, threatened, or excluded. According to the terms espoused by Mae Gwendolyn Henderson in her excellent essay on Black women writers, this means that although the text enters into 'familial' or 'testimonial' address with its Black/female audience, it *doesn't* enter into overtly hostile 'competition' with Black men, white men, or white women.[38] The predominance of race, moreover, in identifying these reader-categories tends to marginalize further the significance of sexuality in text–reader relations: the fact that the novel is addressing straight as well as gay readers almost goes without saying once we have established it is addressing whites as well as Blacks. Sexuality is simply another aspect of the novel's general humanistic 'appeal'.

It is also worth noting, in conclusion, that this humanism is a feature of *plot* as well as address. I have already observed how Celie's relationship with Shug may be seen, by the end of the novel, as simply one factor in her overall growth and development, and the strength and independence she achieves is crucially linked to her improved relationships with others: male and female. What Shug 'teaches' Celie is (literally) how to 'love herself', and this subsequently enables her to take up her proper place within her natural and 'extended' family. The fact that, in the final chapter, Shug is simply one element in a 'family' whose other members are still predominantly heterosexual, means that the lesbianism of the text, as of the Shug–Celie relationship, is very much 'a thing of the past'. Thus the early sexual encounter seems, in retrospect, more like an initiation into masturbation than to lesbianism. In terms of Marilyn Farwell's thesis (see Part I), very little pressure has been put on the text's primarily heterosexual economy. The fact that this is a novel which 'features' a lesbian relationship does not mean that it is, in the last analysis, a very lesbian text.

Wide Sargasso Sea

It might be said, then, that Walker's novel is one in which lesbianism is present at a *thematic level* but absent as a feature of *interlocution*, By contrast, I now hope to demonstrate that although *Wide Sargasso Sea* does not *directly* address a lesbian audience, its 'subtext' interpellates (see Glossary) a *covert* one. There is, indeed, a potential paradox at work here whereby the more 'closeted' texts may be seen to have the more 'intimate' relationship with their lesbian readers. It is the process of 'de-coding' that effectively identifies and privileges the lesbian reader.

Although they are not supported by narratorial direction in the way that they are in Walker's *The Color Purple*, relationships between women are also the bedrock of Rhys's novel. Apart from the childhood relationship between Antoinette and Tia which is, as I shall argue, the most obvious 'site' for a lesbian reading of the text in terms of its narrative action, there is also considerable emphasis on Antoinette's relationships with her real and 'surrogate' mothers (Annette and Christophine), and with the nuns in the convent in Spanish Town who provide her with a temporary refuge from the heterosexual world. The feminine network in which Antoinette's story is thus enmeshed and, in particular, its emphasis on the primacy of mother–daughter relations, means that it, too, invites a 'gynocritical' approach which can, with a little effort, be augmented with the lesbianism of Rich's 'continuum' (see Part I).

Tia is what I remember about Rhys's novel. When first starting work on this new chapter, and casting around in my mind for which texts to use, I recalled that Antoinette's last cry was to the girl she had known as a child: a moment of recognition (for the reader, as for herself) as complete and surprising as the wail of grief that marks the end of Toni Morrison's *Sula*.[39] What is most remarkable about this particular text, however, is how little Tia actually figures in the narrative. She is referred to, indeed, on only three main occasions: the first establishing her intimacy with Antoinette:

> Soon Tia was my friend and I met her nearly every morning at the turn of the road to the river.
>
> Sometimes we left the bathing pool at midday, sometimes we stayed till late afternoon. Then Tia would light a fire (fires always lit for her, sharp stones did not hurt her bare feet, I never saw her cry). We boiled green bananas in an old iron pot and ate them with our fingers out of a calabash and once we had eaten she slept at once. I could not sleep . . . Late or early we parted at the turn of the road. My mother never asked me where I had been or what I had done. (p. 20)

Although it is never spelt out, these days spent with Tia in the wild and overgrown grounds of the Coulibri estate represent the only period of true freedom and happiness in Antoinette's life. In the brief spell before class and racial difference intervene to separate them forever, Antoinette's bonding with a black 'native' allows her to 'belong' to the place and country she would love (despite her enforced alienation) for the rest of her life. This Eden is, however, short-lived, its end foreshadowed by Tia's contemptuous seizure of Antoinette's three pennies (p. 201), and consummated by her action of throwing the stone at Antoinette the night of the fire:

> Then, not so far off, I saw Tia and her mother and I ran to her, for she was all that was left of my life as it had been. We had eaten the same food, slept side by side, bathed in the same river. As I ran, I thought, I will live with Tia and I will be like her. Not to leave Coulibri. Not to go. Not. When I got close I saw the jagged stone in her hand but I did not see her throw it. I did not feel it either, only something wet, running down my face. I looked at her and I saw her face crumple up as she began to cry. We stared at each other, blood on my face, tears on hers. It was as if I saw myself. Like in a looking-glass. (p. 38)

In this second (and most significant) entry, we are given some indication of the intensity of the Antoinette–Tia relationship through a dramatic exposition of the social forces that would not permit it to continue. Even as the two girls represent 'home' to one another (a union predicated on merger and identification), so are they fatally divided by their racial and economic difference. Tia casts her stone, even as she 'steals' Antoinette's pennies, not because she hates Antoinette, but because she herself is threatened by the differences separating them. What her apparent betrayal reveals, however, is only the mark of her own powerlessness. Whilst in their former life together Tia had always been the strong, competent and brave one who 'never cried' (see previous quotation), her tears indicate her effective (social) powerlessness. As women ('poor black nigger' and 'poor white nigger') both Antoinette and Tia are now marked as 'victims', which is why Antoinette sees the 'blood on my face, tears on hers' as a reflection. Reading this episode through a lesbian frame, however, it could be argued that this tragic moment of separation is also a moment of recognition: at the point Antoinette and Tia are wrenched apart, so does their passionate investment in one another become most visible.

Although Antoinette never sees Tia again in person after the night of the fire, she persists in her unconscious where she is bound up with her childhood memories of the Coulibri estate which she refers to repeatedly as 'the most beautiful place in the world'. Throughout her 'marriage' to Rochester, Coulibri clearly represents a place of emotional warmth and freedom whose polymorphous sexuality (see Glossary) (the lesbian sexuality of the popular imagination) he is deeply afraid of. Viewed in this way, Antoinette's considerable sexual appetite during the first weeks of her marriage to Rochester (she is presented as increasingly 'hungry' for it) may be thought of as less affirmatively heterosexual than it first appears: what she is making love to is not Rochester but Coulibri which she loves 'more than a person', yet in which is buried the spirit of Tia.

By recognizing the symbolic interconnection of place and person in Antoinette's sexual and emotional being, her last, desperate cry to Tia becomes less surprising:

> But when I looked over the edge I saw the pool at Coulibri. Tia was there. She beckoned to me and when I hesitated, she laughed. I heard her say, You frightened? And I heard the man's voice, Bertha! Bertha! All this I heard and saw in a fraction of a second. And the sky so red. Someone screamed and I thought, *Why did I scream?* I called 'Tia!' and jumped and woke. (p. 155)

What this final entry reveals is that whilst, on the one hand, Antoinette's memory of Tia is bound up in the shame and humiliation of a difference she has been unable to break free from (her racial identity; her colonial past), she is still, nevertheless, her undiminished object of desire. In this dramatic rescripting of Tia's earlier taunts and challenges, Antoinette makes her choice and proves that she is not afraid. As Rochester commands her to return to the 'safety' of the white, English, heterosexual world, she leaps (back) towards Tia: an action that the lesbian reader can read as a mark of sexual as well as cultural preference.

It is not only Tia, however, who defines Coulibri as a female/lesbian space. What emerges in the course of the novel is how much Antoinette's protective passion for the estate is bound up with her love for 'both' her mothers: how the neglect of her 'natural' mother does not stop her from believing her the most beautiful woman in the world, and how she is prepared to trust Christophine (literally) with her life.[40] It is, indeed, important to note the extent Antoinette is prepared to defend her mother despite the latter's rejections. When she is telling Rochester of her childhood at Coulibri, the beauty of place and person are indistinguishable:

> And then she was so lovely. I used to think that every time she looked in the glass she must have hoped and pretended. I pretended too. Different things of course. You can pretend for a long time, but one day it falls away and you are alone. We were alone in the most beautiful place in the world, it is not possible that there can be anywhere else so beautiful as Coulibri. (p. 108)

And when her relationship with Rochester goes bad, her defence of her mother becomes a defence of herself: both are presented as victims of the same (hetero)sexually abusive patriarchal forces:

> She drank some more rum and went on, 'My mother whom you talk about, what justice did she have? My mother sitting in the rocking chair and speaking about dead horses and dead grooms and a black devil kissing her sad mouth. Like you kissed mine,' she said. (p. 121)

But it is Christophine, her wet-nurse 'surrogate' mother who, of course, epitomizes the female 'magic' of Coulibri: Christophine, with her spells and curses, her 'Obeah' inheritance, whom Antoinette turns to as her last protector and salvation and whom Rochester regards as his nemesis. What is interesting here is the fact that both Antoinette's faith and Rochester's fear are marked by the superstition of cultural difference. The powers that Christophine herself disclaims, they are both desperate to believe in: he, as an 'explanation' for what is happening to him; she, as a way out. For the lesbian reader, moreover, it is clear that Christophine's 'secret recipes' are very explicitly gendered. Whatever substance is used to spike Rochester's wine, he experiences it as a malevolent female 'hormone' that makes him a victim of Antoinette's own, insatiable 'oceanic' sexuality: 'Above all I hated her. For she belonged to the magic and loveliness. She had left me thirsty and all my life would be thirst and longing for what I had lost before I found it' (p. 141). By the time he eventually escapes Coulibri, then, Rochester believes he has been permanently poisoned by malevolent female forces: his testosterone tainted by an excess of oestrogen as the maternal passions bonding Antoinette and Christophine are literally fed into his own blood stream.[41] For Antoinette, meanwhile, it could be argued that the end-result of Christophine's voodoo is simply to confirm and/or establish her lesbian identity. While she goes to Christophine asking for magic that will make her husband love her again, what she gets is something that (indirectly) will stop her loving him (and all men):

> 'Just you touch me once. You'll soon see if I'm a dam' coward like you are.'
> Then she cursed me comprehensively, my eyes, my mouth, every member of my body, and it was like a dream in the large unfurnished room with the candles flickering and this red-eyed wild-haired stranger who was my wife shouting obscenities at me. It was at this nightmare moment that I heard Christophine's calm voice.
> 'You hush up and keep yourself quiet. And don't cry. Crying's no good with him. I told you before. Crying's no good'. (pp. 122–3)

By the end of the 'honeymoon', then, Antoinette is firmly back in Christophine's maternal 'possession' and Rochester a target of her permanent hostility.

Apart from discovering a subtext in its principal narratives, a 'symptomatic' (see Glossary) lesbian reading of Rhys's novel might also attend profitably to details of syntax. Although, as I noted at the outset of this section, this is certainly not a text that is overtly addressed to a lesbian readership, the fluctuating, ambiguous and politically charged use of personal pronouns throughout ('we', 'us', 'them') signals the presence of 'in' and 'out' groupings that is part of 'everyday' lesbian existence. The opening sentence of the novel, indeed, sets up a charged dynamic of 'us' and 'them' within which Antoinette is doomed to flounder the whole of her life: '*They* say when trouble comes close ranks, and so the white people did. But *we* were not in their ranks. The Jamaican ladies had never approved of my mother, 'because she pretty like pretty self, Christophine said'. (p. 15) [my italics]. In the course of the novel, who 'they' are depends upon the different subjects' relationship to whatever constitutes the dominant social group, but it is significant that, for Antoinette, the native Black population is both 'us' and 'they': the people who torched her family home, and the people (Christophine, Baptiste, Tia) who were the closest thing she had to a family. This precarious ambiguity makes itself present in one of her conversations with Rochester in which she is asked who she means by 'they', to which she replies, evasively: 'Christophine was with us, and Godfrey the old gardener stayed, and a boy, I forget his name' (p. 108). Tia, of course, effectively became one of 'them' through her act of casting the stone, but the fact that Antoinette refused to think of her in that way is evident both in her protection of Tia's name ('My head was bandaged because *someone* had thrown a stone at me' [my italics], p. 110) and her own manifest desire to become one of 'them' herself. When Rochester asks her why she hugs Christophine, for example ('I wouldn't hug and kiss them . . . I couldn't', p. 76), she 'laughed for a long time' as a sign of her complicity.

Although this 'out-group' Antoinette seeks to enter could never be thought of exclusively in terms of sexuality, it can nevertheless be likened to the experiences of lesbians and gay men and also to the textualization of homosexuality at the level of syntax. In this respect, indeed, we may think of Antoinette as a notional 'bisexual' who sits uncomfortably between two groups, neither of whom will accept her claim to an 'authentic' identity. For, at the end of the day, it is Antoinette's tragedy that her desire to 'be' ('woman/native/other') is thwarted by the birthright that imprisons her in the dominant culture (white/colonial/heterosexual) that she most despises.[42]

In conclusion, then, I would argue that this destabilizing interrogation of 'identity' (racial, sexual and otherwise) at the level of *syntax*, combined with the text's covert or 'closeted' *address* to a lesbian audience (inviting them to uncover a lesbian subtext in the manner I have just demonstrated) makes *Wide Sargasso Sea* a more subversively lesbian text than Alice Walker's *The Color Purple*. And the heterosexual orthodoxy is further challenged at the level of *plot* where, as we have seen, the sham marriage of Rochester and Antoinette is finally blasted apart by the latter's suicidal leap back/towards Tia. In striking contrast with *The Color Purple* where the lesbian relationship between Celie and Shug gets lost amid the reconstruction of a large, wholesome, heterosexual family, Rhys's novel concludes with a spectacular 'combustion' of this idealized norm. Even if it *is* limited to the level of symbolic revenge, lesbian readers will undoubtedly read Tia's reappearance at the end of Antoinette's life as a powerful challenge to heterosexual coupledom.

III

The fact that I have ended up presenting Jean Rhys's novel as more 'authentically' lesbian than Walker's demonstrates vividly the paradoxes and perversities involved in the practice of this type of feminist criticism. Attending to my own hypothesis (see Part I) in which I suggest that the lesbianism of a text is best understood as a complex interaction of text and reader, I have implied that it is often those texts – like *Wide Sargasso Sea* – which require their readers to 'symptomatically' (see Glossary) uncover lesbian subtexts that are ultimately more subversive than those with an overtly lesbian content and/or address.

There are obvious problems with this. Although I do, indeed, stop short of making this into a generalization (i.e. the most radical texts are always the most closeted ones), there is, I think, a strong possibility that future lesbian criticism will continue to privilege the more recalcitrant texts – the texts that hide and disguise their sexual preference – if only because these appear to demand the more sophisticated reading practices. (The more difficult the challenge, the more the reader/critic is able to 'show off' her skills and competencies.) In this respect, lesbian critics are, indeed, suffering the same problem that has beset all those working on a body of contemporary writings that have become themselves so sophisticated, and so theoretically aware, that the reader has a problem defining their role. A text which *does not* wear its (political) heart on its sleeve is therefore much more rewarding in critical terms and, as I have shown here, will achieve its identity and value (sexual or otherwise) through a dialogue in which the reader becomes *complicit* in the act of production. As various theorists have shown *vis-à-vis* advertising, the harder the reader/consumer *works* to 'unlock' a text's meaning, the more likely she is to value it.[43]

There are, however, plenty of texts which interpellate a lesbian audience very frankly and directly that have achieved the status of lesbian classics. The reason *The Color Purple* fails to fall into this category is, as I hope to have made clear, the result of its more pervasive humanist discourse. Although it is a text with explicit lesbian 'content', and although lesbian readers are clearly invited to 'identify' with this material, there is little *exclusivity of address* that marks them as a 'special' audience. The pervasive universalism of the novel's reader-positioning, combined with the conservatism of the plot, ultimately do much to undermine its claim to a satisfactory lesbian status (cf. Farwell's argument in Part I of this chapter).

The point I am making here, then, is that the two readings I have made in this chapter should not been seen as *representative* of the present and/or future of lesbian criticism. While I do believe that the 'outing' of closeted texts will remain a favoured practice for post-structurally trained literary critics, equally complex readings can, and will, be made of those texts which engage a lesbian audience more directly. No textual audience is, in any case, monolithic *or* static, and lesbian readers should expect to find a certain volatility in their positioning by *any text*: even one which identifies them as its 'preferred' target group. As I have argued elsewhere, much of the excitement (and stress!) of reading depends on the fact that we do not really know, from one moment to the next, how a text is going to position us: whether we will be 'included' or 'excluded' in its address.[44] In terms of lesbian literary criticism, what this means is that the 'out' text *can* provide the reader/critic with as many challenges as the closeted one, once she has learned to observe and attend to the 'fracturing ' that is present in all acts of interlocution.

Whilst I feel strongly, however, that sophisticated lesbian textual analysis is possible across a wide range of closeted and uncloseted texts, my own failure to make a more effective intervention into *The Color Purple* may be taken as evidence that such readings are not possible of *any* text. No matter if it is overt or covert, there has to be some engagement of text and reader that makes sexuality a *contested site*. The problem with Walker's novel is that, as Farwell has argued, it *represents* 'deviant' sexuality without *contesting* the orthodoxy. And this is demonstrated both by the conservatism of the plot, and the fact that *all* specificities of address are subsumed within a universalizing humanist discourse.

However else we might, or might not, come to define it, it thus seems clear to me that 'the lesbian aesthetic' will only be found in texts with which lesbian readers can interactively engage: either through a symptomatic uncovering of 'repressed' materials, or through more overt challenges of address. The status of a text as lesbian depends crucially on its potential for such interaction, and 'the best' (i.e. most satisfying) texts are therefore likely to be those which 'become lesbian' (like their readers!) *through the act of reading itself.*

For the Queer theorists of present and future generations, however, I accept that even such a provisional identity as I am presenting here – an identity predicated on a brief moment of dialogic *recognition* between text and reader – is likely to be regarded as a critical red herring. An interrogation of sexuality and gender in writing must not (always) be 'reduced' to questions of identity. Whilst I have much sympathy with this (at times I felt myself going to desperate lengths to wrestle such identities out of both these novels), my efforts were largely an acknowledgement of the point I made at the end of Part I about the *desire* for identity, in reading – as in life – not going away. The model of lesbian sexuality/texuality I am proposing here is therefore an acknowledgement of the residual cravings for such an identity that I believe will persist even when, as my friend prophesized, 'Queer is everywhere'. Even when we have fully acknowledged the insecure status of our 'being' and 'becoming', as sexed and gendered subjects, there will still be moments when we read books and watch films with the dream of something more permanent, and through the persistence of these desires continue to (re)produce texts and readers which recognize one another as 'lesbian'.

Notes

1. Opinion about which theorists should be included in the category 'Queer' is constantly changing , but the following authors/texts were undoubtedly instrumental in 'destabilizing' all aspects of 'identity politics' within feminist theory: Judith Butler, *Gender Trouble* (Routledge, London and New York, 1990) and *Bodies that Matter* (Routledge, London and New York, 1993); Diana Fuss, *Essentially Speaking* (Routledge, London and New York, 1989) and (as editor) *Inside/Out: Lesbian Theories, Gay Theories* (Routledge, London and New York, 1991); Teresa de Lauretis, *The Practice of Love: Lesbian Sexuality and Perverse Desire* (Indiana University Press, Bloomington and Indianapolis, 1994); Eve Kosofsky Sedgwick, *Epistemology of the Closet* (Harvester Wheatsheaf, Hemel Hempstead, 1991), *Tendencies* (Routledge, London and New York, 1994), and (with Andrew Parker) *Performance and Performativity* (Routledge, London and New York, 1995).

2. For this, and many other judicious observations, I am indebted to Jackie Stacey whose own work has contributed significantly to recent debates about sexuality and desire. See especially 'Desperately seeking difference', in *The Female Gaze*, edited by Lorraine Gamman and Margaret Marshment (The Women's Press, London, 1988), pp. 112–29.

3. Joseph Bristow (ed.), *Sexual Sameness: Textual Differences in Lesbian and Gay Writing* (Routledge, London and New York, 1991), p. 7.

4. Ellen Moers, *Literary Women* (The Women's Press, London, 1977); Elaine Showalter, *A Literature of their Own* (Princeton University Press, Princeton, 1977).

5. Bonnie Zimmerman, 'What has never been: an overview of lesbian feminist criticism', in Gayle Greene and Coppelia Kahn (eds), *Making a Difference* (Methuen, London, 1986), pp. 177–210.

6. Bonnie Zimmerman, *The Safe Sea of Women: Lesbian Fiction 1969–1989* (Onlywomen Press, London, 1989); Gabriele Griffin, *Heavenly Love?: Lesbian images in twentieth-century women's writing* (Manchester University Press, Manchester, 1993).

7. Elaine Hobby and Chris White (eds), *What Lesbians Do in Books* (The Women's Press, London, 1991).

8. It is one of the problems and paradoxes of authentic realist criticism that it requires its textual characters to be 'true to life' and yet 'ideal' (i.e. in the sense of providing positive role models) at the same time.

9. See Adrienne Rich's celebrated essay, 'Compulsory heterosexuality and lesbian existence', in *Blood, Bread and Poetry: Selected Prose 1969–1985* (The Women's Press, London, 1987), pp. 23–75. See also Paulina Palmer's 'The lesbian feminist thriller and detective novel', in *What Lesbians Do in Books* (see note 7 above), p. 16.

10. Bonnie Zimmerman, 'Lesbians like this and that: some notes on lesbian criticism for the nineties', in Sally Munt (ed.), *New Lesbian Criticism* (Harvester Wheatsheaf, Hemel Hempstead, 1992), p. 13.

11. Karla Jay and Joanne Glasgow (eds), *Lesbian Texts and Contexts* (New York University Press, New York and London, 1990). Further page references to this volume will be given after quotations in the text.

12. The term 'expressive realism' denotes a type of literature which (ideally) combines a *mimetic* transcription of 'the real world' with the Romantic idea that it should also convey 'the spontaneous overflow of powerful feelings'. Although critics have presented 'expressive realism' as a *genre*, it is clear that it is really a theory of what writing can, and ought to, achieve. For further discussion see Catherine Belsey, *Critical Practice* (Methuen, London, 1980), pp. 7–14. See also Gillian Spraggs's essay 'Hell and the mirror: a reading of *Desert of the Heart*', in *New Lesbian Criticism* (see note 10 above) which explores some of the problems of this particular value system for lesbian criticism.

13. See Sally Munt's essay on Sarah Schulman, ' "Somewhere over the rainbow": postmodernism and the fiction of Sarah Schulman', in *New Lesbian Criticism* (see note 10 above).

14. For a social and literary history of the period of 'Lesbian Nation' see Lillian Faderman's *Odd Girls and Twilight Lovers: A History of Lesbian Life in Twentieth-Century America* (Penguin, Harmondsworth, 1991), pp. 215–45.

15. Eve Kosofsky Sedgwick, from *Epistemology of the Closet*, in *The Lesbian and Gay Studies Reader*, ed. Henry Abelove *et al.* (Routledge, London and New York, 1993), pp. 45–61.

16. Apart from the 'Queer' lobby, it is important to recognize that many lesbian and gay theorists would be unhappy with Sedgwick's analysis of the two 'tropes' of homosexuality. Jackie Stacey (see note 2 above), for example, has urged me to observe that the case for women desiring each other on the grounds of 'sameness' has been frequently overstated, since *other differences* besides that of primary gender identification (i.e. masculine/feminine) are present in all relationships. The 'dynamic' which causes attraction between two women might be predicated upon race, class, national and educational differences *as well as* the similarities/identifications between them. As I argue in the chapter, however, I think it is fair to say that a number of lesbian literary texts *have* 'celebrated' a version of lesbian desire which subsumes these 'secondary' differences, and *The Color Purple* is a classic example of this.

17. Rich, 'Compulsory heterosexuality' (see note 9), p. 35. See also Nancy Chodorow, *The Reproduction of Mothering: Psychoanalysis and the Sociology of Gender* (University of California Press, Berkeley, California, 1978).

18. See Simone de Beauvoir, *The Second Sex* (Knopf, New York, 1953); H.D., *Her* (Virago, London, 1984); Katherine V. Forrest, *Curious Wine* (Silver Moon Books, London, 1983); Jeanette Winterson, *Oranges are not the only fruit* (Pandora, London, 1985).

19. Jane Rule, *Desert of the Heart* (Pandora, London, 1986); Patricia Highsmith, *Carol* (Bloomsbury, London, 1981).

20. See Rich's framing comments on the reception of her essay in the *Blood, Bread and Poetry* collection (note 9 above), pp. 23–6.

21. See the texts listed in note 1. Page references to these volumes will be made after quotations in the text.

22. Performativity: much of Judith Butler's recent work depends upon the notion that (sexual) identity is constructed through its 'performance'. In *Bodies that Matter* (1993, see note 1) she writes:

> Crucially, then, construction is neither a single act nor a causal process initiated by a subject and culminating in a set of fixed effects. Construction not only takes place *in time*, but is itself a temporal process which operates through the reiteration of norms; sex is both produced and destabilised in the course of the reiteration (p. 10).

23. Biddy Martin, 'Lesbian identity and autobiographical difference[s]', in *The Lesbian and Gay Studies Reader* (see note 15 above).

24. Munt, *New Lesbian Criticism* (see note 10 above), p. xviii.

25. 'Imaginary communities': see Benedict Anderson, *Imagined Communities: Reflections on the Origins and Spread of Nationalism* (Verso, London, 1983).

26. Examples of mainstream TV series which now feature lesbian characters include *Brookside* and *Between the Lines* (both ITV Channel 4).

27. The Onlywomen Press includes a clause in its contract that requires its authors to declare that they are lesbians.

28. Elaine Showalter, 'Feminist criticism in the wilderness', in *The New Feminist Criticism* (Virago, London, 1986). See Chapter 3.

29. See my essay 'Dialogic theory and women's writing', in *Working Out: New Directions in Women's Studies*, ed. Hilary Hinds *et al.* (Falmer Press, Brighton, 1992), pp. 184–93.

30. See Diana Collecott's essay 'What is not said: a study in textual inversion', in *Sexual Sameness* (see note 3 above), p. 95.

31. Alice Walker, *The Color Purple* (The Women's Press, London, 1983); Jean Rhys, *Wide Sargasso Sea* (Penguin, Harmondsworth, 1968). Page references to these volumes will be given after quotations in the text.

32. Pantheism: a spirituality that believes God is in everything, and climaxing, in *The Color Purple*, in Celie's final diary entry: 'Dear God. Dear Stars, dear trees, dear sky, dear peoples. Dear Everything. Dear God.' (p. 242)

33. Hilary Hinds, '*Oranges are not the only fruit*: reaching audiences other lesbian texts cannot reach', in *New Lesbian Criticism* (see note 10 above), pp. 153–72.

34. For a fuller discussion of my theories of 'exclusive address' see the essay 'Dialogic theory and women's writing' (note 29 above) and also my ' "I" the reader: text, context and the balance of power', in Penny Florence and Dee Reynolds (eds), *Feminist Subjects, Multi-media* (Manchester University Press, Manchester, 1995), pp. 160–71, in which I deal with the issue of 'reader jealousy'. These ideas are developed further in chapters on the 'emotional politics of reading' in my forthcoming book *Feminism and the Politics of Reading* (Edward Arnold, London, 1997).

35. The concept of the 'good mother' derives from the work of psychoanalyst Melanie Klein. See Elizabeth Wright, *Psychoanalytic Criticism* (Methuen, London, 1984) for an introductory discussion of her work.

36. This criticism is even more valid with respect to Steven Spielberg's film in which sexual relations between Celie and Shug are given very

limited expression on screen. (*The Color Purple*, dir. Steven Spielberg, 1985.)

37. Harriet Jacobs, *Incidents in the Life of a Slave Girl, Written by Herself*, ed. L. Maria Child, with introduction by Jean Fagan Yellin (Harvard University Press, Cambridge, Mass., 1987).

38. Mae Gwendolyn Henderson, 'Speaking in tongues: dialogics, dialectics, and the Black woman writer's literary tradition', in Cheryl Wall (ed.), *Changing Our Own Words: Essays on Criticism, Theory and Writing by Black Women* (Routledge, London and New York, 1989).

39. Toni Morrison, *Sula* (Bantam, New York, 1980).

40. In her book *Imperial Leather* (London and New York, Routledge, 1995) Ann McClintock discusses the 'doubling' of white mothers and 'native' nurses. See pp. 86–7.

41. It is interesting to observe how threatened Rochester is by the homosexual attention paid to him by one of the Coulibri serving boys as he prepares to leave (pp. 140–2). His angry response can be read as a fear of his own emasculation.

42. 'Woman/native/other': this phrase derives from Trinh Minh ha's excellent book of the same name: *Woman, Native, Other* (Indiana University Press, Bloomington and Indianapolis, 1989).

43. See in particular Judith Williamson's work in *Decoding Advertisements: Ideology and Meaning in Advertising* (Marion Boyars, London, 1978).

44. See the publications listed in note 34 for a fuller discussion of dialogic address and its implications for feminist criticism.

8
Post-colonial feminist theory

Sara Mills

Margaret Atwood: *Surfacing*
Jean Rhys: *Wide Sargasso Sea*
Gayatri Spivak: 'Can the subaltern speak?';
'Three women's texts and a critique of imperialism'
Anne McClintock: *Imperial Leather: Race, Gender and
Sexuality in the Colonial Contest*

I

Perhaps one of the most fundamental shifts in feminist theory in
recent years has been one which we noted in the Introduction and in
the critical sections of Chapters 2 and 7: that is, the move towards a
problematization of the categories woman/women and the notion of
difference. Instrumental in this sea change has been a critique of
Western feminism and its universalizing tendencies.[1] This new focus
has had the effect of clearing productive spaces for feminist theory and
it has led to a different, more complex type of analysis of texts by
Western women writers dealing with colonial and post-colonial subjects.[2] At the same time, because of this move away from Eurocentric
theorizing, feminists have played a major role in mainstream post-
colonial theory and have made gender an important element in
analyses of the writings of colonizing, colonized, and post-colonial
men and women.[3] Colonial and post-colonial discourse theory has
concerned itself, following the work of Edward Said in *Orientalism* and
Culture and Imperialism, with a critique of the processes whereby other
nations are characterized as Other, that is, as negatively different to a
implied Western norm. In terms of textual practice, this work has been
of enormous importance in detailing the rhetorical strategies which
have been employed to Other colonized nations; however, little
attention has been paid to gender issues in mainstream work.[4] It has
been the task of feminist post-colonial theorists to address this issue. I
will give a brief overview of some of the concerns of these feminist

theorists before discussing the critics, Gayatri Spivak and Anne McClintock, whose work I will be drawing on in this chapter.

For many feminists, the colonial period has been characterized by critics as a male domain. Feminist post-colonial critics have formulated revisions of imperial history, foregrounding gender issues both to bring to the surface white women's activities within the imperial zone and to delineate the masculinities which constitute imperialism. This project has not simply been a question of making white women's presence visible, but it has rather been a critical evaluation of their complicity and resistance in the imperial endeavour. It is clear that gender relations within the colonial sphere were different to those within Britain at the time, colonial femininity and masculinity being constructed by different sets of power relations. Women took part in colonial activities in a range of different capacities, as writers, travellers, nurses, missionaries, settlers, wives, and acted in ways in which they could not have done in the British context. They were also represented in different ways both at a textual and more symbolic level.[5]

Feminist post-colonial critics have also concerned themselves with the way that the colonial sphere has been characterized as a sexualized zone; colonial landscapes were described in sexual terms ('virgin territories' which were eager for penetration) and as Anne McClintock has shown, by the Victorian era 'Africa and the Americas had become what can be called a porno-tropics for the European imagination – a fantastic magic lantern of the mind onto which Europe projected its forbidden sexual desires and fears'.[6] This had profound implications for women within the colonial setting, because as many critics have shown, British males sexualized power relations with indigenous women (as well as with men and children); they also produced the figure of the British woman in the colonies as one which was under constant threat of sexual attack by 'native' males.[7] As Jenny Sharpe has shown, this trope of the 'rapable' white woman had a very varied trajectory and seemed to become more important at moments of political unrest in the colonies, serving to displace protests against oppression by inscribing vulnerability on the white female body. Focusing on the representations of the rape and murder of white women in the 1857 Indian Uprising/Mutiny, Sharpe comments: 'the savaged remains [of British women] display a fantasy of the native's savagery that screens the "barbarism" of colonialism'.[8] For feminist theorists in this area of study, it is essential that these gender issues are not simply seen as peripheral – to do with women – but are foundational elements in the construction and maintenance of imperial rule and colonial discourses. Thus, as Anne McClintock states in *Imperial Leather*:

imperialism cannot be understood without a theory of gender power. Gender power was not the superficial patina of empire, an ephemeral gloss over the more decisive mechanics of class or race. Rather, gender dynamics were, from the outset, fundamental to the securing and maintenance of the imperial enterprise. (pp. 6–7).

One of the most important feminist theorists in the field of colonial discourse and postcolonial theory has been Gayatri Chakravorty Spivak, an Indian theorist now based in the United States. She has produced theoretical work integrating feminism, poststructuralism, (particularly, deconstruction) and Marxism, which analyzes both canonical Western literary texts, Western feminist theory, and Indian writing; her work, whilst extremely dense and at times difficult, has proved to be challenging and insightful for many feminists. The critical texts which I will focus on here are her 'Can the subaltern speak?' in my reading of Margaret Atwood's *Surfacing*, and in the analysis of Jean Rhys's *Wide Sargasso Sea* I shall draw on Spivak's article 'Three women's texts and a critique of imperialism', together with the work of Anne McClintock on 'degeneration'.

Spivak begins the article on the subaltern subject, that is, the non-elite colonized subject, by questioning the tendency in poststructuralist theory, at the very moment when it is seemingly destabilizing the Subject, to reintroduce the European subject at the expense of the colonized Other. She argues that poststructuralist theory (she focuses here on the work of Michel Foucault and Gilles Deleuze in particular), often ignores the history of imperialism and the international division of labour when addressing seemingly global issues. Thus, issues are investigated from a Eurocentric perspective, and even when discussing international subjects the First World is placed centre-stage. Whilst posing as theorists concerned with Third World issues, Spivak criticizes Deleuze and Foucault for 'masquerading as the absent nonrepresenter who lets the oppressed speak for themselves' (p. 87). In this process, the 'Third World' subject is described in homogenizing terms and is effectively Othered: as Spivak puts it 'the asymmetrical obliteration of the trace of that Other in its precarious Subjectivity' (p. 76). Giving the example of the changes which took place in Hindu law after British colonialism, she shows that 'a version of history was gradually established in which the [elite] Brahmans were shown to have the same intentions as (thus providing legitimation for), the codifying British' (p. 77). Given this elite collaboration with the colonizers she begins to question the authenticity of the voice of the 'Third World' subject, particularly what she calls the subaltern subject, that is, those who are not members of that elite group.[9] Suggesting that although the elite subject might be the one whose voice most approximates to the First World notions of what the Other is, it is nevertheless necessary to 'insist that the colonized subaltern subject is irretrievably heterogeneous' (p. 79). Spivak goes on to question the notion that the subaltern subject will be necessarily outside colonial determinants, and will constitute a 'pure form of consciousness' (p. 81). And she notes that for the female subject, the issue of representation is even more difficult:

> within the effaced itinerary of the subaltern subject, the track of sexual difference is doubly effaced. The question is not of female participation in insurgency, or the ground rules of the sexual division of labour, for both of which there is 'evidence'. It is, rather, that, both as object of colonialist historiography and as subject of insurgency, the ideological construction of gender keeps the male dominant. If, in the context of colonial production, the subaltern has no history and cannot speak, the subaltern as female is even more deeply in shadow. (p. 83)

She argues that in order to 'speak to (rather than listen to or speak for) the historically muted subject of the subaltern woman, the post-colonial intellectual systematically 'unlearns' female privilege' (p. 91). Thus, Spivak in this article is reflecting upon the role of the critic in establishing new frameworks of analysis, as well as questioning the possibility of locating an authentic voice for the subaltern subject.

Spivak's article therefore poses certain key questions for feminist literary theory. First, it demands that the issue of who represents whom is investigated. In many ways, Spivak is calling into question that stable subject position of the Western feminist, who analyzes 'Third World women' and 'Third World women writers' as objects of quasi-anthropological interest; she is suggesting here that what is necessary is a fundamental critique of the position from which Western feminists speak and analyze. Secondly, this article questions the notion of authenticity; that is, it forces Western feminists to consider their own reasons for locating authentic voices in subaltern subjects, and calls attention to the fact that within this type of Western theory, authenticity is posed as a much simpler, cohesive position than that mapped out for the critic. Finally, it questions the displacement of the figure of the Other by the concerns of the First World subject. At the very moment when Western feminism seems to be considering international questions, it is only from the perspective of its own concerns.[10] These fundamental questions do not remain simply at an abstract level, because they can clearly be used to pose further questions related to textual practice. For example, we might ask what the implications are of including 'Third World' women's writing on our literature syllabuses and reading them as autobiographies. We might ask what our reasons are for including the writing on our courses; this is not to suggest that we remove the writing from our courses but simply that we are clear about what we are doing and why we are doing it. We might analyze the determinants of this writing, in much the same way that we analyze First World women's writing, and not assume that they are 'true' accounts; these subaltern subjects can only speak within the discursive frameworks available to them. We might also consider how we analyze Western women's writing written in the post-colonial period; perhaps Spivak's article might encourage us to focus on elements of the texts which are not in the foreground, but which have been marginalized in the process of representing Western female subjectivity.[11]

Anne McClintock's work is important in mapping out the complex sets of relations between colonized and colonizing subjects; thus her work is less about the critic's role than it is about the discursive representations themselves. Her work is particularly apposite here since she investigates the interlocking nature of 'racial' and sexual purity which is at work in the notion of degeneration which was of such crucial importance for Victorian notions of Britishness.[12] Robert Young has shown that the fear of miscegenation or racial interbreeding was crucial for the construction of a sense of British 'racial' identity; to allay this fear a range of 'scientific' theories developed to suggest that white and Black 'races' were in fact different species who could not or should not intermarry and breed.[13] Drawing on the analogy of the hybrid in the plant world, and the inter-species breeding of animals, most notably the donkey and horse, Victorian racial theorists argued that 'the descendants of mixed-race unions would eventually relapse to one of the original races, thus characterising miscegenation as temporary in its effects as well as unnatural in its very nature' (Young, p. 26). For McClintock, the notion of mixed race people being degenerate was essential to the construction of a notion of the 'civilising mission':

> The degenerate classes, defined as departures from the normal human type, were as necessary to the self-definition of the middle class as the idea of degeneration was to the idea of progress, for the distance along the path of progress travelled by some portions of humanity could be measured only by the distance others lagged behind. (p. 46)

The stereotype of the pure, maternal white woman is essential here as a standard against which the mixed race woman or indigenous woman was measured; as McClintock explains:

> controlling women's sexuality, exalting maternity and breeding a virile race of empire-builders were widely perceived as the paramount means for controlling the health and wealth of the male imperial body politic, so that by the turn of the century, sexual purity emerged as the controlling metaphor for racial, economic and political power. (p. 47)

She goes on to show that: 'The idea of racial "purity" for example, depends on the rigorous policing of women's sexuality; as an historical notion, then, racial "purity" is inextricably implicated in the dynamics of gender and cannot be understood without a theory of gender power' (p. 61).

Thus, while Spivak and McClintock focus on different aspects of post-colonial theory – Spivak analyzing the impossibility of a subaltern subject speaking in her own voice, and calling on Western theorists to acknowledge their Eurocentric critical positions; McClintock focusing on the interlocking nature of representations of sexual and 'racial' purity – they are both concerned to forge a type of theory which stresses the importance of gender to the imperial, colonial and post-colonial project. The implications of their work for textual analysis are varied, as I have mentioned, but here I will concentrate on two aspects only: first, the foregrounding of Western female subjectivity in female-authored texts set within the post-colonial context, and the problems this raises for the privileging of gender over 'race', Western women over indigenous peoples. Secondly, the fact that 'race' and gender are inseparable; thus, in textual analyses of gender, there must always be an implicit consideration of 'race'. Both theoretical positions call on Western feminists to reconsider their textual practices: to analyze precisely what is omitted when Western feminists focus on gender alone.

II

It might seem strange to analyze a text like Margaret Atwood's *Surfacing*, a text by a white Canadian writer about a white Canadian woman's experience, when discussing post-colonialism, since for many people, Canada has not undergone the same type of colonial experience as, say, India or Africa. The settler/invader colonialism of Canada is clearly different in kind, and, in some sense, more complex because of the layering of colonial relations: the Natives were dispossessed of their land by the French and English, but the French-speakers were subordinated to the English-speakers and confined to the geographical area of Quebec in the nineteenth century.[14] Canada has also been the subject of economic and cultural imperialism by the United States. *Surfacing* poses itself as a text which challenges imperialism, because of its representation of imperial America as the source of contagion and pollution. Yet, I hope to show the ways in which the term post-colonial can usefully describe the Canadian situation without as Diana Brydon states 'turning to the post-colonial as a kind of touristic "me-tooism" that would allow Canadians to ignore their complicities in imperialism.'[15] The problems which confront Atwood are ones which confront white Canadian writers as a whole, that of 'establishing their "indigeneity" '.[16] Brydon argues that a concern with post-colonialism provides us with a language and political analysis for discussing the differences between types of, and degrees of involvement in, colonial relations.

Surfacing is often read as a text about a woman confronting her 'naked' self, setting herself free from capitalist and material constraints/desires and in the process experiencing a kind of semiotic epiphany, discovering the truth of her situation (see Chapter 3). However, once viewed within a post-colonial context the detailing of the individual woman's psychic history begins to seem less celebratory.[17] As Firdous Azim has shown, the concentration on a liberal humanist notion of full subjectivity for the Western individualized subject has often been at the expense of the claims to subjectivity or even representation of the 'native'.[18] She argues that:

> The birth of the novel coincided with the European colonial project; it partook of and was part of a discursive field concerned with the construction of a universal and homogeneous subject. This subject was held together by the annihilation of other subject positions. The novel is an imperial genre, not in theme merely, not only by virtue of the historical moment of its birth, but in its formal structure – in the construction of the narrative voice which holds the narrative structure together. (p. 30)

Thus in *Surfacing*, the delineation of the movement towards the 'truth' of the female subject, the protagonist, is unproblematically presented as the 'aim' of the novel. All other consciousness is relegated to the margins – her companions, her family and perhaps more importantly the past and present inhabitants of the seemingly empty space upon which this grandiose psychic drama is played out. The text consistently appropriates for the protagonist stereotypes of Indian religious practices and ways of life, whilst rigorously excluding engagement with indigenous peoples themselves, instead of characterizing them as prehistoric traces and shadowy figures on the margins of the text. This is not a simple critique of representation, a call for Native representation in the text, it is more a calling attention to the 'epistemic violence' which is enacted in the constitution of the white Canadian individual female subject against a backdrop of post-colonial territory. In some ways, the protagonist comes to a position of 'truth' and subjecthood only through appropriating ventriloquized versions of other subjectivities and thus erasing them as subject-positions. The subaltern certainly does not speak in this context; s/he is silenced at the very moment when her/his voice is seemingly most vocal.

The protagonist locates herself as an outsider who, as a child, lived in the area, which we must assume is somewhere in the north of French-speaking Quebec. As an English-speaker and as, effectively, a non-French-speaker, she is denied an 'authentic' relation to her home country. She also represents herself as excluded from their religion and culture, the older people crossing themselves in fear when her mother walks past (p. 54). The French-speakers can, within the terms of the text, claim a less problematic relation to the land, because of their oppression by the English-speaking Canadian state. The protagonist verbalizes a form of ethnic jealousy when describing Paul and his wife, her father's French-speaking neighbours: 'I'm annoyed at them for looking so much like carvings, the habitant kind they sell in tourist handicraft shops' (p. 20), and she feels 'betrayed' when she sees that Paul's wife now has an electric stove rather than a wood-range. For her, the French-speakers are located in the past, even whilst she herself is involved in the changes which are being brought about by American and English-speaking Canadian state intervention. The changes which are being introduced are ones which bear striking resemblances to those meted out by nineteenth-century British imperialism: the loss of a distinct way of life, customs and culture; economic exploitation, so that decisions about resources are made by the colonizing power; exploitation of the region for leisure pursuits such as hunting and fishing by the colonizing power. Moreover, whilst the protagonist tries to distance herself from these changes, she is inextricably linked to them, by the fact of her father's largely unexplained work as a prospector 'mineral rights, that's what he explores, for one of the big international companies' (p. 70), or perhaps he investigated 'trees for the paper company or the government' (p. 79). This is ironic since her father attempted to align himself with the Natives/French-speakers because 'he needed . . . a place where he could recreate . . . not the settled farm life of his own father but that of the earliest ones who arrived when there was nothing but forest and no ideologies but the ones they brought with them' (p. 59). However, whilst this sense of loss on the part of the protagonist can be read as a form of resistance to imperialism, it should also be noted that this naive idealization of the French-speakers erases the role they played in the expropriation of land from Natives.

Thus, within the terms of the text, there are two levels of authenticity which the protagonist cannot achieve in her own right and in her own identity role, that of the French Canadian and that of the Native. Diana Brydon notes the trend within white Canadian literature to focus on Native Canadian stories and subject matter; she comments: 'some native writers in Canada resist what they see as a violating appropriation to insist on their ownership of their stories and their exclusive claims to an authenticity that should not be ventriloquized or parodied.'[19] She argues that

> the current flood of books by white Canadian writers embracing Native spirituality clearly serves a white need to feel at home in this country and to assuage the guilt felt over a material appropriation by making it a cultural one as well. In the absence of comparable political reparation for past appropriations such symbolic acts seem questionable or at least inadequate. (p. 141)

In *Surfacing*, Natives make their presence felt in representational terms through the traces that they leave – the seemingly child-like drawings that they incise in rock faces, which the protagonist's father photographs and copies and which he sends to an archaeologist who includes them in his research work, transforming cultural artefacts into 'colonial' knowledge. When the protagonist finds the drawings she comments:

> I was expecting a report of some kind, tree growth or diseases, un-finished business; but on the top page there's only a crude drawing of a hand, done with a felt pen or a brush, and some notations: numbers, a name. I flip through the next few pages. More hands, then a stiff childish figure, faceless and minus the hands and feet, and on the next page a similar creature with two things like tree branches or antlers protruding from its head. On each of the pages are the numbers, and on some a few scrawled words . . . I can't make sense out of them.' (p. 59)

This representation of the Natives in terms of their traces has several functions in the text. As Mary Louise Pratt has shown, indigenous peoples have often been represented in colonial texts only as traces – the ashes of their camp-fires, the ruins of their buildings, the remnants of their civilizations, their footprints.[20] This has the effect of con-structing them as non-subjects, as Other. In the context of *Surfacing*, it also has the effect of locating Native culture in a prehistoric past only. As Natalie Zemon Davis suggests, it is important to insist on the 'absolute simultaneity of the Amerindian and European worlds rather than viewing the former as an earlier version of the latter', and rather than locating one in the past and one in the present.[21]

The fact that the indigenous inhabitants' drawings are viewed as objects of the anthropological/archaeological gaze by the protagonist's father has the effect of further objectifying them and denying the inhabitants subjectivity. He documents them, listing them, locating them on a map, transforming them into a diagram, but they are given no interpretation by him, and the text does not provide any link between the drawings and a historically located material culture. Even within the archaeologist Dr Robin M. Grove's analysis of the paintings, they are not traced to any particular tribe-band nor are they even approximately dated. They are described as 'reminiscent . . . of the drawings of children' and compared unfavourably with 'European cave paintings' (p. 102). The explanations for these paintings offered by present-day Natives (dismissed in the text as simply 'some say . . . that they are the abodes of powerful or protective spirits') are ignored. Even though Grove notes that the practice of leaving offerings of clothing still persists in remote areas, he suggests instead that 'one gives more credence to the theory that the paintings are associated with the practice of fasting' (p. 102). The drawings are viewed entirely through a Western vector of verisimilitude, whereby they are criticized for 'crudeness' and for not 'representing', following Western realist models. Even though the protagonist does later feel that she can make some sense of them, it is only at a representational level and not at the level of their cultural significance to the culture which produced them: 'I righted the page . . . and it became a boat with people, the knobs were their heads' (p. 101).

In the course of the novel, the drawings become associated with both death and madness. They are made more mysterious because the father meets his death in his search to document them further. And this mysterious quality is emphasized by the protagonist herself who views the drawings as objects of madness, religious reverence and power. She represents the drawings as, at first, being a representation of her father's madness: 'Total derangement . . . the drawing was something he saw, a hallucination; or it might have been himself, what he thought he was turning into' (p. 101). She then feels she will find the 'answer' to her father's disappearance through diving down to one of the sites of the rock paintings, and it is there that she has a hallucination of her father's dead body. It is at this point that her delusions start to unravel and she remembers clearly the 'truth' of her life. Contact with these drawings, at least implicitly, brings about the father's death and the protagonist's 'madness', as well as curing her of her previous 'madness'.

At the point of contact with the paintings she 'discovers' the 'truth' of Native religious beliefs: 'These gods, here on the shore or in the water, unacknowledged or forgotten, were the only ones who had ever given me anything I needed; and freely' (p. 145) and she goes on to say 'The Indians did not own salvation but they had once known where it lived and their signs marked the sacred places, the places where you could learn the truth' (p. 145). However, whilst the protagonist seems to have found a 'true' religion, at the same time she equates it with superstition and childishness, both of these conventional Othering techniques employed in a wide range of colonial texts, as Johannes Fabian has demonstrated.[22] For example when she offers an item of clothing to her newly found gods, she says:

I didn't know the names of the ones I was making the offering to; but they were there, they had power. Candles in front of statues, crutches on the steps, flowers in jam jars by the roadside crosses, gratitude for cures, however wished for and partial. (p. 146)

Thus she is making an analogy between these stereotypical and vague representations of Indian belief systems with a 'simpler' less formalized type of belief within Christianity. She also compares the paintings with her own drawings when she was a child, thus making these cultural artefacts seem to be located at a period of immaturity and arrested development (p. 158). This discovery of the 'truth' of these religious beliefs which the protagonist projects on to the drawings is seen to be her form of resistance to American colonialism: 'the Americans . . . [had] had their chance but they had turned against the gods, and it was time for me to choose sides' (p. 154). This alignment to the Natives is signalled by the fact that she is described as now having 'dark red skin' (p. 175) and she wraps herself only in a blanket. If we interpret this as the point when the protagonist has gone mad, then we are forced to view these religious practices as themselves invalid; if we see this as the point where the protagonist sees the truth, we are led to romanticize and dehistoricize these practices. The protagonist states: 'I tried for all those years to be civilised but I'm not and I'm through pretending' (p. 168). Unfortunately, colonial relations cannot be unravelled simply by an individual act of will.

The only Native subjects who are represented in the book are the family whom the protagonist remembers seeing when she used to pick berries on one of the islands:

I was remembering the others who used to come. There weren't many of them on the lake even then, the government had put them somewhere else, corralled them, but there was one family left. Every year they would appear on the lake in blueberry season and visit the good places the same way we did, condensing as though from the air, five or six of them in a weatherbeaten canoe: father in the stern, head wizened and corded like a dried root, mother with a gourd body and hair pared back to her nape, the rest children or grandchildren. They would check to see how many blueberries there were, faces neutral and distanced, but when they saw that we were picking they would move on, gliding unhurried along near the shore and then disappearing around a point or into a bay as though they had never been there . . . It never occurred to me till now that they must have hated us. (p. 86)

This is a classic colonial description which Others the indigenous inhabitants of a country, objectifying them, describing them in relation to inanimate objects (roots and gourds), describing them as inscrutable and mysterious, having no real location in time and place. They are given no tribe-band; instead they are simply termed 'the others'.

Although this objectifying account is undercut by the realization of their hatred, even this is presented in personal terms, rather than in terms of colonial expropriation. There is also a passing reference to Indian culture when the protagonist describes strategies for dealing with starvation; she refers to the Indian way (of catching fish) 'if there's no bait try a chunk of your flesh' (p. 63) which has the effect of casting Natives as barbaric people who do not feel pain in the way that 'real' subjects do. This notion of Indian barbarism is picked up in an observation by the protagonist about David, who, when he tries to have sex with her, she describes as 'smelling like scalp' (p. 151). This might seem to be simply an accidental and rather odd turn of phrase, but in a post-colonial analysis it is these small elements of lexical choice which are crucial in mapping out the stance taken towards subalternity. In a novel which purports to be about the discovery of links with Natives, this reference to 'scalping' cannot be innocent, and a particular view of the conflicts between the colonizers and the indigenous inhabitants is entailed by the use of such a word.

The land in which the protagonist was brought up is represented as a wilderness and as dangerous, which as Kay Schaffer has shown is very common within the context of colonialism.[23] Within colonial texts, the wilderness is rarely represented as inhabited, but rather as empty space. Even though the protagonist is shown to be competent in this environment, knowing the names of plants, able to kill fish, having memorized survival manuals, it is still represented in the text as a place of danger and fear, for example when her father plays hide-and-seek with them when they are children: 'even when we knew which tree he had gone behind there was the fear that what would come out when you called would be someone else' (p. 50). This fear of the wilderness is reminiscent of the fear pervading British travellers' accounts of African forests, and it is a terror which has a very particular history within Western European colonial culture, which marked a clear distinction between the metropolitan culture and the colonial culture through labelling one civilized and one uncivilized. For those inhabitants of this 'wilderness' not operating within this binary opposition, the fears that the wilderness generates would be of a very material kind, rather than this unspecific paranoia.[24]

Thus, in answer to Gayatri Spivak's question 'Can the subaltern speak?', within texts such as this, the answer is a resounding 'no', since although seemingly subaltern knowledge is present in the text, the subject matter is entirely determined by stereotypes and delusions about Amerindian culture. Native culture is in effect not represented in its own terms, whatever that might be; the subaltern himself/herself is given no place from which to speak and is in effect silenced, generalized into an Othered, unspecific representative figure. The subaltern is

ventriloquized in the appropriation of an 'authentic' voice for the
white Canadian female subject, a common strategy in settler post-
colonial literatures.

Wide Sargasso Sea is set largely in Domenica and the events are
viewed through the eyes of the ex-slave-owning class Creoles, the
mixed race descendants of the British and indigenous peoples. The text is
a reinscription of *Jane Eyre*, reworking and reframing the question of
'race' and sexuality. As mentioned in Chapter 3, in *Jane Eyre*, 'Bertha'
although central to the narrative, only features briefly, and she is
represented in objectifying terms which portray her as barbaric and
animal-like, making her both not-English and not-female. It is this
concern to mark out the limits of a 'proper' 'racial' and sexual identity
with which this analysis will be concerned.

As I discussed in the introductory section of this chapter, the Creole,
or in fact, any mixed-race person, was viewed with horror by Victorian
ideologies of racial and sexual purity. In *Jane Eyre*, Bertha Mason is
portrayed in terms of her liminality 'what it was, whether beast or
human being, one could not tell' (p. 295) and her 'hybrid' state, of
being neither Black nor white, neither indigenous nor British, is
mapped onto this shifting boundary between animal and human.
Gayatri Spivak argues that this rendering indeterminate the animal/
human boundary functions to 'weaken her entitlement under the
spirit if not the letter of the Law'.[25] And as Spivak goes on to note:

> she must play out her role, act out the transformation of her 'self'
> into that fictive Other, set fire to the house and kill herself, so that
> Jane Eyre can become the feminist individualist heroine of British
> fiction. I must read this as an allegory of the general epistemic
> violence of imperialism, the construction of a self-immolating
> colonial subject for the glorification of the social mission of the
> coloniser. (p. 251)

For Spivak, Rhys's recasting of this narrative ensures that 'the woman
from the colonies is not sacrificed as an insane animal for her sister's
consolation' (p. 251).

Some Western feminists, such as Moira Ferguson, have attempted
to read Bertha/Antoinette's position as analogous to slavery, in that
she is 'dispensable property that can be bartered for a respectable
lineage'.[26] Whilst this casting of her position has the effect of high-
lighting the economic reasons for Antoinette's marriage to Rochester, it
is problematic, since using slavery as an analogy entails the obscuring
of the barbarity of the real slavery which operated within the
Caribbean. It might also be added that, although *Wide Sargasso Sea*
does not objectify the white Creole in the way that *Jane Eyre* does, that
is not to say that it is free from colonialist assumptions. I will argue
that in its presentation of the white Creole as a monstrous hybrid, and

in presenting the narrative from the point of view of the Creoles, the text participates in and ratifies colonial knowledge, at the same moment as it appears to be calling that knowledge into question.

Drawing on Anne McClintock's work enables us to reread *Wide Sargasso Sea*, focusing on 'racial' and sexual purity. Whilst many critics have viewed Antoinette as simply a white Creole, the text suggests that Antoinette and her family are much more closely linked to the indigenous community than the text at first implies. Robert Young has described the obsessive charting of the degrees of 'racial' purity in the colonial period and the perception that it was important to quantify and record the distance of mixed-race people from a white norm.[27] The opening paragraph states: 'They say when trouble comes close ranks, and so the white people did. But we were not in their ranks. The Jamaican ladies had never approved of my mother, "because she pretty like pretty self", Christophine said' (p. 15) (see Chapter 7 for a discussion of the use of pronouns in this quotation). This final remark particularly seems to mark out clearly that, whilst spurned by the Black community, Antoinette's family is nevertheless not part of the white community at all and is more closely aligned to the indigenous culture. Here, Annette is being compared physically to Christophine, a native of Martinique. And in describing Christophine, Antoinette says: 'she also came from Martinique'; the 'also' refers to Annette, her mother, who is referred to earlier in the text as 'a Martinique girl' (p. 15), a point which, as Gayatri Spivak has commented, is often ignored by white critics. Daniel Cosway's letter to Rochester also states that Antoinette's mother is a 'young girl from Martinique' (p. 80). This perhaps explains why even when Antoinette gets her 'white pappy' when Mr Mason marries her mother, her mother is still extremely edgy about racial boundaries; as Mason says to Antoinette's mother ' "Didn't you fly at me like a little wild cat when I said nigger. Not nigger, nor even Negro. Black people I must say" ' (p. 28). Antoinette argues strongly against her mother being seen as a 'white nigger': 'Not my mother. Never had been. Never could be' (p. 30), but it seems as if the strength of her protest simply highlights this possibility.

Mixed-race people are described with horror even within the terms of the text; one of Antoinette's attackers, when she is at the convent, is described in the following terms:

> The boy was about fourteen . . . he had white skin, a dull ugly white covered with freckles, his mouth was a negro's mouth and he had small eyes, like bits of green glass. He had the eyes of a dead fish. Worst, most horrible of all, his hair was crinkled, a negro's hair, but bright red. (p. 41)

It is the juxtaposition of features normally associated with stereotypes of whiteness and blackness which cause the horror: red hair with crinkles, a negro's mouth with white skin and green eyes. Each feature is rendered 'ugly', 'horrible', 'dull', 'dead' because it does not occur in its 'proper' sphere. This could be seen to emphasize Antoinette's own internalized racial phobia. It is quite clear that Antoinette also displays features of her mixed-race background, since when she envies the neat, straight hair of one of the white girls in the convent, she says ' "Helene, mine does not look like yours, whatever I do." Her eyelashes flickered, she turned away, too polite to say the obvious thing' (p. 46). The 'obvious thing' which this text cannot speak is that Antoinette's hair displays very clearly the traces of her mixed-race origin. Gayatri Spivak emphasizes this in her analysis of *Wide Sargasso Sea*, that most Western readers of the text actually interpret Antoinette and her family as simply white and do not consider them to be of mixed-race. This focusing on 'muted' elements within the text in a post-colonial reading forces these questions of 'race' to be of utmost importance.

The racial mixing within Antoinette's family seems to be portrayed as resulting in degeneration. Pierre, Antoinette's brother is depicted as sickly and possibly retarded. Daniel Cosway is portrayed as degenerate, a fallen preacher, indulging in drunkenness and idleness. Antoinette and her mother both become mad (even though the text provides 'reasons' for that, the colonial context still exerts a pressure on readers to interpret the madness as a degeneration). Daniel Cosway's letter reiterates the colonial 'knowledge' that all 'hybrids' are tainted: 'This young Mrs Cosway is worthless and spoilt . . . and soon the madness that is in her, and in all these white Creoles, come out' (p. 80). Christophine recognizes the force of this colonial knowledge about 'hybrids' and that for Antoinette to assert the specificity of her condition against this colonial knowledge will need care. Antoinette's difficult negotiations with her own circumstances and her own personal history will be erased in favour of colonial knowledge about the degeneration of those of mixed race. Christophine advises Antoinette: 'Speak to your husband calm and cool, tell him about your mother and all what happened at Coulibri and why she gets sick and what they do to her. Don't bawl at the man and don't make crazy faces' (p. 96). Thus Christophine knows that Antoinette will have to assert the facts of her family's situation in contradistinction to colonial knowledge about hybridity.

Rochester's doubts about Antoinette's 'racial' purity come at the moment when he doubts her sexual purity, and these doubts seem to be intermingled. As Robert Young has shown, fears about racial mixing are, within the colonial context, often projections of desire.[28] When Rochester describes his sexual feelings towards Antoinette on their honeymoon, it is in racial terms: 'one afternoon the sight of a dress which she'd left lying on her bedroom floor made me breathless and savage with desire' (p. 78). This relocation of the term 'savage' within this carefully described racial territory cannot be seen as accidental when viewed from the perspective of a post-colonial analysis. Similarly, when Rochester first meets Amelie, the servant, he states that she is a girl of mixed race; however, once he has had sex with her he suddenly sees her as Black: 'In the morning, of course I felt differently . . . And her skin was darker, her lips thicker than I had thought' (p. 115). Once Amelie is seen as sexually impure by Rochester, he also sees her as 'racially' impure. It is this confusion around racial and sexual purity which the text displays, and as Robert Young states: 'we encounter the sexual economy of desire in fantasies of race, and of race in fantasies of desire' (p. 90). For Rochester, sex is already racialized, and race sexualized.

Rochester fears that Antoinette is not only racially 'impure', that is, not as white as he had been led to believe, but that she has had a sexual relation with Alexander Cosway, himself of mixed race, rumours about which come to him from both Hilda and Daniel. It is after his meeting with Daniel that Rochester starts to see the similarity between Antoinette and Amelie and considers that they may be related (p. 105). Even though the status of Daniel Cosway's racial ancestry is presented as confused in the text (old Mr Cosway does not acknowledge him as his son, Hilda states that the pictures of his parents are of 'coloured' people, Antoinette says that he is called Boyd and not Cosway, and Christophine tells him that Daniel is not a relative of Antoinette), Rochester chooses to believe his story of his past and Antoinette's ancestry because of the force of colonial knowledge. Once he doubts Antoinette's 'racial' purity, he fears for her sanity and that she will become promiscuous: 'She'll loosen her black hair and laugh and coax and flatter (a mad girl. She'll not care who she's loving). She'll moan and cry and give herself as no sane woman would – or could. *Or could*' (emphasis in text; pp. 135–6). This problematics of 'race'/sexual purity is one which the text presents but does not sufficiently disentangle itself from. It is often difficult to know to what extent the text is critiquing what it presents. Perhaps the force of colonial knowledges about 'racial' and sexual purity are still too strong for the text to disengage from them.

The text is also unable to disassociate itself from colonialist views on rebellion. Although the burning down of the house by Antoinette/ 'Bertha' at the end of the book takes on a different meaning when it is viewed in the light of the earlier burning of Coulibri, this first revolt is still firmly located within a colonial perspective. The earlier house-burning could be seen to inflect the latter with a particular edge of revolt and set it within a context of colonial resistance. However, because this novel is written from the perspective of the Creole class, even this first incident has to be forced to speak of resistance rather than rebellion. The causes of the burning of Coulibri are mentioned but ultimately obscured. 'My stepfather talked about a plan to import labourers – coolies he called them – from the East Indies. When Myra [the servant] had gone out Aunt Cora said, "I shouldn't discuss that if I were you. Myra is listening." "But the people here won't work. They don't want to work" ' (p. 30). This move by Mr Mason to import labour and thus displace the freed slaves who worked on the plantations is the cause of the house-burning, and yet during the incident itself the actions of the indigenous population are simply glossed in standard colonialist terms: the causes of the resistance are not mentioned at all, and it is only through careful piecing together of evidence that this causal relation can be established clearly. The participants are portrayed as an uncontrolled mob, 'like animals howling but worse' (p. 32) and Antoinette describes them in the following terms: 'they all looked the same, it was the same face repeated over and over, eyes gleaming, mouth half open to shout' (p. 35). The revolt would be seen very differently from the eyes of the insurrectionists, and it is perhaps significant here that the causes of the house-burning are made so little of. As Laura Donaldson has shown, it is sometimes these small features of logical connection, or in this case the absence of logical connections between the importation of foreign labour and the house-burning, which can point up the underlying imperial perspective of the narrative.[29]

We must also consider the notion of the subaltern here. Antoinette is a member of the white Creole community and yet not accepted by them or by the Black community. Her voice within the context of this text, as a rewriting of a canonical European text, could be viewed as subaltern: she, after all, is given a voice which 'Bertha' was denied. However, because of the view presented of the revolt and the 'knowledge' about miscegenation, I would argue that the views of white Creoles are elided with colonialist knowledge. Antoinette's crisis as a mixed-race subject does not extricate itself from views of hybridity as degeneration. It is through her eyes that we see the mixed-race subject as a spectacle of horror. Even though the very material factors impinging on the production of Antoinette's 'madness' are detailed, throughout the text the notion of degeneration is stressed and insufficiently critiqued.

Christophine could also be viewed in this context as a subaltern subject. Moira Ferguson suggests that we should see the role of Christophine as crucial.

> The first syllable evokes Christ in the context of a culture in which Christianity overlays and becomes syncretized with African belief systems. Christophine in a sense subsumes Rochester and his

values and proclaims the power of Caribbean culture. Implicit in Christophine's name is the firm notion of struggle and revolution against colonial domination. (p. 105)

However, as Spivak has shown, we should not expect Christophine as a character to function completely outside of the ambit of colonialism:

> she cannot be contained by a novel which rewrites a canonical English text within the European novelistic tradition in the interest of the white Creole rather than the native. No perspective critical of imperialism can turn the Other into a self, because the project of imperialism has always already historically refracted what might have been the absolutely Other into a domesticated Other that consolidates the imperialist self. ('Three women's texts', p. 253)

Thus, both of these literary texts, whilst initially offering images and knowledge which challenge colonial stereotypes, nevertheless remain within the boundaries of colonial thought and are complicit with it in some measure. It has proved impossible to trace the voice of a subaltern subject; in various ways these texts silence the subaltern or ventriloquize her/his voice. Whilst both texts move against and challenge colonialist knowledge, they both remain firmly within the realm of the imperialist project.[30]

III

There are a number of features of this type of analysis which need to be remarked upon and which are crucial for the development of a post-colonial textual practice. First, perhaps, the status of the theoretical model itself needs to be considered. Post-colonial feminist theory generally tries to draw together psychoanalytic theory, feminist theory and post-colonial theory. This fusion of theoretical perspectives makes for difficult reading, since it assumes a familiarity with a wide range of theoretical work. It also presents a difficulty for those who are not comfortable with psychoanalysis being used to describe not psychic development and psychic economies but rather the oppressive relations between states which colonialism and imperialism involved. In much of the work by theorists such as Homi Bhabha and Robert Young, Othering is a process which takes place at a psychic level and for them describing Othering at this level enables them to discuss the role of fantasy and stereotype more adequately.[31] The two critics whose work I have drawn on here, Anne McClintock and Gayatri Spivak have attempted to integrate a Marxist-feminist/political perspective with a concern for theorizing the post-colonial, in order to retain some clear political edge in the face of psychoanalytic ahistoricism; however, the complexity of this theoretical work, requiring a knowledge of psychoanalysis, feminism, post-colonialism and Marxism may be off-putting for many readers.

A further problem with this type of analysis is in the term 'post-colonial' itself; as Anne McClintock has noted, the term has been used to refer to such a wide variety of contexts that it is beginning to become almost meaningless. Whilst it is useful to use the term to refer to a variety of different social and economic elements which are the result of imperialism, in fact 'the singularity of the term effects a re-centring of global history around the single rubric of European time. Colonialism returns at the moment of its disappearance.'[32] The term post-colonial is also problematic in that it is 'haunted by the very figure of linear development that it sets out to dismantle' (p. 292). Thus the use of the term runs the risk of erasing history and 'telescoping crucial geo-political distinctions into invisibility' (p. 293). It is clear that 'post-colonial' means something quite different for Canada and for the Caribbean and perhaps it is this difference which future interventions within post-colonial theory will attempt to retain.

Finally, it might be argued that broadening the ambit of feminist theory from a concern with women to a concern with gender and its imbrication with other factors, such as 'race' and class, leads to a dilution of feminist political edge and focus. It could be argued that this chapter has focused on gender itself less than other chapters have. However, McClintock argues that

> race and class difference cannot, I believe, be understood as sequentially derivative of sexual difference, or vice versa. Rather, the formative categories of imperial modernity are articulated categories in the sense that they come into being in historical relation to each other and emerge only in dynamic, shifting and intimate inter-dependence.[33]

It is for this reason that Western feminism must continue to address itself to issues of 'race' and sexuality and further underscores the need for white feminists to take on board the critiques developed by Black feminist theorists.

Notes

1. For a survey article of some of the problems with Western feminism see, Maria Lugones and Elizabeth Spelman, 'Have we got a theory for you? Feminist theory, cultural imperialism and the demand for "the woman's voice",' in *Women's Studies International Forum*, 6/6, 1983, pp. 573–81; Rosemary Hennessy and Rajeswari Mohan, 'The construction of women in three popular texts of empire: towards a critique of materialist feminism', in Patrick Williams and Laura Chrisman (eds), *Colonial Discourse and Post-colonial Theory* (Harvester

Wheatsheaf, Hemel Hempstead, 1993), pp. 462–80, and Chandra Talpade Mohanty, 'Under western eyes: feminist scholarship and colonial discourses', pp. 196–221 in Williams and Chrisman, op. cit. For ease of access, I have tried wherever possible to refer readers to articles/extracts which are collected either in the Williams and Chrisman anthology or in the anthology compiled by Bill Ashcroft, Gareth Griffiths and Helen Tiffin (eds), *The Post-colonial Studies Reader* (Routledge, London, 1995).

2. Although within post-colonial theory there is great debate about the meaning of these two terms, we will take colonial to mean those texts which were written during the period of high British imperialism, roughly from the early nineteenth century to the early twentieth century. Colonial discourse is used as a term which both describes all of these texts, literary and non-literary, and it is also used to describe the critical approach to these texts. See Edward Said, *Orientalism* (Routledge and Kegan Paul, 1978), for one of the founding texts in the study of this field. Post-colonial theory is the critical study of colonial texts and texts which have been written in the wake of colonialism. See Anne McClintock, 'The angel of progress: pitfalls of the term "post-colonialism" ', pp. 291–305 in Williams and Chrisman (see note 1 above) for an overview of some of the difficulties in classifying disparate cultures as post-colonial. In contrast to Bill Ashcroft, Gareth Griffiths and Helen Tiffin (eds) in *The Empire Writes Back: Theory and Practice in Post-colonial Literatures* (Routledge, London, 1989) who argue for the term post-colonial to be used to cover all cultures involved in colonial/imperial relations, both colonizing and colonized, McClintock questions the overgeneralized use of the term, arguing for greater specificity of reference.

3. By and large colonial discourse theory has concentrated its analysis on India and Africa during the mid to late nineteenth century. However, Edward Said's analysis was centred on the 'Orient', and critics such as Peter Hulme and Mary Louise Pratt have discussed South America and the Caribbean (Peter Hulme, *Colonial Encounters: Europe and the Native Caribbean* (Methuen, London, 1986); Mary Louise Pratt, *Imperial Eyes: Travel Writing and Transculturation* (Routledge, London, 1992)).

   For feminist post-colonial work, see Gayatri Spivak, *In Other Worlds: Essays in Cultural Politics* (Routledge, London, 1987); 'Can the subaltern speak?', pp. 66–111 in Williams and Chrisman (see note 1 above); 'Three women's texts and a critique of imperialism', pp. 269–73 in Ashcroft *et al.* (see note 1 above); *The Post-colonial Critic: Interviews, Strategies, Dialogues*, ed. Sarah Harasym (Routledge, London, 1990); *Outside in the Teaching Machine* (Routledge, London, 1993); Trinh T. Minh ha, *Woman Native Other: Writing Post-coloniality and Feminism* (Indiana University Press, Bloomington and Indianapolis, 1989); Vron Ware, *Beyond the Pale: White Women, Racism and History* (Verso, London, 1992); Nupur Chaudhuri and Margaret Strobel (eds), *Western Women and Imperialism: Complicity and Resistance* (Indiana University Press, Bloomington, 1992); Sara Mills, *Discourses of Difference: British Women's Travel Writing and Colonialism* (Routledge, London, 1991); Jenny

Sharpe: 'The unspeakable limits of rape: colonial violence and counter-insurgency', pp. 221–44 in Williams and Chrisman (see note 1 above), and also *Allegories of Empire: The Figure of Woman in the Colonial Text* (University of Minnesota Press, Minneapolis, 1993); Anne McClintock, *Imperial Leather: Race, Gender and Sexuality in the Colonial Contest* (Routledge, London, 1995).

4. Said, *Orientalism* (see note 2 above) and *Culture and Imperialism* (Chatto and Windus, London, 1993).

5. See Jane Haggis, *Women and Colonialism: Untold Stories and Conceptual Absences*, Studies in Sexual Politics (University of Manchester, Manchester, 1988); Joanna Trollope, *Britannia's Daughters: Women of the British Empire* (Hutchinson, London, 1983) and Mills (see note 3 above).

6. McClintock (see note 3 above), p. 22.

7. See Kenneth Ballhatchet, *Race, Class and Sex under the Raj: Imperial Attitudes and Policies and their Critics: 1793–1905* (Weidenfeld and Nicolson, London, 1980); Ronald Hyam, *Empire and Sexuality: The British Experience* (Manchester University Press, Manchester, 1990); McClintock (see note 3 above).

8. Sharpe, 'The unspeakable limits of rape' (see note 3 above), pp. 196–221, and *Allegories of Empire* (see note 3), p. 233; see also Sara Mills, 'Discontinuity and post-colonial discourse', pp. 73–88, in *Ariel: A Review of International English Literature*, 26/3, July 1995; and 'Gender and colonial space', in *Gender, Place and Culture*, 3/2, forthcoming, 1996.

9. Subaltern studies is an oppositional analysis of the history of colonized countries; 'their project is to rethink Indian colonial historiography from the perspective of the discontinuous chain of peasant insurgencies during the colonial occupation' (Guha and Spivak, pp. 78–9). Gayatri Spivak and Ranajit Guha have been instrumental in developing this reinterpretation of history: see Ranajit Guha and Gayatri Spivak (eds), *Selected Subaltern Studies* (Oxford University Press, Oxford, 1988) and Spivak, 'Subaltern studies: deconstructing historiography', pp. 197–222, in Spivak, *In Other Worlds* (see note 3 above). By focusing on dominant texts and other documents, it is possible to make the history of the subaltern surface, although that 'history' is not one formed solely in the interests of the subaltern subject.

10. Since Spivak's article 'Three women's texts and a critique of imperialism' contains within it a reading of Rhys's *Wide Sargasso Sea* I will discuss this article in more detail in the course of the analysis in Part II of this chapter.

11. This follows on from Edward Said's work in *Culture and Imperialism*, especially his analysis of Jane Austen's *Mansfield Park*, where he foregrounds the colonial and slave-labour economic relations which the novel is at pains to erase, and upon which much of the wealth of the characters is based (Said (see note 4 above), Chapter 2: 'Jane Austen and empire').

12. I put the terms 'race' and 'racial' in inverted commas to foreground their constructed nature, and to contest the assumed biological origin of 'racial' categories. See Ella Shohat and Robert Stam, *Unthinking Eurocentrism* (Routledge, London, 1995); David Goldberg, *Racist Culture*

(Blackwell, Oxford, 1993); Paul Gilroy, *There Ain't No Black in the Union Jack* (Routledge, London, 1992), (3rd edn); Vron Ware (see note 3 above).

13. Robert Young, *Colonial Desire: Hybridity in Theory, Culture and Race* (Routledge, London, 1995).

14. In the Canadian context the terms 'Native', 'Indian' and 'First Nations' are used to refer to the indigenous inhabitants who had settled North America before invasion by white settlers. The question of naming indigenous peoples is a vexed one and I thank Jill LeBihan for helping me find appropriate terms. I have used Native or Indian throughout, although within other post-colonial contexts, such as the United States, the use of these terms is not appropriate and other terms have been developed. One of the difficulties in analyzing this novel is precisely the lack of terminology; here the subalterns are homogenized. Within much post-colonial writing, indigenous peoples are referred to by more specific terms: Inuit, Sioux and so on; it is indicative of a lack of address to this question that subaltern subjects within this text are not named either in general or specific terms.

    See, for a brief discussion of questions of Canadian national identity, the Introduction to Roberta Hamilton and Michèle Barrett (eds), *The Politics of Diversity: Feminism, Marxism, and Nationalism* (Verso, London, 1986); and the section in Ashcroft (see note 2 above) entitled 'Theory at the crossroads: indigenous theory and post-colonial reading', pp. 116–54.

15. Diana Brydon, 'The white Inuit speaks: contamination as literary strategy', pp. 136–42', in Ashcroft (see note 1 above), p. 139.

16. Ashcroft (see note 2 above), p. 135.

17. Indeed, reading *Surfacing* within a framework of post-colonial analysis forces us to read the text as one which has been written as a reworking of Conrad's *Heart of Darkness*, rather than simply as a text about a woman's experience. See Jill LeBihan's chapter in Keith Green and Jill LeBihan's *Critical Theory and Practice* on Culture and Identity (Routledge, London, 1996).

18. Firdous Azim, *The Colonial Rise of the Novel* (Routledge, London, 1993).

19. Brydon (see note 15 above), p. 140.

20. Mary Louise Pratt, 'Scratches on the face of the country; or, what Mr Barrow saw in the land of the Bushmen', *Critical Inquiry*, 12/1, Autumn, 1985, pp. 119–44; and *Imperial Eyes* (see note 3 above).

21. Natalie Zemon Davis, 'Iroquois women, European women', pp. 243–58 in Margo Hendricks and Patricia Parker (eds), *Women, 'Race' and Writing in the Early Modern Period* (Routledge, London, 1994); see also Johannes Fabian, *Time and the Other: How Anthropology Makes its Object* (Columbia University Press, New York, 1983) for a thorough examination of the way that locating indigenous subjects in the past constructs them as Other.

22. Fabian (see note 21 above).

23. Kay Schaffer, *Women and the Bush: Forces of Desire in the Australian Cultural Tradition* (Cambridge University Press, Cambridge, 1988).

24. In a recent Radio 4 programme, called American Beauty, 29 November

1995, there was an interview with several of the indigenous Native American inhabitants of Death Valley who tried to rename the area in its original name of Tamasha. They strongly rejected the association of Death Valley with death and desolation, an association determined by the large number of deaths amongst the white settlers/invaders. Instead, they wished to focus on the fact that the desert for them was not an empty, threatening place but was rather a productive, fertile place which had sustained their economies and cultures for centuries.

25. Spivak (see note 3 above), p. 249.
26. Moira Ferguson, *Colonialism and Gender: From Mary Wollstonecraft to Jamaica Kincaid* (Columbia University Press, New York, 1993), p. 94.
27. Young (see note 13 above).
28. ibid.
29. Laura Donaldson, *Decolonising Feminisms: Race, Gender and Empire-Building* (Routledge, London, 1992).
30. For an examination of the differences between colonial and colonialist writing, see Elleke Boehmer, *Colonial and Post-colonial Literature* (Oxford University Press, Oxford, 1995).
31. Young (see note 13 above) and Homi Bhabha, *The Location of Culture* (Routledge, London, 1993).
32. McClintock, 'The angel of progress; pitfalls of the term "post-colonialism" ', pp. 291–304 in Williams and Chrisman (see note 1 above), p. 292.
33. McClintock (see note 3 above), p. 61.

Conclusion

Lynne Pearce and Sara Mills

Although this new edition of *Feminist Readings/Feminists Reading* has attempted to bring the volume up-to-date, we recognize that what it offers readers new to feminist literary theory and criticism is primarily a *historical* overview of a range of approaches and debates that have developed over the past 30 years. As we stated in the Introduction, we believe this genealogy of feminist literary theory is – and will remain – vitally important for all those of us seeking to find, or redefine, our own critical standpoint. No matter how hybrid or heterogeneous our textual practices become, it seems important to remember that all 'feminist readings' bear the mark of a particular *political* commitment and, as such, come with a history attached. And it is only by properly understanding the debates and disputes that have led succeeding generations of critics to adopt, revise and/or reject various positionings that we can attempt to understand, and justify, the ones we have presently arrived at. It also enables us to work on past feminist theories without simply dismissing them; instead, we can see them as developing the problematics which form the basis of our current theoretical concerns.

It is our hope, therefore, that even though readers from the 1990s and beyond are unlikely to adopt the unreconstructed textual practices of, for example, Kate Millett (Chapter 1) or Sandra Gilbert and Susan Gubar (Chapter 4), this sense of evolution will help prevent the slide into a 'postfeminist' consciousness that is oblivious to the material and intellectual struggles that have brought us where we are today. We would argue that even as it is too early to abandon the gynocritical project of reclaiming women writers 'hidden from history' (see Chapter 3), it is also too soon to forget the history of feminist literary theory itself. We need to avoid a situation in which any aspect of feminist thought gets taken (or, indeed, rejected) as a 'given', especially since what now seems crude about many of the early theories is the result of their earnest endeavour to make links between feminist scholarship and women's oppression in the material world.

It is in response to this last point that we would like to reiterate our continued engagement with a broadly defined Marxist-feminist textual practice. As we argued in the Introduction, and in Chapter 6 itself, it seems vitally important for feminists to preserve a sense of how class and economic circumstances have been, and will remain, a key factor in women's oppression. We also feel that Marxist theory still provides one of the best accounts of how that system of oppression operates, and how it may be challenged. Such a belief in the significance of the economic base 'in the last instance' is important to Marxist-feminist literary critics in both their textual analyses of representations of women (see the reading of *Surfacing* in Chapter 6), and in the emphasis they place on the importance of production and consumption in the overall consideration of a text's meaning (see the reading of 'The Yellow Wallpaper' in Chapter 6).

This rehistoricization of the text in its moment of production has, indeed, become a welcome feature of a good deal of recent feminist criticism (see Introduction), including that which comes under the umbrella of colonial and post-colonial criticism (see Chapter 8). Whilst we have expressed some concern about the slide of Marxist-feminism into an ambiguously defined 'Materialist-feminism', therefore, it is heartening to see the pains being taken by feminists of all theoretical persuasions (psychoanalysis included) to attend to the specificities of history and culture in their analysis of texts.[1] Those feminist theorists who draw on Foucault's work are concerned very clearly to reinflect Foucault's work so that it is more clearly historical and focused on contextual features.[2] Perhaps it is the radical modifications of the notion of simple linear history which Foucault has developed which have enabled certain types of Marxist-feminist criticism to re-evaluate its own model of history and context.

The call for historical specificity that has marked the work of so many feminist theorists since the late 1980s, meanwhile, has been commensurate with the call for a recognition of *difference*: only by fully, and finally, acknowledging that (in Hélène Cixous's words) 'there is no general woman, no one typical woman', has feminist theory been able to rid itself of the problematic essentialism (see Introduction) that overlooked differences of race, nationality, class, education, sexuality, disability and so on, in its attempt to homogenize its critique of women's oppression.[3] Chapters 7 and 8 present feminist theories which have been at the vanguard of this movement towards the recognition of difference, alerting us to the many assumptions and blindspots that characterized the earlier feminist criticism *vis-à-vis* its white/First World/heterosexual bias. The work of theorists like Judith Butler, meanwhile, has radically challenged the way we think about difference: instead of the liberal politics which urges us to recognize, and support, the interests of all 'minority' groups, the new Queer theorists have followed the road of the French feminists (see Chapter 5) in calling for an interrogation of *how* systems of difference operate.[4] In terms of textual practice, this has resulted in ever-more subtle and sophisticated analyses of how 'dominant' discourses (like femininity and heterosexuality) are constantly struggling to maintain their privilege against oppositional voices (like homosexuality) which work to expose their precarious provisionality.[5]

This increasing awareness of the significance and complexity of 'difference' has also led many feminists to consider that the early gynocritical project to discover a distinct 'female aesthetic' (see Chapters 3, 4 and 5) is misdirected. Desirable as it might be to justify or, indeed, celebrate the difference of women's writing, it is virtually impossible to *prove* without recourse to essentialist models of biology, language, gendered subjectivity (see Chapter 5) or, indeed, culture (see Chapter 3). To argue for a difference *common* to women writers is, alas, to suppress differences *between* them (see discussions in Chapters 7 and 8). As a consequence, the trend in recent criticism is to register the specificity – historical, cultural and otherwise – of all textual production, and to acknowledge that the role of gender in one text cannot be made into a universal statement on behalf of women writers (or even their subgroups e.g. Black/lesbian) in general.

This new concern for specificity has also coincided with a shift from 'author' to 'reader' as the key element in the production of textual meaning: a movement that was heralded in mainstream literary studies with the publication of Roland Barthes's famous essay 'The death of the author' as long ago as 1968.[6] As we have indicated elsewhere, however, this sea change is one that feminist critics have had to negotiate with care in order to prevent a premature abandoning of the project to get women writers (and, in particular, Black and lesbian women writers) accepted into the canon (see Chapter 7). What recent feminist theory has achieved, however, is a new, anti-essentialist conceptualization of the text–reader relationship that helps to explain and legitimate the reasons *why* women readers choose to read female authors. In contrast to those theories which have attempted to define a feminine aesthetic in terms of an idiosyncratic use of language and form *per se*, feminist reader-theorists have concentrated on how certain textual strategies position their readers in gender-specific ways, and how it is often at the level of *address* that we can account for a text's specifically female/feminist identity.[7] As Lynne Pearce has argued elsewhere: 'women's writing' may, perhaps, best be understood not as writing by women, nor writing about them, but writing *for them*.[8] In retrospect, it is clear to see that the sense of being privileged and/or excluded by certain texts on the grounds of gender and/or other difference is integral to the 'authentic realist' evaluations discussed in Chapter 2. A clearer understanding of the way in which texts and readers interact with one another has helped tremendously in the feminist analysis of textual pleasure; and it can also help to account for why our emotional response to certain texts might *appear* to be at odds with our politics.[9]

In recent lesbian, Black, and postcolonial criticism, meanwhile, this recognition of an interactive relationship between text and reader has been of vital importance to those who wish to hold on to some aspects of 'identity' in their critical practice, whilst avoiding essentialist models of subjective and/or aesthetic difference. As we argued in Chapter 7, the undermining of the category 'lesbian' by Judith Butler *et al.* has left critics with a dilemma as to what, if anything, can be identified as lesbian writing.[10] Our own suggestion, that this, and other forms of textual identity may best be understood as a moment of (perhaps fleeting) recognition between text and reader seems one way out of the impasse. Although neither text nor reader can occupy a permanent lesbian (or other) identity, a temporary reading site may be created.

This leads us back to the opinion, voiced on several occasions in this new edition, that the call to difference that marks so much contemporary feminist theory and criticism must remain tolerant of our desires to retain certain strategic identities and affiliations. We might have abandoned our search for totalizing visions of women's oppressions or female artistic production, but there are certain commonalities and similarities that have to be strategically maintained for feminism as a political and intellectual project to continue.

As we also indicated in the Introduction, the strategic preservation of the category 'feminist' remains vitally necessary in institutional contexts as elsewhere. Whilst a book such as this one may, on one level, be seen to dispute the notion of a unified feminism (even within the relatively narrow field of feminist literary criticism), it is clear that we need to hold on to it as an umbrella term around which to organize politically. In terms of the university curriculum, for example, we would argue that it is still too soon to abandon courses on 'Feminist Criticism' or 'Women's Writing' in favour of a more utopian 'calling into question of gender difference' across the syllabus; and even *within* literary theory courses, it will be necessary to retain a labelled 'feminist' component for some time to come.[11]

Our conclusion, then, is that feminist literary criticism must be preserved as a distinct area of scholarship with its own history, evolution and pedagogic rationale even though 'feminism' itself will become increasingly hard to describe as a unified political movement. The challenge facing each new generation of feminist readers is clearly to find a means of acknowledging the specific contexts in which different critical texts are produced and consumed whilst, at the same time, maintaining the vision and commitment associated with a 'common cause' demonstrated by many of the earlier critics represented in this volume. The fact that we recognize the cause is no longer 'common' in terms of 'experience' does not mean that we should not still regard it as a series of common struggles. Our different, and changing, political priorities might cause us to read texts through very different lens (as the readings performed here will hopefully have shown) but we remain, as feminist readers, committed to making visible the means by which literature can be used to expose, and redress, the oppression of female subjects.

Notes

1. See note 56 in Chapter 5.
2. See Dorothy Smith, *Texts, Facts and Femininity: Exploring the Relations of Ruling* (Routldge, London, 1990).
3. Hélène Cixous, 'The laugh of the medusa', in E. Abel and E. K. Abel (eds), *The Signs Reader: Women, Gender and Scholarship* (University of Chicago Press, Chicago, 1983). Reproduced in *Feminisms: A Reader*, ed. Maggie Humm (Harvester Wheatsheaf, Hemel Hempstead, 1992), pp. 196–202, p. 196.
4. Judith Butler, *Gender Trouble* (Routledge, London and New York, 1990) and *Bodies that Matter* (Routledge, London and New York, 1993).
5. See, for example, Sasha Torres's essay 'Television/feminism: *Heart-Beat* and prime time television', in *The Lesbian and Gay Studies Reader*, ed. Henry Abelove *et al.* (Routledge, London and New York, 1993), pp. 176–85, and Teresa de Lauretis's analysis of *She Must Be Seeing Things* (1987) in *The Practice of Love: Lesbian Sexuality and Perverse Desire* (Indiana University Press, Bloomington and Indianapolis, 1994), pp. 81–148.
6. Roland Barthes, 'The death of the author', in *The Rustle of Language* (Blackwell, Oxford, 1986), pp. 49–55.
7. See *Gendering the Reader*, ed. Sara Mills (Harvester Wheatsheaf, Hemel Hempstead, 1994).
8. Lynne Pearce, 'Dialogic theory and women's writing', in *Working Out: New Directions for Women's Studies*, ed. Hilary Hinds *et al.* (Falmer, Brighton, 1992), pp. 184–93, p. 184.
9. See Laura Mulvey, *Visual and Other Pleasures* (Macmillan, London,

1994); *The Female Gaze*, ed. Lorraine Gamman and Margaret Marshment (The Women's Press, London, 1985); and Lynne Pearce, *Feminism and the Politics of Reading* (Edward Arnold, London, 1997).

10. Judith Butler: see note 4 above.

11. Indeed, the wealth of anthologies/readers of feminist criticism available since the production of the first edition of this book testify to the benefits which many feminists have found in analyzing and re-evaluating the feminist criticism of the past. See for example, Diane Price Herndl and Robyn R. Warhol, *Feminisms: An Anthology* (Blackwell, Oxford, 1991); Catherine Belsey and Jane Moore (eds), *The Feminist Reader: Essays in Gender and the Politics of Literary Criticism* (Macmillan, London, 1989); Mary Eagleton (ed.), *Feminist Literary Criticism* (Longman, London and New York, 1991); Gayle Greene and Coppelia Kahn (eds), *Changing Subjects: the Making of Feminist Literary Criticism* (Routledge, London and New York, 1993); Maggie Humm, *Feminisms: A Reader* (Harvester Wheatsheaf, Hemel Hempstead, 1992); Maggie Humm, *Practising Feminist Criticism: An Introduction*, (Harvester Wheatsheaf, Hemel Hempstead, 1995); Terry Lovell (ed.), *British Feminist Thought: A Reader* (Blackwell, Oxford, 1990); Sneja Gunew (ed.), *A Reader in Feminist Knowledge* (Routledge, London, 1991); see also Isobel Armstrong (ed.), *New Feminist Discourses: Critical Essays on Theories and Texts* (Routledge, London and New York, 1992).

Bibliography

Abelove, Henry, Barale, Michèle Aina and Halkerin, David M. (eds), *The Lesbian and Gay Studies Reader* (Routledge, London and New York, 1993).

Althusser, Louis, 'Ideology and ideological state apparatuses', in *Lenin and Philosophy and Other Essays*, translated by Ben Brewster (New Left Books, London, 1971).

Anderson, Benedict, *Imagined Communities: Reflections on the Origins and Spread of Nationalism* (Verso, London, 1983).

Ardener, Edwin, 'Belief and the problem of women', in Shirley Ardener (ed.), *Perceiving Women* (Malaby Press, London, 1975).

Ardener, Shirley (ed.), *Defining Females: The Nature of Women in Society* (Croom Helm, London, 1978).

Armstrong, Isobel (ed.), *New Feminist Discourses: Critical Essays on Theories and Texts* (Routledge, London and New York, 1992).

Ashcroft, Bill, Griffiths, Gareth and Tiffin, Helen (eds), *The Empire Writes Back: Theory and Practice in Post-colonial Literatures* (Routledge, London and New York, 1989).

Ashcroft, Bill, Griffiths, Gareth and Tiffin, Helen (eds), *The Post-colonial Studies Reader* (Routledge, London, 1995).

Assiter, Alison, *Althusser and Feminism* (Pluto, London, 1990).

Atwood, Margaret, *Surfacing* (Virago, London, 1979 f. pub. 1972).

Azim, Firdous, *The Colonial Rise of the Novel* (Routledge, London, 1993).

Babcock, Barbara, *The Reversible World: Symbolic Inversion in Art and Society* (Cornell University Press, London, 1978).

Bakhtin, Mikhail, *Problems in Dostoevsky's Poetics*, translated by Caryl Emerson (Manchester University Press, Manchester, 1984).

Baldwin, James, 'Everybody's protest novel', in *Notes of a Native Son* (Corgi, London, 1964).

Ballhatchet, Kenneth, *Race, Class and Sex under the Raj: Imperial Attitudes and Policies and their Critics: 1793–1905* (Weidenfeld and Nicolson, London, 1980).

Barrett, Michèle, *Women's Oppression Today: Problems in Marxist-Feminist Analysis* (Verso, London, 1980).

Barrett, Michèle, 'Ethnocentrism and socialist-feminist theory', *Feminist Review*, no. 20, pp. 23–47, 1980.

Barrett, Michèle, *The Politics of Truth: From Marx to Foucault* (Polity Press, Cambridge, 1991).

Barrett, Michèle and McIntosh, Mary, *The Anti-social Family* (Verso, London, 1982).

Barthes, Roland, *S/Z*, translated by Richard Miller (Hill and Wang, New York, 1974).

Barthes, Roland, *Roland Barthes by Roland Barthes*, translated by Richard Howard (Hill and Wang, New York, 1977).

Barthes, Roland, 'The pleasure of the text', in Susan Sontag (ed.), *Barthes: Selected Writings* (Fontana, London, 1982), pp. 404–14.

Barthes, Roland, 'The death of the author', in *The Rustle of Language* (Blackwell, Oxford, 1986), pp. 49–55.

Batsleer, Janet, Davies, Tony, O'Rourke, Rebecca and Weedon, Chris, *Rewriting English: Cultural Politics of Gender and Class* (Methuen, London, 1985).

Baym, Nina, *Women's Fiction: A Guide to Novels by and about Women in America 1820–1970* (Cornell University Press, London, 1978).

Beecher Stowe, Harriet, *Uncle Tom's Cabin* (1852), authoritative text ed. Elizabeth Aminatis (Norton, New York, 1994).

Beer, Patricia, *Reader I Married Him, a Study of the Women Characters of Jane Austen, Charlotte Brontë, Elizabeth Gaskell and George Eliot* (Macmillan, London, 1974).

Bell, Currer, 'Biographical notice of Acton and Ellis Bell' (1850) reproduced in Penguin edition of *Wuthering Heights* (Penguin, Harmondsworth, 1982), pp. 30–6.

Belsey, Catherine, *Critical Practice* (Methuen, London, 1980).

Belsey, Catherine, *John Milton: Language, Gender, Power* (Blackwell, Oxford, 1988).

Belsey, Catherine and Moore, Jane (eds), *The Feminist Reader: Essays in Gender and the Politics of Literary Criticism* (Macmillan, London, 1989).

Benstock, Shari, *Textualizing the Feminine* (University of Oklahoma Press, Norman, 1991).

Berger, John, *Ways of Seeing* (Penguin, Harmondsworth, 1972).

Betterton, Rosemary, *Looking On: Images of Femininity in the Arts and Media* (Pandora, London, 1987).

Bhabha, Homi, *The Location of Culture* (Routledge, London, 1993).

Bloom, Harold, *The Anxiety of Influence* (Oxford University Press, New York, 1973).

Boehmer, Elleke, *Colonial and Postcolonial Literature* (Oxford University Press, Oxford, 1995).

Boumelha, Penny, *Thomas Hardy and Women: Sexual Ideology and Narrative Form* (Harvester, Brighton, 1982).

Bowie, Malcolm, 'Jacques Lacan', in John Sturrock (ed.), *Structuralism and Since* (Oxford University Press, Oxford, 1979), pp. 116–53.

Bristow, Joseph (ed.), *Sexual Sameness: Textual Differences in Lesbian and Gay Writing* (Routledge, London and New York, 1991).

Brontë, Emily, *Wuthering Heights* (Penguin, Harmondsworth, 1982 f. pub. 1847).

Brontë, Charlotte, *Jane Eyre* (Penguin, Harmondsworth, 1982).

Brownstein, Rachel, *Becoming a Heroine: Reading about Women in Novels* (Penguin, Harmondsworth, 1982).

Brydon, Diana, 'The white Inuit speaks: contamination as literary strategy', in Bill Ashcroft *et al.* (eds), *The Post-Colonial Studies Reader* (Routledge, London, 1995), pp. 136–42.

Burton, Deirdre, 'Through glass darkly: through dark glasses', in Ron Carter (ed.), *Language and Literature: An Introductory Reader in Stylistics* (Allen and Unwin, London, 1982), pp. 195–217.

Butler, Judith, *Gender Trouble: Feminism and the Subversion of Identity* (Routledge, London and New York, 1990).

Butler, Judith, *Bodies that Matter* (Routledge, London and New York, 1993).

Butler, Marilyn, 'Feminist criticism, late 80s style', *Times Literary Supplement*, 11–17 March 1988, pp. 283–5.

Cameron, Deborah, *Feminism and Linguistic Theory* (Macmillan, Basingstoke, 1985).

Carter, Angela, *The Magic Toyshop* (Virago, London, 1982, f. pub. 1967).

Carter, Angela, 'Notes from the front line', in Micheline Wandor (ed.), *On Gender and Writing* (Pandora Press, London, 1983).

Carter, Angela, Interview with Moira Paterson, 'Flights of fancy in Balham', *The Observer*, 3 November 1986, pp. 42–5.

Chapman, Rowena and Rutherford, Jonathan, *Male Order – Unwrapping Masculinity* (Lawrence & Wishart, London, 1988).

(charles), helen, 'Whiteness – the relevance of politically colouring the "non" ', in Hilary Hinds (ed.), *Working Out: New Directions for Women's Studies* (Falmer, London, 1991), pp. 29–35.

Chaudhuri, Nupur and Strobel, Margaret (eds), *Western Women and Imperialism: Complicity and Resistance* (Indiana University Press, Bloomington, 1992).

Chesler, Phyllis, *Women and Madness* (Allen Lane, London, 1974).

Chester, Gail and Nielsen, Sigrid, *In Other Words: Writing as a Feminist* (Hutchinson, London, 1987).

Chodorow, Nancy, *The Reproduction of Mothering: Psychoanalysis and the Sociology of Gender* (University of California Press, Berkeley, 1978).

Christ, Carol, 'Margaret Atwood: the surfacing of women's spiritual quest and vision', *Signs*, Winter 1976.

Christian, Barbara, *Black Women Novelists: The Development of a Tradition* (Greenwood Press, London, 1980).

Cixous, Hélène, 'The laugh of the medusa', in E. Abel and E. K. Abel (eds), *The Signs Reader: Women, Gender and Scholarship* (University of Chicago Press, Chicago, 1983) and also in *Feminisms: A Reader*, ed. Maggie Humm (Harvester Wheatsheaf, Hemel Hempstead, 1992), pp. 196–202, p. 196.

Cixous, Hélène, 'Sorties', in Elaine Marks and Isabelle de Courtivron (eds), *New French Feminisms* (Harvester Wheatsheaf, Hemel Hempstead, 1980) pp. 90–8.

Cixous, Hélène and Clément, Catherine, *The Newly Born Woman*, translated by Betsy Wing (Manchester University Press, Manchester, 1986 f. pub. 1975).

Clément, Catherine, *The Weary Sons of Freud* (Verso, London, 1987).

Collecott, Diana, 'What is not said: a study in textual inversion', in Joseph Bristow (ed.), *Sexual Sameness: Textual Differences in Lesbian and Gay Writing* (Routledge, London, 1991).

Cornillon Koppelman, Susan (ed.), *Images of Women in Fiction: Feminist Perspectives* (Popular Press, Bowling Green, Ohio, 1972).

Coward, Rosalind, *Female Desire: Women's Sexuality Today* (Paladin, London, 1984).

Coward, Rosalind, 'This novel changes lives', in Mary Eagleton (ed.), *Feminist Literary Theory: A Reader* (Blackwell, Oxford, 1986), pp. 155–60.

Coward, Rosalind and Ellis, John, *Language and Materialism: Developments in Semiology and the Theory of the Subject* (Routledge and Kegan Paul, London, 1977).

Crawford, Mary, 'Identity, Passing and Subversion', in Celia Kitzinger and Sue Wilkinson (eds), *Heterosexuality* (Sage, London, 1993), pp. 44–5.

Culler, Jonathan, *Structuralist Poetics* (Routledge and Kegan Paul, London, 1975).

Culler, Jonathan, 'Reading as a woman', in *On Deconstruction* (Routledge and Kegan Paul, London, 1983), pp. 43–64.

Daly, Mary, *Gyn/Ecology* (The Women's Press, London, 1978).

Daly, Mary, *Pure Lust: Elemental Female Philosophy* (The Women's Press, London, 1984).

Davis, Lennard J., *Resisting Novels: Ideology and Fiction* (Methuen, London, 1987).

de Beauvoir, Simone, *The Second Sex* (Knopf, New York, 1953).

de Lauretis, Teresa, *The Practice of Love: Lesbian Sexuality and Perverse Desire* (Indiana University Press, Bloomington and Indianapolis, 1994).

Diamond, Arlyn and Edwards, Lee R. (eds), *The Authority of Experience: Essays in Feminist Criticism* (University of Massachusetts Press, Amherst, 1977).

Donaldson, Laura, *Decolonizing Feminism: Race, Gender and Empire-Building* (Routledge, London, 1992).

Donovan, Josephine (ed.), *Feminist Literary Criticism: Explorations in Theory* (University of Kentucky Press, Lexington, 1975).

Durant, Alan and Fabb, Nigel, *Literary Theory in Action* (Routledge, London, 1990).

Eagleton, Mary, *Feminist Literary Theory: A Reader* (Blackwell, Oxford, 1986); new edn 1996.

Eagleton, Mary (ed.), *Feminist Literary Criticism* (Longman, London and New York, 1991).

Eagleton, Terry, *Marxism and Literary Criticism* (Methuen, London, 1976).

Eagleton, Terry, 'Pierre Macherey and Marxist literary criticism', in G. H. R. Parkinson (ed.), *Marx and Marxisms* (Cambridge University Press, Cambridge, 1982).

Eagleton, Terry, *Literary Theory: An Introduction* (Blackwell, Oxford, 1983).

Eagleton, Terry, *Against the Grain: Essays 1975–1985* (Verso, London, 1986).

Eagleton, Terry, *Ideology: An Introduction* (Verso, London, 1991).

Easton Ellis, Brad, *American Psycho* (Picador, London, 1991).

Ehrenreich, Barbara and English, Deirdre, *For Her Own Good* (Pluto, London, 1979).

Ellmann, Mary, *Thinking about Women* (Harcourt, New York, 1968).

Evans, Mari (ed.), *Black Women Writers* (Pluto, London, 1985).

Fabian, Johannes, *Time and the Other: How Anthropology Makes its Object* (Columbia University Press, New York, 1983).

Faderman, Lillian, *Surpassing the Love of Men: Romantic Friendship and Love Between Women from the Renaissance to the Present* (Morrow, New York, 1981).

Faderman, Lillian, *Odd Girls and Twilight Lovers: A History of Lesbian Life in Twentieth-Century America* (Penguin, Harmondsworth, 1991).

Faludi, Susan, *Backlash: The Undeclared War against Women* (Chatto and Windus, London, 1992).

Felman, Shoshana, 'Women and madness: the critical phallacy', *Diacritics*, vol. 5, no. 4, 1975.

Felski, Rita, *Beyond Feminist Aesthetics* (Hutchinson Radius, London, 1989).

Feminist Review, no. 23, *Socialist Feminism: Out of the Blue*, 1986.

Feminist Review, no. 31, *The Past Before Us: 20 Years of Feminisms*, 1989.

Ferguson, Kathy E., *The Man Question: Visions of Subjectivity in Feminist Theory* (University of California Press, Berkeley, 1993).

Ferguson, Moira, *Colonialism and Gender: From Mary Wollstonecraft to Jamaica Kincaid* (Columbia University Press, New York, 1993).

Fetterley, Judith, *The Resisting Reader: A Feminist Approach to American Fiction* (Indiana University Press, Bloomington, Indiana, 1988).

Florence, Penny and Reynolds, Dee (eds), *Feminist Subjects, Multi-Media: Cultural Methodologies* (Manchester University Press, Manchester, 1995).

Forrest, Katherine V., *Curious Wine* (Silver Moon Books, London, 1983).

Foucault, Michel, *The Order of Things: An Archaeology of the Human Sciences* (Vintage/Random, New York, 1973).

Foucault, Michel, *Discipline and Punish: The Birth of the Prison*, translated by Alan Sheridan (Vintage/Random House, New York, 1979).

Foucault, Michel, 'What is an author', in J. V. Harari (ed.), *Textual Strategies: Perspectives in Post-structuralist Criticism* (Methuen, London, 1980), pp. 141–60.

Foucault, Michel, *The History of Sexuality* (Pelican, Harmondsworth, 1981), vol. I.

Foucault, Michel, *Madness and Civilisation: A History of Insanity in the Age of Reason* (Tavistock, London, 1981).

Frankenberg, Ruth, *White Women, Race Matters: The Social Construction of Whiteness* (Routledge, London, 1993).

Friedan, Betty, *The Feminine Mystique* (Penguin, Harmondsworth, 1965).

Fuss, Diana, *Essentially Speaking: Feminism, Nature and Difference* (Routledge, London and New York, 1989).

Fuss, Diana (ed.), *Inside/Out: Lesbian Theories, Gay Theories* (Routledge, London and New York, 1991).

Gallop, Jane, *Feminism and Psychoanalysis: The Daughter's Seduction* (Macmillan, Basingstoke, 1982).

Gallop, Jane, *Reading Lacan* (Cornell University Press, Ithaca, 1985).

Gamman, Lorraine and Marchment, Margaret, *The Female Gaze: Women as Viewers of Popular Culture* (The Women's Press, London, 1988).

Gilbert, Sandra and Gubar, Susan, *The Madwoman in the Attic: The Woman Writer and the Nineteenth-Century Literary Imagination* (Yale University Press, New Haven, 1979).

Gilbert, Sandra and Gubar, Susan, *The War of the Words* (Yale University Press, New Haven, 1988), vol. 1.

Gilman, Charlotte Perkins, *The Yellow Wallpaper* (Virago, London, 1973) and 'The Yellow Wallpaper', in Ann Lane (ed.), *The Charlotte Perkins Gilman Reader* (The Women's Press, London, 1981), pp. 3–20.

Gilroy, Paul, *There Ain't No Black in the Union Jack* (Routledge, London, 1992, 3rd edn).

Goldberg, David, *Racist Culture* (Blackwell, Oxford, 1993).

Green, Keith and LeBihan, Jill, *Critical Theory and Practice* (Routledge, London, 1996).

Greene, Gayle and Kahn, Coppelia (eds), *Making a Difference: Feminist Literary Criticism*, (Methuen, London, 1986).

Greene, Gayle and Kahn, Coppelia (eds), *Changing Subjects: The Making of Feminist Literary Criticism* (Routledge, London and New York, 1993).

Greer, Germaine, *The Female Eunuch* (Paladin, London, 1971).

Griffin, Gabriele, *Heavenly Love? Lesbian Images in Twentieth-century Women's Writing* (Manchester University Press, Manchester, 1993).

Griffin, Susan, *Woman and Nature* (The Women's Press, London, 1984).

Grosz, Elizabeth, *Jacques Lacan: A Feminist Introduction* (Routledge, London and New York, 1990).

Gubar, Susan, ' "The Blank Page" and the issues of female creativity', *Critical Inquiry*, vol. 8, Winter 1981.

Guha, Ranajit and Spivak, Gayatri (eds), *Selected Subaltern Studies* (Oxford University Press, Oxford, 1988).

Gunew, Sneja (ed.), *A Reader in Feminist Knowledge* (Routledge, London, 1991).

Haggis, Jane, *Women and Colonialism: Untold Stories and Conceptual Absences*, Studies in Sexual Politics (University of Manchester, Manchester, 1988).

Hall, Radclyffe, *The Well of Loneliness* (Virago, London, 1982 f. pub. 1928).

Hamilton, Roberta and Barrett, Michèle (eds), *The Politics of Diversity: Feminism, Marxism and Nationalism* (Verso, London, 1986).

Hardy, Thomas, *Tess of the d'Urbervilles* (Macmillan, London, 1974, f. pub. 1891).

Hartmann, Heidi, 'The unhappy marriage of Marxism and feminism: towards a more progressive union', in Lydia Sargent (ed.), *The Unhappy Marriage of Marxism and Feminism: A Debate on Class and Patriarchy* (Pluto, London, 1981).

Haug, Frigga (ed.), *Female Sexualization*, translated by Erica Carter (Verso, London, 1987).

Hawthorn, Jeremy, *Cunning Passages: New Historicism, Cultural Materialism and Marxism* (Edward Arnold, London, 1996).

H.D., *Her* (Virago, London, 1984).

Henderson, Gwendolyn Mae, 'Speaking in tongues: dialogics, dialectics and the Black women's literary tradition', in Cheryl Wall (ed.), *Changing our Own Words: Essays on Criticism,*. *Theory and Writing by Black Women*, (Routledge, London and New York, 1989).

Hendricks, Margo and Parker, Patricia (eds), *Women, 'Race' and Writing in the Early Modern Period* (Routledge, London, 1994).

Hennessy, Rosemary, *Materialist Feminism and the Politics of Discourse* (Routledge, London, 1993).

Hennessy, Rosemary and Mohan, Rajaswari, 'The construction of women in three popular texts of empire: towards a critique of materialist feminism', in Patrick Williams and Laura Chrisman (eds), *Colonial Discourse and Post-colonial Theory* (Harvester Wheatsheaf, Hemel Hempstead, 1993), pp. 462–80.

Herndl, Diane Price and Warhol, Robyn R., *Feminisms: An Anthology of Literary Theory and Criticism* (Rutgers University Press, New Brunswick, NJ, 1991).

Highsmith, Patricia, *Carol* (Bloomsbury, London, 1981).

Hinds, Hilary, Phoenix, Ann and Stacey, Jackie, *Working Out: New Directions for Women's Studies* (Falmer, London and Washington, 1991).

Hinds, Hilary 'Oranges are not the only fruit: reaching audiences other lesbian texts cannot reach', in Sally Munt (ed.), *New Lesbian Criticism* (Harvester Wheatsheaf, Hemel Hempstead, 1992), pp. 153–72.

Hirsch, Marianne and Fox Keller, Evelyn (eds), *Conflicts in Feminism* (Routledge, London and New York, 1990).

Hobby, Elaine, *Virtue of Necessity* (Virago, London, 1988).

Hobby, Elaine and White, Chris (eds), *What Lesbians Do in Books* (The Women's Press, London, 1991).

Hulme, Peter, *Colonial Encounters: Europe and the Native Caribbean* (Methuen, London, 1986).

Humm, Maggie, *Feminist Criticism* (Harvester Wheatsheaf, Hemel Hempstead, 1987).

Humm, Maggie, *Feminisms: A Reader* (Harvester Wheatsheaf, Hemel Hempstead, 1992).

Humm, Maggie, *Practising Feminist Criticism: An Introduction* (Harvester Wheatsheaf, Hemel Hempstead, 1995).

Hutcheon, Linda, *A Poetics of Postmodernism: History, Theory, Fiction* (Routledge, London and New York, 1990).

Hyam, Ronald, *Empire and Sexuality: The British Experience* (Manchester University Press, Manchester, 1990).

Irigaray, Luce, *Speculum of the Other Woman*, translated by Gillian C. Gill (Cornell University Press, Ithaca, 1985).

Irigaray, Luce, *This Sex Which is Not One*, translated by Catherine Porter, with Carolyn Burke (Cornell University Press, Ithaca, 1985).

Irigaray, Luce, *Je, Tu, Nous: Towards a Culture of Difference* (Routledge, London, 1993).

Irigaray, Luce, *I Love You: Sketch of a Possible Felicity in History* (Routledge, London, 1995).

Jacobs, Harriet, *Incidents in the Life of a Slave Girl, Written by Herself*, ed. L. Maria Child (Harvard University Press, Cambridge, Mass., 1987).

Jacobus, Mary, 'Tess: the making of a pure woman', in Susan Lipschitz (ed.), *Tearing the Veil: Essays on Femininity* (Routledge and Kegan Paul, London, 1978).

Jacobus, Mary (ed.), *Women Writing and Writing about Women* (Croom Helm, London, 1979).

James, Louis, *Jean Rhys* (Longman, London, 1978).

Jardine, Alice, *Gynesis: Configurations of Women and Modernity* (Cornell University Press, Ithaca, 1985).

Jardine, Alice and Smith, Paul (eds), *Men in Feminism* (Methuen, London, 1987).

Jay, Karla and Glasgow, Joanne (eds), *Lesbian Texts and Contexts* (New York University Press, New York and London, 1990).

Jones, Ann Rosalind, 'Julia Kristeva on femininity: the limits of a semiotic politics', *Feminist Review*, no. 18, November 1984, pp. 56–78.

Joyce, Patrick (ed.), *Class* (Oxford University Press, Oxford, 1995).

Kamuf, Peggy, 'Writing like a woman', in Sally McConnell-Ginet (ed.), *Women and Language in Literature and Society* (Praeger, New York, 1982), pp. 284–97.

Kamuf, Peggy, 'Femmeninism', in Alice Jardine and Paul Smith (eds), *Men in Feminism* (Routledge, London, 1987), p. 96.

Kaplan, Cora, 'Radical feminism and literature: rethinking Millett's *Sexual Politics*', *Red Letters*, vol. 9, 1979, pp. 4–16.

Kaplan, Cora, 'Pandora's box: subjectivity, class and sexuality in socialist-feminist criticism', in Gayle Greene and Coppelia Kahn (eds), *Making a Difference* (Methuen, London, 1985).

Kaplan, Cora, 'Keeping the color in *The Color Purple*', in *Sea Changes* (Verso, London, 1986), pp. 176–87.

Kaplan, Cora, *Sea Changes: Culture and Feminism* (Verso, London, 1986).

Kaplan, Cora and Light, Alison, 'Feminist criticism in the eighties', a paper given at Framing Feminism at the Institute of Contemporary Art, London, 12 January 1988.

Klein, Melanie, *Envy and Gratitude* (Virago, London, 1988 f. pub. 1975).

Klein, Melanie, in Juliet Mitchell (ed.), *The Selected Melanie Klein* (Peregrine, Harmondsworth, 1986).

Kristeva, Julia, 'La femme ce n'est jamais ça', *Tel Quel*, vol. 14, Autumn 1974, pp. 19–24.

Kristeva, Julia, 'A partir du polylogue', interview with Françoise van Rossum Guyon, in *Revue des Sciences Humaines*, December 1979, pp. 495–501.

Kristeva, Julia, *Desire in Language: A Semiotic Approach to Literature and Art*, ed. Leon S. Roudiez, translated by Thomas Gorg *et al.* (Blackwell, Oxford, 1980).

Kristeva, Julia, *Powers of Horror: An Essay on Abjection*, translated by Leon S. Roudiez (Columbia University Press, New York, 1982).

Kristeva, Julia, 'Women's time', in Toril Moi (ed.), *The Kristeva Reader* (Blackwell, Oxford, 1986), pp. 188–211.

Kristeva, Julia, 'The adolescent novel', paper presented to the Warwick conference on Kristeva's work, May 1987.

Kristeva, Julia, 'A question of subjectivity – an interview', in P. Rice and P. Waugh (eds), *Modern Literary Theory: A Reader* (Edward Arnold, London, 1989), pp. 128–34.

Kuhn, Annette, *Women's Pictures* (Routledge and Kegan Paul, London, 1982).

Kuhn, Annette, *Family Secrets* (Routledge, London and New York, 1995).

Lacan, Jacques, 'Seminar on *The Purloined Letter*', translated by Jeffrey Mehlman, in *Yale French Studies*, vol. 48, 1972, pp. 38–72.

Lacan, Jacques, 'The agency of the letter in the unconscious or reason since Freud,' in *Écrits: A Selection*, translated by A. Sheridan (Tavistock, London, 1980).

Landry, Donna and MacLean, Gerald, *Materialist Feminisms* (Blackwell, Oxford, 1993).

Lovell, Terry, *Consuming Fiction* (Verso, London, 1987).

Lovell, Terry, *British Feminist Thought: A Reader* (Blackwell, Oxford, 1990).

Lugones, Maria and Spelman, Elizabeth, 'Have we got a theory for you? Feminist theory, cultural imperialism and the demand for "the woman's voice" ', in *Women's Studies International Forum*, 6/6, 1983, pp. 573–81.

Lunn, Eugene, *Marxism and Modernism* (Verso, London, 1985).

Macdonnell, Diane, *Theories of Discourse* (Blackwell, Oxford, 1986).

Macherey, Pierre, *A Theory of Literary Production* (Routledge and Kegan Paul, London, 1978).

Marks, Elaine and de Courtivron, Isabelle (eds), *New French Feminisms* (Harvester Wheatsheaf, Hemel Hempstead, 1980).

Martin, Biddy, 'Lesbian identity and autobiographical difference(s)', in *The Lesbian and Gay Studies Reader*, ed. Henry Abelove (Routledge, London, 1993).

Marxist-Feminist Literature Collective, 'Women's writing: Jane Eyre, Shirley, Villette, Aurora Leigh', *Ideology and Consciousness*, vol. 1, no. 3, Spring, pp. 27–48.

McClintock, Anne, 'The angel of progress: pitfalls of the term "post-colonialism" ', in Patrick Williams and Laura Chrisman (eds), *Colonial Discourse and Post-colonial Theory: A Reader* (Harvester Wheatsheaf, Hemel Hempstead, 1993), pp. 291–305.

McClintock, Anne, *Imperial Leather: Race, Gender and Sexuality in the Imperial Contest* (Routledge, London, 1995).

McConnell-Ginet, Sally (ed.), *Women and Language in Literature and Society* (Praeger, New York, 1982).

Meaney, Gerardine, *(Un)Like Subjects: Women/Theory and Fiction* (Routledge, London and New York, 1993).

Meehan, Johanna, *Habermas and Feminism* (Routledge, London, 1995).

Meese, Elizabeth, 'Theorising lesbian: writing – a love letter', in Karla Jay and Joanne Glasgow (eds), *Lesbian Texts and Contexts* (New York University Press, New York, 1990), pp. 70–87.

Millard, Elaine, 'Reading as a woman', in Douglas Tallack (ed.), *Literary Theory at Work* (Batsford, London, 1986).

Miller, Hillis J., *Fiction and Repetition* (Blackwell, Oxford, 1982).

Miller, Nancy K., 'Changing the subject: authorship, writing and the reader', in *Feminist Studies/Critical Studies* (Indiana University Press, Indiana, 1986), pp. 102–20.

Miller, Nancy K., *Getting Personal: Feminist Occasions and Other Autobiographical Acts* (Routledge, London, 1991).

Millett, Kate, *Sexual Politics* (Virago, London, 1977).

Mills, Sara, 'Alternative voices to orientalism', *Literature Teaching Politics*, no. 5, 1986, pp. 78–91.

Mills, Sara, 'No poetry for ladies: Gertrude Stein and Julia Kristeva', in David Murray (ed.), *Literary Theory and Poetry* (Batsford, London, 1989).

Mills, Sara, *Discourses of Difference: An Analysis of Women's Travel Writing and Colonialism* (Routledge, London and New York, 1991).

Mills, Sara, 'Knowing y/our place: a Marxist feminist stylistic analysis', in M. Toolan (ed.), *Language, Text and Context: Essays in Stylistics* (Routledge, London, 1992), pp. 182–208.

Mills, Sara, 'Discontinuity and post-colonial discourse', in *Ariel: A Review of International English Literature*, 26/3, July 1995, pp. 73–88.

Mills, Sara, *Feminist Stylistics* (Routledge, London, 1995).

Mills, Sara, 'Working with sexism: what can feminist text analysis do?', in Peter Verdonk and Jean Jacques Weber (eds), *Twentieth Century Fiction: From Text to Context* (Routledge, London, 1995), pp. 206–19.

Mills, Sara, 'Gender and colonial space', in *Gender, Place and Culture*, 3/2, forthcoming, 1996.

Mills, Sara (ed.), *Gendering the Reader* (Harvester Wheatsheaf, Hemel Hempstead, 1994).

Mills, Sara (ed.), *Language and Gender: Interdisciplinary Perspectives* (Longman, Harlow, 1995).

Minh ha, Trinh T., *Woman Native Other: Writing Postcoloniality and Feminism* (Indiana University Press, Bloomington and Indianapolis, 1989).

Mitchell, Juliet, *Psychoanalysis and Feminism* (Penguin, Harmondsworth, 1975).

Modleski, Tania, *Loving with a Vengeance: Mass-produced Fantasies for Women* (Methuen, London, 1984).

Modleski, Tanya, *Feminism without Women: Culture and Criticism in a 'Postfeminist' Age* (Routledge, London and New York, 1991).

Moers, Ellen, *Literary Women: The Great Writers* (The Women's Press, London, 1976).

Mohanty, Chandra Talpade, 'Under Western eyes: feminist scholarship and colonial discourses', pp.196–221 in Patrick Williams and Laura Chrisman (eds), *Colonial Discourse and Post-colonial Theory* (Harvester Wheatsheaf, Hemel Hempstead, 1993).

Mohanty, Chandra Talpade, Russo, Ann and Torres, Lourdes, *Third World Women and the Politics of Feminism* (Indiana University Press, Bloomington and Indianapolis, 1991).

Moi, Toril, *Sexual/Textual Politics: Feminist Literary Theory* (Methuen, London, 1985).

Moi, Toril, 'Feminism, postmodernism and style: recent feminist criticism in the US', paper given at Strathclyde University, 1989.

Moi, Toril (ed.), *The Kristeva Reader* (Blackwell, Oxford, 1986).

Moi, Toril (ed.), *French Feminist Thought* (Blackwell, Oxford, 1987).

Montefiore, Jan, *Feminism and Poetry* (Pandora, London, 1987).

Monteith, Moira (ed.), *Women's Writing: A Challenge to Theory* (Harvester Wheatsheaf, Hemel Hempstead, 1986).

Morris, Pam, 'Locutions and locations: more feminist theory and practice', in *College English*, vol. 49, no. 4, April 1987, pp. 465–76.

Morris, Pam, *Literature and Feminism* (Blackwell, Oxford, 1993).

Morrison, Toni, *Sula* (Bantam, New York, 1980).

Morrison, Toni, *Beloved* (Chatto and Windus, London, 1987).

Mulhern, Francis (ed.), *Contemporary Marxist Literary Criticism* (Longman, Harlow, 1992).

Mulvey, Laura, 'Visual pleasure and narrative cinema', *Screen*, vol. 16, no. 3, 1975, pp. 6–18.

Munt, Sally, 'Somewhere over the rainbow: postmodernism and the fiction of Sarah Schulman', in Sally Munt (ed.), *New Lesbian Criticism* (Harvester Wheatsheaf, Hemel Hempstead, 1992).

Murray, Dave (ed.), *Literary Theory and Poetry: Extending the Canon* (Batsford, London, 1989).

Nead, Linda, *Myths of Sexuality* (Blackwell, Oxford, 1988).

Newton, Judith Lowder and Rosenfelt, Deborah (eds), *Feminist Criticism and Social Change* (Methuen, London, 1985).

Norris, Christopher, *Deconstructive Criticism* (Methuen, London, 1982).

Oliver, Kelly, *Womanizing Nietzsche* (Routledge, London and New York, 1994).

Olsen, Tillie, *Silences* (Virago, London, 1980).

Ostriker, Alicia, 'The thieves of language: women poets and revisionist mythmakers', *Signs*, vol. 8, no. 1, Spring 1982, pp. 66–78.

Ostriker, Alicia, *Stealing the Language: The Emergence of Women's Poetry in America* (The Women's Press, London, 1987).

Paglia, Camille, *Sexual Personae: Art and Decadence from Nefertiti to Emily Dickinson* (Yale University Press, New Haven, 1990).

Paglia, Camille, *Sex, Art and American Culture* (Penguin, London, 1994).

Palmer, Paulina, 'From coded mannequin to bird woman: Angela Carter's magic flight', in Sue Roe (ed.), *Women Reading Women's Writing* (Harvester Wheatsheaf, Hemel Hempstead, 1987).

Parmar, Pratibha, 'Black feminism: the politics of articulation' in Jonathan Rutherford (ed.), *Identity: Community, Culture, Difference* (Lawrence and Wishart, London, 1990).

Pearce, Lynne, *Woman/Image/Text* (Harvester Wheatsheaf, Hemel Hempstead, 1991).

Pearce, Lynne, 'Dialogic theory and women's writing', in Hilary Hinds *et al.* (eds), *Working Out: New Directions in Women's Studies* (Falmer Press, Brighton, 1992), pp. 184–93.

Pearce, Lynne, *Reading Dialogics*, (Edward Arnold, London, 1994).

Pearce, Lynne, ' "I" the reader: text, context and the balance of power', in Penny Florence and Dee Reynolds (eds), *Feminist Subjects, Multi-Media: Cultural Methodologies* (Manchester University Press, Manchester, 1995), pp. 160–70.

Pearce, Lynne and Stacey, Jackie (eds), *Romance Revisited* (Lawrence and Wishart, London, 1995).

Pearce, Lynne, ' "Written on tablets of stone?" Jeanette Winterson, Roland Barthes and the discourse of romantic love', in Suzanne Raitt (ed.), *Volcanoes and Pearl Divers: Essays in Lesbian Feminist Studies* (Onlywomen Press, London, 1995).

Pearce, Lynne, *Feminism and the Politics of Reading* (Edward Arnold, London, forthcoming 1997).

Penfold, Susan and Walker, Gillian, *Women and the Psychiatric Paradox* (Oxford University Press, Oxford, 1984).

Phillips, Anne, *Hidden Hands: Women and Economic Policies* (Pluto, London, 1983).

Piercy, Marge, *Woman on the Edge of Time* (The Women's Press, London, 1979).

Pinkney, Darryl, 'Black victims: black villains', *New York Review*, 29 January 1987, pp. 17–20.

Plaza, Monique, 'Phallomorphic power and the psychology of women', translated by M. David and J. Hodges, *Ideology and Consciousness*, vol. 4, Autumn 1978, pp. 5–36.

Pollock, Griselda, *Vision and Difference: Femininity, Feminism and the History of Art* (Routledge, London, 1988).

Pratt, Anais, 'Surfacing and the rebirth journey' in Arnold E. Davidson and Cathy N. Davidson (eds), *The Art of Margaret Atwood: Essays in Criticism* (Anansi, Toronto, 1981), pp. 139–57.

Pratt, Mary Louise: 'Scratches on the face of the country; or, what Mr Barrow saw in the land of the Bushmen', *Critical Inquiry*, 12/1, Autumn, 1985, pp. 119–44.

Pratt, Mary Louise, *Imperial Eyes: Travel Writing and Transculturation* (Routledge, London, 1992.).

Pribram, Deirdre (ed.), *Female Spectators: Looking at Film and Television* (Verso, London, 1988).

Probyn, Elspeth, *Sexing the Self: Gendered Positions in Cultural Studies* (Routledge, London and New York, 1993).

Radcliffe-Richards, Janet, *The Sceptical Feminist: A Philosophical Enquiry* (Routledge and Kegan Paul, London, 1980).

Ragland-Sullivan, Ellie, 'The imaginary', in Elizabeth Wright (ed.), *Feminism and Psychoanalysis* (Blackwell, Oxford, 1993), pp. 173–6.

Ramazanoglu, Caroline, *Up Against Foucault* (Routledge, London and New York, 1993).

Register, Cheri, 'American feminist literary criticism: a bibliographical introduction', in Josephine Donovan (ed.), *Feminist Literary Criticism, Explorations in Theory* (University of Kentucky Press, Lexington, 1975), pp. 1–28.

Rhys, Jean, *Wide Sargasso Sea* (Penguin, Harmondsworth, 1987 f. pub, 1966).

Rich, Adrienne, 'Compulsory heterosexuality and lesbian existence', in *Blood, Bread and Poetry: Selected Prose 1969–1985* (The Women's Press, London, 1987).

Roe, Sue, *Women Reading Women's Writing* (Harvester Wheatsheaf, Hemel Hempstead, 1987).

Roiphe, Katie, *The Morning After: Sex, Fear and Feminism* (Penguin, Harmondsworth, 1994).

Root, Jane, *Pictures of Women – Sexuality* (Pandora, London, 1984).

Rose, Jacqueline, *Sexuality in the Field of Vision* (Verso, London, 1986).

Rule, Jane, *Desert of the Heart* (Pandora, London, 1986).

Ruskin, John, *Sesame and Lilies* (Homewood, Chicago, 1902).

Russ, Joanna, *How to Suppress Women's Writing* (The Women's Press, London, 1984).

Said, Edward, *Beginnings: Intention and Method* (Basic Books, New York, 1975).

Said, Edward, *Orientalism* (Routledge and Kegan Paul, London, 1978).

Said, Edward, *Culture and Imperialism* (Chatto and Windus, London, 1993).

Sandoval, Chela, 'Third world feminism: the theory and method of oppositional consciousness in the postmodern world', in *Genders*, no. 10, Spring 1991, pp. 1–24.

Sargent, Lydia (ed.), *Women and Revolution: The Unhappy Marriage between Marxism and Feminism* (Pluto, London, 1981).

Sawicki, Jana, *Disciplining Foucault: Feminism Power and the Body* (Routledge, London and New York, 1991).

Sedgwick, Eve Kosofsky, *Between Men: English Literature and Homosocial Desire* (Columbia University Press, New York, 1985).

Sedgwick, Eve Kosofsky, *Epistemology of the Closet* (Harvester Wheatsheaf, Hemel Hempstead, 1991).

Sedgwick, Eve Kosofsky, *Tendencies* (Routledge, London and New York, 1994).

Sedgwick, Eve Kosofsky and Parker, Andrew, *Performances and Performativity* (Routledge, London, 1995).

Selden, Raman, *A Reader's Guide to Contemporary Literary Theory* (Harvester Wheatsheaf, Hemel Hempstead, 1985).

Schaffer, Kay, *Women and the Bush: Forces of Desire in the Australian Cultural Tradition* (Cambridge University Press, Cambridge, 1988).

Sharpe, Jenny, 'The unspeakable limits of rape: colonial violence and counter-insurgency', in Patrick Williams and Laura Chrisman (eds), *Colonial Discourse and Postcolonial Theory* (Harvester Wheatsheaf, Hemel Hempstead, 1993), pp. 221–44.

Sharpe, Jenny, *Allegories of Empire: The Figure of Woman in the Colonial Text* (University of Minnesota Press, Minneapolis, 1993).

Sheba Collective (ed.), *Serious Pleasure: Lesbian Erotic Stories* (Sheba, London, 1989).

Shohat, Ella and Stam, Robert, *Unthinking Eurocentrism* (Routledge, London, 1995).

Showalter, Elaine, *A Literature of their Own: British Women Novelists from Brontë to Lessing* (Princeton University Press, Princeton, 1977).

Showalter, Elaine, 'Feminist criticism in the wilderness', in Elaine Showalter (ed.), *The New Feminist Criticism: Essays on Women, Literature and Theory* (Virago, London, f. pub. 1981).

Showalter, Elaine, *The New Feminist Criticism: Essays on Women, Literature and Theory* (Virago, London, 1986).

Showalter, Elaine, *The Female Malady: Women, Madness, and English Culture* (Virago, London, 1987).

Smedley, Agnes, *Daughter of Earth* (Virago, London, 1977).

Smedley, Agnes, *Battle Hymn of China* (Pandora, London, 1974).

Smith, Barbara, *Towards a Black Feminist Criticism* (Out-and-out Books, New York, 1980).

Smith, Dorothy, *Texts, Facts and Femininity: Exploring the Relations of Ruling* (Routledge, London, 1990).

Spacks, Patricia Meyer, *The Female Imagination. A Literary and Psychological Investigation of Women's Writing* (Allen and Unwin, London, 1976).

Spence, Jo, *Putting Myself in the Picture* (Camden Press, London, 1986).

Spencer, Jane, *The Rise of the Woman Novelist* (Blackwell, Oxford, 1986).

Spender, Dale, *Man Made Language* (Routledge and Kegan Paul, London, 1980).

Spender, Dale, *Women of Ideas and What Men Have Done to Them* (Ark, London, 1982).

Spender, Dale, *Mothers of the Novel* (Pandora, London, 1986).

Spivak, Gayatri Chakravorty, 'Three women's texts and a critique of imperialism', in Henry Louis Gates (ed.), *'Race', Writing and Difference* (University of Chicago Press, Chicago, 1985).

Spivak, Gayatri Chakravorty, 'Imperialism and sexual difference', in *Sexual Difference Conference Proceedings* (Oxford Literary Review, Southampton, 1986), pp. 225–40.

Spivak, Gayatri Chakravorty, *In Other Worlds: Essays in Cultural Politics* (Methuen, London, 1987).

Spivak, Gayatri Chakravorty, *The Post-colonial Critic: Interviews, Strategies, Dialogues* ed. Sarah Harasym (Routledge, London, 1990).

Spivak, Gayatri Chakravorty, 'Can the subaltern speak?', in Patrick Williams and Laura Chrisman (eds), *Colonial Discourse and Postcolonial Theory* (Harvester Wheatsheaf, Hemel Hempstead, 1993), pp. 66–111.

Spivak, Gayatri Chakravorty, *Outside in the Teaching Machine* (Routledge, London, 1993).

Spivak, Gayatri Chakravorty, 'Three women's texts and a critique of imperialism', in Bill Ashcroft *et al.* (eds), *The Post-colonial Studies Reader* (Routledge, London, 1995), pp. 269–73.

Spraggs, Gillian, 'Hell and the mirror: a reading of *Desert of the Heart*', in Sally Munt (ed.), *New Lesbian Criticism* (Harvester Wheatsheaf, Hemel Hempstead, 1992).

Stacey, Jackie, 'Desperately seeking difference', in *The Female Gaze*, ed. Lorraine Gamman and Margaret Marshment (The Women's Press, London, 1988), pp. 112–29).

Stacey, Jackie, *Star Gazing: Hollywood Cinema and Female Spectatorship* (Routledge, London, 1994).

Stanley, Liz (ed.), *Feminist Praxis: Research, Theory and Epistemology in Feminist Sociology* (Routledge, London, 1990).

Stanley, Liz, *The Auto/Biographical I* (Routledge, London, 1994).

Steedman, Carolyn, *Landscape for a Good Woman* (Virago, London, 1986).

Suleiman, Susan (ed.), *The Reader in the Text* (Princeton University Press, New Jersey, 1980).

Szasz, Thomas, *Ideology and Insanity* (Calder and Boyars, London, 1973).

Tallack, Douglas (ed.), *Literary Theory at Work: Three Texts* (Batsford, London, 1986).

Tallack, Douglas (ed.), *Critical Theory: A Reader* (Harvester Wheatsheaf, Hemel Hempstead, 1995).

Trollope, Joanna, *Britannia's Daughters: Women of the British Empire* (Hutchinson, London, 1983).

Voloshinov, Valentin, *Marxism and the Philosophy of Language*, translated by L. Matejka and I. R. Titunik (Harvard University Press, Cambridge, Mass., 1986 f. pub. 1929).

Walker, Alice, *The Color Purple* (The Women's Press, London, 1983).

Walker, Alice, 'Writing *The Color Purple*', in M. Evans, (ed.), *Black Women Writers* (Pluto, London, 1985), pp. 453–7.

Ware, Vron, *Beyond the Pale: White Women, Racism and History* (Verso, London, 1992).

Waugh, Patricia, *Feminine Fictions: Revisiting the Postmodern* (Routledge, London and New York, 1989).

Waugh, Patricia, *Practising Postmodernism/Reading Modernism: Gender and Autonomy Theory* (Edward Arnold, London, 1992).

Weedon, Chris, *Feminist Practice and Post-structuralist Theory* (Blackwell, Oxford, 1987).

Whitford, Margaret, *Luce Irigaray: Philosophy in the Feminine* (Routledge, London, 1991).

Widdowson, Peter (ed.), *Re-Reading English* (Methuen, London, 1982).

Wilcox, Helen, McWatters, Keith, Thompson, Ann and Williams, Lynda (eds), *The Body and the Text: Hélène Cixous, Reading and Teaching* (Harvester Wheatsheaf, Hemel Hempstead, 1990).

Williams, Linda, *Critical Desire: Psychoanalysis and the Literary Subject* (Edward Arnold, London, 1995).

Williams, Patrick and Chrisman, Laura (eds), *Colonial Discourse and Post-colonial Theory* (Harvester Wheatsheaf, Hemel Hempstead, 1993).

Williams, Raymond, *Marxism and Literature* (Oxford University Press, Oxford, 1977).

Williamson, Judith, *Decoding Advertisements: Ideology and Meaning in Advertising* (Marion Boyars, London, 1978).

Willis, Susan, 'Black women writers: taking a critical perspective', in Gayle Greene and Coppelia Kahn (eds), *Making a Difference: Feminist Literary Criticism* (Methuen, London, 1986), pp. 211–37.

Winterson, Jeanette, *Oranges are not the only fruit* (Pandora, London, 1985).

Wittig, Monique, 'One is not born a woman', in *Feminist Issues*, vol. 1, no. 2, Winter 1981, pp. 41–8.

Wittig, Monique, *The Straight Mind and Other Essays* (Harvester Wheatsheaf, Hemel Hempstead, 1992).

Wolf, Naomi, *The Beauty Myth: How Images of Beauty are Used Against Women* (Vintage, London, 1991).

Wolf, Naomi, *Fighting Fire with Fire: The New Female Power and How It Will Change the 21st Century* (Chatto and Windus, London, 1993).

Woolf, Virginia, 'Professions for women' – *The Death of the Moth and Other Stories* (Harcourt, Brace, New York, 1942), pp. 236–8.

Woolf, Virginia, *A Room of One's Own* (Granada, London, 1977).

Wright, Elizabeth, *Psychoanalytic Criticism: Theory into Practice* (Methuen, London, 1984).

Wright, Elizabeth (ed.), *Feminism and Psychoanalysis: A Critical Dictionary* (Blackwell, Oxford, 1992).

Young, Robert, *Colonial Desire: Hybridity in Theory, Culture and Race* (Routledge, London, 1995).

Zemon, Davis Natalie, 'Iroquois women, European women', in Margo Hendricks and Patricia Parker (eds), *Women, 'Race' and Writing in the Early Modern Period* (Routledge, London, 1994), pp. 243–58.

Zimmerman, Bonnie, 'What has never been: an overview of lesbian feminist criticism', in Gayle Green and Coppelia Kahn (eds), *Making a Difference* (Methuen, London, 1986), pp. 177–210.

Zimmerman, Bonnie, *The Safe Sea of Women: Lesbian Fiction 1969–1989* (Onlywomen Press, London, 1989).

Zimmerman, Bonnie, 'Lesbians like this and that: some notes on lesbian criticism for the nineties', in Sally Munt (ed.), *New Lesbian Criticism* (Harvester Wheatsheaf, Hemel Hempstead, 1992).

Glossary

All definitions are partial. We have provided these brief definitions to help the reader who is new to feminist theory. However, it should be remembered that most of the terms are the subject of contestation within feminist theory and our definitions of these terms should not be regarded as the only interpretation of them.

Some comment is needed on the use of inverted commas throughout this book. In post-structuralist criticism it has become common practice to put within inverted commas those terms which you are treating with a certain amount of suspicion: terms like 'feminine' and 'race', which appear to have a common sense meaning, and which for theoretical and practical reasons need to be questioned.

alienation a Marxist term used to describe the process whereby the worker gives up their labour in exchange for wages and thus becomes a part of the capitalist machine; the worker no longer experiences the satisfaction of producing goods themselves, but feels distanced from production. Marxist critics, for example Theodor Adorno, stress the alienated nature of reality in contemporary society and argue that the work of art acts within reality to expose its contradictions.

androgynous having characteristics of both sexes. In feminist criticism the concept has been used, particularly by Virginia Woolf, to describe writing which demonstrates both 'masculine' and 'feminine' characteristics.

Anglo-American feminism feminists based in America or Britain who developed a form of reading practice which stressed the importance of representations on women's sense of self.

antithesis the second element in Hegel's dialectical system which is in opposition to the first proposition or thesis (*see* thesis and synthesis).

Anxiety of Authorship this phrase is Sandra Gilbert and Susan Gubar's adaptation of the critic Harold Bloom's concept of 'the anxiety of influence'. Bloom's theory describes the relation of the young poet (ephebe) to his poetic father figure (precursor). The unconscious of the younger poet becomes imprinted by that of the poetic father figure. Only by overturning this influence can the younger poet become free to write. Gilbert and Gubar argue that for the female author a male percursor creates an even more debilitating barrier to creativity. The barrier is so great that she doubts not only what she writes, but her ability to write at all.

authentic realist a view of texts which sees them as relating closely to experience, both of the author and of the reader (*see* Chapter 2).

author intentionality *see* intentionality.

base within Marxist theory, it is assumed that economic relations underlie or predicate all other relations; this is the economic base (*see* superstructure).

biological essentialism an assumption that the differences between the sexes are determined by specific biological differences and not socially-constructed gender. Thus women are seen to be essentially different from men.

binary opposition a characteristic of Western thought which casts qualities as direct opposites, for example: black/white; male/female; nature/culture. A great deal of feminist and poststructuralist work has aimed to show that these terms are not 'true' oppositions, but depend on each other in order to have meaning.

canon this term is used by theorists to refer to that body of literary works that has become established as the proper texts to study on literature courses. It is marked by a preponderance of what feminists describe as 'dead white men's writing'.

castration complex *see* Oedipal phase.

classic realism texts which employ various conventions of realism such as particularized description, character development and closure, to create the illusion of 'real life'. The classic realist genre includes many well-known nineteenth century novels such as those by George Eliot and the Brontës.

closure the term used to describe resolution, at different levels, at the end of a text. If a text is seen to 'resist closure', this might indicate that it is self-consciously subverting the expectations of classic realism.

colonial discourse the group of texts, both literary and non-literary, which were produced by British writers within the British colonial period (*see* post-colonial).

confessional a type of writing, described by Michel Foucault in *The History of Sexuality*, which displays models of behaviour associated with the oppressed: that is, revealing information about oneself to those in positions of power.

consciousness-raising since the 1960s, women have met in groups to discuss the nature and means of their oppression, often through the stimulus of literary and other texts (*see* authentic realism). Such groups helped women understand the political nature of the difficulties they faced and realize that their sufferings were not individual. This new solidarity became the basis of feminist activism, both on a local and a global scale.

cultural essentialism assumes that women can be spoken about as a group because they share the same cultural experiences. In the writings of feminists like Elaine Showalter (*see* Chapter 3) this model of difference was initially preferred because it seemed less essentialist than models based on biology or psychology (*see* biological essentialism), but theorists soon recognized that it is equally problematic to assume that women of different 'race', class, nationality, education, sexuality and historical moment share a common culture.

deconstruction   this term was originally coined by the French theorist Jacques Derrida to describe a method of reading which focuses on the structure and operation of the text rather than on its content. The method undermines the notion of definite meaning in language, because an examination of any single word or concept reveals that it is only understood in relation to its opposite (*see* binary oppositions), or by its difference from other words or concepts. Developing the work of Ferdinand de Saussure, Derrida demonstrates the arbitrary nature of the language system, thereby calling into question the meanings it attempts to convey (*see* differance). Deconstructive criticism has thus been particularly concerned to show how texts undermine their authors' intentions.

determinism   a term to describe something preordained; for example, 'biological determinism' means that someone behaves in a certain way because of a biological predisposition.

differance   a word used by Derrida. His misspelling is deliberate, drawing attention to the written (rather than verbal) nature of language. It is a play on the two meanings of the French verb *differer*: to differ and to defer. Language depends on the difference between signs (words) as the basis of meaning (*see* difference below). The sense is deferred as one word refers to another word in an endless play of meaning, as is illustrated by our use of a dictionary which always sends us to another word and never the source 'object'.

difference   this term is used by Saussure to denote the way that meaning depends on the minimal contrast (difference) between words, rather than any correspondence between an object and the word used to name it. Language is not a naming device but a system of differences with no positive terms (i.e., no one term can be singled out to have its meaning in isolation from other words).

discourse   a term associated with the theorist Michel Foucault, used to designate established ways of thinking together with the power structures that support them (for example, the 'discourse of science', the 'discourse of patriarchy'). Discourses are the product of social, historical and institutional formations. The existence of 'discursive practices' within a society allows for certain subject positions to be taken up. Modes of discourse are established and modified over time and ideas of class, gender, race, individuality, etc. are determined by them. A discourse depends on shared assumptions, so that a culture's ideology is inscribed in its discursive practices (*see* below). Discourses embody power relations, and social meaning often arises at the point of conflict between different discourses. For example, concepts of gender result from the struggle between the legitimized discourse of patriarchy with the marginalized discourse of feminism (*see* Macdonnell, Bibliography).

discursive construct an element in a text or 'real life' which is created because of the pressure of the rules of discourse (*see* discourse).

dominant group a term developed by Shirley and Edwin Ardener (*see* Bibliography and Chapter 3) to refer to the group in society which controls the way that people in that society view and define themselves through language.

double-voiced discourse a discourse in which two voices co-exist in competition or tension with one another, or which address two audiences simultaneously (*see also* polyphony).

dual systems theory a theory developed within Marxist feminist thought to enable the analysis of the oppression of women from a perspective which includes both capitalism and patriarchy.

eclectic using elements from different theories or practices to work out a new position.

écriture féminine a term associated with the French Feminists (*see* below and Chapter 5) and used to refer to writing practices which might be seen to be specifically 'feminine'. Hélène Cixous, whose own experimental writing may be regarded as an example of *écriture féminine*, has dismissed attempts to define or theorize the concept but, in her work, as in that of Julia Kristeva and Luce Irigaray (*see parler femme*) connections are drawn between the non-linear or 'irrational' nature of women's writing and their gender-specific 'privileged' access to the repressed, unconscious stages of psychic development.

epiphany a moment of spiritual enlightenment and/or self-realization in literature.

epistolary a novel written in the form of letters to and from characters.

essentialism the assumption that there is an 'essence' of woman which all women share.

Eurocentrism the assumption, often unacknowledged, that European values, culture, governmental and economic systems, etc. are in essence superior to those of other cultures. (*See* Shohat and Stam in Bibliography and discussion in Chapter 8.)

female subjectivity within psychoanalytic theory there is an assumption that all female subjects position themselves in a similar manner in relation to the Symbolic Order and resolve the Oedipal crisis in a similar way; because of this, psychoanalysts assume that it is possible to describe the range of subject positions which females can adopt.

feminine whilst male and female can be more clearly seen to be based on biological differences, feminine and masculine refer to the way society encourages us to identify in terms of gender. Feminine has also been used by Julia Kristeva to mean a position of marginality, of being outside the mainstream, which is available to both males and females, and from which they can write (*see* masculine and gender).

feminine aesthetic a concept used by theorists who wish to prove the specificity of women's writing in terms of either language, style, address or, indeed, themes based on cultural difference.

feminine mystique a concept developed by Betty Friedan (*see* Bibliography) to describe the way in which women have been restricted to the role of wife and mother through the force of powerful ideologies and discourses that have circulated throughout patriarchal culture.

feminist critique   feminist analysis of male-authored texts.

feminist poetics   an analysis of the way texts work from a feminist perspective. Drawing on Jonathan Culler's work in *Structuralist Poetics* (*see* Bibliography), feminists often use 'poetics' to refer to an analysis which concentrates on the language structures in the text.

feminist practice   used in the context of this book to describe the activity of performing theoretically-informed feminist readings of literary texts.

first generation feminist   those involved in the revived Women's Movement of the 1960s. The problem with the term is that it implies that there were no feminists before; whereas there have been feminists since at least the seventeenth century (*see* Elaine Hobby, Bibliography).

first person narration   when a text is narrated using the first person 'I', for example 'I have only lived in this town for a short while . . .'.

foreground   a linguistic term which means to place at the centre of attention.

foreshadowing   when an event which occurs later in a text is alluded to, as an indication of what is to come.

French feminism   this usually refers to Kristeva, Wittig, Irigaray and Cixous, but there are many other interesting theorists working in France, (*see* Toril Moi, *French Feminist Thought*: *see* Bibliography).

gender   is a socially-constructed masculine or feminine role as opposed to the biologically-determined difference (i.e. sex).

gender studies   an analysis of masculinity and femininity, drawing on feminist theory and Women's Studies (*see* Chapman, Bibliography).

genre   a grouping of texts which have similar (and quite specific) literary codes and conventions; for example, the detective novel, melodrama, epic romance. Poetry, fiction and drama are probably better classified as different modes of writing rather than genres although the latter application is commonplace.

gyandry   a term which Gilbert and Gubar use as a rewriting of the term 'androgyny' which they feel privileges the male, because of its etymology (*see* Chapter 4).

gynocriticism   a term which refers to the practice of turning away from the analysis of male-authored texts to an analysis of female-authored texts and their specific difference from one another (*see* Chapter 3).

heterogeneous   composed of diverse elements.

heterosexism   a range of 'commonsense' ideologies that assumes that heterosexuality is the norm and that all other forms of sexual behaviour are deviant and perverse (*see* homophobia).

hommelette   a term which Jacques Lacan developed to describe the pre-Oedipal psychic condition of the child. He plays upon a pun in French (*hommelette* = little man and omelette) in that the child is both an adult in the making, with sexual desires, but also a dispersed consciousness which does not distinguish between self and other clearly. S/he is thus like a runny egg witout clearly-defined subject boundaries (*see* Chapter 5).

homogeneous   composed of a single element, unified.

homophobia   a fear and/or dislike of homosexuality which manifests itself in various forms of discrimination and prejudice, both personal and institutional.

humanist   *see* liberal humanist.

identity politics is the politics predicated upon a particular identity (e.g., gay, lesbian, Black) and which has been contested by Queer theorists who have made the poststructuralist de-centring of the subject central to their critique (*see* Chapter 7).

ideology a system of beliefs (or illusions) that determines the way in which people live. Ideology expresses itself through numerous forms of visual and verbal communication which 'interpellate' individuals into an imaginary relation to the world in which they live and through which, in capitalist and patriarchal society, they can thus be exploited (*see* Althusser, Bibliography). There are many similarities between ideology and discourse (*see* above), but it is important to remember that they belong to different theoretical frameworks and vocabularies (Marxist and Foucauldian).

images of women this type of criticism concerns itself with analyzing the representations of women in visual and verbal texts, often as part of a sexual-political critique. See, for example, Josephine Donovan (*see* Bibliography).

Imaginary in Lacanian psychoanalytical theory this is a period which roughly corresponds to Freud's pre-Oedipal phase, but which is associated particularly with the mirror stage of psychic development. Although this stage is actually the child's first move towards individuation, its recognition of itself in a mirror is accompanied by a sense of plenitude and authority. The pleasure it gains in waving its hand and seeing its hand wave back is also connected to its feelings of unity with the mother who, like the mirror image, responds to its actions and demands. In adult life this state of imagined unity and control thus becomes a touchstone of (unfulfilled) desire (*see* Chapter 5 and Symbolic Order below).

intentionality traditional literary criticism proposes that one of the aims of the critic is to recover the aims of the author. Recent critics like Foucault and Barthes have discussed the problems with this (*see* Bibliography).

interpellation literally this means 'calling by name'. It is a term taken from the Marxist Althusser, to describe the process by which people are given positions within an ideological frame. The person is constructed in language and individuals recognize (or misrecognize) themselves in the positions assigned them within ideology, i.e., they are 'called' to adopt certain roles and do so unquestioningly.

interrogate this term is used to refer to the radical process of questioning carried out by modern literary theory on literary texts rather than simply 'reading' them. It is a more rigorous and 'suspicious' process.

interlocutor the person who is addressed. In literary analysis this may refer either to characters in the text or the reader.

ISA/Ideological State Apparatus This is an umbrella term employed by Althusser to refer to the educational system, the law, the family, literature, art, the media. All these systems reinforce the dominant ideology of a particular culture and are instrumental in constituting people as subjects (i.e. positioning people within that ideology).

Lacanian psychoanalysis Lacan developed a theory of psycho-analysis based on the work of Freud and deSaussure. For an accessible description of his work, see Deborah Cameron's *Feminism and Linguistic Theory* and also Malcolm Bowie (*see* Bibliography).

lack   a psychoanalytic concept which is much disputed by feminists, but a convenient short-hand for the various sexual, psychological and political disadvantages supposedly suffered by females because of their uncomfortable and precarious position within the Lacanian Symbolic Order (*see* below). It may also be associated with penis-envy within a Freudian vocabulary.

Law-of-the-Father   Lacan, in stating that the phallus is the primary signifier, says that this has effect not only in language, but in all institutions and aspects of life. He traces this back to the Oedipal crisis.

lesbian continuum   Adrienne Rich (*see* Bibliography) has suggested that rather than a 'deviance' lesbianism should be regarded as the state towards which all women would tend, were it not for the ideology of 'compulsory heterosexuality', because of their primary affiliation to their own mothers. Rich's theory also defines lesbianism as an emotional rather than a specifically sexual bonding between women.

lesbian separatist   is the term given to those Radical Feminists (*see* below) who believe that the only way for women to fundamentally challenge the forces of patriarchy is to withdraw from it (in various ways, and to different extents), and to have as little to do with men as possible. Lesbian separatism is now seen as very much a movement of the 1970s, but has been instrumental in colouring the popular opinion of lesbians (and, indeed, of feminists) as 'man-haters'.

liberal humanist   this term is applied loosely to describe a philosophical position (and, by extension, a branch of literary criticism) where 'man' and his experience are the centre of interest. Literary texts can be shown to have universal significance, speaking for all time, of an unchanging transcendental human nature. Within this system, certain values and emotions (e.g., love) are considered outside of social relations and historical change. The Eurocentrism of this position has been investigated by among others Shohat and Stam (*see* Bibliography).

logocentrism   Derrida uses this term to describe a Western tradition of philosophy that places at its centre the logos, translated as 'word', which also stands for rationality or truth. It is a system of thought that places emphasis on the power of language to deliver the full truth and presence of some external feature. It privileges the spoken over the written word, content above form, and implies that meaning is independent of the language that produces it. It assumes an absolute foundation, outside language itself, which 'anchors' or organizes language so as to fix particular meanings to particular words. Differance (*see* above) is the term that Derrida sets against logocentrism.

Marxist-feminist   a practice or theory which considers both gender and class to be essential components of an analysis.

masculine   the socially constructed elements of an individual which are associated with males; in writing practices, the term is often used to mean that writing which attempts closure and stresses its own authority and rationality (*see* feminine and gender).

masquerade   it is similar to mimicry, but within feminist theory has come to signify an adoption of the roles assigned to women by men. Irigaray (*see*

Chapter 5) suggests that by self-consciously 'performing' femininity, its constructedness may be radically contested and undermined (*see also* performativity).

materialism or historical materialism is the central tenet of Marxist theory, stressing that institutions and socio-economic relations create social conditions rather than any metaphysical agency (that is: material relations are the primary element and consciousness is secondary to this). It is opposed to idealism, systems of thought based on metaphysics. In literary criticism, the focus is on the modes of literary production and consumption, and social conditions which determine access to these.

matriarchy a society where the line of descent is traced through the mother's family, but can be used to refer to a society where women have some power.

mimicry Irigaray's term for imitating a male model of writing in order to demonstrate its failing. Simply by imitating, mimicry has the effect of subverting the male text.

miscegenation the interbreeding of groups of people ('races'), thought within the Victorian period, to result in degeneration of one of the groups .

modernist a vague grouping of texts (from a period around 1880–1930) which experiment with language and with form; for example, the writing of Gertrude Stein and Virginia Woolf.

muted group groups in society which are relatively inarticulate, because meanings are controlled by the dominant group (*see* dominant group).

narrator the character or position from which the story is told.

New Criticism textual criticism associated with the American academics John Crowe Ransom, Cleanth Brooks and R. P. Blackmur, amongst others. Its emphasis is on the linguistic structure of the work and its verbal complexities as an object in itself without reference to its historical context or the psychology of either the author or the reader.

New Historicism a form of criticism which attempts to set a text within its socio-cultural and textual context.

nom-du-père *see* Law-of-the-Father.

not-said this term depends on Pierre Macherey's 'symptomatic' approach to the literary text, whereby locating the 'lack' in the work, what it cannot articulate, becomes the means of detecting that which threatens and undermines its conscious project. The process whereby the 'unconscious' of a text is formed is thus directly paralleled to the child's entry into the Symbolic Order where all that which 'cannot be spoken' is repressed.

Oedipal phase in Freud's psychoanalytic theory, the point in a child's development where the Father enters, forcing the child to give up its unity with its mother and recognize sexual difference. Lacan identifies this point with the child's entry into language, so that as well as recognizing sexual difference the child becomes aware that the language system is also based on difference. The male child suppresses his desire for the mother, on realizing that he may, like her, be castrated by the Father; he aligns himself therefore with the Father. The female child suppresses her desire for the Father, and aligns herself with the Mother, and the lack she suffers because of 'castration' is filled by the desire to have a baby herself. Some feminists have viewed this account of Oedipal socialization as flawed and have stressed the metaphorical nature of the alignment with those of one's own gender. See the work of Melanie Klein and Julia Kristeva (*see* Bibliography).

Other this term has multiple meanings in Lacanian psychoanalytical theory. Most simply it means the difference which stimulates desire. It is used to denote that which creates the sense of lack (*see* above) in the subject and initiates desire. The primal Other is the role of the father within the Oedipal triangle. This introduces a gap between desire and its objects that cannot be filled. Lacan suggests that the key discovery of Freud is that we bear this Otherness within ourselves. In post-colonial theory, the Other refers to the colonized country and its inhabitants described by Westerners.

other in the writing of French feminists it is the tendency of Western discourse to posit the feminine as the other in relation to the masculine that is at issue. Thus, the masculine becomes the positive against which the feminine is defined as negative (i.e. not-man).

parler femme   see *écriture féminine*.

passing the means, conscious or unconscious, by which a subject, culturally defined according to one set of norms (e.g., Black, working class, lesbian), presents herself (or is perceived) in such a way that she is mistaken as belonging to another group with a different social and cultural status (e.g., white, middle class, heterosexual).

patriarchy is that social organization which produces and guarantees superior status for the male and inferior for the female. It is a political concept in that it governs power-structured relationships in which one group is controlled by another.

penis-envy Freud's much maligned account of the way girls recognize a difference between themselves and their boy-peers (*see* Oedipal phase). Juliet Mitchell suggests that rather than reading Freud's account as the girl's envy for the penis, it is possible for feminists to read it as the girl's envy of the boy's social advantages (*see* Bibliography).

performativity is the concept associated with Judith Butler's work on gendered and sexual identity (*see* Bibliography) which argues that no identity is given, fixed or permanent but is produced and sustained only through constant reiteration or performance. Because neither 'femininity' nor 'heterosexuality' are 'natural', for example, individuals have to work hard at producing them. The visible sign of this labour is related to the concept of **masquerade** (*see* above) and is the basis for much of the activism associated with the **Queer** movement.

phallogocentrism   *see* logocentrism.

phallus the symbol of difference at the heart of the language system is the distinction phallus/lack of phallus and from this follow the other differences which form our language system male/female, head/heart, culture/nature, sane/mad and so on. It is the phallus that can be seen to be the central or primary signifier in the language system, since it is the sign of difference and dominance.

pluralism a theoretical position which suggests that more than one position or theory is possible in the reading of a text. It is not necessary to assume that all possible theories or positions are equally valid in all situations, but does not, like traditional criticism, assert that only one view is right.

polymorphous perversity the sexuality of the child in the pre-Oedipal period. This sexuality is not centred on the genitals but takes pleasure in the anal and oral regions particularly, though pleasure is also experienced over the whole body.

polyphony a term developed by Mikhail Bakhtin (*see* Bibliography) to refer to the many voices which exist in a text. Conventional criticism sees the text as coming from one source, spoken by one voice. Bakhtin, however, sees the text as a collection of voices, competing for dominance or existing in tension.

post-colonial a term used to describe the situation in countries which have undergone a colonial relation with Europe in the past. This is not to assume that the colonial experience is the most salient feature in those countries' histories. Post-colonial discourse theory aims to analyze this legacy of colonial intervention and its effects on current cultures.

post-feminism a position of having worked one's way through feminist theory and politics to such an extent that the basic tenets of feminism can be taken as read. It can also mean a (much disputed) position where feminism itself is no longer necessary because all its objectives have been gained.

postmodernism may refer to (a) an aesthetic practice (b) an historical period (i.e., we live in a period of post-modernity) or (c) a mode of cultural analysis, many of whose central tenets are shared with **poststructuralism** but whose politics and political project are frequently unclear (including its relationship to feminism). As an aesthetic practice, literary postmodernism is frequently associated with texts which self-consciously experiment with language, and which pastiche different styles of writing without wishing to form a unified whole or make specific points by so doing.

poststructuralism is used as a general term for recent developments in literary theory. It is the working out in practice of the implications of Derrida's rewriting of Saussurean linguistics, and is marked by an insistence on the instability of meaning and of the **humanist** model of **subjectivity**. It also moves away from an emphasis on the structures which texts share (as in Structuralism), and encompasses recent applications of psychoanalytic criticism such as that based on the theories of Jacques Lacan, as well as Michel Foucault's work on discourse.

pre-Oedipal the stage of development of a child before the Oedipal crisis where the child experiences reality as an undifferentiated mass of sensations (*see hommelette*).

prescriptive it is a type of writing which tells you what to do. Prescriptive feminist theory suggests to writers ways in which they might improve their work in terms of representations of women (*see* Cheri Register, Bibliography).

primary signifier *see* Law-of-the-Father.

primary text this is the term generally applied to the literary text under examination. However, as noted in the Introduction, we disagree with the notion of a theoretical text remaining untouched by the reading process. We hold that the theoretical text as well as the literary text is constructed and altered in the process of reading.

pro-feminism the position men can adopt if they wish to play a part in the feminist debate. It means that they can show their solidarity with

women's work by reading feminist theory etc., while not directly
intervening.

psychodynamics   a term used in psychoanalytical readings of literature to
describe the way a text is written with reference to psychological
predispositions, for example, gender.

pulsions   Kristeva's term for the psycho-sexual drives which function
within the pre-Oedipal stage of childhood development. These pulsions
move across the child's experiencing of the world; they can be thought of
as waves of emotion or sensation which flow through the child in a
rhythmic way.

Queer Theory   is the name that has been adopted by certain contemporary theorists to describe a radical re-thinking of how gender and sexuality
operate. Rejecting the essentialism implicit in the terms 'gay' and 'lesbian'
critics like Judith Butler and Eve Kosofsky Sedgewick (*see* Bibliography)
have argued for the provisonality of all (sexual) identity and shown how
the supposedly positive terms like 'femininity' and 'heterosexuality' have
to constantly work to 'prove' themselves (*see* performativity).

'race'   this is a contested term, in that some groups of theorists assume
that there is a cultural or biological essence to racial identity, whereas
others see race as a term which is used only to exclude certain groups of
people (*see* Robert Young, Bibliography).

Radical Feminism   believes that patriarchy alone is the root of women's
oppression, and that resistance must take the form of a radical dismantling
of the patriarchal system.

repressive state apparatus   within Althusser's work, the institutions
which are established to maintain the status quo (the police, prisons,
judiciary, etc.).

resisting reader   a term developed by Judith Fetterley (*see* Bibliography)
to describe the type of strategies which a female reader can adopt when
reading a male-authored text. She says that because these texts address us
as men, we have to 'side-step' the address, and construct an alternative
form of reading or reading practice.

role model   in authentic realist criticism and images of women criticism,
it is thought to be important for women readers to see examples of female
characters who are strong. When reading, it is thought that women
identify with these characters, and use them as forms of aspiration. Whilst
realizing the importance of this for many women, it is a term which needs
analysis, since this is not the only way women have for constructing a
sense of self.

romantic friendship   a term developed by Lillian Faderman to describe
the passionate but hypothetically non-sexual friendship which women
have with each other (*see* Bibliography).

Saussurean linguistics   Ferdinand de Saussure's system of linguistics has
been very influential in structuralist and post-structuralist thought. An
accessible account of his work is available in Deborah Cameron: *Feminism
and Linguistic Theory* (*see* Bibliography) (*see* sign).

secondary text   this term is generally applied to theoretical texts (*see*
primary text).

second generation feminist   feminists who were not involved in the first
wave of the revived Women's Movement in the 1960s, and therefore did

not go through the political struggles of first generation feminists, but who developed forms of feminist theory based on their work.

second person address when the text addresses the reader as 'you'.

semiotics (semiology) is the science of signs (or, broadly, language) as first proposed by Ferdinand de Saussure.

semiotic Julia Kristeva uses the term to refer to flow of pre-linguistic rhythms or **pulsions** experienced by a child before it acquires language (i.e. before it enters the 'Symbolic'). The rhythmic pulses are themselves a sort of language which is repressed once the child learns to speak, since our linguistic system is not capable of expressing everything the child experiences. But the semiotic is not totally repressed. It lies beneath the **Symbolic Order** and can make itself evident in the movement of word play of avant-garde or modernist writers marked by rupture, absences and breaks in symbolic language (*see* Chapter 5).

sexual politics a theory of patriarchal power relations outlined by Kate Millett in her book of the same name (*see* Chapter 1) and associated primarily with her analysis of the misogynistic representation of women in male-authored texts.

sign is the term used in Saussurean linguistics to describe a unit of language comprised of the concept (the signified) and its form (the signifier, that is the words on the page, or sounds in the air). It is arbitrary and creates meaning in its difference from other such signs rather than by any correspondence to the material world. So, for example, the word 'cat' is used arbitrarily to mean a small, furry animal – there is no actual relationship between the word and the object. We know the meaning of 'cat' because we have not said 'mat' or 'dog'.

sisterhood a form of bonding between women, irrespective of race, class or other differences. It is an identifying of one's interests with other women (*see* consciousness-raising, womanist and woman-centred). Sisterhood as a concept was important in the 1960s and 1970s but has been problematized since then because of Western women's assumption that their priorities were shared by all other women (*see* Chapter 8).

specularized other the speculum is a curved mirror which reflects back a distorted image. For Irigaray, woman is man's specularized other.

split-subject a term used in psychoanalysis in opposition to the idea of the unified subject, that is, the notion that each individual is in control of her thoughts, desires and intentions. In psychoanalysis the subject is the site of conflicting impulses, and is an amalgam of diverse urges, desires and thoughts.

structuralism a group of theorists, Lévi-Strauss, Barthes, Genette and Propp amongst others, who were interested in analysing the basic structural components of texts, reducing groups of texts to their lowest common denominator; for example, seeing what all fairy tales had in common in terms of their structure.

structuration a term used in psychoanalysis to describe the way that individuals come to see themselves in a way which is determined by ordered forces whose roots are in the psyche. For example, the structuration of desire refers to the fact that desire does not simply spring from the individual 'naturally' but is structured by forces beyond her control.

subaltern   non-élite colonial subjects – those groups, like peasants, who do not have so much contact with the colonial powers and from whom resistance often springs.

sub-genre   a division within genres; for example, feminist detective novels are a sub-genre of the detective genre.

subject   since most psychoanalysts do not believe in a unified individual consciousness, they use the term 'subject', which does not suggest wholeness or control in the same way as 'individual' does.

subjectivity   what is involved in becoming a subject, and occupying subject-positions. It is akin to the notion of consciousness, but is less unitary, since one individual occupies several subject positions.

superstructure   within Marxist theory, societies consist of an economic base which determines all other structures, such as education and culture. These other structures are termed the superstructure (*see* base).

Symbolic Order   in Lacanian theory this is the stage of development children enter when they acquire language. Language imposes a social order on the child's experience. In the process, some of the child's experience prior to the acquisition of language is lost because it cannot be expressed in language and is thus repressed into the **unconscious**. The phallus is the 'transcendental signifier' in the Symbolic Order, not because it contains any absolute meaning, but because it marks the child's separation from the **Imaginary** (*see* above).

symptomatic reading   a form of analysis which views the text as displaying a range of symptoms which can be analysed by the critic.

synthesis   the third element in Hegel's dialectical system, which resolves the conflict between thesis and antithesis (*see* thesis and antithesis).

text   a term which can refer to all types of writing, both literary and non-literary.

theory/theoretical   a position which provides a way into a text because of already thought out 'schemas' or models of the way texts work. These models are at a more generalizable level than an intuitive response to individual texts, and are seen to hold true of a range of texts.

thesis   the first element in Hegel's dialectical system; a first proposition within an argument which is then challenged by its opposition, or antithesis (*see* antithesis and synthesis).

third person narration   a novel is told in the third person if the focus of attention is on the actions of 'she' or 'he', for example: 'She wrote him a brief letter'.

unconscious   within psychoanalytic theory, the subject consists of the conscious mind (the thinking subject which appears to be in control), and the unconscious (that zone within the individual where repressed desires are expelled). The unconscious is not accessible to examination but its existence can be traced through the eruption into the conscious of modified elements from the unconscious (in dreams, in slips of the tongue, and in symptoms).

un-said   *see* not-said.

utopian   concerned with a depiction of a distant, ideal future world.

wild zone   a term used by the anthropologists Shirley and Edwin Ardener to describe that section of women's experience which is not available to men (*see* Chapter 3).

woman-centred   a text or practice which consciously addresses itself to women and which focuses on women's experience.

womanist   a term developed by Alice Walker that avoids the race-blindness implicit in the term 'feminist' (since other feminisms need to define themselves as non-white, such as Black feminism). Womanist writing identifies itself as writing to other Black women, and is concerned to focus on their experience. An example of 'womanist prose' can be found in Alice Walker's *In Search of Our Mothers' Gardens* (Virago, London, 1983).

writing the body   a form of writing developed by **French feminists** (*see écriture féminine*) which concentrates on the analogies between the writing process and the functions of the female body.

Index